The Church with a Human Face

The Church
with a Human Face

*A New and Expanded Theology
of Ministry*

Edward Schillebeeckx

SCM PRESS LTD

Translated by John Bowden from the Dutch
Pleidooi voor Mensen in de Kerk.
Christelijke Identiteit en Ambten in de Kerk,
published by Uitgeverij H.Nelissen BV,
Baarn, Holland, 1985

Schillebeeckx, Edward
The church with a human face : a new and
expanded theology of ministry.
1. Clergy—Office—History
I. Title II. Christelijke indentiteit
en ambten in de kerk. *English*
262'.14'09   BV660.2

ISBN 0–334–01956–7

First published in Britain 1985
by SCM Press Ltd,
26-30 Tottenham Road, London N1
Second impression 1989

Phototypeset by Input Typesetting Ltd
Printed and bound in Great Britain at
The Camelot Press Ltd, Southampton

Contents

Part Five
The Church with a Human Face

Preface

In its first and second editions, my book *Ministry*[1] was still too much a work consisting of originally separate articles, even though I had worked through them again for the new publication. These circumstances in which the book came into being caused unnecessary misunderstandings among some readers.

Those who read my books will also be aware that although *Ministry* was enthusiastically approved by many people, since it was published it has also provoked criticism of me here and there, both from theologians and from the official *magisterium*. Perhaps as a result of particular anxieties, some of which are understandable and some of which I find incomprehensible, a number of critics (for example W.Kasper, A.Vanhoye, P.Grelot and to a large extent also the Roman Congregation for the Doctrine of Faith) seem to have been blind to what I actually said in the book. I myself was struck by the way in which some of them (perhaps rather hesitantly) were in fact really saying the same thing as I was, and yet criticizing me at the same time. The criticisms that they made usually related to small points of detail (some of them very small; while these were always valuable in the context of a comprehensive verdict on my book, they did not really affect my basic positions). I am particularly grateful to the patristic scholar H.Crouzel for his serious criticisms of detail, which moreover are certainly in place in an accurate and objective interpretation of what I have actually said in my book (this can hardly be said of the comments of some of my other critics). I shall take full account of *justified* criticism in the present book; the truth is served by that, and the truth is my concern.

Because their pastoral concern has led theological friends from abroad, too, to press me to make a specific reply to ungrounded criticisms or criticisms of positions which I nowhere defended in my earlier book, I have slightly changed my theological timetable for a while in order to return to the problem of ministry in the

Roman Catholic Church and the crisis surrounding it, which is a cause of grief for many people – sometimes even a scandal. Unfounded criticism can damage the pastoral usefulness of experiments in the church. Hence this *new* book on 'ministries in the church'.

Precisely in view of this particular impasse and its ecumenical implications, I have ended this new book with a critical assessment of the third part of the Lima Report, about 'Ministries in the Church', as a challenge to all Christians issued by the early, still undivided church.

Nijmegen, 1 January 1985   Edward Schillebeeckx

*Factus sum insipiens
vos me coegistis*

(II Cor. 12.11, Vulgate)

Introduction:
Why this new book? A test case?

(a) The aim of my earlier book, *Ministry*

In both the first and the second, expanded, edition of *Ministry* I began from the specific situation in which Christian churches now find themselves – in positions for and against. In many respects a great many people – members of believing communities and ministers – find their experiences in the present situation negative. The dominant conceptions about the practice and the theology of the ministry seem to be robbing the gospel of its force in communities of believers – an experience which is shared by quite a number of Christians and ministers. Moreover, in all areas we can see an increasing shortage of priests. These facts often have serious consequences where traditional views are maintained. The Sunday celebration of the eucharist is trivialized (the laity preside over a kind of pseudo-eucharist, with hosts which are brought from elsewhere; this both takes the heart out of the celebration that in fact takes place and regards consecrated hosts in a magical way). Moreover, not only nor even primarily in Holland, one can see all kinds of attempts to get out of this dead end.

For the theologian, this raises the question: what is possible and desirable, and even pastorally urgent, for Christians and the church, in such developments? To find an answer, the theologian turns to the life of the church down the centuries. He or she then discovers that the church is always affected by new social and historical developments in the world – sometimes to its advantage and sometimes less so. This raises the question: why should this process of trial and error and pastoral exploration suddenly come to an end in our day, perhaps to the detriment of the vitality of the gospel in the churches? There is a theological problem here which calls for theological illumination. My starting point in dealing with it is the view that much, but not everything, is possible in a community of Christ. Ministries in the church have their own specifically sacramental significance, which in my view was also accepted by the Reformation, though it did not use the technical term 'sacrament' in this context. Moreover, one can never give an absolute cut-and-dried formulation of what is specifically normative for Christians, since this can only be found in changing historical forms. If such a norm is made absolute, then 'the normative element' is itself caricatured; despite everything, this normative element is to be found only *in* these historical forms, never detached from the historically contingent context. Where such a development takes place, absolute authority is accorded, for example, to the actual practice of the ministry at the time of the New Testament (as in biblicism, in either right-wing or left-wing fundamentalism), or to the view of the ministry held, for example, by Saint Sulpice, the modern image of the priesthood down to our day.

A historical investigation teaches the theologian that on the basis of the sacramental reality of the 'community of God', the exercise of ministry in the church has taken different forms over the course of history. At the same time it becomes clear that according to sociological laws, in an established church which needs a church order, the various forms, including that of ministry, develop a tough structure and in the long run no longer fit different situations. Changes in the forms of ministry never seem to be deliberate in the first place, but only appear as a consequence of social changes in the church and the world: the rise of a new spirituality, different views of the church, society and the world. By this theological approach to 'socio-historical facts' and especially by demonstrating the pluralism in them, I have sought to show that even today, changes in the practice of the ministry can be quite legitimate in the light of the gospel (in the sense of being legitimate dogmatically) and that from a pastoral perspective they may even be said to be necessary for the vitality of the gospel in Christian communities at the present time. Of course opinions may differ over the question of pastoral necessity, but there is no need to brand someone a heretic who points this out and indicates the possibilities within the church. Perhaps I might add that in *Ministry* I did not argue for illegality in any way, but tried to *make understandable*, both theologically and pastorally, those illegal practices which are in fact carried on. I did this both in order to get rid of excrescences and to open up ways to the recognition of new possibilities in the church.

Ministry was also intended for those to whom the 'classical' image of the priest is so familiar and so beloved - that is why so many spiritual and material sacrifices are still made for it – in order that they can also reconcile themselves emotionally to changes in the familiar image of this practice and to other emphases relating to conceptions of the ministry. It can be liberating to discover from historical material that in other times the accents did not lie where they do now. Moreover, many of today's changes are not as drastic as some people fear; indeed, taken together they are very modest. In my view, at any rate, fear about any change whatsoever in this area goes back to the view of the priesthood held by Père de Bérulle in the seventeenth century, though some moves in this direction can be detected in the Middle Ages and the early church. At the heart of this view lies the conviction that Jesus Christ was a priest on the basis of his divine and not his human nature. If we see, rightly, the church's ministry as 'sharing in the priesthood of Christ' (Thomas Aquinas) against this background, the source of the sacral ontologizing of the ministry is clear. But if one bases the priesthood of Jesus not on his deity but on his humanity – and in the nineteenth century J.H.Newman argued for this – then the ministry, too, takes on another dimension with a no less truly Christian, sacramental significance. The ultimate aim of my first book about ministry was to clarify this.

(b) The aim of this new book

In *Ministry* I drew a very sharp distinction between the conception of the ministry in the first Christian millennium and that in the second. At that time, and especially in the second edition of this book, I called this an *overall* (i.e. unqualified) schematization of past history. I still believe this to be true as a general appreciation. Of course, differences in spirituality, in conceptions and forms, even of ministry, never take place suddenly. They come about over the course of centuries, often imperceptibly, with a good deal of overlapping in which the old and the new stand side by side. Moreover, one can see what became characteristic and striking in the second millennium take shape as early as the end of the fourth century. So this overlapping can last for centuries. It already begins at the end of the first century. Throughout this process over two Christian millennia there are of course *quite fundamental* shifts, but no definitive or radical break can be established. Thin but real threads of continuity remain, as I already saw in *Ministry*.

In this perspective it would be better to present the overall scheme of the two millennia following the New Testament in a more sophisticated way, as follows – though it is still schematic throughout:

1. Conceptions of ministry in the second century;

2. A fundamental shift between the second and the end of the fourth century: the mystique of the consecrating priest perceptibly gains ground;

3. Feelings and experience in the church in the early Middle Ages and the feudal period;

4. The thirteenth century, the time of the mediaeval bourgeoisie and the writers of great *Summas*, which systematized in a somewhat 'timeless' way the practice and the view of the ministry which had in fact come into being;

5. The Council of Trent and its influence (really only the influence of the canons of the ministry) in the Counter-Reformation;

6. The image of the priest in the modern period: de Bérulle and his Oratory, Saint-Sulpice, Pius X, XI, XII.

I envisaged this scheme even when I was writing *Ministry*, though not in such a sophisticated way. What I there call 'the fundamental opposition between the two Christian millennia' is thus to be seen as a schematization of what in my view is the evident opposition between two extremes, namely the first century (despite breaks which appeared in the time before Nicaea) and the conception of the ministry in modern times, from the seventeenth to the twentieth century: in other words, between the *beginning* of the first millennium and the *end* of the second. By means of the basic historical facts and converging indications I now want to make the 'theological programme' of this first work much deeper – to offer help both to my brothers and sisters in our calling and to all members of the churches.

(c) Ministry from a socio-historical and a theological perspective

Some criticisms of *Ministry* have shown me that many people find it difficult to say farewell to what I regard as a persistent form of dualism: they put what can be clarified by sociology and/or history into a kind of theological storm-free zone within which a community of Jesus Christ nevertheless rightly experiences that ministry is 'from above': grace from God. Confronted with socio-logical or historical facts, believers then say to sociologists or historians: that's all very well, but ministry is *not only* a sociological or a historical fact. This can rightly be a protest against a socio-logical and historical reduction of ministry. But there is also such a thing as theological reductionism, which puts the character of the ministry as grace alongside and above its socio-historical reality. In that case the *not only* betrays the ambiguity of this dualism: certainly, two separate dimensions are recognized, only attainable from different perspectives and only capable of being articulated in two different languages (scientific language and the language of faith); however, these are then projected side by side on to the same level of reality. It is precisely there that the error lies. We are always concerned with one and the same reality: the form which has grown up through history and which can be explained sociologically or historically (in this case, of ministry) is precisely what the believer experiences and expresses in the language of faith as a specific manifestation of grace: a successful, less successful or improper response of the believing community to God's grace. There is no 'surplus of revelation' behind or above the socio-historical forms of ministry. Critics of my book forget that. Do they have more, 'supernatural meaning'? Do they want to think in 'supernaturalist' terms – in which case they are being untrue to the gospel? A dualism of this kind seems to make 'ministry', as a datum of faith, immune to historical and socio-logical analysis.

However, my criticism is that *on the level of reality* there is no way of distinguishing the two. Although it transcends the forms in which it is expressed, grace can only be found *in* the historical or sociological form, not beyond it or above it. So if we study ministry historically or sociologically, then in fact, as believers, we are looking from a special perspective to see whether the responses given by the church to God's grace are good or inad-equate. This implies the need to look for critieria for assessment *from more than one period of the church's history*. The sociological and indeed the historical outlines differ from the theological outline: epistemologically they form two different theoretical frameworks within which nevertheless *one and the same* datum is approached.

Even historians sometimes forget this. As historians, they too, rightly, work with a theoretical framework and have specific interests. Why should a theologian, too, not study the past in the perspective of a theological theory, with a theological interest? Of course, in this work he or she must stand on firm historical ground, as otherwise this kind of theologizing will hang in the air. The procedure of a theologian also differs from that of a historian in that in and during his historical investigation he is doing theology. If we suppose that historical investigation and thematic theology mark two different phases, then in my view we are opting for a hybrid combination of positivism and purely 'speculative' theology.

Of course a theologian is in search of real history. Moreover, for example in the interpretation of historical texts, he or she must be open to historical criticism, since this can have theological consequences. That is the reason why I have invited historical criticism. However this must be criticism of my own book, and not of what others say with reference to it. A theologian is concerned with the precise content of the reality of faith at all times, good and bad. For me, ministry represents and is such a reality of faith. Precisely its specific historical character can mean that the continuity of the full content of the gospel cannot be demonstrated *without breaks*. Within the broad tradition of the church one cannot pass lightly over counter-traditions which are part of the very life of the church, forgotten truths which are constantly recalled and criticized afresh, and which have a considerable role in theological thematizing. The pastoral intention of *Ministry* was to bring out again the validity of forgotten truths and thus counter the pauperizing of ministry. This intention is developed in the present book.

(*d*) Sensitivity to hermeneutics and ideological criticism in the light of present-day negative experiences with ministry

In criticisms of my book *Ministry*, the criticism of Pierre Grelot in particular is clearly directed at my hermeneutical method.[1] However, as other reviewers of Grelot's book have pointed out, this exegete has interpreted my hermeneutical approach perversely: he attributes positions to me which I never defended in my book. I do not blame him for never having read any of my books or articles on hermeneutics; I do blame him for regarding a 'Hermeneutical Intermezzo' in *Ministry*, in which I try to anticipate a possible objection, as a formal discussion of hermeneutics.

I myself have repeatedly argued that we can only perceive *interpreted* facts, experiences and 'history' (which is precisely what Grelot says on pp.42-7, but then he seems to hold it against me –

why?). He finds occasion for his criticism in my use of the word 'dogmatic' (which, given the context, I clearly intended in the sense of 'dogmatistic' and not 'dogmatic' in the Christian theological sense of the word) and then nevertheless suggests that when dealing with the New Testament one is never approaching it purely as a 'profane historian'. According to this author a believing historian must evidently already be able to find in the Bible insights of faith which are explicitly put into words later, as a result of his participation in faith in the Christian tradition. In that case, why is historical study still necessary? Certainly, every historian must be well disposed to texts that he seeks to analyse, as the two authors cited by Grelot, H.Marrou and P. Ricoeur (and I myself), have repeatedly stressed. But for the historian of the New Testament, says Grelot, what is needed 'in the faith and praxis of the church is a lucid will to communicate with the experience of the apostolic church, in accordance with the structural forms outside which the desire for the *sequela Jesu* would lose all authenticity' (Grelot, p.49). All this does not apply in any way to the historian, but it does apply to the believing theologian. And even then, it does so only with one proviso (which Grelot forgets): in the New Testament the Christian churches (for all their apostolicity, a point on which I am in full agreement with him, as will be evident later in the book) are still in search of the most appropriate structures. Grelot, however, seems to put forward later structures which developed through history as a model for the historical study of the New Testament. This seems to me to be quite unsound exegesis, both scientifically and in terms of faith.

The basis of Grelot's incorrect interpretation is his mistaken understanding of the term 'illegality' which I use. He gives the impression that I want to base this illegality on the Bible. He says that I 'promote illegality so that it becomes a legitimate Christian and apostolic possibility in the church' (Grelot, p.55). That is to stand things on their head. I am looking to see whether the *content* of certain practices is illegal, not just in terms of canon law but also in terms of the New Testament, so that they are theologically impossible. And if this content does prove possible in terms of the Bible, my request is for some changes in present canon law, as the present situation in the churches clearly calls for it. There is no mention in my book of a biblical foundation of illegal practice, whether in my intentions or in the text as it stands objectively.

As a result of clearly noting expressions of discontent, in

Ministry I looked for the many possibilities which seem to be acceptable to forms of organization in ministry – within the fundamental unity and apostolicity of the New Testament (my standpoint of faith). I do that because for me, as for Grelot, the New Testament is *norma normans*. Nor is my intention biblicistically to return in our time to the still vague lack of differentiation in the New Testament ministries. I do that, because in communion with the apostolic churches (which is what Grelot rightly asks of a believer) I can see how in the light of God's Spirit the churches implemented the institutionalizing of ministries in the communities in a varied and flexible way, depending on the specific wants and needs of the various communities of believers in different cultural areas, albeit under the profound influence of Graeco-Roman culture of that time. So here we find a normative model showing especially how, in what ways, the church even now can attune its ministries and organize itself in accordance with the real needs of a 'community of God'. So I am in no way adopting a purely canonical standpoint, as Grelot (p.55) claims. If that were the case, the whole of the historical exposition would have been unnecessary and from the negative experiences of today over the ministry I would have come directly to the conclusion that in some points canon law needs to be changed. End!

However, I made this long historical detour in order to show that precisely such changes are possible for Christians, i.e. without any infringement of the *salva eorum substantia* (of Trent), the essential soundness of the sacrament. In other words, I did it to show that the changes are possible both biblically and theologically, and are also desirable, perhaps even pastorally urgent. To say that I am arguing on biblical grounds for practices which are illegal (in terms of present canon law) is to stand my book on its head. It is the illegal practices that are *in fact* going on which have set me thinking as a theologian. That is something different from what Grelot claims.

Apart from the unjustly perverse interpretation of my book by Grelot, a general (more sympathetic) objection could nevertheless run: 'Are you not reading history *with an eye to* the present problems associated with the ministry?' My first retort to that is, 'Of course'. But at the same time I would deny what seems to be being suggested by the objection. For that is the claim that old documents can be read 'neutrally'. Whereas for me the method followed is the only reason why history is worth the difficulties of reading it, tradition becomes a living tradition because facts that had been forgotten can again be called to mind, expounded and interpreted. We cannot cross out our own present, push it on one side or disregard it. Anyone who believes that is wrong, in supposing such a thing is possible. For in that case people are not even aware of their own concealed interests. Consciously or unconsciously, people look at historical documents in the light of present-day questions, suppositions and hypotheses, and above all in the light of 'negative experiences'. The critical problem is whether one simply looks to history to confirm one's own already established views or whether one allows them to be put to the test by history.

Anyone who reads a book written perhaps two thousand years ago is himself or herself addressed by this book; he or she reads it in the light of his or her own questions and hypotheses, whether or not he or she is aware of the fact. Only a 'dogmatic' reader reads into the past what happens in his own street. Today's questions, formulated consciously and openly, are quite different from disguised prejudices; they are the necessary, albeit inadequate, prerequisite of being able to read old texts with an eye to their significance for us now. The past is not a computer from which stored information can constantly be drawn afresh. That view is historicism, a false view of history. On the other hand the reader must allow the texts to be 'texts', i.e. must respect them in their consistency. This is the only way in which he or she can get an answer from the texts to present-day questions, even if it is an indirect one, an answer which by understanding meaning may give meaning and at the same time offer criticism. We need creative trust in the texts, without anticipating 'dogmatically' what their meaning is for us. It is a matter of beginning from contemporary questions and allowing ourselves to be addressed by the texts from within their own structure. Present and past now form a dialectical process, for the simple reason that we readers are part of the same human history as that in which the texts were written. The story began long before we took up its thread. Someone once said that the last thing that a fish would perceive (if it attained reflective awareness) would be the water in which it lived: the 'today' of its own milieu. This is so familiar and obvious that the fish does not even notice it. So, too, everyone spontaneously reads the past through the prism of the present, his or her own present with its particular questions, presuppositions and hypotheses. To read a text critically and thus 'objectively' (in accordance with the material in question) is therefore also to be aware of all this: the uncritical reader is the one who wants to read a text 'unhistorically' and claims that he or she can exclude his own present in reading it.

Anyone who is unfamiliar with this hermeneutical structure of our human historical consciousness looks 'scientistically', i.e. ideologically, at the past, because in that case contemporary views are often legitimated unconsciously by reading the text, since they play an uncontrolled role in that reading.

Thus the practice of particular Christian, and above all critical, communities was the stimulus and the challenge to this study. Does this mean that the actual alternative practices of these Christian communities and their leaders in relation to ministry become the 'norm and truth', and thus determine the reading of earlier texts? Not at all: that would be pure empiricism or prragmatism. Even pastoral effectiveness is not decisive in matters of truth: in this sense I reject the so-called principle of 'orthopraxis' as a principle of truth. (In that case the 'orthopraxis' of a thorough-going Nazi would also validate the 'orthodoxy' of Nazism as truth! I.e., thorough-going belief in a doctrine does not of itself make that doctrine true or sound.) The actual practice of Christian communities, legally or illegally, depending on the norms of canonical church order, is the *interpretandum*, i.e. what must be justified in theory, or can perhaps be criticized. For the theologian, what is called Christian practice is never a direct norm, but the agenda, i.e. that which he or she must clarify *secundum scripturas*, in the light of the great Christian tradition. On its side, practice must never wait for the permission of theologians before it gets going. That is certainly true. Whether justifiably or not, practice follows from faith (i.e. the spontaneous or implicit 'theory'), and so practice does not precede faith, but theology. However, the theologian must make a reflective investigation of the very 'spon-taneity' of this practice of faith, because this spontaneity can unconsciously admit uncritical elements. A certain practice can even wrongly be regarded as a 'practice of faith'. The theoretical justification of the theologian can also demonstrate by a reference to scripture and tradition, with a practical and critical end in view, whether the practice is in fact the expression of the movement of the Holy Spirit or rather that of the whims of personal preference. A successful justification demonstrates whether what is in fact happening is directed by the Holy Spirit. Thus the theologian turns into theory, in a critical way, what is presented in the effective practice of Christian communities and their leaders today as a concrete solution to urgent pastoral needs. By nature the theologian is always the 'latecomer' in respect of Christian practice, which precedes him. But in his own time this latecomer is extremely necessary and irreplaceable, especially when it comes to demonstrating in a rational way whether this practice is authentically Christian. An intuitive certainty here is not enough, and could open up the way to all kinds of arbitrariness. To the theologian, the actual practice of Christians and Christian communities is for the time being simply a possible sign of faith; he or she investigates whether it is a real sign of faith. This secondary but necessary demand for theological reflection thus clearly presupposes the practice of the community. But no practice of any kind is legitimated solely by itself. Only theological theory can demonstrate whether the direction of the practice is *orthos*, right (*orthopraxis*), in the light of the inspiration and orientation of the great Christian tradition, even if this practice should be completely new. You do not change the world or the church by 'ideas', and to change the world or the church is not of itself salvation, truth or happiness. *What* are the changes? That is the critical question. In a theological justification of them the theologian plays an irreplaceable role, unless practice is to become a runaway horse. We are therefore concerned with what I said above was the 'logos' or 'Christian reason' of practice. But once this is assured, the practice of the Christian community is in fact the sphere in which theology is born, and theory is at the same time a function of practice. However, we would have an ideology if theology were put *directly* – i.e. without the mediation of hermeneutics and in accordance with its own laws, laws in this sense independent of all practice – at the service of practice, whether that of the grass-roots communities or of the church authorities. That would theoretically amount to opportunism.

Still, there is more (and this additional element played an implicit, though real, role in *Ministry*). To look to the past for the nature of ministry as a reality of faith, i.e. as something belonging to the essence of the church, in no way represents a search for an abstract essence as distinct or even distinguishable from its historical and cultural forms, far less a purely 'value-free' historical reconstruction. Even in the New Testament there is an interaction between the building up of the community of faith and its social and cultural context. There is no surplus of revelation above or in addition to specific historical forms. Anyone who is in search of 'more supernatural meaning' in this sense, as some people seem to require, is in the end in search of an un-Christian supernaturalism.

The theological meaning (e.g. of ministry) intended by believers must be found precisely in and through the concrete historical forms of ministry, good or bad. In this search, experiences of contrast play a large role: are the specific forms of ministry given in history liberating or enslaving and alienating for the believing community? So while I do history as objectively as possible, I do it in the light of a specifically Christian remembrance, that of Jesus' promise of coming freedom (not arbitrariness) for all. To look for social and historical factors which have contributed to the formation of both particular practices of ministry and particular forms of theology of ministry is, from a Christian perspective, to look from present positive and negative experiences of ministry to what the ministry of the church really means. It is not a question here of difficulties which are of course bound up with the exercising of any ministry (including secular ministry)! Negative historical experiences of contrast come into play in which (from a sociological perspective) the failure of ministry to function is felt to be a painful experience and in which (from a theological perspective) the liberating character of the gospel is not experienced in every respect. Hermeneutically it is in no way *a priori* a matter of a pure actualization of biblical or church history in connection with ministry. Rather, precisely with a view to being faithful to the gospel, it is a matter of a biblical, emancipatory, critical evaluation of this history in the light of contemporary negative experiences of ministry.

Of course the theologian does not have the last word here, but he or she does have a special contribution to make in the formation of what might be called the 'consensus of believers', which sooner or later is expressed by the pastoral *magisterium* of the church and which is presented in the light of the historical power of the many experiences of ministry in the history of the church as a *question posed by the gospel* to the official church.

Part One

Jesus Christ and his Messianic Communities

1. Jesus' historical identity as reflected in the messianic Jesus movement

Not only the Old Testament but also Jesus' own disciples are determinative for our understanding of Jesus, just as a second generation of Christians is determinative for the understanding of earlier 'apostles and prophets', on which according to Eph.2.20 the church is built.

The New Testament is about the story of a Jew who appeared in our human history and who, after his death, was confessed by fervent followers as 'Christ, God's only Son, our Lord'. In that story we read how certain people reacted to the historical phenomenon of Jesus and how as a result they began to lead a new life. We also read how other people, in an equally radical reaction, fiercely rejected this same Jesus and even removed him from the scene by executing him. Through the New Testament we can discover, as in a reflection, the essential historical outlines of who Jesus was, how he lived and what inspired him. For these Christians were ready to follow him, while others exterminated him. We have no writings from Jesus himself, no direct 'documents'; a portrait of him is handed down to us only as reflected through his followers.

Jesus' followers were first called 'Christians' in the great Syrian mission community of Antioch (Acts 11.26). Although to begin with this name was probably used by outsiders, it already indicates a group-identity of certain Jews which was already clearly recognizable in Antioch: these were especially Jews and Jewish proselytes who confessed Jesus as the Christ and followed him in Jewish integrity.

The later disciples sought to understand for themselves what Jesus had meant for his first disciples and what he meant and could mean for their own life here and now. At least in part, this first process of interpretation led to what we call the New Testament. It is clear from the accounts in the New Testament that what emerged from Jesus' earthly life was of such a nature that it led either to radical discipleship or to an equally fierce rejection. 'Who do you say that I am?' therefore takes on a theologically significant meaning. This is the view of the canonical New Testament itself.

Moreover, we can see that the whole history of Christianity consists of a constant ongoing process of interpretation in which Christians are constantly confronted afresh with other situations and problems in the church, within spheres of culture which also change. Confident in the tradition of faith which has been handed down to them, though nevertheless also critical – given new situations – they involve themselves in what has been passed on by previous generations. A diachronic survey of all these interpretations of Christians and their actual practice indicates what Christian identity is.

The response of Christians in faith to Jesus' appearance among us is the confession that a human individual, Jesus of Nazareth, is Christ. Therefore a historical interest in the man Jesus has theological significance *par excellence*. Here we have in no sense an expression of an intrinsically liberal historical interest but the authentic Christian anti-docetic character of any proper christo-logical or messianic reaction to Jesus of Nazareth, albeit in the conditions of our heightened modern Western 'historical consciousness'.

First of all I shall turn to what gave Jesus and his followers an identity of their own.

(a) The time and place of Jesus' historical appearance

Although Jesus' life came to its end and climax in Jerusalem, the main part of his life was spent in a triangle bordered by Capernaum, Bethsaida and Chorazin, on the north of the Sea of Galilee, which was then ideal for bathing in because of its clear and pure water. The climate there is sub-tropical, and at that time the area was densely populated, well-known for its agriculture: the grain (wheat) of Chorazin was famous. From here fishermen swarmed over the lake to catch fish and to trade. Somewhat further north lay the borderland of the tetrarchy of Herod Antipas

and the tetrarchy of his step-brother Philip: Caesarea Philippi.
And north-west of this were Tyre, Sidon and, at the same distance
to the north-east, Damascus. So from Nazareth Jesus did not
move in the direction of Jerusalem for his preaching and healings,
but more to the north, to the district which with the prophecies
of Isa.8.23; 9.1-2 (see Matt.4.15-16) could be described as 'Galilee
of the Gentiles', the borderland between 'Israel' and the 'land of
the Gentiles', above all in Jesus' time – as Jewish sources also tell
us. One hour's journey from Nazareth lay Sepphoris, the Galilean
capital of the time, with its Greek theatre and gymnasium (for
sports events), destroyed in 4 BC but rebuilt by Herod Antipas
during Jesus' lifetime as a fortress. (During Jesus' lifetime this
Herod Antipas – 4 BC to AD 39 – was the governor of Galilee and
Peraea. From AD 26, Pontius Pilate was the Roman governor or
procurator. The emperor Augustus died when Jesus was about
eighteen, and was succeeded by the emperor Tiberius, in whose
reign Jesus was crucified, as we also know from the Roman
historian Tacitus.)

Politically speaking, this was a tumultuous period for Palestine.
In the difficult days after the death of Herod the Great (4 BC),
the emperor Augustus sent his general Sabinus to Palestine to
supervise the succession. However, he humiliated the Jews, who
therefore attacked the Roman troops of Sabinus in Jerusalem on
the feast of Pentecost. This was the beginning of a serious
revolt. Judas the Galilean gathered together sympathizers in the
neighbourhood of Sepphoris; they took weapons from the royal
arsenal: this was the beginning of the Jewish revolt (recalling that
of the Maccabees). When Varus, the governor of Syria, to which
Galilee was annexed, heard of this, he came from Antioch with
two legions to restore order throughout Palestine. Sepphoris, the
capital, was burnt to the ground and its inhabitants sold as slaves.
From there the troops went to Jerusalem, which was besieged by
Zealots. These fled before the superior Roman forces. Varus made
raids throughout the land and at that time had scores of Jews
crucified.[2]

Herod Antipas had Sepphoris rebuilt, but also erected a new
capital elsewhere which he called Tiberias, after the name of the
Roman emperor.

In the year AD 6 (at that time Jesus was about ten years old) the
emperor sent the legate Quirinius with the first procurator of
Judaea, Coponius, to Syria with a commission to hold a census
in Judaea – not in Galilee. In terms of taxation, this amounted to

estimating incomes and possessions in this region. Judas the Galilean again went into action, but without much success. Then the militant wing of the Pharisees split off into a separate, 'Zealot' party. After that the movement remained underground until the troubles which began in AD 66 flared up into the Jewish War (66-72).

After thirty-seven years of freedom from Roman troops, the now permanent military presence intensified the political situation in the time of Jesus.

In the time of Jesus the temple of Jerusalem, whose high priests were appointed by the Romans and had become corrupt, lackeys of the Romans, had long ceased to be the true centre of authentic Jewish piety, as Ezra had dreamed. This role had been taken over by the synagogues spread throughout the country. These were an invention of the Pharisees (so-called above all by their opponents the Sadducees; the Pharisees preferred to call themselves 'scribes' or 'the wise'). With regret, the priestly élite at Jerusalem saw that moral authority no longer lay with them but with the Pharisees and their rabbis, though these had no political power. In contrast to the Sadducees, who revered the principle of *sola scriptura* - only the written Law, without commentary – the Pharisees also recognized the *halakah* alongside the Torah. The *halakah* was a hermeneusis or exposition of the Law which brought it up to date. The Pharisees translated the Law in new situations so that it applied to these new situations – so they were not fundamentalists. Whereas the Sadducees were the party of the rich and powerful, the Pharisees were more the party of the poor and unprivileged. Following the line of the prophets, they wanted the conversion of the heart to be expressed in righteousness and love in all social relationships in Israel. It was the Pharisees who, since the Second Temple, had brought a new understanding of God and religion to Judaism. The highest expression of religion was not the priestly cult, but righteousness and love. The kingdom of God could not come to perfection unless righteousness prevailed in all social relationships. The Pharisees were not against the liturgy, but official temple liturgies had to be combined with social justice and mercy – the theme of the prophets of old. Nevertheless the Pharisees were opposed to the violent solution to situations of injustice proposed by the Zealots, above all under an occupation.

Of course they were as hostile to Rome as the Zealots, but they pursued another method which, given the military superiority of

Rome, was politically wiser at the time. Their tactic was never to become involved in a direct conflict with Rome but to oppose the local collaborators, especially the priestly caste in Jerusalem. In this way they shifted the centre of moral power and established synagogues throughout the land. Rabbinic Judaism developed spontaneously out of the Pharisaic movement. The synagogues, also house communities, at that time themselves called *ecclesiae* (along the lines of Graeco-Roman associations), were the central religious institutions of Judaism in the time of Jesus, opposed to the corrupt temple of Jerusalem. Finally, the Pharisees also stressed table-fellowship within the house as a symbol of the power of the people, whom they therefore called 'priestly and royal', in opposition to the priestly élite.[3]

The whole of this religious policy of the Pharisees was supported by a new concept of God which goes back to the old covenant theology: God, YHWH, is personally very close to the people and therefore to the individual. For the Pharisees, 'Our Father who is in heaven', *abinu she-bashamayim*, was the one who was always near, for all the distance and religious fear which surrounded him. He was *makom*, the one who was always present. The more time goes on, the more I begin to see how the Pharisaic movement made 'the phenomenon of Jesus' historically possible, despite the original and creative features of Jesus. The unfavourable connotations of the term 'Pharisees' to be found in the New Testament must be seen in the light of the situation after the Jewish War (66-72), when Pharisaic rabbinism to some degree became a fossilized orthodoxy, and synagogue and church had become involved in a large number of conflicts.

After 72 the Sadducees, the Zealots and the Essenes disappeared from the scene completely. Probably some of the Essenes became Christians. Only the Pharisees were left to be the religious leaders of the people. Also because of the fact that the first three persecutions of the Greek-speaking Christians (who were nevertheless Jews) were not launched by the Romans but by Jewish contemporaries and because of the equally probable fact that the first Roman persecution of the church under Nero in Rome took place at Jewish instigation, the New Testament writers took over an anti-Pharisaic terminology from the Sadducees, who had then disappeared from the scene. However, the discussion over this anti-Pharisaic tendency in the New Testament is still far from over. Our knowledge of the Pharisees in Jesus' day is very indirect and comes from much later sources.

The historical lesson that we can learn from the attitude of the Pharisees in Jesus' day is this: the clear hostility of the Pharisees to the Zealots, which is also shared by Jesus, still does not tell us in any way that the Pharisees and Jesus were 'politically neutral' or apolitical. They were very aware of the injustice of the occupation and the exploitation of the people by the Romans. It is difficult to distinguish personality and situation. Both the line taken by Eisler-Brandon-Carmichael-Maccoby[4] that Jesus was a Zealot and the line taken by Cullmann-Grant-Hengel-Yoder[5] that Jesus was apolitical towards the Romans are historical caricatures. For all his differences, as a 'political revolutionary' Jesus clearly stood in the tradition of the Pharisees. We have a clear echo of this in the Synoptic Gospels: 'Jesus said : "You know that those who are regarded as rulers of the people rule with an iron hand and that the great misuse their power over them. This is not to be so with you"' (Mark 10.42-43; Matt.20.24-25; Luke 22.24-27). These are no Zealot tactics, but for Jesus too the God of Israel is not the symbol of the religious legitimation of situations of injustice and of the *status quo*, but a God of liberation. This Jewish belief in God itself contains an intrinsic emancipatory solidarity.[6]

(b) The ministry of Jesus: message and life-style

Precisely what do we know historically about Jesus? On the basis of independent traditions we know that he was born in the time of the prince Herod, known as 'the Great'. Herod died in 4 BC. So Jesus was born four or five years before the date from which the Christian calendar is calculated. He was crucified under Pontius Pilate, who became procurator in AD 26.

The time of Jesus' so-called 'public' life was very short. According to responsible investigations it was at most a year and a half. So it was a brief flash in our human history. We do not know what happened to him before this year and a half; we can only guess on the basis of information from the Jewish environment of the time. He was probably born in Nazareth. Only with his baptism by John the Baptist do we arrive at a point at which he appears in history for us. This event is also of decisive importance for the understanding of his ministry. All the traditions which exegetes call 'Jesus traditions' begin with this event, though we do not know what took place at that time in the consciousness of Jesus. We can of course regard the fact that he allowed himself to be baptized by John as an indication that he had the certainty of a programme, or better a calling, which he had thought through personally, and that in it he identified the God of Israel as the one who had called him. Precisely this awareness permeates the whole of his work, from the baptism to the cross. His commitment is unconditional commitment to this God. Jesus claims to speak and act in the name of precisely this God who had always known his Jewish people. However, in Jesus' days the priestly caste saw to it that this belief in God functioned in society in such a way that 'the poor of the land' became the victims. Jesus wanted to show how the reality of 'God' had to function throughout life among the people of Israel.

When after his baptism (and perhaps after the imprisonment of John the Baptist) Jesus himself began to preach, in contrast to John the Baptist as a *travelling preacher*, it very soon became clear that this proclamation was essentially a message of the kingdom of God, i.e. of the rule or the government of God: God's rule as salvation for men. Jesus gives a religious solution to a specific political problem. In those days, when 'religion' and 'social and political life' could not be distinguished as they can be in modern Western society, religion was essentially, in one way or another, a political matter. Moreover, the concept of the 'rule of God', the kingly rule, is itself a political one. 'Kingdom of God' is something very different from imperial rule, something very different from the actual politics of 'the great' in the days of Jesus. The *term* 'kingdom of God' was recognized at that time by all Jews. However, this does not mean that Jesus preferred to take up these current terms. He gave this one a very personal content and even radicalized the new, Pharisaic 'intimacy' of the relationship between God and man. To put things very crudely, three versions of the kingdom of God were current in his day.

1. Above all in the apocryphal writings (the Psalms of Solomon; IV Ezra), the kingdom of God is seen as the restoration of the national political theocracy in Israel, the restoration of the kingdom of David. Since the time of Judas the Galilean this term was also connected with the Zealot opposition to foreign rule: the Zealots or Sicarii wanted to establish the rule of God by force.

2. In the circles of 'the community of the poor' in Qumran the thought lived on of an eschatological, transcendent and universal rule of God over all people. God himself would come to establish a thousand-year kingdom of peace after his judgment over the people and the downfall of 'this world', i.e. the evil world. Only initiates who knew the signs would escape the wrath of God. They too recognized a time of armed revolt.

3. Finally, there was the rabbinic and Pharisaic conception of a provisionally hidden kingdom of God in the hearts of the lovers of the Torah, a kingdom which on the other hand had to take shape in social righteousness in Israel. Without righteousness the kingdom of God cannot come to completion. Men and women are co-creators of the kingdom of God. The *malkuth YHWH* or kingdom of God comes to fulfilment in faithful observance of God's will, i.e. the Torah or law and the *halakah* (the interpretative tradition). Conversion, repentance or change, and observance of the law again make possible the rule of God in oppressed Israel and in the long run (it was thought, if not in the near future) would break the foreign rule. Thus doing God's will accelerated the coming of the kingdom. Finally, the Lord would exercise universal rule over all people who accepted belief in YHWH, 'the one'.

Historically, Jesus' own concept of the rule of God is closely related to that of the Pharisees. However, for him this rule is something original and distinctive. It emerges from the 'Our Father' that Jesus, like the Pharisees, sees a close connection between 'Your kingdom come' and 'Your will be done' completely on earth, as happens in heaven. Only by his parables, healings and the whole of his kingdom does Jesus indicate how he sees this kingdom. For Jesus the kingdom is to be found where human life becomes 'whole', where 'salvation' is realized for men and women, where righteousness and love begin to prevail, and enslaving conditions come to an end. Jesus makes the reality of the kingdom of God imaginable in terms of a common participation in a festive and splendid banquet in which cripples, the poor and the social outcasts can share. Clearly connected with this is the fact that he ate illegally (in religious terms) with people from his own environment and specifically also with outcasts from the society of the time. Here Jesus radicalizes and transcends the Pharisaic notion of table fellowship. In the communal eating together Jesus implements by his own concern for his fellow Jews something of the coming reality and thus anticipates the kingdom of God which begins to exist where under the spell of Jesus people themselves become new.

The coming kingdom is a kingdom *of God*. So it is not at the disposal of men and women, though they may have its privileges (see Mark 4.26-29). Nevertheless this kingdom takes concrete form in human action. That kingdom is not wholly present, once and for all, but wherever and whenever Jesus performs his work of salvation in his fellow men and women. Where Jesus appears, the sick are cured and human communication is restored. In Christian history salvation has often been expressed one-sidedly as something that relates only to inwardness, to the human soul. However, the Old Testament and the Pharisees already understand it to be strongly focussed on the whole of human reality, and Jesus makes this visible by his action: physical and social life are also part of the sphere of the offer of wholeness of life or salvation. Jesus also shares these human needs and they determine his behaviour.

The kingdom of God is a new world in which suffering is done away with, a world of completely whole or healed people in a society no longer dominated by master-servant relationships, quite different from that under Roman rule. For this very reason Jesus turns especially to the poor. 'Salvation is preached to the poor.' To a great degree Jesus' action consisted in establishing social community, opening up communication, above all where 'excommunication' and rejection were officially in force: in respect of public sinners, publicans making themselves rich from the poor, lepers and others, whoever and whatever were 'unclean'. These are the ones whom he seeks out, the ones with whom he eats. Jesus also singles out women, though they do not belong, like the men, to his group (although a later phase in the New Testament to some degree removes the distinctive character of Jesus' attitude to women).[7]

In all this Jesus is aware that he is acting as God would do. He translates God's action to human beings. His parables speak of the one lost sheep, a lost coin, a lost son. By his actions Jesus wants to make clear to his fellow believers who are irritated at his dealings with the unclean that God turns towards lost and vulnerable people: Jesus acts as God acts. So with him there is a claim that in his actions and words God himself is present.

To act as Jesus does is the praxis of the kingdom of God; it also shows what the kingdom of God is: salvation for human beings.

Thus the actions of Jesus, including the New Testament miracle stories, stand alongside his proclamation. Historically there can be no doubt that in the early church phenomena were produced by those who proclaimed the gospel of Jesus which in the judgment of his contemporaries were miracles. However, it is quite impossible, in view of the present form of the texts as they have been handed down to us, to get behind them to an event in the life of Jesus which can be demonstrated historically. On the other hand it is a fallacious argument to conclude from this impossibility of arriving at a truly historical Jesus-event that nothing took place in Jesus' life which could lead to the origin of these stories. Precisely the opposite is the case. The individual stories reflect the awareness of the narrators that Jesus performed miracles, even if they expressed this awareness in forms which do not correspond to our understanding of these events. It is certain that in their encounters with him people were healed, that in his company they experienced fullness of life in a way which immeasurably transcended their other daily experiences. 'If in the power of God I cast out demons, then the kingdom of God has come among you' (Matt.12.28). In this context the miracles are signs of the 'whole' or sound world of the kingdom of God which becomes present in them. Moreover, the proclamation of the nearness of the kingdom of God and Jesus' miracles belong indissolubly together. That the healing ministry of Jesus and the whole of his life-style, freeing people from need and distress, are part of his commission is also shown by the fact that Jesus does not send out his disciples purely with the task of handing on his message but also with the task of 'healing people and making them whole' (see Mark 3.14-16; 6.7ff.). The people who could experience salvation from God in Jesus were also themselves called to do what Jesus did after him, even to a still higher degree (see John 14.12), in unconditional love for their fellow human beings. The foundation of the career of the disciples lies in the course which Jesus himself followed in history.

Though the travelling teacher whom people called rabbi explained the Law, which he too saw as the will of God, for the benefit of men and women even more than the Pharisees did, he did fail to affect Herod Antipas and the priestly authorities. Historically, the tradition according to which Simon the Pharisee warned Jesus of the risk to his life which he ran from Herod Antipas (Luke 13.31) is particularly credible, above all because of the bias against the Pharisees to be found in many New Testament texts after AD 70. However, the murder of John the Baptist also made Jesus think. According to the historian Flavius Josephus, Herod Antipas had John beheaded because he sowed political unrest by attracting people to him, and that compelled the Romans to intervene. (On the other hand, this does not exclude the other motive which the New Testament gives for the murder.) Herod also feared popular unrest because of the appearance of Jesus, above all after the so-called cleansing of the temple.

In this Jesus performed an action which was clearly directed against the priestly rulers of the temple, who enriched themselves by the poverty of religious people. Historically, the issue here was less a matter of Jesus' anger over the desecration of the temple as the house of God by the trade practised there than of Jesus' sudden holy anger because this was the very place where the poor were deprived of their rights and exploited. The 'mystical' side here clearly has a political element. This was also an action which affected the immediate masters of the priestly caste, the Romans. This fact (which is also illustrated by the constant anger over the temple in those days, above all on the part of the Diaspora Jews) of itself clearly indicates that Jesus was not apolitical or unaffected by the Roman oppression of the people; only that he saw this in a different way from the Zealots. At all events, at a certain moment, as a result of all these factors, Jesus understood that his career too must include rejection and an ignominious death. In one way or another, perhaps in the dark night of faith, but aware of his task, Jesus related his imminent death to his preaching of the kingdom of God. Despite this threat of death, at all events he remained faithful to his message and deliberately said farewell to his followers at a festal meal. After that he was executed, by a Roman crucifixion *sub Pontio Pilato* (there is good reason for that standing in the Christian creed). By any account, this is also a political factor.

This is a broad outline sketch of the life of Jesus, something like a historical reconstruction, as far as that can be done in the light of the New Testament, 'meta-' or 'supra-dogmatically'. It makes clear that one of the most certain facts from the life of Jesus is that he expressed the reality of God as he saw it through his message of the kingdom of God and his action in accordance with it, personally, in a very special and distinctive way. He made clear the content of this message about the God who loves humanity by means of his parables, in which conversion and alternative possibilities of life are offered: the praxis of the kingdom of God. Moreover, this content was also demonstrated through Jesus' life-style and action, through his dealings with men and women which opened up communication, even with tax-collectors and public sinners; through his offer of salvation from God in table fellowship and his interpretation of the law, the sabbath and the temple in favour of humanity. Finally, and not least, it was expressed in his fellowship with the small group of disciples.

The nucleus of the whole of this ministry is the God of human beings, concerned for humanity, who wants to make us people of God, in turn, like God, concerned for other people. What is striking about Jesus is his liberating 'humanization' of religion which nevertheless remains the service of God, faithful to death: service to God and humanity. Here there is no question of a choice between the two – God and humanity. Jesus' whole life was a celebration, a doxological celebration, of the rule of God and at the same time an orthopraxis, action in keeping with this kingdom of God, i.e of God who wants to come into his own in human history, for the happiness of human beings in a society in which *shalom* prevails. The link between the two – the kingdom of God and the life-style of Jesus – is, as Jesus understood it, so inward that precisely in his actions and way of life Jesus shows something of the kingdom of God. This is an important historical fact – with not a few theological implications. Historically, the living God of Israel is clearly the flashpoint of the life of the man Jesus; with him something comes near to men and women which Jesus himself calls the 'kingdom of God' (see Matt.12.28): God himself who comes into his own in the man Jesus for the advantage of fellow men and women. This gives rise among men and women to a new relationship to God, and the comprehensible and visible side of this new relationship is a new type of relationship among men and women within a community of peace, which brings liberation and opens up communication.

(c) Jesus, confessed by his followers as the Christ

Does the christology of the church add anything to this historical picture of Jesus? Or does it simply make explicit, with the help of key concepts from the Old Testament and later Hellenistic Judaism, what was really already present in this historical picture of Jesus? Or are things even more complicated? Finally, one can ask whether, without God's final judgment on Jesus, we ourselves can come to a definitive judgment on him and identify him truly without a special action on God's part. In that case there would ultimately be an appeal to a decision of faith.

The Christian churches confess of the man Jesus whom I have just described that he is 'Christ, Son of God, our Lord'. Have we here left the Jesus of history or even replaced him by a myth? Or can an earthly figure as attractive as Jesus of Nazareth be ultimately defined in his authenticity and originality other than 'in mythical terms' (unlike the people of the nineteenth century, we no longer regard 'myth' as a bad word!)?

(i) The choice of faith

No one can lay a foundation other than that which is already laid: Jesus Christ (I Cor.1.11; see also Mark 12.10ff.; Acts 4.10,12). This is the starting point and the foundation of New Testament faith, which could not be founded otherwise. It is a decision of faith, nevertheless founded on the special character of the Jesus of history.

What applied in the case of the kingdom of God applies equally to the term messiah (*meshiah*), the Lord's anointed, the Christ.

Originally this title belonged in the context of the monarchy of ancient Israel. Israel's king from the Davidic dynasty was understood to be the Lord's anointed (Pss.2.2; 18.50; 20.6; 84.9; 132.10,17). But here we must not look for the immediate occasion of the attribution of the title Messiah to Jesus. The arguments from ancient scripture in the New Testament clearly belong to the period after Easter. However, this old concept underwent a whole development, and not long before Jesus' day this development ended in the so-called early Jewish concepts of the Messiah. With some provisos one may rightly speak of a Jewish messianic expectation, although the most specific texts belong to the royal ideology of Jerusalem and Judah. However, the real early Jewish messianism had its roots in religious and political developments which arose through the Hellenistic religious persecution under Antiochus IV Epiphanes (175-164 BC) and also in the time of the Maccabees and Hasmonaeans (167-63 BC). At that time there sprang to life a romantic recollection of King David and his great kingdom, in which nostalgia was coupled with religious and political freedom and independence, which people were still able to enjoy for a while after the first conquest of the Near East by Rome (129-63 BC). The crisis period for Judaism between the persecution of Antiochus IV and the end of the Bar Kochba revolt (at the time of Jewish apocalyptic, 167 BC to AD 135) is the real background to the early-Jewish, religious and political messianism.[8]

At that time messianism was not a simple but rather a fluid concept: ideas of a high priestly Messiah, a royal Messiah and a prophetic Messiah were going the rounds. In a rough sketch we could categorize ideas at the time of Jesus rather like this:

1. A popular expectation of the Davidic Messiah as depicted in

the Psalms of Solomon (cf. Ps.Sal.17 and 18; Test. Levi 17,18) with a strong Pharisaic colouring. Related to this, but distinct from it, is the concept of the Messiah from prophecy and wisdom: Solomon is wisdom, and as such is 'Son of David', a king who brings peace and heals humanity (see Ps.72).

2. The expectation of two messianic figures in Qumran, a priestly Messiah from Aaron and a political Messiah from Israel (1 QS 9.11; CD 12.19; 14.19; 19.10; 20.1).

3. The figure of 'the Son of man' (Dan.7; Eth.Enoch, Similitudes, 37-71), which took on messianic features and in so doing received a new content.

Given the varied nature of this concept of Messiah, we must take into account that Jesus himself could also give a new significance to messianic thinking or 'christology' by his own experience and reflection, and also as a result of the reactions of his disciples, especially as none of the current conceptions can be applied to Jesus as they stand. Therefore in filling out what made Jesus Christ, we cannot begin from already existing messianic concepts, although these form the Jewish background to the New Testament concept of Messiah to which Jesus himself reacted in his own way, also as a Jew. Jesus himself may have changed this concept decisively; the multiplicity of this concept also allows that.

(ii) Jesus of Nazareth is Christ

Originally the term 'Jesus Christ' was not a proper name but a double name which at the same time expressed a confession, namely, the confession of the earliest community in Jerusalem: the *crucified* Jesus is the promised Messiah, the eschatological anointed of the Lord: 'God has made him Lord and Messiah' (Acts 2.36; cf. Rom.1.3-4). In Hellenistic Gentile Christianity, which did not understand ths Jewish background, 'Christ' became an ingredient of Jesus' name, Jesus Christ, and the question then shifted to become : In what sense is Jesus Christ Son of God? Paul usually speaks of 'messiah Jesus': Christ Jesus.

That Jesus Christ is a confessional name characterizes the basic structure of all christology: this confession is the foundation and the origin of the whole of the New Testament. Without this confession we would never have heard of Jesus of Nazareth. That Jesus has become known in our history in this way is essentially also a result of this Christian confession. But the confession points to the historical Jesus. The confession has the form it does because Jesus of Nazareth was the sort of person who could evoke it. All the statements about Jesus in the New Testament, even when they are recollections of historical facts from Jesus' life, have a confessional character. People talked about Jesus because they believed in him and not out of idle historical curiosity. And that is also and already the case with what exegetes call the Jesus tradition. In this sense a meta-dogmatic christology is *a priori* impossible, though that does not mean that we cannot and must not look for a 'meta-dogmatic' reconstruction of the historical Jesus. However, no historical reconstruction, however pure, can bring us to 'Christ'. Here we have the underivable mediation of the New Testament or 'apostolic' confession. And this confession comes first in any christology, if it is to be Christian and not a 'Jesuology'.

Still, just as important here is the fact that this confession concerns a historical person with a very specific context in our history, Jesus of Nazareth – no one else and no mythical being. Therefore the historical question of Jesus is also a theologically relevant one. Christology without a historical foundation is empty and impossible. In modern times this appeal to history is at the same time an expression of Christian opposition to ideological misuse of the name of Jesus Christ, since the way the church uses the name Christ is subject to criticism from the perspective of Jesus: his message and the distinctive character of his life-style, to the death.

The identity of 'the historical man Jesus' with 'the Christ of faith' is a basic affirmation of the New Testament.[9] These are not exclusive alternatives, but form a unity in tension without which Christianity ceases to be Christianity and the gospel ceases to be the gospel. The Jesus tradition is as it is precisely because Jesus himself was the kind of person that he appears to be in the tradition, albeit to those who became disciples, followed him and formed the church. This is to a large extent confirmed by textual analysis and comparative studies with the Jewish and pagan environment. Despite all his rooting in Jewish and above all Pharisaic culture, Jesus clearly had an independent, original profile of his own. Despite and specifically within his historical roots he seemed to his Jewish followers to be 'new'. In this sense, in his historical life, Jesus was in the eyes of the believers a Christian, the first fruits of Christianity. But at this point any form of later Christianity is subject to the criticism of the *Jewish* Jesus of Nazareth, though in my view not to the criticism of Judaism.

Thus to identify Jesus essentially calls for a decision of faith.

However, this decision of faith presupposes more than a mere historical view of the person of Jesus whom we know simply by the New Testament interpretation of faith.

(iii) Jesus and the structure of the Christian creed

If we analyse the Christian confession of faith, we see in it a structure which at the same time points us directly to the historical Jesus. Christians experience in the man Jesus a definitive and universal significance for (*a*) their understanding of God and (*b*) the salvation of the whole of history and humanity, and, precisely here, for the salvation of the individual human life. In this respect Christians are 'Jewish'. To confess Jesus as the Christ is both a response to the question of God and a response to the question of human salvation, in an indissoluble unity. In the last resort *we* must say who Jesus is: 'Who do *you* say that I am?' Jesus subjects us to the influence of a 'christology' or 'messianology', but this is possible only on the basis of the roots which lie in Jesus, recognized through and in following him, becoming his disciples. That is the purpose of the whole of the New Testament.

What is always permanently striking in the New Testament (as has already emerged from this brief 'portrait' of Jesus) is the essential relationship between the person of Jesus and his message of the imminence of what Jesus calls the kingdom of God. There is an intrinsic connection between message and proclaimer, just as there is an intrinsic connection between the message and Jesus' activity in consistency with it. With his person, his message and his way of life Jesus stands surety for the God who liberates and loves humanity.

This already emerges from a first hearing of his parables and from a first look at his way of life. Jesus does not say to the little Zacchaeus who had climbed a tree to see Jesus as he went past, 'God loves you' (as modern fundamentalist posters shriek at us in the crush of our railway stations). Something quite different happens. Jesus goes to Zacchaeus' house, sits at table with him, and by his liberating action, which opens up communication, and his dealings with the 'excommunicated', shows Zacchaeus quite specifically that God loves him. Something is opened up which transcends humanity: as a result of his liberating contact with Jesus, Zacchaeus gives away half his possessions to the poor. He is a new man. Precisely because Jesus on the basis of his experience of God put this turning to humanity into practice radically and without compromise, he deliberately went to his death and accepted this death planned by his fellow men as the extreme price and consequence of the truth of his message and action in accordance with it.

That the man Jesus guarantees God's love of humanity is clear from the way in which Jesus understands God: he is a God whose liberating action Jesus not only proclaims but also implements and makes visible in his own action. He calls God 'Abba', Father, which points to a very close, almost human intimacy; and also to the fact that he learned his message and the nature of his action from God himself (in the Jewish family 'the Father' is the authority and the teacher): Jesus acts as God acts.

As reflected in the man Jesus, the Unnameable and Inexpressible One, in the face of whom all religions become speechless, takes on specific contours: he is a God who reveals himself and does not want to dwell in the clouds, although this revelation takes place in the finite and thus ambiguous veiling of true humanity, that of Jesus (and does so within an androcentric society). Therefore the Jesus of Nazareth who is identical with 'the Christ of faith' confronts us most profoundly with the question of God, with a God concerned for humanity and no other God. Precisely here, human salvation, salvation from God, becomes visible. For from Jesus' message, his life-style and his death, it became clear to believers that the God of Jesus, the God of Israel, accepts men and women wholly and seeks to renew them in their relationships to themselves and to others in a world fit for humans to live in. The specifically Christian experience of what is called 'the transcendent' is the experience of this divine affirmation which needs humanity in order finally to be able to affirm oneself and others and to be free to unfold a better history (*iustificatio*).

All this of course presupposes that Jesus himself also lived from the conviciton that he was loved and recognized by God. The Christian tradition expressed this subsequently with more pointed words in the language of faith: Jesus is in a relationship of Son to God as Father, 'Son of God'. However, the foundation for the possibility of the use of this name by the church lies in the historical reality of Jesus himself,[10] above all in his 'abba' experience which, in contrast to 'this world' – Jesus' own turbulent time – was the source of his message and life-style marked by turning towards suffering humanity.

Moreover, Jesus wants to make people share in his relationship with God: being loved and constantly loved again by God. 'Yes, you may live' – as is said about him in the apostolic testimony: 'This is my well-beloved Son.' Elsewhere we hear the words 'My and your Father' (John 20.17), i.e. my Father who has become your Father through the baptism of the Spirit. Thus by his proclamation and way of life to the death, Jesus has opened up a new relationship of human beings to God and in so doing has established a new relationship of one human being to another in the world in which they live. A christology which passes over this fails to recognize the true humanity of Jesus *in which* – not above it or below it – God's own reality becomes visible. Here, too, there is no question of a surplus of revelation. To follow Jesus is at the same time also to follow in the footsteps of his belief and trust in God which ultimately lie at the basis of this life. A christology with 'the death of God' as a background is historically and theologically passé. In that case Jesus is no longer Jesus of Nazareth, the Jesus of history, but a cipher for human projections.

On the other hand, it is inappropriate theologically to ask, 'Who or what is Jesus in himself?' That is an abstraction. The relationship of Jesus to his disciples and also to us today, in other words the significance of Jesus for us, is included in the question 'Who do you say that I am?' But this question, which is also topical for us today, nevertheless at the same time concerns the historical Jesus of Nazareth, and not a cipher. Therefore the distinction which Schubert Ogden makes between the 'empirical-historical' and the 'existential-historical' Jesus is very misleading,[11] although he is right to point out that theologians often ask the wrong questions.

All this brings out something very important. Jesus' message of and about God is so integrated into his dealings with fellow human beings, in action, liberation and communication, that his proclamation and his way of life interpret each other reciprocally, while together they renew and change the given situation and those involved in it, making them free for their fellow human beings in love and solidarity – like Zacchaeus, who after his liberating encounter with Jesus allowed the poor to share in his possessions.

In turning both to the rich tax-collector and to vulnerable children, the sick or the posssessed, cripples and beggars, Jesus makes directly evident what he is talking about, and in this way, here and now, he anticipates eschatological salvation: the kingdom of God. His way of being, speaking and acting cannot be detached from the reactions of others to it. He proclaims the

reality of God as salvation for men and women who, in contact
with him, at the same time experience salvation to the full. In his
human existence, by his human action, Jesus affirms God as the
reality which saves and liberates human beings.

The identity of Jesus must therefore also be read out of and in
the salvation which is realized in other human beings thanks to
him. The Gospels bear witness to that. In the repentance and
renewal of human life through and in contact with Jesus, we
begin to see who Jesus himself is and what he does. Therefore
the New Testament witness is essentially part of the response to
the question who Jesus was, and can be also for us.

All this is possible only if God was in fact the foundation for
Jesus and his way of life. However, only God can bear witness
(albeit always by means of believing men and women). This
brings us to the death and resurrection of Jesus. Here too, it
is impossible to separate what happened with Jesus and the
conversion which came in reaction to Jesus, the change and
renewal in those who came into contact with him, though it is
equally impossible to identify them.

(iv) The crucifixion

In the Christian tradition, Jesus' crucifixion becomes a central
kerygma and dogma, although in the New Testament there are a
whole series of passages in which no believers' interpretation of
Jesus' crucifixion are given.

However, we may say that the Christian proclamation of the
saving significance of the crucifixion of Jesus goes back to the
basic tenor of Jesus' own proclamation. This becomes clear in a
subtle way from the Gospel of Mark. Many commentators rightly
see the 'messianic secret' as a construction by Mark, but in so
doing they sometimes forget that this construction does have a
foundation in the life of the historical Jesus, viz., his restraint in
connection with the title 'Christ', Messiah. Mark addressed his
Gospel to a community which already believed in Jesus *Christ*.
He had to make clear to this Christian community that Jesus
had interpreted his own mission in a way which in no sense
corresponded to existing messianic expectations. This title can be
applied to Jesus only if what 'Messiah' means is defined afresh.
It was in fact the crucifixion of Jesus which reverified this term
Messiah: the crucified and rejected Jesus is the Christ. That is the
first confession of faith. Therefore the crucifixion is central in the
New Testament, and rightly so. Mark 8.27-33 is significant here.

The scene of the first 'passion prediction' is set near Caesarea Philippi in the context of Jesus' question, 'Who do men say that I am?' Peter replies and goes on to say, 'I myself believe that you are the Messiah.' But at that point, according to Mark, Jesus immediately tells them to keep quiet about it (to shut their mouths!) and he himself fills in the concept of Messiah with the words, 'the Son of man must suffer many things, be rejected and die.' The words come from after Easter, perhaps, but they are not without roots in the historical Jesus. Here, on the basis of the way in which it is given new content by Jesus' proclamation and life-style, we also have a redefinition of the term 'Christ': it is used of a man who dies in 'unconsecrated ground', outside the walls of the holy city. Even during his lifetime Jesus had broken through the walls separating the sacred from the profane. The fact that in the New Testament narrative of Jesus' passion, witnesses said something to the effect that this man had said that he would destroy the temple and rebuild it in three days, is clearly connected with Jesus' proclamation about the nature and person of God's own being and the nature of his own messianism. Like God, Jesus preferred to identify himself with the outcast and the rejected, the 'unholy', so that he himself ultimately became the Rejected, the Outcast.

This identification is indeed radical. So there is continuity between Jesus' life and his death. Precisely for that reason, Jesus' saving significance comes to a climax in his death. The theologumena used in the New Testament and indeed later to describe this reality of salvation to certain people within their own culture should not be confused with the specific reality of salvation itself. The redefinition which Jesus gave of both God and man, in and through his proclamation and way of life, takes on its supreme and ultimate significance in his crucifixion: God is present in human life where to human vision he seems to be absent. On the cross God shared in the brokenness of our world.

This means that God determines in absolute freedom, from eternity, who and how he will be, namely, a God of human beings. In his own being he is a God for us! It is very difficult to find a distinction between God in himself and God for us in the New Testament. (This has theological consequences; it does not fit with the affirmations of 'process philosophy' and its theological adherents, although it fits in with their fundamental concerns.) Clearly there is a theological redefinition of various concepts of God in the New Testament; there is also a redefinition of humanity. God accepts humanity without any condition from our side, and precisely as a result of this unconditional acceptance he transforms men and women and brings them to conversion and renewal. His is love without conditions. Therefore the cross is also a judgment on our own selfish views; on our ways of experiencing what it means to be human and what it means to be God. Here we have an ultimate and definitive revelation of God's humanity, the heart of Jesus' message of the kingdom of God: God who comes into his own *in* the human world, for human happiness. God does not lay down any conditions for us human beings or for Jesus himself for his redeeming and liberating presence: 'God reconciled the world to itself in Jesus' (II Cor.5.19). Human beings put Jesus to death, but this execution is at the same time God's supreme self-revelation.

(v) Resurrection – reality and belief

Of course this christology (= this Christian messianism) only became clear to the first Christians, who were all Jews, by virtue of, and within, their 'paschal experience'. For all the continuity there is a break here. Only a new action by God can connect Jesus' historical life, over the break of his death, with 'the Christ of faith', with the confession, 'he is truly risen'. In the resurrection from the dead, God's end-time action over Jesus, the crucified one, God's own judgment on, and also his relationship to, Jesus and his message, his life-style and his death, become clear to the believer. Easter faith implies and presupposes a new action from God towards the crucified Jesus. Here in the first instance is an expression of the way in which God himself is related to Jesus – as received in and interpreted by his disciples. Paul in particular understood this well when he observed explicitly in connection with those in Corinth who denied the resurrection of Jesus: 'Some evidently have *no sense of God*' (I Cor.15.34). Therefore the reality of the resurrection, which is the only way in which belief in the resurrection is called to life, becomes the test both of the understanding of God proclaimed by Jesus and our soteriological christology (= messianism). Here it becomes evident that Jesus' way of life and death did not happen in vain. In the resurrection God authenticates the person, the message and the whole career of Jesus. He puts his seal on it and speaks out against the human judgment on him. Through and in this Christian faith in the resurrection of Jesus, the crucified but risen Jesus remains active in our history. Here, too, the principle applies (though in another

way) that the 'in itself' and the 'for us' cannot be separated. Jesus'
own resurrection, his sending of the Spirit, the origin of the
Christian 'community of God' living from the Spirit and the New
Testament witnesses of faith provide a mutual definition of one
another and are indissolubly bound up together, although at the
same time they are not the same things. One can say that the
communities of God which came into being on the basis of the
resurrection of Jesus are what is meant *at the deepest level* in the
New Testament by 'the appearances of Jesus'. The crucified but
risen Jesus appears in the believing, assembled community of the
church. That this sense of the risen, living Jesus has faded in
many of them can be basically blamed on the fact that our churches
are insufficiently 'communities' of God (though of course there
are other factors). Where the church of Jesus Christ lives, and
lives a liberating life in the footsteps of Jesus, the resurrection
faith undergoes no crisis. On the other hand, it is better not to
believe in God than to believe in a God who minimizes human
beings, holds them under and oppresses them, with a view to a
better world to come. In this heartbeat we can hear an echo of the
message of Jesus of Nazareth in all his goodness and life.

2. Church communities, 'living from the Spirit'

The experience of God's concern for humanity which emerges
from the message and the life-style of Jesus was the origin of the
first wave of the Jesus movement which was composed above all
of Hebrew (Aramaic) speaking Jews who had become Christians;
they looked for the coming of Jesus, the judge of the world.
However, in the New Testament in fact we come to hear of the
segments of the old Christian Jesus movement above all through
Greek-speaking Diaspora Jews who had become Christians. In
their milieu this Jewish, Christian movement became a universal
mission church.

 For these Christians, the experience of the historical Jesus was
not the direct foundation of their faith, their church or their
mission (they had never met him); that role was played by their
baptism in the Spirit, baptism in the name of Jesus. The God of
these Christians was and is the God who did not leave Jesus in
the lurch after his death, but made him the 'life-giving Spirit' (I
Cor.15.45). Christians who are baptized in him are therefore
pneumatici. This was already the old view of the church held by
the Hellenistic Jewish Christians in Jerusalem – the group around

Stephen. These were driven out of Jerusalem at an early stage. Many of them went via Samaria to Syria, above all to Antioch. There they ultimately founded the first great church mission commmunities. It was there that Paul, too, went to be taught after his conversion.

The pre-Pauline view of the church in these circles (to which Paul made some corrections, though he was basically in sympathy with it) was very widespread in the early church. Granted, we know this view from the New Testament only indirectly: through Paul and Paulinism, through Acts, through certain traditions in the Gospel of Mark and through other texts in the New Testament. However, its presence in early Christianity is clear.

The solidarity and equality of all Christians 'in the Spirit' (Acts 2.17-18; II Cor.5.17), 'living through or in the Spirit' (Gal.5.25; 6.1), 'new creation' (Gal.6.15; II Cor.5.17) were the key phrases of this 'Antiochene-Christian', Jewish-Christian missionary movement and its theology. This ecclesiology had its source in the baptism in the Spirit, the foundation of all church life. Paul was to accuse this pneumatic movement of denying the resurrection. But what seems to have been historically involved was not so much the resurrection as a specific form of present or already realized eschatology: through the baptism of the Spirit these believers lived as though they were already redeemed, in a new world and in the fullness of time. Therefore they were not concerned for the 'old world', not really involved in it. For them this old world had become irrelevant. At least within the community of believers they were already living 'in a new world', completely alienated and 'not at home' in the world outside.

A few passages from Acts 19.1-7; 18.24-19.1 are very illuminating for this early Christian view of the church. There seem to have been disciples of Jesus who were baptized by John the Baptist but nevertheless were also given special instruction 'about all that concerned Jesus' (Acts 18.25); evidently they were up in the so-called logia tradition about Jesus. But they had heard nothing about the Spirit! Apollos was one of this group, and therefore had to be instructed. He had to receive the baptism of the Spirit, the basis of all pneumatic and indeed ecstatic experience in the community. Thus Apollos did not know anything of the 'Antiochene' pneuma christology. We find the contrast between baptism with water and baptism with Spirit from the Q tradition onwards (Matt.3.11; Luke 3.16), in all levels of the New Testament (Mark 1.8; John 1.26,31,33; Acts 1.5; 11.16; I Cor.13.13). Acts (2.17-

21) relates the prophecy of Joel to the whole of the Christian community: all who received Christian baptism formed the one prophetic and pneumatic people of God: they were equal partners, without any domination in relationships.

This pneuma-christological wisdom messianism, summed up by Paul in 'Christ is God's power and wisdom' (I Cor.1.24), in fact goes back to a very widespread early Christian pre-Pauline theology of the church: 'You are in Messiah Jesus, who for us is the wisdom of God' (I Cor.12.30). Hence the Antiochene name Christians, people who are in Christ Jesus who himself is full of pneuma: 'No one can say "Jesus is Lord" save through the Holy Spirit' (I Cor.12.3). The wisdom christology is also the nucleus of all the wisdom hymns quoted by Paul and Paulinism (Phil.2.6-11; Col.1.15-20; Eph.2.14-16; I Tim.3.16; also Heb.1.3; I Peter 3.18,22; even, this time in masculine Logos terms, in the pre-Johannine hymn John 1.1-14, worked over by John). Messiah Jesus, Wisdom Jesus, Logos Jesus: for all their Christian character these are typical statements by Hellenistic Jews. Christology is, in Jesus, a corrected form of Jewish messianism.

At that time the whole Mediterranean coast was full of pneumatics, above all of religious enthusiasts, often of Eastern origin. The Christians, too, expressed their specifically Christian experience in very contextual terms of experience from the surrounding culture. However, for them all this was based on the 'paschal' Pentecostal experience of the baptism of the Spirit.

Paul, converted to Christianity, was confronted above all with this form of early Christianity. It is not for nothing that even post-Pauline traditions speak about the church as being built on 'apostles *and prophets*' (see Eph.2.20). Nevertheless, Paul was to make some corrections to this tradition. It is striking that he always makes the pre-Pauline hymns the vehicle for ethical admonition (see II Cor.8.13f.). Despite the 'already', which he too resolutely affirms, Paul wants to put emphasis above all on the 'not yet' of redemption. In this way he corrects a present eschatology and thus reduces irrational ecstatic elements in the pneumatic movement to more sober proportions. For all their experience, as members of Christian communities, of living in a new world (which is also Paul's view), according to him Christians had to be brought back into what at the same time needed to be done in this world; to live as human beings in this world. Without any eye, of course, for the critical task of a Christian in secular social and political spheres (this was perhaps a consequence of his legacy from the pneumatic Antiochenes), Paul also wants to set the pneumatic Christ movement firmly on the ground, where evidently other than Christian laws hold, e.g. a civil government, a particular system of families and of work, and so on. According to Paul, the pneumatics must also be involved in that. However, Paul does not see the consequences of being a Christian in this earthly context; at least, he does not see them critically, in social and political terms. Therefore for Paul a slave could be free in the community but remain a slave in the world, while from their perspective many pre-Pauline pneumatics were not affected by the world at all, and sometimes did not even want to work.

Paul was opposed to this. As Christians – moved by the Spirit – they are already living in the community in a new free world (that applies just as strongly to Paul himself). But Paul wants the free Christians also to be seen to live in the world as human beings. And rightly so. According to Paul, however, they must do this as integrated members of Graeco-Roman society (except when this puts pressure on their faith). Paul makes this choice for pastoral reasons. If (Paul's argument goes) Christians are good citizens of the Roman Hellenistic empire, in the state system, the work of Christian mission will benefit in the long run. Many of Paul's admonitions are prompted by such motives of pastoral mission: not giving offence to others, for these are potential Christians. This is an expression of contextual pastoral strategy, not kerygma or dogma. This choice on the part of Paul clearly opens up possibilities of other Christian options. These are no binding norms for present-day Christians.

'The power of the Spirit', the key-word of the old pneumatic Christ movement, was the basic conviction of this generation of Christians. Every member of the community had *de facto* authority in the community on the basis of his or her own inspiration by the Spirit – even at that time the leading authority in the Christian churches was institutionalized, on the basis of the baptism of the Spirit and the pneumatic phenomena which followed from that and led to the formation of communities. Paul came to know this originally egalitarian view of the church as a brotherhood and sisterhood from pre-Pauline traditions. The view of the church warmly shared by Paul is crystallized in Gal.3.28; a kind of Christian charter of freedom, which according to present-day exegetical studies is not an invention of Paul but an earlier baptismal tradition from the Hellenistic-Jewish, pre-Pauline communities:

For you are all children of God,
for all of you who are baptized in Christ
are clothed with Christ.
There is no longer Jew nor Gentile,
There is no longer slave nor free man,
There is no longer man nor woman,
but you are all one in Christ Jesus (Gal.3.26-28).

I do not intend to go into the reasons why these verses should be seen as a pre-Pauline tradition and indeed as a solemn declaration over those who have been newly baptized: exegetes are now virtually unanimous over this interpretation.[12] The tradition goes back to the old pneuma-christology.

The Greek literally reads, 'the male and the female no longer exist' – a clear reference to the Septuagint translation of Gen.1.27, 'male and female created he them'. In this line of thought the baptism of the Spirit is the eschatological restoration of an order of creation with an equality which was destroyed historically and in society – it is 'new creation' (Gal.6.15). The baptism of the Spirit removes historical discriminations. The three categories of those discrimininated against are clear from the Jewish-Christian perspective: the Gentiles (discriminated against in favour of the Jews), the slaves (discriminated against in favour of the free), and women (discriminated against in favour of men). Nowadays we could add yet more categories. In principle, Christian baptism completely removes all these social and historical oppositions within the community of believers. Of course this is a performative and not a descriptive statement; however, it is a statement which expresses the hope which needs to be realized now, already, as a model in the community.

In I Cor.12.13 Paul refers to this same baptismal tradition; however, he leaves out the clause 'neither male nor female', evidently because of the difficulties which had arisen in the Corithian communities over the emancipation movements for women which had already come into being there (see I Cor.11.2-16; I Cor.7). Paul says there that the difference between man and woman exists, but must be done away with 'in the Lord' – a somewhat ambiguous remark. However, we should also bear in mind here that Paul is reacting against a premature enthusiasm stemming from a present eschatology which seeks to minimalize or pass over the 'not yet' of redemption.

Nevertheless, here, in contrast to the pre-Pauline tradition (Gal.3.28), there are again privileges for the male (I Cor.11.7f.), albeit in Paul for pastoral and strategic reasons. According to him, in the eyes of the Gentiles the free Christian behaviour of the Corinthian women could damage the reputation of the Christian community. Paul takes the same attitude over slaves: in the community of faith they are free, but in society they remain slaves. In his opposition to the present eschatology Paul has not thought through the secular social consequences of the 'now already'. So here too, for us, other Christian options are possible.

Despite all the pastoral strategy which is well-disposed to the Roman world, nevertheless in Paul we can still feel the original power of the whole of the liberating tradition of Antioch and the early church: 'Where the Spirit of the Lord is, there is liberty' (II Cor.3.17; Gal.5.13; it has also influenced Mark 10.6). According to Paul and the whole of the New Testament, at least within Christian communities of believers, relationships involving subjection are no longer to prevail. We find this principle throughout the New Testament, and it was also to determine strongly the New Testament view of ministry. This early-Christian egalitarian ecclesiology in no way excludes leadership and authority; but in that case authority must be one filled with the Spirit, from which no Christian, man or woman, is excluded in principle on the basis of the baptism of the Spirit.

We shall now trace the trajectory of the formation of groups in these church communities built on the pneuma of Christ.

Part Two

The Practice and Theology of Ministry in the Early Communities of Christian Believers

Introduction

1. Jesus entrusted the further proclamation of the kingdom of God to his disciples. Like Jesus himself, his followers, to begin with in Palestine, led the life of travelling preachers, in expectation of the speedy coming of the kingdom of God. Some echoes of this can be detected in what is now called the Logia tradition, the so-called Q source. Above all in a subsequent phase, Christianity extended into Hellenistic Christian Jewish missionary communities, also directed towards the Gentiles. The more the church spread, the tighter became institutional forms; they also became more thought-out, i.e. more uniform. I shall try to follow this development in broad outline.

2. This Part has two sections. In the first section I shall give a socio-historical analysis of the form of organization in these communities. In the second section I shall take up this analysis from an explicitly theological perspective, without forgetting the first section.

The difficulty with ventures into social history is that there are no such things as 'facts', even the 'hard facts' which sociologists are fond of positing. There are only interpreted facts. We can only arrive at facts within changeable theories which we make ourselves. There thus seem to be facts which in one way or another are based on the theoretical plan or which in the long run ovrthrow this theory. Although one can produce all kinds of criticisms of even established theories with reference to socio-historical facts, a purely empirical approach, without a theory, is of course a chaotic and senseless enterprise. Moreover, here implicit theories, like that of 'common sense' or, in connection with the ministry, of later developments in the church, begin to play a role. The advantage of an approach from facts in the light of a theory is that such an approach can at all events be falsified or proved wrong. Social history presupposes theoretical models in one way or another, implicit or explicit. It is better that they should be explicit.

The problem which immediately arises is: which theory? There are always a large number of models on offer – above all models of conflict or integration. There is also the question *cui bono?*. What interest do you seek to serve with a particular socio-historical investigation? The critical question is: what do you stand for? What do you choose? For me as a theologian this is clear, and I have even sought to indicate this 'partisan' choice in the title of this book: it is a plea for humanity in the church. In my view this was Jesus' own choice: humanity's cause is God's cause and God's cause is humanity's cause. As an institution, the church is the servant of the true salvation, the true happiness, of men and women. Moreover the church as an institution can be measured by the liberating power of the gospel. It can also be criticized. According to the New Testament there must be a fundamental solidarity and equality among Christians, without master-servant relationships, though this does not in any way exclude authority and leadership in the community.

So my interest is in the baptismal declaration from the New Tetament: 'there is neither Jew nor non-Jew, freeman nor slave, man nor woman'. On this basis it is no wonder that until well into the second century Christians were regarded by Gentiles as subversive elements in society: freed and free men and women.

This book is concerned, therefore, with an interpretative description of facts, in which I am principally interested in the group process as a liberating system of communication. To demonstrate how authority and leadership were exercised in the early Christian churches I shall therefore look above all for situations of conflict and see how these were resolved and decided. The relationship of the Christian group to the social and cultural context is also important. This is not the same for Christians in Greece as it is for Christians in Egypt or Asia Minor. The different theological accents which one finds in many early Christian communities also determined the form which people gave to the community and its ministers. The semiotic insight that cultures, like any grouping, form a complex 'web of meanings',[1] the mutual connections between which can be studied so that one can read their intentions from them, will also help us in this investigation, if only in criticizing ideologies.[2]

Section 1: **A socio-historical approach, though not without theological importance**

1. Authority and leadership in the early church

(a) *Ekklesia*: communities of Christian believers

In everyday Greek of this time *ekklesia* denoted the assembly of the free (male) citizens of a *polis* or city to hold elections; this was also the case later, when this right to vote had become a formality, merely an acclamation. However, groups with strong internal ties, like the first Christians, soon developed their own jargon, which was independent of current semantic fields. Through the Septuagint translation of the Old Testament, which translated the Hebrew *qᵉhal* YHWH, 'assembly of (or around) the Lord', sometimes as '*synagoge* of the Lord' and sometimes as '*ekklesia* of the Lord, it came about that the first Christians only used the term *ekklesia* of themselves and never the term *synagoge* (except in James 2.2). They did so in a variety of contexts: for the 'free association' of Christians assembled 'at the house of X'; also for the various house communities of a city, 'the church which is in Corinth'; they also used it for the Christian communities in several cities and finally for all the Christians in the world. Here they were following a Hellenistic Jewish usage of *ekklesia*. To translate *ekklesia* 'church' is therefore in one sense an anachronism. Expressions like 'the *ekklesia* of the Thessalonians' or 'of the Laodiceans' (I Thess.1.1; II Thess.1.1; Col.4.16), or the expression 'a particular city holds a church' (I Cor.11.18; see also 14.19,23,28,35), still betray the background of the current Greek use of the term. However, the New Testament word *ekklesia* does not just mean the actual assembly of Christians, but above all the Christian group itself, whether local or dispersed as many house communities all over the then world. Paul speaks in the plural of *ekklesiai*: the *ekklesiai* of a province (the Christians in Galatia, Asia Minor, Macedonia or Judaea: I Cor.16.1; 16.19; Gal.1.2; II Cor.8.1; I

Thess.2.14), but also of 'all *ekklesiai* of the Gentiles' (Rom.16.4) and of 'all *ekklesiae* of Christ' (Rom.16.16) or '*ekklesiai* of God' (I Cor.11.16,22; I Thess.1.4).[3] Above all in the post-Pauline letters (Colossians; Ephesians) the word *ekklesia* is often used to indicate the universal Christian movement.[4] Old expressions like 'the *ekklesia* of God' alongside 'the *ekklesia* of Jews and Greeks' (I Cor.10.32) are also typical; they are nevertheless used of a local community, as in 'the *ekklesia* of God which is in Corinth' (I Cor.1.2). The consciousness of belonging to a universal people of God, typical of the earliest early Christian communities, clearly comes from Jewish roots.

(b) Looking forward: *ekklesia – dioikesis – paroikia*

Some critics of my book *Ministry* accuse me of using the term 'local church' vaguely and indeterminately. For these critics the local church is only the bishopric or the diocese, in the present canonical sense of the word. Here they clearly overlook the fact that in this sense diocese is used generally and univocally only after the thirteenth century.

The term *dioikesis*,[5] 'diocese', comes from *dia oikos*, and in secular Greek terminology this usually means the household. *Hoi epi tei dioikesei* were the members of the Athenian magistrature, a kind of official department or Ministry of Finance. However, among the Romans *dioecesis* meant more the *subregio* or district of an admistrative *provincia*. Later, under the emperor Diocletian, there was some reordering here. In those days, probably about 297-298, dioceses were no longer subdistricts of a province, but the term comprised different provinces. Together the various dioceses then formed a prefecture (the Empire consisted of four prefectures – Italy, Gaul, Illyrium and the East – and there were twelve dioceses). At the head of each diocese there was a *vicarius* (viz., of the emperor, who in this way wanted to hold the concentration of power of the four prefectures in check). The use of the term *vicarius Christi*, later used of all bishops (before the term came to be reserved for the Pope) is in no sense strange here.

The ecclesiastical use of this Graeco-Roman term 'diocese' with its historical fluctuations is also clearly determined by the political side, i.e. the use current in the *polis* of the day. In canon 2 of the Council of Constantinople (381) there is mention of 'bishops of the *dioecesis Asiana*'; various bishops from all over Asia thus belonged to one diocese. So also in the Council of Chalcedon, canon 9. Historically, the term diocese was only used in the sense known to us in the fourth century, for the first and only time, in Roman Africa; however for a long time this remained the distinctive characteristic of this area (Councils of Carthage 390, canon 5, and 397, canon 42). There the diocese is the territory covered by an episcopal administration. (Following civil practice, this also included a stress on the strict autonomy of the districts.) Moreover, we hear from Africa that a bishop of one diocese has no say in the diocese of another bishop (Council of Carthage, 397, canon 20). Here the emphasis is not so much on the territory as on the *plebs* – i.e. the diocese is the population of a diocesan territory, falling under the pastoral government of a bishop. In the East this was called eparchy, which there coincided with the civil province. At its head was a metropolitan, who thus had various bishops under him. The term *dioikesis* comes from the secular form of organization among cities in the Roman empire.

Originally, as I said, people talked about 'the *ekklesia* which is in Corinth, in Ephesus and in Rome', and so on. At an early stage the term *paroikia* was used for this: *he ekklesia he paroikousa Romen*,[6] the church which dwells in Rome. Therefore people began to call the church which dwelt there itself *paroikia*. Thus *paroikia* is the local church. However, from the fourth century onwards, *parochia* was used to denote the area under the control of a bishop, in other words 'diocese' in its present usage. For centuries *paroikia* and diocese were used side by side, right down to the mediaeval texts (though then the usage was more archaic).

When all kinds of religious centres which were secondary to the metropolis came into being alongside the episcopal cities, these centres of faith, dependent on the episcopal, capital see, were – remarkably enough – called dioceses or *paroikiai*. Thus 'diocese' was also used for regions which had no bishop, while on the other hand a bishop could have control of various dioceses. Does this vague and indetermined element in the term local church come from me, or does it lie in the historical facts? (I ask this question in passing, for some of my critics to answer.)

In 517, in the Synod of Epaone in Gaul, canon 8, there was still mention of a presbyter who holds a diocese (*presbyter dum diocesim tenet*),[7] while canon 7 of the same synod speaks of *presbyteri parrochiarum*,[8] parish priests. Thus diocese and parish are still synonymous. Granted, in the case of the synods of Gaul we can note a certain tendency towards the traditional use of *paroikia*, as a synonym for diocese: here *parochia* gradually becomes what we now know: the parish with its pastor. But this becomes established only in the Middle Ages.

Moreover in the first millennium, at least in the West, diocese often had the vague meaning of what we now call a church province. Thus the present church province of the Netherlands could be called a diocese in the sense that was still alive even in the ninth century.[9] Diocese also has the meaning of a territory under a metropolitan or archbishop. Only after the thirteenth century was the older Latin-African meaning of diocese to come into force everywhere definitively; after that all divergent meanings fell away. In the eleventh century (1092), at the beginning of Roman centralization, Urban II reserved for the Apostolic See the right to establish dioceses, join them together or split them up.[10] Thus there is no theological reason to take the term local church *per se* as being identical with bishopric. This is a legitimate development in the life of the churches, but it is not a historically necessary development or a dogmatic one.

All this is not just a question of vague, shifting terminology; it also reflects actual historical situations. In the second century and later bishops were bishop of a city; in other words the diocese and parish in our sense did not yet exist. Only at the end of the early period and the beginning of the Middle Ages did what we now know as a diocese come into being, divided into parishes, with a degree of independence and each with its own *curatus* or pastor, who because of his office (and not as a delegate of the bishop) led his parish in all things.

The parish became a *feodum* of the pastor, whereas earlier, in the early Christian metropolitan system, all churches were the property of the bishop. The feudal significance of this parochial division clearly emerges from what is said of a mediaeval bishop: *parochiam appello, populum primitias, oblationes et decimas persolventem*:[11] 'I call a parish the people that provides first fruits, sacrificial gifts and tithes.'

The conclusion is that there is no theological reason whatsoever for identifying the local church in itself with the bishopric in the modern sense; its significance is connected with history and canon law. But that means that no dogmatic conclusions can be drawn from it.

(c) Christian 'free fellowships' gathering in house communities

(i) He kat'oikon ekklesia: *Christian house communities*

The early church made the *oikos*, that is, the Graeco-Roman city family house, the pastoral basis of the whole of the Christian movement: 'the *ekklesia* which meets in the house of Aquila and Priscilla' in Ephesus (I Cor.16.19); 'the *ekklesia* which meets in the house of Prisca and Aquila' in Rome (Rom.16.5); 'the *ekklesia* which meets in the house of Philemon' in Colossae (Philemon 2); 'the *ekklesia* which meets in the house of Nympha' in Laodicea (Col.4.15). From then on there are repeated references, direct or indirect, to the same phenomenon (I Cor.1.16; I Cor.16.15-16; Acts 12.12-17; 16.15; 16.31-34; 18.8; see also John 4.53; Acts 10.2;11.14; perhaps also Rom.16.10-11,14,15; I Cor.1.11; Phil.4.22). The basic structure of the earliest communities of Christian believers was the same as what was then the basic unit of civic life in the cities, namely the household. The *kata* in *he kat'oikon ekklesia* was used of groups which were based on a particular household, to be distinguished from (a) the whole church, which also sometimes gathered (I Cor.14.23; Rom.16.23; see I Cor.11.20) and (b) the whole of the Christ movement, which is also called *ekklesia*.

The *oikos* or household of that time had greater cohesion than our modern family. Servants, slaves and others also belonged to 'the house'. There were also non-Christian households where Christians gathered (Rom.16.10,11,14,15), and houses in which the father of the house was a Christian, like Philemon, while his slave, Onesimus, was not.

The consequences of this structure of the early Christian communities are clear from a socio-historical perspective. As a result the Christian groups were integrated into an already existing network of 'face to face' relationships, both internally (other members of the household, relatives, servants) and externally (friends, acquaintances, clients – the *clientela* – and often people with the same profession or calling). On the other hand the result of this structure was that because there were different households in a city (e.g. Corinth) it was easy for 'parties' to come into being (see I Cor.1-4; also in the Johannine communities: III John).

In the early church the house community or 'the household of the faith' (Gal.6.10) was the beginning of Christianity in a particular city or province in the Graeco-Roman empire. The house was the place where there was preaching or instruction, and also the place where people ate and drank together, celebrated the eucharist, and so on. These were mostly well-to-do citizens who had become Christians and put their house at the disposal of the community, and often also gave it financial support. Although socially, these leaders, men and women, owners of large houses, belonged to the better classes, the communities themselves consisted of all kinds of levels of the population, with the exception of the upper crust of society. We find this kind of house community in existence even down to the third century; in the fourth century it became possible to have separate church buildings.

In the Roman Hellenistic household the *paterfamilias*, the father of the house, was the unspoken authority, and the structure of the family in antiquity was markedly hierarchical, with a patriarchal order, and in this respect was also the basis of the welfare of the whole of Greek and Roman society. By contrast, initially in the Christian household or house community this hierarchical model was radically broken up (we find a difference in the post-Pauline developments to which the Pastoral Epistles bear witness, see below). Early Christianity was a brotherhood and sisterhood of equal partners: theologically on the basis of the baptism of the Spirit, and sociologically in accordance with the Roman Hellenistic model of free societies, called *collegia*, who also assembled 'at the house of NN'. Therefore it was not the Graeco-Roman codes of the *oikos* but the form of organization of the more democratic or egalitarian (religious and non-religious) *collegia* or associations which lent itself as a model for the earlier Christian house communities. In the empire there were numerous of these associations, also of a religious kind, above all many kinds of eastern cultic associations.

The fact that houses of certain Christians occupied a central role as a place where the life of the *ekklesia* was lived (although to begin with the Jewish Christians also used to go to the Jewish temple) has unmistakeable sociological consequences for understanding their missionary work.

Here our modern, personalistic conceptions about individual conversions fall short. In the New Testament we repeatedly hear that this or that Jew or Gentile went over to Christianity 'with all his house' (e.g. Acts 16.15; 16.31-34; I Cor.1.16). The consequence of this is (from the modern perspective of social psychology) that the motivation to become a Christian also differed among many of the members of the house. Often, though not necessarily, people became Christians en bloc, because the *paterfamilias* had become a Christian. This could often happen more from house solidarity, with, from a religious point of view, a whole gradation in inner commitment and personal conviction.

Although originally and for a long time the *oikos* was the place where Christians felt themselves to be the *ekklesia*, and gathered together, to begin with the household was not the fundamental principle of organization and structure (i.e. the beginning of church order) in the communities of Christian believers. For to begin with the building up of the Christian community did *not* follow the ethically legitimated, hierarchical model of the Romano-Greek household, as this was prescribed and respected in the *Peri Oikonomias* (guidelines for the ordering of the household) which then applied – Aristotle also wrote one. At any rate, this *oikos* principle does not explain the various and different patterns of leadership and authority in the Christian communities: the authority of many others from outside was in many ways greater than the authority of the *paterfamilias* of the house; these external authorities included the apostles and their fellow workers and also many teachers and prophetic figures in the communities. Nor does the *oikos* principle provide an explanation of the strong, more than local sense of unity – *koinonia* – of all Christian house communities, not only in one city but also in the same province, and far beyond.

(ii) Ekklesia *as* collegium *or free association in the Graeco-Roman world*

At that time the Roman Hellenistic empire had a wealth of associations and clubs, guilds and fellowships. It is also striking that even in the second century, Roman imperial officials, including anti-Christian writers, see the many Christian *ecclesiae* or assemblies in terms of a 'free association': *collegium quod est in domo Sergiae Paulinae*[12] – the model of a free association which 'gathers at the house of NN'. Membership of such an association depended on free decision and initiation. Often, and this was also the case in all kinds of Eastern cultic communities in the empire, these associations brought together people who held the same office or practised the same profession (although the Christian *collegia* were socially very mixed indeed). In accordance with old custom their workplaces and shops were also close together: the street of leatherworkers, the street of the smiths, and so on. Paul, a tentmaker, was happy to live in Corinth with the prosperous tentmakers Prisca and Aquila (Acts 18.2-3). The associations also practised cultic activities and had regular meals together. The burial of members was looked after and paid for by the club itself, and each year there were memorial celebrations for departed members of the association. These associations were for the most part dependent on *patroni*, men or women, male or female guardians who offered financial support. This is also clearly the case in the New Testament with people like Stephanas (I Cor.16.15-18) and Phoebe, *diakonos* and *prostatis* of the community (Rom 16.1-12). Paul asks the community to pay a bit more respect to the benefactors of the house communities (I Cor.16.15-18), a fact which within a pneumatic experience of the church points to criticism from the church community of the actual violation of the egalitarian brotherhood or sisterhood, for whatever reasons, however understandable.

The civil and religious associations of the time had a free 'democratic' form of organization. In questions of procedure and organization they often took over the structure of the civil government, often even its official titles, though each club had its own jargon. To begin with, the Christian communities certainly did not deliberately adapt themselves to the existing structures of these *collegia*. For apart from the terms *episkopos* (Phil.1.1) and *diakonos* (Phil.1.1; Rom.16.1) in the authentic letters of Paul all the technical terms which were current in these *collegia* are absent, above all the term *synagoge* (as the name for the gathering of these societies). At the same time the name *episkopos* does seem to be borrowed from these free associations.[13] The associations developed their own legal systems for dealing with internal conflicts. This was done by both the Jewish and the Christian free associations. The Jewish Christian associations came into being in a very specific cultural context.

In addition to these Graeco-Roman *collegia*, the community structure of the Jewish Diaspora also served as a model; however, the Jewish synagogue was itself modelled on the structures of these Graeco-Roman free associations. It is not so much a matter of deliberate borrowings, but even less of a creation out of a cultural *ex nihilo*. The formation of Christian groups also took place in a cultural context: this shows all the sociological features of the formation of groups in antiquity; in other words, distinctiveness, but many analogies with other forms of group at the time can be recognized without difficulty by social historians.

(d) Structures of authority in communities of early Christian believers

No group can exist long without some institutional structures. This is a well known sociological law. In this sense 'free churches' cannot be found anywhere, even by sociologists, among the early communities of Christian believers. Sooner or later all these communities had to face the question, 'How are conflicts resolved in your community or fellowship? Who is in charge of it?' We have most knowledge of the pre-Pauline, Pauline and post-Pauline community structure, though these are only one sector of the early Christian churches.

(i) How were conflicts resolved?

The first fundamental conflict arose in Antioch at the beginning of the missionary work of Barnabas and Paul. On the occasion of a conflict, Barnabas and Paul go to Jerusalem to speak there with the leaders of the earliest community, the mother church from which the Christian movement arose. Paul says that his decision to go to Jerusalem came to him 'by revelation' (Gal.2.2). In Acts 15.2, Luke says on the other hand that the *ekklesia* of Antioch ordered Paul to go to Jerusalem. This need not be a contradiction. At that time a response by someone or other in Antioch, a prophetic member of the community, or even the drawing of lots, could be regarded as revelation. It is certainly striking that the Jewish Christians do not present this difference to the Jewish synagogue in Antioch but to the 'eminent members', people of repute (*hoi dokountes*), the pillars of the Christian community in Jerusalem. Even before there is any mention of a formal schism between synagogue and church, Christians are aware of their distinctiveness, as a free association. Perhaps Acts does presuppose a later situation in the complex church organization in Jerusalem: as in other religious associations, according to Luke the whole of the community had already assembled there, led by a council of elders or presbyters (*gerousia*) in order to come to a decision, along with 'the apostles' who already during Jesus' earthly life had followed him and after his death believed in his resurrection. Thus we can best put the apostles within the then model of the *prytania* or *decania* in the free fellowships of this time (though at that stage they were not religious). The Jerusalem *ekklesia* or decisive gathering came to a solution which satisfied all parties: converts from the Gentile world need not be circumcised. However, there is a difference between Paul's account of this event and that in Acts. According to Luke a solemn decree is promulgated there on the authority 'of the apostles and the *presbyteroi* along with the whole of the *ekklesia*' (Acts 15.22), a procedure current in the free associations of the time.[14] By contrast Paul does not see this as any kind of decree or edict, but as an agreement between two equal parties, with the 'men of note' (Peter, James and John from Jerusalem) on the one side, and Barnabas and Paul on the other. The agreement, he says, is sealed 'with the hand of fellowship' (Gal.2.9). Paul and Luke have clearly different views of church structures!

Despite this official – some people call it a synodal – agreement, soon afterwards a newer and fiercer incident developed, the outcome of which was fatal for Paul, despite his theological equality. Jewish and non-Jewish Christians ate together in Antioch; when Peter arrived there, like a good Christian he generously joined in. However, when 'certain of James's people' arrived from the Jerusalem mother church, not only the Jewish Christians, but also Peter and, the worst blow for Paul, even Barnabas (Gal.2.13b) refused to sit at one and the same table with non-Jewish Christians – i.e. non-Jews. Paul was abandoned and left in isolation (Gal.2.11-13). As a 'spiritual' Christian from Antioch he could no longer understand this behaviour of the men of note, whose lofty reputation therefore seemed to him to be couched purely in human terms (Gal.2.6). The 'freedom of the children of God' was radically contradicted by this behaviour of the men of note: the very nature of pneuma christology, indeed of Christian faith, was put in question.

What had happened in the meantime, since the agreement in Jerusalem? We do not know. But there are many reasons for supposing that the departure of the mediator, Peter, from Jerusalem (Acts 12) left all the power in the mother church in the hands of members of Jesus' family, the clan of James. Even Peter, who knows better, yields to these people. After that, he disappears into the mist of early Christianity. Historically it is certain that this conflict between Paul and Jerusalem was resolved at the expense of a schism in the Christian community of Antioch. Paul, deeply disillusioned by this whole event, leaves the mother community of Antioch as a result, to some degree detaches himself, and directs his missionary activities thenceforward to

Asia Minor and Greece. Barnabas, too, goes his own way, apart from Paul.

This conflict teaches us a great deal about the structure of the church. The Christian *ekklesia*, in Antioch and also in Jerusalem, has become a separate group within Judaism, with its own leaders independent of Judaism, although their respective authority is still very fluid and unclear. Moreover, there is a clear concern to bring the Christian movement in the many churches on to one and the same wavelength. However, conflicts are resolved by particular Christians coming together, talking, and sorting them out. Moreover, we can see that there is constant 'movement' between the various different local communities, above all through delegations which are given a special name, viz. *apostoloi ekklesiōn*, i.e. messengers or legates whom one church sends to another (II Cor.8.23). Rather later, perhaps when journeys are not always possible or are advised against for strategic reasons, 'apostolic letters' perform this function of correction. To begin with there was no formal procedure for resolving conflicts. Of course it is a fact that certain leaders arose throughout this group development, usually through the authority of what they said and their Christian conduct. Precisely their active participation in the resolution and settling of conflicts consolidated their authority successfully. Also, all this led to the discovery of more formal ways of creating a church government.

On the other hand, for Paul his fiasco in Antioch marked the beginning of a development which took him more in his own (Pauline) way towards a clear and deliberate, distinctive way of organizing the missionary work of the gospel. Certainly he remained in contact with Jerusalem and in unity with it, but along with his fellow workers, independently of Jerusalem, he developed his own forms and techniques in order to maintain contact throughout all the churches which he or his fellow workers had founded and to preserve unity among them all.

Sociologically speaking, this initial universal blossoming of earlier Christianity called for one form or another of social control. Moreover, Paul gives all kinds of instructions through visits, through legates or through personal letters. These were subsequently circulated to all the Pauline sister churches and read out in many house communities. Thus there came into being the authority of a tradition. In *his* churches, Paul was the authority. So he intervenes from Achaea in the church of Thessalonica (churches of the province of Macedonia); he sends his fellow-worker Timothy to strengthen the communities and to search and discover precisely what is going on (I Thess.3.1-5). When the good news has reached him from Timothy he sends a letter, along with Silvanus and Timothy, to the churches of Thessalonica (I Thess.1.1). Paul clearly works with a team. The authoritative models for Christian behaviour are said in this letter to be Christ, the apostles and other groups of Christians - just as the Christians of Thessalonica are also themselves *topoi* or a model for yet other Christian communities. The bond between the apostle Paul and the churches which he has founded is a constantly recurring theme in his letters. From then on these letters also functioned in the catechizing of new converts. This gave rise to a Pauline tradition of Christian doctrinal, ethical and disciplinary instruction which applied in all the Pauline churches.

We see the same thing happening in conflicts in Galatia (Galatians) and also in Corinth (I and II Corinthians). In Corinth Paul wants to, indeed has to, defend his own authority above all against those whom he sarcastically calls 'super-apostles' (II Cor.12.11). Above all this last conflict is concerned with the question who exercises authority in the churches of God. I Corinthians was written by Paul himself in order to consolidate his apostolic authority in all the churches founded by him and his fellow workers in the face of a Christian authority from elsewhere which has a different theological orientation (I Cor.9.1-18; 15.1-11). Evidently another great teacher had been active alongside Paul, when he was not in Corinth, namely Apollos, a most eloquent Christian, an orator with a splendid physique and charismatic talents. And although Paul speaks (rhetorically) about many parties, I Cor.1-4 shows unmistakably that in reality the real issue was whether he or Apollos was to be the authority in this community. Paul indeed had a handicap (what handicap is impossible to determine historically). Presumably he was unimposing physically, and this fact was played on by the opposing party around Apollos, to Paul's disadvantage and along the lines of a 'christology of glory' in the present.

Some local leaders, including Stephanas, patron of a certain house community in Corinth, wrote Paul a letter in which they explained the difficulties which had arisen there (see I Cor.7.1,25; 8.1; 12.1; 16.1,15-18). Elsewhere, however, we hear that Paul was informed about these conflicts through the patroness of a Corinthian church, Chloe, who had come to Ephesus on business

(I Cor.1.11). Or did this indirect information perhaps confirm and add detail to what he had learned from the official letter? Paul perhaps heard from Chloe that some supporters of the charismatic Apollos did not take any notice of his advice; they completely doubted his wisdom when confronted with the handsome, charismatic Apollos. We hear from Paul's letter that they did not want to see Paul again in Corinth (I Cor.4.18). Thus even in Pauline communities, Paul's authority could be challenged by Christians of another theological trend. Here we only have the account of the winners.

Of course it is also clear that authority was also established in early Christian communities by the Christianity taught by the teacher, while others, who also gave instruction, lost authority as a result of their behaviour. That was Paul's argument. There was still no room for formal, juridical authority. Questions of jurisdiction in authority cannot be seen anywhere in all these conflicts.

There were also other conflicts in Corinth, often with a social background including discrimination between poor and rich, even in the context of eucharistic meals (I Cor.11.17-34) – the 'liberated' behaviour of Corinthian women who challenged the Graeco-Roman household code on the basis of Christian freedom (I Cor.11-14) – the question of eating meat offered to sacrifices (I Cor.8.1-11.1). Quite apart from these socially determined problems in the emancipated city life of the port of Corinth, the phenomenon of prophecy and glossolalia, speaking in tongues, had become a pressing problem (I Cor.14.1-25). Here notions of church authority were involved. From a social point of view, these pneumatics gained influence in the church. Paul found it difficult to deny their authority: he himself accepted the authority of the Spirit. The direct appeal to being led by the Spirit was a real, albeit sometimes ambiguous, form of authority within the pneuma christology. Paul therefore lays stress on discipline and rational comprehension (I Cor.14.40). Paul, who always had an eye to the Gentiles (for him they were potential Christians), did not want to scare them away from Christianity by the behaviour of Christians which was irrational in the eyes of Hellenistic Romans (I Cor.14.23). For pragmatic reasons he stresses that male and female prophets in the church should take account of the current Graeco-Roman codes relating to hair-style and clothing, including those specific to one sex (I Cor.11.2-16). Finally, he forbids women in a prophetic trance (as also happened in Gentile pneumatic milieux) to let down their bound-up hair (I Cor.11.2-16). Here we are confronted more with a breach of ancient culture than with the gospel, albeit within a specific church context.

(ii) Competence – local and more than local

In contrast to the second century, in which all the stress comes to be placed on the local (episcopal/presbyteral) authority which is established or to be established, the actual authority in the pre-Pauline, Pauline and post-Pauline churches was a still vague, albeit already structural totality of local and more than local authorities, though the boundaries between the two are fluid. Where new local churches were founded from outside, their founders continued to be authoritative in the community – sometimes even taking up residence – even when they went on further to found new churches, and even ranking above authorities who lived in the place.

1. More-than-local leadership and church service. In the Pauline and post-Pauline communities, pride of place is given to the mention of 'apostles'. In these communities Paul in principle was regarded as the highest authority. Precisely because he exercised such an authority we are still in possession of many of his letters, which in fact are the oldest of the Christian writings known to us. Without this authority exercised by Paul over others certain Christians would not have kept his letters! On his side Paul recognizes that alongside him there are many local leaders, teachers, prophets and evangelists. But what he regards as most important is the link between the founder of a church (Paul and his fellow workers) and his communities. Although there is some rhetoric in this, his comment in a letter to the Corinthians is characteristic: 'For although you had scores of trainers (*paidogogoi*) in Christ, you have only one father. I am the one who has brought you to life through the gospel in Christ Jesus' (I Cor.4.15). It emerges from this that there are different competences, but Paul demands the highest authority over his community, which evidently was challenged as such by others more than once. 'Although I am not an apostle for others, for you I am certainly so, for in the Lord you are the seal on my apostleship' (I Cor.9.2). In this view Paul's apostolic authority cannot be detached from the apostolic community itself, which was called to life by Paul and accepted his authority in faith. In the light of the apostolic tradition in which Paul knows himself to be firmly established, he tolerates no invaders on his own ground. Here Paul's formal authority is clearly subordinate to accepted authority with an apostolic content.

Luke himself reserves the title apostle exclusively for the Twelve (with one exception, probably arising from a different source, Acts 14.4,14). Paul is not included. However, we know little or nothing of the activity of these Twelve in earliest Christianity apart from Peter, although there are divergent traditions (some of them in the New Testament) which point to the Twelve as the authority of their own tradition – down to the third century.

Historians and theologians are agreed that at the time of Paul apostle was no formal office. The term apostle belongs with the first constitutive phase of the origin of the church communities. The apostles were the undisputed authority throughout the church's mission. In Greek, apostle means something like ambassador, someone sent by God (see II Cor.5.20). Of course in the Septuagint this is also the significance of the classical prophets in Israel (in Gal.1.15-16 Paul refers to Jeremiah). In his defence of his own apostleship Paul points to the 'Damascus Road event', his direct sending to the Gentiles, by virtue of a call from the risen Jesus, though not through the earthly, historical Jesus.

Paul's principle was only to be active in cities where theoretically there were still no Christian communities, and therefore in an area to which other Christian leaders could not lay claim. Perhaps this was the lesson he had learnt from his conflict with Peter, Barnabas and the 'people from James' at Antioch. However, other Christians in no way adopted this Pauline standpoint of territorial delimitation and often crossed the path which Paul had reserved for himself. Of course Paul recognized the authority of people 'who were apostles before I was' (Gal.1.17). However, apart from a few conflicts with these 'original apostles' we do not find them playing any role in Paul's mission, except through the 'tradition which he received', a fundamental datum. He even says that from now on he has no message for these people. Apart from Peter, 'I have seen no other apostles apart from James, the brother of the Lord' (Gal.1.19).

Moreover, in addition to the 'original apostles', Paul also seems to know a broader concept of apostleship: Jesus appeared 'to Cephas and after that to the Twelve' and 'then he appeared to James and after that to all the apostles' (I Cor.15.5,7). Are 'the Twelve' the same as 'all the apostles'? I doubt it. Paul also, strangely, calls the Christian opponents who appeared in Corinth when he was away 'apostles' (II Cor.11.5,13), though he sarcastically calls them 'super-apostles', pseudo-apostles 'who parade as apostles of Christ'. Paul also presumably regarded as apostles the reformers in Galatia who cherished other Christian views and according to Paul undermined his work, although technically he does not give them this name: for Paul an apostle is really *sent by God* (*apostolos*) and therefore can never undermine his apostolic work!

We find 'apostle' with a wider significance above all in expressions like *apostoloi ekklesiōn* (II Cor.8.23; Phil.2.25-29; 4.18). Here it is not, at least directly, God who sends an ambassador, messenger or legate to another church. (These are also called 'fellow workers'.) Certain Christians, highly respected or with certain capacities, receive a certain commission from a church – in II Cor.8.23 in order to oversee the collection for poor Christians in Jerusalem, a point of honour in Paul's care of his churches. Thus Epaphroditus, 'your apostle', is also sent to Philippi as Paul's fellow worker (Phil.2.25): as a messenger, but not without authority, albeit within the limits of the task assigned him.

Alongside 'the apostles', Paul's fellow workers do have a special authority over the local community and its local leaders. From the beginning the Pauline work of mission was a collective undertaking on the part of the mission church in Antioch and was itself to begin with under the direction of Barnabas, who had already been a Christian for a long time, and not of Paul. Certainly we can speak of an apostolic mission team – collegial leadership – in the Pauline communities, despite Paul's dominant, central place in it (in psychological terms as well). Nevertheless, G.Schille has pointed out,[15] in my view rightly, that the original Christian mission was collegial throughout; this is evident above all from the different sets of names, in which the first name is often the leader of the team (Stephen in Acts 6.5; Barnabas in Acts 13.1; Sopater in Acts 20.4; see also the lists in Rom.16.21-23; 16.6-12; Col.4.7ff.; Philemon 23-24; Titus 3.12-13; II Tim.4.10ff.). The team comprised at most five to seven members. Moreover, a team is often the leader of a city community of believers, from which surrounding cities are evangelized. At the 'top of the mission' there is therefore a blurred transition between local and more than local authority (perhaps in the same team of persons).

The functions of the fellow workers of the apostles were therefore partly local and partly more than that, though often from one fixed base. Sometimes they join in writing Paul's letters. Thus 'Paul, Timothy and Sosthenes' write I Thessalonians (1.1); in Philippians (1.1) we find the names of 'Paul and Timothy' at the head; and the names of Paul and Timothy also head the post-Pauline letter Colossians (1.1); I Corinthians begins with the names of Paul and Sosthenes (1.1); II Corinthians (1.1) bears the names of 'Paul and Timothy'. When Paul speaks in these contexts, not of brother or sister but of 'our brother and our sister', this means his personal fellow worker and not just a 'fellow Christian'. These are brothers or sisters in the collegial leadership of Pauline communities.

In Paul's name, Timothy goes from Athens to Thessalonica in order to deal with difficulties there: the constitutionally difficult Paul got on with him best. Paul also sends him to Philippi (Phil.2.19-24). Titus also performed the same role as mediator in settling difficulties in Corinth (II Cor.2.13; 7.6-16), as did Tychicus in Colossae (Col.4.7). Paul himself was in no way a mediator!

The fellow workers of the apostle also often include the 'first-fruits', i.e. the first converts in a district, a city or a province; moreover these often put their house at the disposal of Christians. Stephanas and Gaius already perform this role in Corinth. They were the first-fruits in the whole of the province and therefore have authority and leadership in the community.

The significance of people like Prisca and Aquila is again different from that of earlier fellow workers, although these too have more than purely local significance. They were patrons of Paul and also of local house communities, but also often went on evangelical journeys. According to Acts 18.26 they were 'teachers' (husband and wife) who were greatly respected and had authority in many churches. From then on there are also many other fellow workers whom we know only by name and who in fact are local leaders, although they are called fellow workers of Paul. All in all, we find about eighty personal names in the authentic letters of Paul of whom it can be said that they 'toiled for the community' in one way or another, as teachers (male or female), leaders (male or female) of house communities, as evangelists and prophets, as deacons or whatever, either in local communities or as itinerant preachers of the gospel. However, even this last distinction is not adequate or clear cut. Local leaders were also sent out to civically subordinate, neighbouring towns in order to found new communities there. Colossae and Ephesus were not founded by Paul as Christian communities. Epaphras, Paul's fellow worker, founded the Christian community of Colossae (Col.1.7-8; see 4.12).

The personal relationship between Paul and those who were called his fellow workers differed widely; often it was temporary and sometimes also permanent. After what happened in Antioch the bond between Paul and Barnabas was completely broken: each went his own way. Apollos, who according to Acts apparently had hands laid on him in Corinth, becomes 'a prophet' (Acts 19.1-6), together with some others. Paul later sees this Apollos as his opponent (I Cor.). Timothy and others, however, remain faithful to Paul all their lives, though this in no way means that Timothy or Titus did not also influence Paul! At all events, they are the ones who often bring divisions between Paul and the Pauline communities to a satisfactory conclusion where Paul failed.

So in the Pauline communities there was a complex, fluid network of local and more than local structures and authorities. All together they order the *ecclesiae*, although there were really no official titles connected with leadership or authority. All this grew out of a pneumatic vitality and prophetic power of the Spirit.

2. Local leadership and service. Although there was some fluidity in the concepts of local and more than local leaders, there was something like a 'residential' leadership in the local communities, though in the Pauline communities these almost never bear the technical titles which we find at the time in all the free communities which assemble 'at the house of NN'. In these associations there was a whole jargon of names for special functions, and people often took over the secular titles from city associations, with all kinds of adaptations. However, in Paul's Christian 'free associations', while we see different forms of ministry and also of local leadership, they never have official names in his own letters. We never find among the Pauline communities *arche*, the contemporary Greek term for a ministry in the *polis* or city, or synonyms like *time* (official authority which is to be feared or to be esteemed highly). Socio-historical approaches, which in fact uncover analogies, must be kept in check by the content of the faith by which these Christian 'free associations' live.

Of course we can see a gradual and steadily developing, more uniform, differentiation of leading ministries in the local communities – in terminology as well. To begin with, i.e. in Paul's first letter, the earliest Christian document known to us, the leading ministries are completely undefined, 'We ask you, brothers, to respect those who work among you, who lead you (= preside and guarantee or make financial provision for you) in the Lord, who instruct you, and to show them more than usual love because of their work' (I Thess.5.12). All of the three tasks which are summed up here are covered by the one term; thus this does not denote three different ministries, but what Christian community leaders and those who inspire a Christian group should in fact and must do. That Paul has to ask the community to show these people special respect indicates at least a degree of latent opposition towards non-egalitarian attitudes from a brotherhood and sisterhood in the church which was originally egalitarian. But so far, stereotyped terms for this ministry in the church have not yet come into being (see also Rom.12.8-9, nevertheless a letter written after I Thess., Gal. and I and II Cor.). In the text of the letter to the Christians of Rome cited above, Paul speaks of different gifts, those of prophecy, instruction, that of admonitory revival, of care for the poor and of leadership. Leadership is understood here in a narrow sense, perhaps relating to government and administration or even to financial acumen, as a service distinct from prophecy, instruction, and so on. At all events, leadership can also denote patronage, i.e. the service performed by guardians of both sexes set over the church (*proista-menoi*) by which these, like Phoebe, gain authority in the churches (as also in the 'free associations' of the time).[16]

There is certainly still no formal procedure, not even a special liturgical framework, for the selection and appointment of specific leaders, prophets or teachers in the communities. A survey of the many ministries in fact exercised in and for the communities may add more realism to the specific life of the earliest communities, at least in the Pauline sectors of the church:[17]

I Cor 12.28-30	I Cor 12.8-10	Rom.12.6-8	Eph.4.11 (c. AD 90)
apostles	wisdom	prophecy	apostles
prophets	gnosis	diaconia	prophets
teachers (catechists)	faith	teachers	evangelists
miracle workers	gifts of healing	admonishers	pastors
healers	miracles	benefactors	teachers
givers of support	prophecy		
those giving	distinguishing		
leadership	the spirits	those who show	
speaking with		mercy (financial	
tongues and		support?)	
the interpreters	speaking in tongues		
	and the interpreters		

Common to these different social roles in the local communities is that they are all called charismata, gifts – indeed, gifts of God, Christ or the Spirit. The various lists show that there was great freedom in the official structural ordering of the communities, and also that spontaneously a degree of church order arose everywhere, however varied. Here concern (above all in the lists in Corinthians) was less with people and their status in the church than with what they actually do to create Christian communities – i.e. their specific functions. In the face of the developing multiplicity (which would also have brought status along with it) Paul seeks to neutralize the difference in status: above all he wants to stress the unity of a Christian group, by virtue of a series of variegated ministries. However, he makes room for diversity, despite all his demands for everyone to join in building up the community.

For all the difference between these three lists (as a fourth I have included Ephesians, which is certainly post-Pauline, to clarify a tendency which is becoming obvious in the early church), a certain tendency towards formalization and uniform specialization is evident. That becomes clear first of all from the primary sequence: 'apostles, prophets and teachers (catechists)' (I Cor.12.28). We hear from Gal.6.6 that although some community leaders were also financial benefactors of the community, there were also other forms of community leadership which were themselves financially supported by other authorities and communities. Above all the list in Ephesians, as also the title of the letter to the Christians of Philippi (1.1), shows that 'formalization' of the ministry was also becoming stronger in Pauline communities. Is this not a development in accordance with sociological laws? That is what happens in the building up of every community, even that of a religious community. To begin with, the social roles in a community are not institutionalized. However, the intrinsic dynamics of the community call for it. And that was also the case in the Christian communities: initially vague and varied up to the turn of the century and even in the first half of the second century, the signs of a uniform institutionalization become clearly visible, from the Pastoral Epistles and in the letters of Clement and Ignatius (see below). On the other hand we cannot say that the actual development towards an increasingly uniform type of organization goes back in a straight line to the distinctive Pauline tendency to formalization which we nevertheless perceive also in the Pauline churches. Many factors have played a part in the tendency towards a uniform model; the premises for this have certainly not lain exclusively in the Pauline communities themselves. Ultimately there come into being a formal series of titles for ministers and for ministry in the church, and even some rules and criteria for the selection of candidates for ministry. Ministry in the formal sense is ultimately seen as essential for the sound ordering of a Christian community.

It becomes clear from this socio-historical account which can be constructed from the sources at our disposal that – apart from the exceptional authority of the apostolic or prophetic founders of or inspirers of a Christian community – the sharp distinction between local and more far-reaching authority (to put things cautiously) is historically not too clear; nor is the difference between Christian pneumatic authority and local authority. There are a variety of reasons for this, sometimes social or intellectual. Recognizable or demonstrable manifestations of being moved by the Spirit are relevant to authority in the community. So are the social and intellectual status of individuals in the community; the first converts in a city or district; personal acquaintance with the apostle who founded the church; and a variety of local and more than local people of note. These authorities – with their broad and sometimes questioned significance – built up the community, but the mutual tension between them was often the cause of internal conflicts. The church was in search of its own Christian structures.

Quite apart from theological theorizing, this is the sociological image presented by the early Christian communities of which we have the best historical knowledge, those from before Paul, from Paul's time and from after him. The characteristics of their internal order were unmistakably connected with the theological content of the Christian Graeco-Roman free associations which had their centre 'in the house of X', despite at least some Christian differences arising from Christian cultural criticism.

With no premeditation, these communities (though children of their time) automatically took over certain forms of organization both from their earlier past in the Jewish synagogue and their life in a Graeco-Roman polis – sometimes spontaneously, but nevertheless with christological criticism.

Here all kinds of recent studies have broken through some modern traditional clichés. Quite apart from the first mission from Jerusalem to Galilee, the collection of the earliest Christian communities that we know best from the Pauline literature gives a good cross-section of the social composition of a Graeco-Roman city, in any area. The two extremes are lacking in these earliest churches: there are no Christians from the upper crust of these Graeco-Roman cities and none from the lowest sector of the city population. The social composition of the Pauline communities lies between the two extremes, although it also comprises slaves and freemen. To what extent? We do not know. Many 'internal theological' conflicts in the early churches, above all those founded by Paul, arose as a result of the socially variegated strata or the varied social stratification of these Christian communities. Many theological problems even then had a social and political background.

This socio-historical survey, modest though it may be, of the early Christian communities (which are almost exclusively Pauline) can in itself suggest that we should adopt a critical and restrained attitude towards a normative theological approach to the church and its ministries. As I said in the introduction, we must not interpret dualistically socio-historical vocabulary and the Christian language of faith, despite their fundamentally different perspectives, as though each was in fact expressing a different reality. Now, in the language of faith – albeit with a constant socio-historical interest – we shall look in detail at the same reality. First, however, we must present a retrospective survey.

(iii) Summary

A socio-historical approach shows us that in the earliest and best-known forms of church organization (Pauline and pre-Pauline – just one sector of the early Christian churches) there was no difference between ministries (*officia*) and services (*munera*). In the richly-varied life of these communities of believers there is sound authority or leadership, both at a local and a more than local level, on the basis of mission, catechesis, prophecy, liturgy and many kinds of other activities through which particular Christians make their faith their work in order to build up the community. These ministries are of many kinds. Christian authority also has to be substantiated: there is still no formal authority apart from the Christian content, i.e. the authority, of what people have to say in terms of authentic Christianity and the apostolic heritage, although above all with Paul there is an appeal to his formal authority precisely as one called by the Lord. However, for the substance of this formal authority he refers to the Lord and to the 'apostolic tradition' received through him. Where he cannot do this, Paul speaks in his own name, and with the force of his own arguments, which are not always convincing. He himself is aware of that 'No matter what they think', he himself even has to say, 'at least this is what I think about it' (I Cor.7.4a), or, when he feels that his arguments will not convince anyone, he says, 'At any rate this is not usual with us, nor in the other churches' (I Cor.11.16). Even apostolic authority knows of gradations in binding force. There were also conflicts of authority. Here there were battles as to who had *authentic* authority. Leadership in the church consists in exercising all kinds of functions *with the authority of the gospel* (theologically speaking – see the following exposition – this means in the name of Christ and guided by the Spirit). Authority in leadership (in all types of group formation) is one of the forms of building up the church, though many other factors contribute to it. Moreover, structures of leadership arise gradually and in very changing forms; above all they differ very much between one region and another.

Within this totality 'leadership' is a service, but it is not to be distinguished from all other instruments of the 'tradition': proclamation, worship, diakonia and so on. 'Authority' is not yet a formal matter; it cannot be distinguished from all other functions and instruments of the paradosis or tradition. All the leading ministries are a diaconia, a service to the community; it is a matter of the one *episkope* (Acts 1.19) in what is of course a *Christian* community – one that confesses the Messiah Jesus; but as in the formation of any group, the functions which build up the community are divided into many tasks, and their specific structure can change depending on the regional context in which the Christian community of believers finds itself here and now. It is the church community of believers itself which helps and supports the many services of ministry, in relation to and together with many instruments of tradition. 'Leadership', authority, therefore cannot be thought of apart from other perhaps more tranquil forms of tradition, paradosis or the transmission of faith to the present generation and the one to come, namely instruction, prophecy, liturgy, admonition, whatever comes through the original witnesses to Jesus, and so on. The *id quod traditum est*, the paradosis or original Jesus movement, is the matrix or the nursery of the whole of this event. However, from a sociological point of view, above all after the death of the earliest generation, there is a tendency to be Christian, to follow Jesus, and to unify and institutionalize the ministries of the church more strongly, and with it a tendency to embody them liturgically in one or another of the apostolic ministries and also to give them an institutional framework. That is what happens in communities, even in religious ones! This will take us to the theological reflection on this social development in the differentiation of systems as it can be found in the New Testament. First of all, however, we must look within the New Testament at the further development of ministry in the post-apostolic period in terms of social history.

From the beginning of Christianity there was also anti-Paulinism in the early church. The 'people from James' were clearly opposed to Paul's position that Gentiles could become Christians without being circumcised. These Christians in the Jerusalem community, within Judaism, continued to practise circumcision. However, after the Jewish War we hear no more of the community in Jerusalem, which leads some scholars to suppose that they perished during the war: others think that they fled.

There is some doubt as to whether one can speak in historical terms of a Cephas party in Corinth (I Cor.); however, some exegetes point to traditio-historical connections between the anti-Paulinists in Corinth and the leaders in Jerusalem.[18] Of course it emerges from Galatians that Paul's apostleship was not in fact recognized by the Jerusalem synod.

Jewish Christianity in the second century did not recognize Paulinism; that is a fact. Above all the Greek homilies of the Pseudo-Clementines, which were authoritative at that time, deny Paul any apostolic legitimation on the grounds that he was not taught by the historical Jesus. According to this exposition Paul distorted the true gospel by robbing the Torah of its force. Only with Irenaeus did anti-Paulinism disappear from the early church, but at that time there were no longer many Jews in the church.

After all kinds of ups and downs and some redaction (including post-Pauline interpolations into the authentic letters of Paul) the *corpus paulinum* became an official authority in and for the whole church, as part of canonical scripture; it was included along with other non-Pauline Christian writings after a process of tradition which went on for two centuries. Thus the mainstream church connected the pneuma christology with the historical Jesus via the logia tradition. It thus made it impossible for pneumatology to lose its christological basis and be just generally religious, without a christological foundation.

2. Authority and leadership in the post-apostolic New Testament communities of believers and in the early church

(a) The shift from 'house communities' to 'the household of God'

The shift that we see emerging at the end of the New Testament and even more in the first half of the second century is not so much a transition from formerly charismatic to subsequently institutional leadership as a consolidation and strengthening of the local leadership, which has appropriated the doctrinal authority of the former prophets and teachers. The question was the same as before: who has authority in the community? At the end of the first century we see that the conflict between authorities in the communities was decided in favour of believers who took the title of 'episkopos' (presbyter) and deacon. The tendency to reserve all authority exclusively for them becomes clear. Above all, the power of the *patroni*, sponsors, of both sexes, was gradually neutralized and the phenomenon of Christian prophets, widespread within the early church and accepted and respected almost without criticism, was gradually removed. The presbyter-episkopos and presbyter now appropriated to themselves this prophetic authority, although this conflict between the hierarchical leadership of the church, which was becoming official, and prophecy (on the basis of the baptism of the Spirit) was to last for centuries and often formed the real background of heretical and anti-heretical polemic.

The beginning of this tendency can be seen in a number of letters. The Pastoral Epistles (I and II Timothy; Titus) and along the same lines I Peter regard the time of 'the apostles (and prophets)' as past. Timothy and Titus do not call themselves apostles, but evangelists, who want to secure the authority of the Pauline tradition, i.e. sound doctrine.

Although people still continued to meet in house communities, the phrases now used are 'the household of God' (I Tim.3.15); 'the great house' (II Tim.2.20), of which the presbyter/episkopos is the *paterfamilias*, the leader, along with all the presbyterion. He is depicted as the good householder and spouse, 'husband of one wife' after the model of the Graeco-Roman *oikos* (I Tim.3.2; Titus 1.7ff.). Here the strictly hierarchical structures of the *oikos* of the time are taken over, in contrast to earlier situations in which

the house communities were a free association of equals with
nevertheless many kinds of authorities, on the basis of a contribution inspired by the Spirit. Now Christians had to subject
themselves to the one authority.

The *presbyterion* or presbyteral council seems to have been an
administrative council, which consisted of heads of households,
both male and female. *Episkopos* always occurs in the singular;
this perhaps indicates a rotating function taken over by one of the
presbyters: in this function he is head of the presbyteral council
(as was also always the case in the Roman Hellenistic free
associations).[19] In I Tim.5.17 we find a difference between the
presbyters and the presbyter-president, viz. a presbyter who is
also good at administration and is therefore paid double. The
functions of the president are here the same as those which
elsewhere in the Epistles are assigned to the *episkopos*: to instruct
and teach. Thus in the Pastoral Epistles the *episkopos* is one of the
presbyters, but evidently not all presbyters can be called *episkopos*.

On the other hand, from now on women have to keep silent in
services. This is more prescriptive than descriptive comment, and
it seems to presuppose what was earlier a different practice.
Moreover, the instruction of women is now restricted to the
teaching of women by women, which again indicates a different
custom earlier (I Tim.2.11; Titus 2.3-5 are therefore not contradictory). The pastoral reason is always that non-Christians, who are
familiar with a rigid and hierarchical household, must not be
offended by the Christian life-style, which at these points differed
from the cultural pattern in the empire (cf. I Tim.6.1 in connection
with slaves; in 3.1 it is said that those holding office must have a
good reputation 'among those who are not members of the
community'). All this is not to be written off immediately as the
uncritical assimilation of Christians to the conditions of their
Gentile society. Pastoral concerns play the main role here.
However, from the perspective of early Christianity and the
gospel, a great danger for the church lurks in this pastoral strategy.
It was to emerge in later times when the *ordo*, the group of
ministers in the church, was in fact equated with the Roman *ordo*
of senators, not least in prestige and status,[20] and the bishops
were equated with princes and kings, from then on with all the
insignia of state.

The shift to a later stage of the New Testament can still best be
seen in the introduction of the Hellenistic Jewish 'household
codes' (inspired by the Graeco-Roman world): these appear for

the first time in Col.3.18-4.1; then also in Eph.5.21-6.9; I Peter 2.3-3.7. Here Christians take over the non-Christian, pagan patriarchal houshold code of the Graeco-Roman family with only a few Christian adaptations. In this code, Gal.3.28 – 'neither male nor female, slave nor free' – is shattered. From then on Christians took over the hierarchy, as this was also an ethical matter of honour and a mark of civic virtue in their cultural environment. The wife was subservient to the husband and the slave subject to the free *paterfamilias* – although these social and political relationships must have been smoothed over by an all-permeating, Christian, spirit of love. However, within these hierarchical relationships from then on obedience was the key word. Here we hear clearly 'the voice of the well-to-do', though it is only to be heard in the New Testament in one section of the early church, viz. in the post-Pauline tradition of Asia Minor (of course I Peter is based on the authority of the Petrine tradition, but this letter also contains many Pauline elements). Christians in Asia followed the model of Jewish Hellenism there for missionary purposes.[21] I Peter above all gives a good illustration of the specific problems of the isolated Christian minority groups in Asia. This letter prefaces the code concerning the way Christians must behave towards Gentiles in the empire, towards slaves, in marriage and towards one another, with the words: 'Lead an exemplary life among the Gentiles; then those who now revile you as evil doers will on closer inspection glorify God and your good works...'(I Peter 2.12). Pastoral aims always prevail, also in expressions like 'subject yourself to all human institutions for the Lord's sake' (I Peter 2.13). These are not dogmatic or ethical statements, but pastoral guidelines in a very definite historical context. We know from Tacitus how Jewish proselytes were regarded as culturally subversive in the empire because of their life-style, which differed from the Graeco-Roman codes.[22] Christians in Asia therefore modelled what were earlier egalitarian relationships in the Christian house communities increasingly on the pattern of the prevailing hierarchical code of the pagan houshold, precisely in order to be able to live peacefully as Christians in a culture which was alien to Christianity. This is the eternal problem of contextual adaptation and critical independence based on the gospel (because it is critical inculturization it may not necessarily be successful). However, here the *status quo* of the Hellenistic Roman social and political institutions, including slavery and the subjection of women, was taken over, despite the protest against it in the light of the gospel from the early Christian churches and their baptismal declarations.

(b) The rigidification of the model on the basis of theological legitimation

Adaptations of a religion to its cultural environment which are often unavoidable in cultural terms are often given a subsequent religious legitimation. Contingent legacies (sometimes open to criticism) are then given an ideological substructure. We also see this sociological law at work in Christianity, even in the New Testament. The hierarchy in the Graeco-Roman household (*oikos*), with its explicit aspects of androcentrism, power and subjection, is not only taken over, as we already saw in the Pastoral Epistles, but at least in Eph.5.21-6.9 is then legitimated on theological grounds. The subordinate relationship of *Eva Ecclesia* to *Adam Christus* is a legitimate *theological* theme, but it became the illegitimate model of the *social* subjection of the woman to the man, even 'in all things', however much Christian love might soften this household code and the relationships of subjection which were accepted in civic society. In fact the critical power of the gospel lies precisely in this last factor, a power which, however, was only to break through social subjection at a late stage of church history and which even now has not broken through completely. Of course love is the normative biblical and critical element in this letter; not the demand for subjection which appears on the surface, and which precisely as a result of this context is open to criticism from the gospel.

In the roughly contemporaneous non-canonical Christian writings and those which appear rather later, towards the end of the first century and the beginning of the second, we see the tendency which began in the Pastoral Epistles and in Ephesians growing even stronger as a result of a gradually increasing theological legitimation of relationships of subjection and power which are essentially contrary to the gospel.

The Letter of Clement[23] is about the nomination and deposition of ministers. It is a letter from the church of Rome, written by a presbyter who calls himself Clement, to the church of Corinth. Its occasion was the fact that certain presbyters in Corinth had been deposed from office by 'youngers' (youths, new converts or deacons?). The letter says that this is illegitimate because these presbyters were chosen with the assent of the whole community: that was traditional. Moreover, they had performed their task well. If they had behaved outrageously, they should therefore be deposed, according to the ancient rule which was still valid, by the community as a whole; the Spirit has been poured out on all members of the community (I Clem.2.2). Thus the community itself must decide what is to be done (54.2). So Clement knows the earlier traditions. Nevertheless the letter calls the initiative of the community in Corinth in deposing certain presbyters a downright revolt. A tension between an earlier church order and a new and coming order can already be noted in this letter from the early church. The letter suggests that the deposed ministers derive their leadership from the apostles (42.2ff.). At all events, the letter shows how church order at this time was made more precise and institutionalized more tightly.[24] The men of Corinth, heads of households, are praised because they maintain church order (1.3; 21.6-9). The writer derives the theological substructure of presbyteral church order from 'nature' and 'the order of creation' (56.16). This is the theological legitimation. On this basis the rebels must again be made obedient (57.1-3). The contrast which is drawn is significant: 'the young, the worthless, those of no reputation' in the community rebelled against 'the renowned, those older and more prudent' (3.3; 1-3). By contrast, the women are praised for their obedience (6.3; 21.7; 54.1; 55.3-6). The keyword is not so much freedom as obedience.

Rather later, the theological legitimation becomes even stronger, viz. in Ignatius of Antioch. Here too *episkopos* occurs in the singular, but he is distinguished more clearly than in the New Testament from the presbyters and deacons; now he is evidently the permanent, truly episcopal president of the presbyteral college – and thus of higher rank.[25] The *episkopos* in the letters of Ignatius is the centre of all church unity. He is personally supported by deacons, and along with his presbyters he governs the church. It is striking that the authority of the bishop, the presbyters and the deacons is not derived from the apostles via an apostolic succession. Rather, these ministers are the earthly type of a heavenly prototype or model:[26] the bishop represents God; the deacons are Christ himself, and the presbyters are the apostles (Magn.6.1; Trall.3.1). The authority of the bishop comes directly from an archetypal relationship between the one heavenly God and the bishop, God's representative on earth.

Just as in Graeco-Roman literature there was said to be, 'one God, one emperor, one imperium', so the principle in the church was now, 'one God, one bishop, one church'. Although the bishop of Magnesia still appears to be young, he must nevertheless be treated as one clothed 'with the authority of God the Father' (Magn.3.1). The bishop is president in the community 'in God's place', while the council of presbyters takes the place of the apostolic college; the diaconate is entrusted with the service of Christ himself 'who from eternity is with the Father' (Magn.6.1). Here deacons still seem to be senior to presbyters. Just as Jesus did nothing without the Father, so Christians may do nothing without their father bishop, God's representative. So the bishop is put as it were outside and above the believing community. Of course he does not have sovereign power in his own right or independently, nor does he have it from the believers. He receives this ministry 'from the love of God the Father and the Lord Jesus Christ' (Philad.1.1). What the bishop decides wins divine approval (Smyrn.8.20), for God the Father is 'the *episkopos* of everyone' (Magn.6.1).

This system of authority and subjection – hierarchy – thus receives a theological and christological, ideological substructure. There is clearly a shift here, and another picture of the church emerges. The earlier forms with often also a more than local authority undergo a shift. The earlier authorities in prophecy and teaching are now swallowed up and incorporated into the authority of the one local bishop. The 'apostle' is a once-for-all phenomenon, limited to the first disciples of Jesus;[27] however, the earlier prophetic authority of all believers now becomes a property of the office of the bishop. According to this view, the bishops are not so much successors to the apostles as to the prophets.[28] The aim is clear. Prophecy, which still lives on in the community (on the basis of the baptism of the Spirit), with undoubted authority in the church, can in fact hardly be denied, even by Ignatius, but it is as it were assigned by him to the episcopate and annexed by it. In the Pastoral Epistles the prophets remain alongside the presbyters and the *episkopos* what they had always been in the early church (I Tim.4.1). The Shepherd of Hermas (perhaps written in Rome) also points to the abiding significance of true prophets (*Mandates* 11.9). However, soon after the New Testament a struggle arises in various places between the developing hierarchy of the church (in the Hellenistic Roman and later Byzantine sense) and the older authority of the prophets. In the letter to the Philadelphians (97.1-2) Ignatius claims with some passion ecstatic prophecy for himself as bishop. He makes a reference to prophetic authority precisely in order to lend power to his own function as *episkopos*, for what the prophetic Spirit made him say was, 'Do nothing without the *episkopos.*' Ignatius is clearly making a plea for the tripartite system of ministry in the church as a new church order, which seeks to do away with the former authority of other institutions and concentrate the power in the one bishop.

Now whether we put Ignatius' letters in the first or the second half of the second century (some indications are in favour of the latter), it must be conceded that although the threefold ministry - bishop, presbyter and deacon – was not a historical reality in the New Testament itself, at least before its official canonization, it does have the backing of New Testament authority. It is the result of historical decisions.

In other writings of the early church the presbyteral church order (with an *episkopos* president and in this sense an episcopal church order) co-existed peacefully with earlier forms of church order, like the teachers and the prophets. The Didache (a church order written at the end of the first century, perhaps in Syria) is a clear example of this. Here the prophets still have a central place and real authority in the church, an authority which must be above all criticism.[29] Their prophetic spirit must not be tested (11.7); that would be an unforgivable sin against the Holy Spirit. However, the behaviour of prophets, viz. 'in the service of the Lord' is a criterion for prophetic authenticity (11.7-8). The Didache compares the prophets with (the status of) the Jewish high priest. They preside at the eucharist and may formulate the eucharistic prayer in a free way but 'in the Spirit' (10.7). Only if there is no prophet does the leadership in the liturgy go over to other local ministers. The later, final redaction of the Didache therefore allows the community to nominate *episkopoi* and deacons to preside at the eucharist if no prophet is present (15.1), 'so that you too perform for yourself the ministry of prophets and teachers'. The earlier prophets and teachers were evidently the appropriate people to preside at the eucharist. Nowhere in the New Testament is it said explicitly who presides at the eucharist (except perhaps in Acts 13.1-2). It emerges from old, non-canonical writings that this function was traditionally performed by the prophets and teachers. However, we should not forget that in the house communities there was initially no difference between the 'diakonia of the word' and the 'diakonia of the table' (eating and drinking together, with a eucharistic conclusion). 'Serving the table' (Acts 6.2; see 16.34; Luke 10.40; 12.37; 17.8) included presiding at the eucharist. Later, the two ministries became separate and were entrusted to different people: 'work in proclamation and instruction' (I Tim.5.17) and 'those who serve (at table)' (I Tim.3.8ff.).

3. Conclusion

Fourth-century Christians were aware that there was a marked difference between the life of the earliest church and what subsequently began to emerge as church order between the second and the fourth centuries, a development of which there are clear signs as early as the letters of Ignatius of Antioch (the dispute over the date of some of these letters does not affect this). They expressed it in terms of a break in church order. This is not just my own subjective view but is documented at the time in writing. We read this in Ambrosiaster. He says that in the early church anyone could teach and baptize (*omnes docebant et omnes baptizant*), but that later a different church order was introduced, for 'when all do everything, that is irrational, vulgar and abhorrent' (*coepit alio ordine et providentia gubernari ecclesia, quia si omnes omnia possunt, irrationale esset et vulgaris res vilissima videretur*).[30] Thus the author clearly notes the difference, but lets the later church structures prevail over those in the New Testament, which as a Roman jurist he obviously feels to be too popular. Here speaks a Roman jurist, Ambrosiaster, long after the pneuma christology of the New Testament.

It can hardly be denied that originally there were times when ministry in the church was exercised on the basis of the baptism of the Spirit, the pneumatic power of which was manifested more clearly in certain believers than in others. The first were themselves leaders, teachers and liturgists of the ecclesial communities of believers. This historical result brings us to the theological problem of the relationship of the baptism of the Spirit (*sacramentum baptismi*, somewhat later split into baptism and confirmation) to the spiritual charisma of the ministry (*sacramentum ordinis*). The most important aim of the next section is the theological investigation of this.

Section 2: **A theological approach, though not without sociological interest**

More than thirty years of biblical studies by commentators and theologians on ministry in the church, above all in the New Testament, have made a good deal clear over against the earlier so-called speculative theology, though some questions still remain unanswered. Above all in recent years feminist exegetes have made a notable contribution and have brought to light aspects in the New Testament which had escaped male eyes.

1. The founders of communities and those 'who labour among you, lead you and admonish you' (I Thess.5.12; see Rom.12.8-9)

Apart from apostleship proper, the Christian communities did not receive any kind of church order from the hands of Jesus when he still shared our earthly history. Furthermore, 'the Twelve' were the symbol of the approaching eschatological community of God, which originally was not yet organized for a long-term earthly history. This primary, fundamental datum of the New Testament must already make us very cautious; we must not be led astray into speaking too casually about 'divine ordinances' and particular dispositions in respect of the ministries in the church community of believers, at least without reference to church history. On the other hand it is also a fact that what 'Christian prophets' said was at that time attributed to 'the heavenly Christ, the Lord'. The Spirit of Christ inspired these prophets.[31] Historians do not have the last word here.

Since according to the self-understanding of the first Christians the community of believers is a "community of God',[32] a 'community of Christ',[33] and a 'temple of the Holy Spirit',[34] it is obvious that what developed spontaneously from the community of faith (as we would now put it, in accordance with the socio-logical laws of group formation) was rightly and spontaneously experienced by the communities as a 'gift of the Lord' (Eph. 4.8-11; I Tim. 4.14; II Tim 1.6). The New Testament, bubbling over with praise for 'blessings from above', does not know the later contrast between what comes 'from below' and what comes 'from above'. On the contrary, the whole community is the temple of the Spirit, the body of Christ. Unless the whole community is unfaithful to the Lord in word or deed, what arises spontaneously from the community of Jesus is at the same time experienced as a gift of the Spirit. (Of course, this easy way of speaking also has a problematical reverse side, just as the later opposition between 'from above' and 'from below' also has a very problematical reverse side.)

Within the New Testament, the texts compel us to make a distinction between two periods or phases which, though distinct, nevertheless flow into each other: these are the time of the 'apostles' and the post-apostolic period, though the latter is still within the New Testament. It is a fact that the first communities were founded by the first disciples of Jesus. However, while the concept of 'apostleship' has a clearly defined nucleus, it is more fluid at the periphery. 'The Twelve' (later this becomes 'Peter with the Eleven') is a category which more than probably goes back to the earthly Jesus himself. It is a symbol of Israel's twelve patriarchs and tribes, and of the whole of Israel as a sign of the eschatological community of mankind. Luke above all (at a much later stage) worked out in his two books the concept of the 'apostolate' theologically in terms of the Twelve, in such a way that in fact he had some difficulty in recognizing Paul as an authentic apostle. Paul, at any rate, had not accompanied Jesus throughout the whole of his public ministry from his baptism in the Jordan until his death and the Easter experiences of the apostles afterwards (see Acts 1.21f.). However, in addition to this key concept of the Twelve, the primitive Christian concept of apostleship also includes many of the first Christians who had come forward before the founding of the first communities or before the building up of newly founded communities. To begin with there were also many enthusiasts here who in the earliest Christian period (and already in the old Q tradition) were called 'prophets' and also evangelists, bearers of the gospel. Later, Eph. 2.20 speaks of 'apostles and prophets' as the foundation of the earliest Christian communities. Perhaps these prophets had not founded the communities themselves, but they were of great significance for their development. So in addition to the Twelve (about whose individual roles we know virtually nothing, apart from James and, to some extent, Peter), there were other 'apostles' who in fact presided over the birth of the first communities. At

any rate, we should not forget that barely three years after Jesus'
death (i.e. before Paul had become a Christian), intractable
difficulties had arisen in Jerusalem, specifically between the
Aramaic-speaking Christians – 'the Hebrews' (Acts 6.1) – and the
Greek-speaking Jewish Christians there – 'the Hellenists', the
followers of Stephen. The occasion for these difficulties may have
been some neglect on the part of the Aramaic-speaking Christians
in providing material help to the Greek-speaking Jewish-Christian
members of the community (Acts 6.15). However, all the signs
are that the cause of this conflict lay deeper, because from the
beginning the Greek-speaking Jews had other, wider expectations
than the representatives of the Jerusalem tradition, and they
introduced these broader views into Christianity. The conflict was
finally resolved when 'apostles, together with all the community'
(Acts 6.2) appointed seven members of the Greek-speaking Christian community in Jerusalem[35] to look after the Greek-speaking
Jewish Christians in Jerusalem. Given Luke's interpretation (Acts
6.1-4), it is to some extent understandable that they were later
called 'deacons', though this is historically incorrect; these so-
called deacons, above all Philip 'the evangelist' (Acts 21.8), who
was one of their number, did everything that the apostles did. In
fact they were in a sense 'new apostles', although the Jerusalem
community retained some oversight over their activity (Acts 8.14).
Moreover, it was these Greek-speaking Jewish Christians who
were persecuted by the Jewish Sanhedrin, while the Aramaic-
speaking Christians were left undisturbed. Because of the
persecutions they finally fled to Samaria and further north, to
Syria. On the way these fugitives (especially under the leadership
of Philip) founded many communities.[36] It is above all because
of them that Christianity spread with such surprising speed
throughout the whole of the ancient Near East. It was also from
this group (remember Ananias in Antioch, Acts 22.12; 9.10-12;
9.17f.) that the later apostle Paul received his first initiation into
the gospel of Jesus Christ. This Paul, after Barnabas, was to
become the great bearer of the tradition and the pioneer of many
Christian communities (though not the only one), above all of the
communities about which we have the best historical information.
By contrast, as is well known, not least because of conflicts within
the early church, we have only scanty information about those
communities which remained outside the influence of Paulinism
(probably the so-called Matthaean and Johannine communities).

The Twelve, and the other 'apostles' and prophets (cf. Acts 13.1-3), understood themselves to have been sent by their dead but risen Lord in the cause of Jesus, i.e. continuing the proclamation of the coming kingdom of God (see also Acts 20-25), and to be bound up with the action and the whole historical career and death of Jesus of Nazareth. The first communities received the faith from them on the basis of the personal experiences which most of them had had of Jesus, from his baptism in the Jordan until his death, and their own Easter experiences afterwards.[37] Other founders of communities had obtained the content of their faith from what they had been told by older Christians, just as Paul had not known the earthly Jesus. On the basis of their origin and foundation, the Christian communities were therefore also characterized by apostolicity: they were apostolic churches. This essential characteristic was later to be taken up into the so-called apostolic creeds.[38] Of course, logically and also historically, apostolicity became an explicit theme only after the death of the apostles, in particular in the New Testament post-apostolic period, in which ecclesiology, the doctrine of the church and its ministry, was worked out more clearly. At any rate, when the apostles had died, the communities were more clearly conscious that they owed their Christian character to these founders. In other words, their foundation was apostolic (in a general sense) and they therefore had to build further upon it. The second generation of Christians, who had come to know Jesus through the mediation of the 'apostles', began to call themselves apostolic in roughly the same way as, for example, the followers of Benedict began to call themselves Benedictines, i.e. not immediately, but at a later stage. For the New Testament apostolicity is in the first instance a distinguishing title for the Christian community itself on the basis of the 'gospel of Jesus the Christ' which was proclaimed to the community by the first disciples of Jesus, i.e. the gospel of reconciliation and the forgiveness of sins (see II Cor.5.17-21; Matt.18.15-18; John 20.21ff.).

In fact, for the most part these founders of communities were not local community leaders, but proclaimers of the gospel of Jesus, who were constantly on the move. However, Paul in particular sees a permanent *koinonia* or bond between founder and community (Gal.6.6; Phil.2.30; 4.14-17), which applies both in his own case and that of his fellow workers. It was natural that when these missionary apostles moved on, their functions of leadership

and co-ordination should be taken over by obvious and spontaneous leaders in the various communities (often the first
converts and the first fellow workers, male or female, of the
apostle); of course there is historical evidence for this. In the
earliest writings of the New Testament, Paul already says to a
community he has founded: 'We beseech you, brethren, to respect
those who labour among you, lead you in the Lord and admonish
you, and to esteem them very highly in love because of their
work' (I Thess.5.12; see also Rom.12.8f.). It is evident from
this admonition of Paul's that within the communities, which
understood themselves as brotherhoods, without rank or status,
spontaneous leaders sometimes came up against the opposition
of the brethren. Paul resolves the difficulty by pointing to the
multiplicity of charismatic gifts given to members of the
community, which include the gift of leading the community
(in many different forms). Each has a particular task in the
community. Although it is recognized as a particular charisma,
the gift of leading the community still has no significance as a
'ministry' of the church; it is one of the many services which all
the members of the community owe to each other, and each
person cannot do everything. Thus originally the leaders of the
community do not seem to have had any special name for their
ministry ('those who labour among you, lead you and admonish
you'). But the fact that there were local leaders in the communities
even during the lifetime of the apostles, albeit ultimately under
the oversight of the apostles, is historically undeniable. The
leaders of the community also refer to these apostles when
difficulties arise which they are uncertain how to resolve. Hence
Paul's answer to a series of questions which had reached him
from the community in Corinth (I Cor.7.1, see above).[39]

Local leaders of communities are not always the same as those
whom Paul calls his 'fellow workers' (Rom.16.3; I Thess.3.2; II
Cor.8.23) 'in the work of the Lord' (I Cor. 15.58), fellow workers
whom he evidently chose carefully and tested (see Phil. 2.19-24).
They also seem to have included local community leaders, whom
he mentions above all at the beginning of his letters (I Thess.1.1;
I Cor.1.1; II Cor.1.1; Philemon 1) or in the closing greetings (I
Cor.16.19f.; Rom.16.3ff; Phil.4.21; Philemon 23f.). Paul calls his
fellow workers *sunergountes* (co-workers) and *kopiountes* (those
who share concern and toil for the communities: I Thess.5.12; I
Cor.16.16), '...who have devoted themselves to the service of the

saints', i.e. the community. The consequence of this is that, 'I urge you to be subject to such men and to every fellow worker and labourer' (I Cor.16.16). Paul laid the foundation (I Cor.3.10); they, the fellow workers, must continue to build upon it (*epoiko-domein*), but they therefore also share in apostolic authority and privilege (above all I Cor. 9.6,11f.; I Thess.5.12-14; I Cor.16.10-12) which Paul claims for himself on the basis of the Word of God which he proclaims (II Cor.10.8; 13.10; I Thess.2.13; 4.8). Over against but in the community, apostle and fellow workers are 'co-workers with God' (I Cor.3.9).

Paul gives pride of place among services within the community to prophesying and instruction (I Cor.14.6; 12.28; Rom.12.6-8); so after the apostles he goes on to name 'prophets and teachers' as fellow workers of the apostles: 'And God has appointed in the church all kinds of people, first apostles, second prophets, third teachers' (I Cor.12.28).[40] This mention occurs in the middle of a list of other services in the church: that of leading the community does not yet have the full significance of what ministry will later come to signify; at least, there was no reflection on this as long as the apostle was still alive. 'Prophets and teachers' were evidently general and technical terms in primitive Christianity for these incipient local leaders and pioneers in the Christian communities. We find them again not only later (when technical terms for the ministry had come into circulation), in Luke (Acts 13.1f.) and even in II Peter 3.2.; 1.12-21, and moreover also in communities of a Matthaean type (Didache 15.1f.), but also in the intermediary period in the community at Ephesus ('apostles and prophets', Eph.2.20, and 'pastors and teachers', Eph.4.11).[41]

As I have said, the names or titles for the community leaders and those who work with the apostle are still in no way fixed. Paul speaks of 'those who labour for the community', of 'those who are over you', in the sense of members who have special responsibility for the community (I Thess.5.12), i.e. making their faith their work; in Philippi, general Greek terms are used: *episkopoi* in the sense of overseers, and their 'helpers' (deacons, but not in the technical sense). The technical names can differ, as is clear from a comparison between I Thess.5.12; I Cor.12.28 and Phil.1.1; and it is impossible to describe precisely what all these 'ministers' do for the sake of the ministry: they build on the foundation laid by Paul, each one according to his own gifts and talents. However, some are assigned a special place. In the Pauline communities, Timothy and Titus in particular, and also, though less clearly,

Silvanus and Sosthenes, are notable in this respect, even according to the authentic letters of Paul, and, moreover, at a very early stage (I Thess.3.2; I Cor.4.17; 16.10; II Cor.7.6,13,14; Phil.2.19ff.). Like Paul, these fellow workers of the apostle have authority in the community (I Thess.5.12), and even over the local leaders of the community (e.g. over the overseers and helpers of Phil.1.1, to whom Paul wants to send Timothy, Phil.2.19-24). Paul's immediate fellow workers are evidently senior to local community leaders (II Cor.8.16ff.,23).

Phil.2.19-24 is of special importance in this respect. Philippians is an authentic letter of Paul (though there is dispute as to whether it is not a later combination of two different authentic letters of Paul's). It is evident from this letter that Paul is reckoning that his life may be nearly at an end (Phil.2.17). He therefore envisages sending Timothy to Philippi as 'his successor', responsible for care of the communities; he insists that in the last resort Timothy has the same authority as he does, as a faithful fellow worker, firm in the same faith. Although there is no 'legalism' here, Paul shows a certain concern over what will later be called 'apostolic succession'. The sending of Timothy (Phil.2.19-24) is a commission which goes above the local leaders and bears all the marks of being a 'succession' to the apostle Paul. However, the basis of this succession is 'the community of faith' between Paul and Timothy. Only the Pastoral Epistles will reflect on this further.

Finally, in the first New Testament phase it is also striking that Paul himself never mentions 'presbyters'. However, in certain church communities presbyteral order is very old, even pre-Pauline. After the Twelve, in Jerusalem it was above all James, 'the brother of the Lord', who was revered as the great leader; but he was surrounded by a college of presbyters (following the pattern of the Jewish synagogue). He and these presbyters make important decisions for the community (Acts 11.30; 21.28; see 15.2). Presbyteral church order was somewhat later to spread widely from Jerusalem and then from the community in Rome.

2. Ministry: the specific crystallization of a universal charisma of the Spirit into a gift of the Spirit reserved for certain Christians with a function in the church

(a) 'On the foundation of the apostles and prophets' (Eph.2.20; 4.7-16)

Only after the disappearance of the first generation, above all the apostles and prophets, did the theological problem of ministry explicitly present itself to all communities, above all after the Jewish War. Moreover some commentators connect Eph.2.20; 4.7-16 with a crisis of authority after the death of the apostles. Paul was also preoccupied with the question when he thought that his end was near (Phil.2.19-24). In the post-apostolic period ministry not only took on more specific, though still changing features, but at the same time became the object of theological reflection. In other words, a theology of ministry came into being, though people were less interested in actual structures of ministry or in uniform titles for ministers.

The original founders of the communities had died; what was to be done next? On closer inspection, the use of pseudonyms or *noms de plume* – which at an earlier time was often interpreted in a rather unfavourable light – gives us a positive insight into this problem. At a time when the local leaders had lost the great bearers of their traditions and the pioneers in their community, Paul, Peter, James, a certain John, and so on, they could best 'legitimate' their own leadership to their fellow Christians by stressing that they were simply carrying on the work, the gospel, of the apostles and prophets, those who founded the community and gave it life. When these leaders then in turn wrote letters to their communities, they did so in the name of the apostle who was the great traditional figure of their community. For example, the letter to Ephesus and the Pastoral Epistles are written as though they came personally from the apostle Paul. But the theology of 'the Pauline ministry' which they contain makes it clear that they represent post-Pauline reflection on what Paul in fact proposed: they are along the lines of Paul's own self-understanding. Precisely for that reason, the letters were written in the name of Paul. In changed circumstances they report tradition with the authority of Paul. This custom of pseudon-ymity[42] (widespread throughout the ancient world), makes the basic intention of these letters clear: the letters seek to carry on the 'apostolic tradition'; they build on the apostolic foundation which Paul had laid. So too in the Letter of Peter: probably a certain Silvanus (I Peter 5.12), who himself had formerly been one of Paul's fellow workers (I Thess. 1.1; Acts 15.40; 18.5), is writing his letter in the name of Peter, because this community is in the apostolic line deriving from Peter (albeit with many Pauline elements). And since Silvanus had a personal predilection for Paul, we also find in this tradition an attempt to harmonize Paul and Peter (II Peter 3.15f.).

Thus pseudonymity conceals a whole theology of the ministry which has been thematized in one way or another in these same letters. This is already clear in the Deutero-Pauline letter to the Christians of Ephesus. In this letter, which is post-apostolic, but still in the New Testament, the theology of the ministry is central, at least as a background. Ephesians 4.7-16 (which perhaps falls into two parts, Eph.4.7-10 and 4.11-16) contains part of a theology of the ministry in which we can clearly see the transition from the apostolic to the post-apostolic period. After the death of the 'apostles and prophets', who are now called the foundation of the church (Eph.2.20), the leaders of the community, here called 'evangelists, pastors and teachers' (Eph.4.11; cf.2.20 and 3.5), must continue to build on this foundation which had already been laid. Pastors and teachers seem to have been the local leaders, whereas evangelists were missionaries or delegates sent out by the community to found new communities in the province. Henceforward these post-apostolic leaders of the communities were characterized by two indivisible qualifications. On the one hand, like the apostles (I Cor.4.1; Rom.10.14f.,17), they work in the name of Christ and are in his service. However, the new development compared with the first Christian generation is that on the other hand those who hold office in the church know that they are under obligation to the apostolic heritage (Paul had already said something like this: his fellow workers are bound to the foundation that he had laid, I Cor.3.5-15). In the name and the service of Jesus Christ, they feel themselves responsible for the 'apostolic and prophetic foundation of the communities', because here a guarantee is given that they truly remain 'communities of Jesus'. This was at the same time a period in which particular Christians, forgetting their historical origin, engaged in vigorous 'speculation', affected as they were by the syncretistic atmosphere of those days. The historical significance of the stress in the post-apostolic period on the 'apostolic heritage' thus amounted to a reference to original experiences of real people who had arrived at a surprising new life through their encounter with Jesus. In the wake of the apostles and prophets, or modelled on them, apostolicity points among other things to the distinguishing mark of the community as being discipleship of Jesus in teaching and life-style. The post-apostolic leaders have to be concerned for this apostolic origin of Christian experience, which in fact stems from the gospel, from which the communities need to live; in other words, for Christian identity. Their ministry – now the church's ministry – is thus experienced as a special ministerial charisma in the service of the community, as the transformation into a specific specialist ministry of what is the task of everyone who is 'baptized in the Spirit'.

At the beginning of this transitional period the church's ministry was in no way detached from the community or so to speak set above it; ministry is clearly incorporated into the totality of all kinds of services which are necessary for the community (Eph.4.11). The peculiarity of this ministerial charisma is that the ministers and the whole of the community have the responsibility for keeping the community in its apostolicity or apostolic origin and orientation, i.e. in the gospel: the gospel of Jesus the Christ. Moreover, it is the task of the ministers (though here another interpretation is possible, depending on how the Greek sentence is punctuated) 'to equip the saints (= Christians) for the work of ministry' (Eph.4.12). If we end this clause after 'pastors and teachers', then as ministers these are also responsible for co-ordinating and encouraging all forms of service in the community. In any case, all forms of official ministry must be directed towards 'building up the body of the Lord' (Eph.4.12b), the church. Of course the tendency which is perceptible in the period between I Cor.12.28ff. and the Deutero-Pauline Eph.4.7-16 moves in the direction of stressing the service of the ministers in the church over against those which are not connected with the ministry (cf. also Eph.4.7-16 with Col.2.19).

Proclamation, leadership and building up the community in accordance with its apostolic foundation: this is unmistakably the theology of the ministry in Ephesians. Ephesians does not say how these ministers are appointed; how one became a leader of the community was not as yet a problem: it was a purely incidental matter. Of course ministers were called on to preserve the apostolicity of the communities, which had to remain 'communities of God' or 'of Jesus'. Here it was the requirement of apostolicity, rather than the mode of appointment, which was theologically relevant.

Does this view, above all of the ministry in the specific historical form of the presbyterate, go back to Paul himself? Presbyteral church order was unknown in the Syrian capital of Antioch, whose Christian community sent out Paul and Barnabas, their original leader, elsewhere, at least in the Antiochene community, although they will have been aware of the presbyteral order in Jerusalem. In Antioch there is mention only of 'prophets and teachers' (Acts 13.1). However, Barnabas came to this already established community *from Jerusalem*, where there was a presbyteral church order. Now where Acts uses the term 'presbyter' in a Christian connection, we seem to have an element of the tradition which antedates Luke. In six places he mentions presbyters alongside the original apostles, albeit exclusively in connection with the Apostolic Council (Acts 15.2.,4,6, 22f.; 16.4). In Acts 11.30 there is mention only of presbyters who, according to Acts 21.18, assemble around James in order to hear Paul's report of the state of affairs. However, there are only two mentions of presbyters in Acts outside Jerusalem, in Asia Minor (14.23, for Lycaonia and Phrygia, and 20.17 for Ephesus). Now in Acts 14.23, Luke says that Barnabas and Paul appointed presbyters during their first missionary journey from Derbe in Lycaonia to the southern coast of Asia Minor. There have been arguments over the historicity of this account for over a century.[43] On the one hand people refer to the fact that the authentic letters of Paul know nothing of presbyteral church order; on the other it is argued that apart from Galatians, no authentic letters of Paul are addressed to communities in Asia Minor, whereas according to Acts this is precisely the place where presbyteral church order was well known and in existence in about five local communities. Historically it cannot be denied that certainly in the time of Luke the presbyterate was very widespread, outside Jerusalem above all in Asia Minor and in Crete (see I Tim.; Titus; I Peter). We can, however, understand Acts 20.17 if we remember that the Christian community in Ephesus was not founded by Paul but by unknown Jewish Christians, which may explain the presence of the presbyteral church order there. In Acts 20.28 Luke wants to identify the unknown term *episkopos* with the well-known term presbyter; he is thus connecting two traditions. Moreover, there is a connection between the Christian presbyter and the Jewish institution of the

synagogue presbyter (see Acts 14.23). (There were also presbyteral dignitaries in the pagan temples of Asia Minor.) Given that
Barnabas – who at that time was still the leader of the mission
from Antioch to Asia Minor – came from Jerusalem, there is every
reason to suppose that he brought the presbyteral model from
Jerusalem to Asia Minor. Thus Acts 14.22f. does not in any way
need to be regarded as unhistorical.

Historically, it can no longer be denied that towards the end of
the first century there was a church order according to which a
group of 'presbyters' was responsible for the leadership and
pastoral care of the local communities (see Acts 14.23; 20.17,20-
30; I Peter 5.1; I Tim.3.1-7; 5.17-22; Titus 1.5-11; James 5.14; II John
1.1; III John 1.1; also in the extra-canonical literature: I Clement
44; Didache 15.1). The presbyters are also called *episkopoi* without
any perceptible difference, among other reasons because they
had the function of oversight (*episkope*)[44] and care. Furthermore,
the difference between prophetic preachers and teachers is also
very small. In I Tim. 5.17 presbyters who not only preached but
also taught seem to be held in double esteem. Some scholars
rightly suppose all kinds of shifts in the meaning of the term
'presbyter', which as time went on increasingly took over the
content of the earlier prophets and teachers. Now the presbyter
is prophet and teacher. The shift is evident in the *Didache*. It
speaks of 'prophets and teachers' (13.1f.; 15.2), but the difference
is small and obscure, since the prophet also instructs (Didache
11.10f.), just as the difference between apostle and prophet (11.3-
6) is also fluid because it is said of an apostle who stays too long
in a community (at the community's expense) that he is a false
'prophet'. Perhaps the only difference between prophet and
teacher is that the prophet is a non-residential teacher (Didache
10.7-11.1), so that there is not always a prophet present in the
community (Didache 13.4). Thus in the Didache 'prophet' does
not have, or no longer has, the significance of predominantly
ecstatic enthusiasm, but that of teaching in word and deed. It is
precisely this content of prophesying and teaching which was
taken up into the term 'presbyter' when some degree of institutionalization developed in various communities.

(b) Ministry in the Gospel of Mark

In the Gospel of Mark, belonging to the community of believers
is understood as a way of being a disciple of Jesus, with a marked
emphasis on Jesus' suffering and death as an execution by men.

The Gospel of Mark is the account of a crime, though in it (as B.van Iersel is fond of saying) there is no attempt to identify the criminals (they are already known from the start); the author acts as a detective to initiate the readers into the identity of the victim of the crime, Jesus of Nazareth. Who is this Jesus and why was he murdered? That is the problem which is raised.

Mark certainly knows a Jesus who evokes faith because he refuses to perform miracles and speaks with authority, but in his view this does not reveal the christological or messianic character of this faith. For Mark, to follow Jesus above all means to join Jesus on the way of suffering, though for a just cause. This evidently reflects the specific situation of the communities to which Mark addresses his Gospel. However, this can take two directions: (*a*) to offer comfort in the gospel to a community which is being tested, suffering and perhaps persecuted: 'the disciple is no better than the master'; (*b*) it can also be a reaction to a pneumatic community which worships a glorious messiah and trivializes the saving significance of Jesus' suffering and death – which is also a characteristic of Paul's reaction. Suffering for the sake of the gospel, the good cause of humanity (and not suffering for the sake of suffering) lies at the heart of this Gospel, and in Mark's composition this is evidently not understood by Jesus' disciples, the Twelve! The threefold prediction of Jesus' suffering in the Gospel of Mark is a masterful composition (Mark 8.22-10.52). Each time the disciples understand the prediction wrongly (Mark 8.34-38; 9.33-37; 10.42f.). Each time Jesus corrects them. Peter, who confesses Jesus bravely as Messiah, is promptly told to keep his mouth shut, because he interprets Jesus' messiahship wrongly. For Mark, Jesus' greatest service is his readiness to give his life when men take it from him. The supreme service for the disciples, too, is to bear witness to this in word and deed. Mark in his day bears witness that for many people, becoming a Christian involved social uprooting; as a result they were rejected by their immediate cultural environment, indeed by their own families. That is the way in which we should read the Markan texts: 'One brother will hand over another to be killed...' (Mark 13.12). According to this context the heart of the conflict lies in the *oikos*, in the pagan household in which some people became Christians. Mark does not ask for this conflict to be smoothed over pastorally, but for perseverance in it (13.13).

The whole of the long account of the nature of true discipleship (8.20-10.52) and the three prophecies of the passion are inserted between two miraculous healings of two blind people (8.22-26; 10.46-52). For Mark, the regaining of sight by these blind men becomes a model for true discipleship of Jesus: suffering, hate and being condemned, and finally living with God (resurrection). In 8.34-38, Jesus, who corrects the misunderstanding of the apostles each time it arises by teaching them all over again, addresses all the Christians who follow him, but in 9.33-37; 10.42-45 he addresses the Twelve and instructs them in true service. Here the real question is who has authority in the Christian community.[45] The greatest in the community must be the least, the servant of all (9.35). As an example Jesus takes a child – like the slave, the most insignificant member of the Graeco-Roman household. In Mark, Jesus turns social relationships upside down. However, the disciples do not understand this either, and so Jesus goes into it more deeply in 10.42-45. The sons of Zebedee, James and John, ask to be allowed to sit in the two supreme places of honour when the kingdom comes, on the right and left hand of Jesus (an echo of the struggle for power in the earliest church?, 10.35-37). Jesus' answer is that non-Christian, pagan leadership is based on power and ruling with an iron fist, but Christian leadership of a community must be service: ministers must be slaves, serve (10.42-44), as did Jesus (10.45).

Mark here is clearly in the tradition of early Christian communities, in which there was leadership and authority, but no official status of power in contrast to subjection. As many exegetes have already observed, in the Gospel of Mark there is some criticism of the Twelve. They seem to misinterpret not only Jesus but their own apostolic ministry. When the crisis comes, all Twelve flee and leave Jesus alone. Mark is unmistakably criticizing a particular false christology, probably (like Paul) an enthusiastic christology or christology of glory which reveres Jesus almost exclusively as the powerful miracle worker or perhaps political and national Messiah, but which again forces Jesus' message, teaching and suffering into the background. Thus Mark seeks a christology, ecclesiology and leadership of the church with a different orientation. However, we cannot identify historically the opponents against which Mark's polemic is directed. His Gospel does, though, point to a conflict in the early church between authority 'after the manner of the Gentiles' and 'Christian authority', after the manner and pattern of Jesus. The fact that Mark has some women disciples of Jesus following him right to the cross (though at a distance, 15.40-41), while all the male disciples fled, stresses the ecclesiological criticism in his Gospel. These women are the true disciples of Jesus; they have followed (*akolouthein*) Jesus from Galilee to Jerusalem (15.41) and served (*diakonein*) him right to the cross. Moreover, in Mark women are the only witnesses to the message that 'He is risen' (16.1-8), just as it was also a woman who was the first to recognize the 'messianic necessity' of Jesus' suffering and thus his true messiahship (14.1-9). It was not Peter, whose messianic confession was in fact heretical and was rejected by Jesus as a statement of Satan. Obviously New Testament criticism, which is predominantly a male preserve, needed feminine exegetes to open up these aspects of the Gospel.[46]

To conclude, Mark is not interested in the structural forms, nor even in the theology, of the ministry, but in the ethics and spirituality of ministers of the church.

(c) Ministry in the Gospel of Matthew

In addition, for example, to the Corinthian communities, where there is no mention of presbyters, we see something of this kind especially in the so-called Matthaean communities. Already in the Gospel of Matthew it is stressed that in the community (which understands itself as a brotherhood in which all differences of rank and status have disappeared) no one may call himself 'rabbi, teacher or father' (Matt.23.8-10); Jesus alone is the teacher of the communities (Matt.23.8). However, fundamentally this is the view of all the primitive Christian communities. Even Paul's apostolate was a *diakonia* or service, not a matter of ruling (II Cor.1.24; I Cor.3.5; Rom. 11.13; II Cor.3.3-9; 4.1; 5.18; 6.3f.); it is above all 'a ministry of reconciliation' (II Cor.5.18; see II Cor.3.4-6). Throughout the New Testament ministry is nowhere conceived of as a structure in accordance with the worldly model of 'leadership', in the sense of rulers being over subjects. On the contrary, as all three synoptics say (Mark 10.42f.; Luke 22.25; Matt.20.25f.), 'It shall not be so (as is the case with worldly rulers) among you'.

Throughout the New Testament, leadership is service or *diakonia* (I Cor.16.15f.; 12.28; II Cor.3.7-9; 4.1; 5.18; 6.3; II Tim.4.5; Eph.4.11f.; Col.4.17). The same thing applies even when the presbyteral ministry of leadership comes more into prominence: 'I exhort the presbyters among you... tend the flock of God of which you are the pastors; keep it in accordance with God's will: from the heart and not under constraint, with dedication and not from the desire for gain. Do not domineer over those who are entrusted to your care, but be an example for the flock' (I Peter

5.1-4).[47] Thus the particularity of Matthew cannot lie here. Of course, like all the earliest Christian communities, his Gospel is familiar with 'prophets and teachers' or 'wise men' (see Matt.5.12; 7.22; 10.41; 11.25; 13.52; 23.8-10,34). However, it is striking that the Gospel of Matthew is very cautious, and issues polemic against 'false prophets'(7.15f.) and 'false teachers' (5.18f.), which presupposes the authentic functions of prophet and teacher in his community. But Matthew wants a community 'of the little' (*mikroi* is a key word throughout his Gospel), and this subjects the actual practice of leading the community, above all in the way of the world, to severe criticism. This is connected with Matthew's view of the church, whose members are 'sons of the kingdom of God' (Matt. 13.38), but still under the proviso of the judgment (Matt.25.31-46); this is a church 'made up of good and evil' (22.10; see 13.36-43; 18.7). Matthew will not tolerate 'office bearers' whose conduct is not in accord with the kingdom of God: Matthew is concerned with 'the kingdom of God and his righteousness' (Matt. 6.33), i.e. the kingdom of God and the life-style which conforms to this kingdom, and this last is revealed in actions with fellow human beings (Matt.7.21-23; 25.31-46). Matthew goes on to depict both the good and the weak sides of the immediate disciples of Jesus; they are paradigmatic types of all Christians, the Christians in Matthew's own community: believers, certainly, but above all 'of little faith' (Matt.6.30; 8.26; 14.31; 16.8; 17.20). The way in which Peter is typified points in the same direction (Matt.4.18; 10.2; 14.28-31; 16.17-19,24-27; 18.21f.); here Peter is the prototype of the community leader, the first, the spokesman for the whole community (16.18f.; 20.20-27). Following the lines of the Q tradition, Matthew also states that the disciple is not above the master (Matt.10.24f.); being a follower of Jesus involves bearing the cross (10.17-25; 16.21-28; 20.22f.). Thus Matthew expresses a special form of criticism of the ministry because he is critical of the church, which still stands under the eschatological proviso. However, this Gospel is certainly, indeed explicitly, subject to the teaching authority of Peter.

At all events, the Gospel of Matthew points to the existence of a still free, earlier system of 'prophets and teachers' – on the basis of the baptism of the Spirit – and does not seem to be familiar with presbyteral church orders; so this freer system - at least in ministry – seems to have existed longer in some areas of the Syrian churches than in many other Christian communities. Of course this freer system of 'prophets and teachers', based on the baptism of the Spirit, had many disadvantages for a developing church, particularly in conflict with false teaching. The Didache, itself closely related to the Matthaean tradition, is particularly important here. It is generally accepted that this 'Didache of the Apostles' falls into two parts, written at different times (Didache 1.1-11.2; 11.3-16.8). This document speaks of 'apostles' (11.4-6), 'prophets' (11.7-12) and 'teachers' (13.2), and the author is principally concerned to distinguish the authentic office-holders from false apostles, prophets and teachers, who are motivated by the desire for gain. We find the early Christian titles, apostles, prophets, teachers (I Cor.12.28), clearly enough here; following the line of Eph.2.20, apostles and prophets belong together in a special way (Didache 11.4-12). 'Apostles' here in no way refers to the old first apostles, but to those holding office in contemporary 'Didache communities'. Their task is *kergyma* (the proclamation of the gospel) and *didache* (interpreting the gospel for present circumstances). In addition to their ordinary and extraordinary (perhaps 'apocalyptic') teachings, the prophets also seem to have their own function at the breaking of the bread and the eucharistic celebration which follows (Didache 11.9, in connection with chs.9 and 10). The community is required to be able to distinguish between true and false prophets and teachers (11.7-12). The teachers share with the prophets 'the ministry of the word', though here the teachers do not seem to enjoy the same prestige as the prophets (in the Letter of Barnabas, which has an affinity with the Didache, the teaching of the prophets is distinguished more precisely from that of the teachers: Barn.18.1). After this exposition Didache 15.1f. suddenly says, '*thus* choose *episkopoi* and *diakonoi* worthy of the Lord... for they too fulfil the ministry of prophets and teachers among you;... they are among your prominent figures, along with the prophets and teachers.' This clearly points to later, changed circumstances in the Didache communities. In fact, in Didache 9 and 10 the writer had described the whole of the liturgy of the breaking of the bread and the subsequent celebration of the eucharist (in which *prophets* preside: 'let the prophets celebrate the eucharist as they will', Didache 10.7). However, it is evident from 14.1 that since then a change had been introduced into this service. Henceforth what we have is a weekly meeting on Sunday, followed by a eucharist, and moreover this is now preceded by a common, liturgical penitential celebration. For this reason ('thus' says Didache 14.1), each community must choose overseers (*episkopoi*) and helpers (*diakonoi*) - how it is not said – so that this more frequent and extended celebration of the eucharist may be prepared for in an orderly way, and may be carried out properly. Thus the *episkopoi* and their helpers are here at the service of the prophets (and teachers) who (continue to) preside at this liturgy; these newcomers – presbyters and deacons – share in the liturgical leadership or in the ministry of these prophets and teachers, or replace them. For that reason, 'they too must be held in honour (by the community) in the same way as the prophets and teachers' (Didache 15.1f.). Thus in these communities at least the ministry of *episkopoi* and *diakonoi* is introduced to take some burdens from the prophets and teachers who lead the community (with all that this involves). So here we have a quite different context for new ministries from what we find, for example, in presbyteral church order in I Clement, written to the Christians of Corinth.

Consequently, even after the New Testament, church order remains very varied in the different communities. The fact that the Didache emphatically points out that overseers and helpers must be held in as much respect in the community as the prophets and teachers perhaps points towards a certain restraint on the part of these communities towards these new ministries. In these communities, perhaps of a Matthaean type, the old order (prophets and teachers) was clearly of longer standing than 'presbyter', and there was even a degree of animosity towards the (later) introduction of *episkopoi* and *diakonoi*. The so-called Apocalypse of Peter (from the same line of tradition) later issues sharp polemic against the new institutional form of church order in the ministry. We should not make light of this *fact*, the recollection of an earlier church order, among what were regarded as heretical Christian sects at a time when the 'great church' was practising what was regarded as a new church order. However, on the other hand it is striking (arguing for the 'early catholicizing' of the early church) that all the communities of this type disappeared completely in the course of the second century, often falling victim to Christian Gnostic sects.

In historical terms, it emerges from this situation that a community without a good, matter-of-fact pastoral institutionaliz-ation of its minstry (a flexible development of it in changed circumstances) runs the risk of losing for good the apostolicity and thus ultimately the Christian character of its origin, inspi-ration and orientation – and in the last resort its own identity. Ministry is connected with a special concern for the preservation of the Christian identity of the community in constantly changing circumstances. Paul already says, 'All things are lawful, but not all things are helpful.' This is the lesson to be learned from the history of the 'Matthaean communities', which evidently defended in a one-sided way the charismatic approach against any diaconal specialization and thus institutionalization of it. The historical information we can discover about these communities must also make us ask whether the Great Church, which was in fact becoming world-wide, left sufficient room for those communities which did not follow a Pauline direction, and seem to have continued to look for all salvation from a charismatic leadership by pneumatic believers in the ministry through the Spirit. As a result they were forced to the periphery of the Great Church, which was in the process of becoming an institution. This history should therefore teach us a twofold lesson: the dangerous and creative recollection of the necessary unity in tension between the charisma of all believers and institutionalized limitation of this same charisma.

(d) The 'testament of Paul' to the community leaders according to Luke's interpretation

In Acts 20.17-38, Luke makes Paul summon the community leaders (here called presbyters) to him for his definitive farewell to his community in Ephesus. In the subsequent testament made by the apostle to the local community leaders who are following in his footsteps, Luke gives a good picture of the later New Testament conception of the ministry. Of course, we can find many parallels to it elsewhere (e.g. in the Pastoral Epistles and in 1 Peter, but also already in Paul's authentic letters).

This testament can be summed up in five points.

1. After the death of the apostles and the other founders of communities, the ministry of leaders of the church is a gift of grace which they have received from the Lord (Acts 20.28: 'The flock in which the Holy Spirit has made you guardians, to feed the church of the Lord').

2. This service consists in bearing witness to 'the gospel of the grace of God' (Acts 20.24).

3. Like Paul, the minister is one who 'preaches the kingdom' (Acts 20.25): he must devote himself to the cause which Jesus espoused, the kingdom of God which becomes manifest in the action and life of the community as it is inaugurated in the message

and the action of Jesus, in which this kingdom of God becomes the object of concrete experience.

4. This witness or 'martyrium' often also acquires the significance of a 'witness to death', as it did with Jesus and many of the apostles who were killed. The apostle, the minister, even the Christian, is not just the witness of Jesus' suffering (see I Peter 5.1f.), but also a witness by virtue of his own suffering (a tradition which can be found in Mark; in I Peter 5.1f.; in Hebrews; see also II Tim.4.6f., and of course in many subsidiary New Testament traditions). Until well into the second century, 'the witness' or martyr, i.e. a Christian who had confessed Jesus as Christ before the civil authorities and as a result, according to Roman norms, was already guilty of a capital offence, *ipso facto* became an official witness to the apostolic tradition (regardless of whether he had actually been executed). According to some documents from the second century this qualified him to be a church leader, an authentic witness to the apostolic tradition, if he was accepted by a community. When this happened, the confessor did not need any *ordinatio* or institution through the laying on of hands (which in the meanwhile had become obligatory, according to canon law).[48] Suffering and withstanding torture for the sake of faith in Jesus the Christ had 'consecrated' him as an authentic witness of the apostolic tradition; to put it in anachronistic terms: he had become a 'priest', a witness and guarantor of the apostolicity of the Christian community. The Christian who has suffered and been tested is thus the obvious candidate for the ministry. The Epistle to the Hebrews has made this a theme in terms of Jesus' own and unique priesthood. Although from a Jewish point of view Jesus was a layman, through his solidarity in suffering with his people he is a true high priest.[49]

5. In the spirit of Luke, who himself repeatedly was able to speak of Christian joy, we can add to this testament that according to the Pauline conception of the ministry, the minister is in the last resort someone who 'contributes to the joy (of the community)' (II Cor.1.24). In any case, all who 'labour for the community' proclaim the message of reconciliation (II Cor.5.18ff.): the joyful tidings of liberation and of a God who is concerned for mankind and for humaneness. Even in suffering, ministers are those who bring joy.

(*e*) Ministry in the Johannine tradition

Above all in John 13-17, the evangelist limits his instruction to a more intimate group of disciples. In contrast to the Gospel of Mark, John does not put the emphasis formally on suffering as a disciple of Jesus, but on service in love.

The contrast between hate and love dominates the whole of this Gospel. 'The world' hated Jesus and murdered him for the sake of the gospel that he brought. Thus the world also hates Jesus' disciples who bear witness to him (John 15.27; 17.14). But just as 'God loved the world' (John 3.16) and is himself love (I John 4.8), so too Jesus was love, a love which gave its life for its friends (John 15.13). That is also the task for those who want to follow Jesus. So these show that they are not of this world, which is without grace and without life. Disciples may not share in the hate and power of this world.

Above all in the account of the foot-washing,[50] John indicates the spirituality needed by disciples who seek to make their faith their work. Jesus, the Master, washes the feet of his disciples and thus stands the social norms of fashion on their head (John 13.1-17). As in the Gospel of Mark and other contexts, so too in John it is Peter who cannot understand this at all (John 15.3; 17.17). Leaders of the community must perform the work of slaves; without this service of love no one shares in Jesus' work of service. There speaks the Johannine Jesus.

Does Johannine theology say anything specific about the structures of ministry in the church? Exegetes differ in their judgments. According to E. Schweizer and others,[51] there were no structures of ministry here, far less particular charismata of individual believers. With only the Fourth Gospel to go on, we would have to say that in this Gospel the existence of the ministry is neither denied or confirmed; we simply hear nothing about it. However, the Johannine Epistles from the same milieu are clearly thoroughly familiar with the presbyteral ministry (II John 1.1; III John 1). In the meanwhile more precise studies have made it clear that while the Johannine communities were familiar with a structured ministry, this was a ministry without any claim to authority, to such a degree that to begin with Johannine theology was opposed to authority in teaching and discipline being invested in the ministry. This was in contrast to other Christian communities. For this very reason, the structure of the ministry in Johannine theology is strongly relativized. For these communities, a direct and personal bond with Jesus was determinative for Johannine ecclesiology or the doctrine of the church. The consequences of this for their conception of the ministry emerge clearly.

According to Johannine theology, all believers possess the Spirit. As those who are reborn (John 3.3-9), they are endowed with pneumatic power. Moreover the Risen Jesus appears to all the disciples and not just to the Twelve (see also 20.21-22). In the power of the Spirit all believers can forgive sins (20.10-23). As in the pre-Pauline communities so too the Johannine communities of believers consist of partners of equal status, where only the Spirit of God, the Spirit of Christ, has authority and gives leadership. This Gospel has a clear contrast between 'the beloved disciple'[52] and Peter, the spokesman of the Twelve, who by his conduct contradicts the nature of true discipleship (18.17-29). Peter was not present at the origin of the Johannine community 'under the cross'; the beloved disciple was, and he was witness to Jesus' resurrection even before Peter (20.2-10; 21.7).

John 21.15-19 above all contrasts service in love with hierarchical authority. Of course on the one hand the Fourth Gospel is familiar with the group of the Twelve (John 6.70); however, it is striking that in contrast to the Synoptic Gospels it does not give any list of twelve names, nor does it have any account of the calling of the Twelve. On the other hand, in II and III John there is mention of 'the presbyter', a community leader who writes these letters. For some commentators this is the most important presbyter,[53] and the community is tending towards a mono-episcopal church order, but this is difficult to reconcile with the collective witness given by these letters (see below). Others look in the direction of the notions of the presbyter to be found in Papias and Irenaeus,[54] but according to these last the presbyters teach with authority; here presbyters were the generation of teachers who came after the eyewitnesses and taught with authority because they derived this authority through their link, as immediate successors, with those who had themselves seen and heard Jesus. However, in Johannine theology the presbyters simply have no authority of themselves. This is connected with the doctrine of the church and the Spirit in these communities. Here the Paraclete is regarded as the only teacher (John 14.26; 16.13); the human teachers, even 'the beloved disciple' (the bearer of the tradition of these communities) are simply witnesses of the tradition which was interpreted by the Paraclete (19.35; 21.24; I John 2.27). After the death of the beloved disciple these communities understand that the work of the Paraclete is continued by the followers of the beloved disciple who had handed down the tradition to them.[55] The presbyter of the second and third letter thus speaks as a member of a collective 'we' which bears witness of what has been seen and heard in the beginning (I John 1.1f). Here at any rate, this collective 'we' is not the whole of the Johannine community (as is the case in other texts in I John), but a group of those who interpret and hand down the tradition and who address the communities as 'you' – the little children (I John 1,1-5; cf. the 'we' of John 21.24 with I John 1.1f.). This presbyter speaks as a long-lived representative of the Johannine school; he can say, 'What *we* have seen and heard from the beginning', not because he himself was an eyewitness but because he knows himself to be close to the school of the disciples of the beloved disciple. The continuity of links in this one chain becomes clear: Jesus saw God; the beloved disciple saw Jesus; the Johannine school shares in this tradition. M.de Jonge rightly says that the *pluralis apostolicus* goes over into a *pluralis ecclesiasticus* which is, however, incomprehensible without the *pluralis apostolicus*.[56] When the Gospel of John was written, the witness of the beloved disciple was enough (John 19.35; 21.24). However, when the Johannine letters were written, the situation in the Johannine communities had changed. Two parties in conflict with each other claimed to be the authentic interpreters of the one tradition of the beloved disciple. As a member of the Johannine school 'the presbyter' (who writes these letters) tries to convince his opponents of their deviation from this great tradition. He cannot do more than this, because he can only bear witness and cannot speak with authority; at all events, the Johannine Christians have no need to be taught by men (I John 2.27); that is what false prophets do (I John 4.1). The opponents of the writer of the letter probably called theselves 'prophets and teachers'. Was this also the earlier form of Johannine church order, as, for example, in the Matthaean communities? Or was this simply the situation of the secessionist opponents? At all events, the concept of the Paraclete who is always at work (John 14.16) relativizes both the delay of the parousia and the significance of the ministry in the church. For Johannine theology it is never such a bad thing that Jesus went away, for at Easter he would return in the Paraclete (John 16.7), who teaches all things (14.26) in truth (16.13). The Spirit itself bears witness along with the witness of the Johannine believers (15.26f.). This is typically Johannine. The chrism or anointing of I John 2.20,27, the gift of Christ to all believers, is not a charisma of enthusiasm and ecstasy but a capacity, given through the Spirit, for all believers to interpret the (Johannine) tradition faithfully.

However, according to I John 3.24-4.6,13, in conflicts it is necessary to test this spiritual interpretation. According to I John 5.6-8 the criterion here is that the witness of the Spirit is bound up with the witness at the baptism in the Jordan (water) and at the death of Jesus (blood) – clearly directed against the Johannine secessionists. I John thus stresses what the Gospel of John had to some extent left in the background, namely that Jesus himself is the Paraclete (John 14.16 speaks of 'the *other* Paraclete'). The only reference in I John to the Paraclete is I John 2.1f., and here Jesus himself is called Paraclete, viz. in his function as the one who speaks for us to the Father and the one who atones for sin. Following the line taken by the Fourth Gospel, in reaction against opponents, I John wants to connect the Paraclete even more strongly with Jesus, who is 'from above'. This presbyter, the writer of this letter, identifies the Paraclete with the 'pneumatic Christ' and thus with Jesus of Nazareth who appeared on earth, was baptized in the water of the Jordan and glorified on the cross.

In contrast to both Pauline theology and the Matthaean communities, in which error is countered with an authoritative statement by the apostle Paul or later by the presbyters, or by Peter, the Johannine presbyter (more in the direction of Mark) does not seem to have this authority; here the Paraclete is the only authoritative teacher, and he is given to all believers without exception. This relativizes the ministry of the presbyters (moreover, even the beloved disciple is never called 'apostle': he is not one of the Twelve, and even after his death there is no need to replace him: see John 21.20-23).

It emerges from all this that the Johannine presbyter is unable to correct his opponents *by the authority of his office*. In Johannine terms, he can only refer to the inner leading of the Holy Spirit (I John 2.20): '*you all* (*pantes*, not the variant reading *panta*) have knowledge' (see also John 2.27, to be compared with John 14.26). The authority of the presbyter lies in his collegial membership of the 'we' as an instrument of the Spirit: they, the secessionists, have disrupted this community. Therefore this presbyter can only seek a test from the Holy Spirit to see who is right here and who are the false prophets (I John 4.1-3). The criterion here is 'Jesus Christ, who has come in the flesh' (I John 4.2f.; cf. I John 4.6). The secessionists in no way deny the earthly Jesus, nor do they transfigure him in docetic fashion, but they do deny the saving significance of the earthly Jesus, and above all the saving significance of his death. However, as a good representative of Johannine theology the presbyter knows that such a testing is of little use, since 'the world' (and that is the Johannine secessionists: I John 4.5; II John 7) listens to opponents (I John 4.5). For Johannine theology worldly success is a contra-indication for Christianity (John 3.19;14.17;15.18f.;16.8-10;17.23,26; I John 2.9,18).

In III John the church situation has become even worse. Here the presbyter is in conflict with another Johannine presbyter, Diotrephes. In this conflict we can see clear signs of two divergent views of authority[57] in connection with the question raised on each side: How can we best preserve Christians from error? (For each of the two presbyters the other is the false teacher.) The presbyter sends a delegation to bear witness before Diotrephes to the true tradition (II John 5-8,12). He does not have the authority to depose Diotrephes; he can only refer to the inner worth of the witness and thus simply challenge Diotrephes (III John 10). However, for the other, the delegation consists of false prophets. Diotrephes, presumably the leader of one of the many Johannine house communities, is thus confronted with the problem of good and false prophets (here the situation is the same as it was in Matthew and in Didache 11). However, of his own accord he decides not to receive those who in his view are false prophets. For the presbyter of III John this is an abuse of the status of presbyter: Diotrephes allows his interpretation of the Johannine tradition to be the highest authority and so 'puts himself first' (III John 9). In other words, here a church leader, in opposition to the Johannine ethos, has taken a step towards 'the authority of the ministry', as this was accepted in most non-Johannine communities. III John protests against this.

If the additional chapter, John 21, was written at about the same time as, above all, I John, some interesting consequences follow.[58] Here the fate of the beloved disciple is presented as part of a divine plan; he is in no way inferior to Peter, even though he does not die the death of a martyr. On the other hand, the author of John 21 commends Peter as an authority to his Johannine readers: he is in no way anti-Petrine. But about six texts in the Gospel of John (13.23; 18.15f.; 20.2-10; 21.7; 21.20-23; 19.26f.) show that Peter, the paradigm of the apostolic church, did not understand Jesus so thoroughly and so profoundly as the beloved disciple, the paradigm of the Johannine communities. John 21 indeed underlines the pastoral role and the authority of Peter over all the church, but only after Peter has been subjected to the Johannine criterion of love (three times: John 21.15-17). This is the principle of the direct and personal bond, in Johannine theology, between each believer, even those in authority, and Jesus. This then becomes the basis of all pastoral authority in the church, just as in the end Johannine theology is forced by the situation to accept it. Here is a symbolic description of two forms of church (for the beloved disciple is not himself assigned the role of an authority, as is Peter). Only in John 21 do the Johannine communities accept the full 'authority of the ministry', at least as founded on the personal bond in love to the one norm Jesus Christ.

Thus in Johannine theology there is certainly a structure of ministry, but to begin with this was in no way a teaching authority. Only gradually does Johannine theology arrive at the experience that a mere reference to the anointing of each believer with the Spirit (I John 2.27) is insufficient to keep the community true to the gospel. John 21, above all, is witness to the fact that in the end even the Johannine church accepts the authority of ministers in teaching and discipline, but nevertheless makes these church structures relative. The picture of the vine and the branches, i.e. a direct and personal bond with Jesus (a theme which marks the whole of the Fourth Gospel) remains the basis for all church authority as well. For the whole of Johannine Christianity the primary thing is the living presence of Jesus, the Risen One, in every Christian, thanks to the indwelling of the Paraclete. As canonical writing, therefore, the Johannine corpus (even before the Gospel of Mark) is a biblical admonition against any legalistic garb for church authority. After the Johannine Epistles we find no further sign of Johannine communities in the second century; they were taken up into the apostolic Great Church or slipped over into gnostic sects. In the 'Great Church', church authority exercised by human beings became a sign of divine authority.[59]

(f) Ministry in the Pastoral Epistles; I Peter; James

The Pastoral Epistles, I Peter and James, in different ways already sketch out for us some clear contours of this institutionalization of the church's ministry.

For the Pastoral Epistles Paul is the great bearer of the tradition in whose footsteps the community means to tread. Thus at one point the ministry of the church is even presented as an explicit institution made by Paul himself, since there it is Paul himself

who lays hands on the presbyters (II Tim.1.6), in contrast to I
Tim. 5.22 (see I Tim.4.14, and remember what is said about
Barnabas in Acts 14.22f.). In these Pauline churches, henceforth
certain Christians, in whom the community sees a charisma from
the Lord, are appointed, instituted to the ministry by presbyters
or local leaders who are already present. This happens through
laying on of hands[60] by a college of presbyters and a word from a
prophet (the later *epiclesis* at all consecrations). Thus in these later
Pauline communities the feeling developed that the continuance
of the leadership of the apostolic community, or the church,
by ministers should also be secured in an institutional form.
Although the community itself is also responsible for the choice
of its leaders on the grounds that here its own authenticity in
terms of the gospel is at stake, the special function of the leaders
of the community (in whatever form) is nevertheless brought
more into relief. Because of the importance of this task, all kinds
of criteria for admission are established (I Tim.3.1-13); this is a
kind of ethics and spirituality of the ministry. Although subject
to these criteria, however, all Christians have the right 'to aspire
to this office' (I Tim.3.1). The post-apostolic leaders of the
communities themselves clearly formulated their own self-understanding: they wanted to walk in the footsteps of the apostles and
prophets. Hence we read in the superscriptions of the Pastoral
Epistles: 'Paul to Titus – to Timothy – his true child in the common
faith' (Titus 1.4; see I Tim.1.2; see already Paul himself: I Thess.3.2;
I Cor.4.17; I Cor.16.10; Phil. 2.22; II Cor.7.6,13,14). Both Timothy
and Titus (clearly ministers of the church, though never called
episkopos or *presbyteros*, are called 'true children' of the apostolic
faith in order to stress the legitimacy of their ministry. The
qualification 'true' is added with good reason: their faith is built
on the apostolic heritage, and therefore they are the authentic
guarantee of the apostolicity of the communities.

Thus in the Pastoral Epistles the ministry is not formally, as
such, a norm; the norm is the *paratheke*, the 'pledge entrusted' (I
Tim.6.20, which also ends the letter, and II Tim.1.14, which also
begins it). In II Tim.1.10-14 we are told of the specific content of
this deposit which is entrusted to Paul, viz. the gospel (1.11; see
also II Tim.2.8), as the apostles have interpreted it. The Pastoral
Epistles call this interpreting the gospel the *didaskalia*, the teaching
(I Tim.1.10; II Tim.4.3; Titus 1.9; 2.1, etc.). In Titus 2.10 we
therefore find the phrase 'the *didaskalia* of God our Saviour'. For
these letters Paul is the great *didaskalos* or teacher of the divine

gospel (I Tim.2.7; II Tim.1.11). The Pastoral Epistles thus show (following what Paul himself had said about Timothy and Titus) a special interest in the continuity of the apostolic tradition, the main theme of these three letters. Primarily the concern is quite definitely not so much with an unbroken succession or continuity in the ministry as with an unbroken succession in teaching, in the apostolic tradition. II Timothy 2.2 states this explicitly: 'The teaching which you have heard from me before many witnesses entrust to faithful men who will be able to teach others also.' The succession in question here is clearly that of the apostolic gospel: Paul receives it from God (I Tim.1.11: Paul himself spoke of himself and his fellow workers as *theou synergoi*, fellow workers with God, I Cor.3.9); for his part Paul hands it down to Titus and Timothy (I Tim. 6.20; II Tim.1.13f.), and these must in turn hand on the same liberating gospel to trustworthy Christians, ministers in the church (II Tim.2.2). Thus the focal point is clearly handing on intact the apostolic gospel, 'the pledge entrusted'. The ministry as a service is subordinate to this continuity or succession which is apostolic in content; there must always be ministry in the church for the sake of continuity. Ministry is necessary for the sake of the gospel. Paul himself had already said, 'How are men to believe in him of whom they have never heard? And how are they to hear without a preacher?'(Rom.10.14). For this reason different commentators have rightly said that in the Pastoral Epistles the central feature is not the principle of the ministry, much less the structures of the ministry (which remain vague), but *the principle of the apostolic tradition*. This is expressed even in the rite of the laying on of hands, which these letters want to see introduced and which is already beginning to become a tradition in these churches. For here, too, there is primarily no question of the transference of ministerial authority, but of the charisma of the Holy Spirit, which will help the minister to hand down and preserve in a living way the pledge entrusted to him and to make him able to proclaim the apostolic tradition intact (I Tim.4.3f.; II Tim.1.6,14). Ministry is necessary, even qualified ministry (Titus 1.5-9), in order to keep the community on apostolic lines: 'the community of Jesus'.

What ministries are needed? The Pastoral Epistles do not seem to be interested in this; this falls outside the normative *didaskalia*. In fact, in the communities to which these letters are addressed there are already specific differentiations in ministry, but we can discover virtually nothing about the precise sphere of competence of each. Thus there are : 1. *deacons* (I Tim.3.8-13; II Tim.4.5), though we are never told what their function is. They are simply urged to be good and required to be *homines probati*, tested by the community (I Tim.3.10); when anything is said about their work, this virtually coincides with what is said about the *episkopoi*. 2. In addition there is a college of *presbyteroi* (I Tim.4.14), who 'preside' over or lead the community (I Tim.5.17; Titus 1.5). Among them are evidently people who are active above all 'in the word and teaching' (I Tim.5.17), the teachers or catechists of former times; this even seems to be a function which carries with it the right to recompense (I Tim.5.17f.), although this last is a universal basic rule in the New Testament (see Matt.10.10; I Cor.9.1-18; II Cor.11.7-11). We are told nowhere whether there were also 'presbyters' who did not preside and did not teach. 3. Finally, two texts mention an *overseer* or *episkopos* (I Tim.3.2; Titus 1.7). It is also said of him that he 'teaches and directs' (Titus 1.9; I Tim.3.2). Is the *episkopos* a presbyteros, perhaps head of the presbyteral team? What specific function does he perform? These letters give us no information on such questions. They are evidently not at all interested in the specific structure of the ministry.[61] It is here that we find the great difference from the interest which will develop later, e.g. already in the letters of Ignatius, in which the structures of the ministry occupy a central place, and the spheres of authority are well defined in terms of church order.[62] Furthermore, in clear contrast to the Pastoral Epistles, I Clement (42.4,5, compared with 44.1f.) already calls the office of *presbyteros-episkopos* a divine institution. By contrast, the Pastoral Epistles do not give us any norm whatsoever as to how the ministry must in fact be structured and differentiated; they simply say that the ministry is needed to preserve in a living way the apostolicity of the community's tradition. Only this last point is theologically relevant; giving it specific form is thus evidently a pastoral question, which the church must consider afresh on each occasion.[63]

Through the introduction of the laying on of hands (above all after the disappearance of the prophets from the church), these letters obviously want to ensure that there is always a ministry in the church. This laying on of hands, with prayer, is therefore founded on, or anchored in, the sacramental church. The building up of the community undergoes further historical development, in apostolic continuity, even after the first and second scriptural phases.

In the letter of James the presbyteral church order is taken for granted. 'Is any among you sick? Let him call for the elders of the church, and let them pray over him, anointing him with oil in the name of the Lord' (James 5.14).

For the New Testament period, we can say that from Jerusalem and, somewhat later, from Rome, presbyteral church order replaced the undifferentiated church order of the first period throughout early Christianity also and perhaps above all in the Pauline communities. I Peter is typical of the disappearance of the type of church with an undifferentiated ministry, in which 'prophets and teachers' were the most prominent figures, in favour of the institution of a presbyteral leadership of the church. It was probably written from the community of Rome to churches in Asia Minor, on the eve of a persecution of the church there (perhaps under the emperor Domitian). In I Peter 1.1-4.11 there is clear mention of a charismatic origin of ministries, evidently on the basis of the baptism of the Spirit, but in the second part of this letter, from I Peter 5.1-5 on, there is an unmistakable mention of a presbyteral church order. Here the two types of church still stand side by side. However, in a situation of possible church persecution (I Peter 4.14-16), the writer still sees salvation and preservation for the threatened community in a strict, presbyteral church order, although this college of pastors is subject to the norm of the 'arch-pastor, Jesus' (I Peter 5.4).

We must therefore note that there is a clearly uniform development in the direction of a presbyteral church order as a uniform type of ministry between Acts 20.28 (see also 14.23); II Tim.3.1; I Peter 5.1-5 and I Clement 44.1ff. It would be a good thing to add here that, in view of the importance of the church's ministry for preserving Christian identity, at that time above all over against 'gnostic' errors, interest in the other charismata in the community (which was constantly maintained by Paul) almost disappears in the Pastoral Epistles and many post-apostolic writings of the New Testament. Without wanting to move in the direction of conservatism, given the threat of persecution and heretical errors, the Pastoral Epistles above all clearly have a preference for the teaching ministry as the only means of preserving Christian identity. Paul's trust in the Spirit which dwells in the whole of the Christian community, leads it and carries it along (shaken though it often was by the community) is only peripherally present in the Pastoral Epistles. Thus in communities of believers the great concern is with humanity.

3. Ministry in newly founded churches

With some prompting from Acts, a particular – one-sided – picture
of Paul's apostolic journeys and foundation of new communities
has established itself among many Christians. Roughly speaking,
it goes like this. With his eye on the parousia of Jesus as the Lord,
which was to come very soon, Paul is said to have travelled
feverishly, and even with an irrational impulse, from city to city.
At each place he delivered a few basic sermons (not without all
kinds of adversities) and then continued his journey to other
areas. The final goal of this hurrying apostolate was ultimately
moved from Asia Minor to Rome.

However, this conception of things, which is still current, does
not fit in either with verifiable historical facts or with Paul's own
view of what he was doing.

Apart from the first mission from Antioch, via Cyprus to Cilicia
in Asia Minor, in which of course Barnabas and not Paul was the
formal leader, and during which the gospel was in fact proclaimed
in some smaller cities (Paphos, Perga, Pisidian Antioch, Iconium,
Lystra and Derbe), it seems historically clear that where Paul
himself was the formal leader his work was planned out very
thoroughly. His pastoral aim was clear, to found a solid Christian
community, and on average that required him to spend two years
in a place. He chose the cities very carefully, staying only in the
main cities of the then provinces, east and west, of the Roman
empire (which was the 'world' or ecumene of the time), or at least
in cities which at that time had a very central position because
of their geographical, economic and cultural-political situation
(above all as international ports), as places which attracted people
and gave access to a large hinterland. After building up such
communities, when he departed Paul left a solid group behind
him which in turn could be an active centre from which the
mission could be carried on in cities both nearer and further away
– for Paul, the church is mission. The model for this was evidently
the flourishing community of Antioch, itself a vital centre of
mission, from which Barnabas and Paul had undertaken their
first apostolic journey, under the aegis of the community.

If we consider the most important places in Paul's mission, we
can recognize situations akin to that of Antioch, which had been
founded as capital of the Seleucid empire. Thus Philippi was a
very important Roman colony in Greece, one of the points of
contact between Greece (Macedonia) and the wider Western

world. The same was true of Thessalonica; it was the capital of the province of Macedonia. Next came Corinth, capital of the province of Achaea (central and southern Greece), a city with a metal and ceramics industry and also a city with great culture: chariot racing, music and athletics; in Paul's time it was the great city of Greek culture, paganized though and through. Corinth was also the centre for banking in Greece and Rome. Ephesus should not be forgotten: although it was not formally the capital of the proconsulate of Asia (officially, this was Pergamum), it was nevertheless the residence of the governor of Asia, with very close relations with Corinth. At that time Ephesus was one of the largest cities in the world with an important, busy harbour; moreover it was a city famous the world over because of its Artemisium, a temple of Diana (in the Roman version) or Artemis (in the Greek version), herself a Hellenistic reinterpretation of the age-old Asiatic Alma Mater or 'Great Mother', the divine symbol of fertility. This temple building (the largest anywhere in Hellenistic times) was one of the seven wonders of the ancient world; its roof was supported by 127 Ionian pillars. As a result of this Ephesus was the ancient Mecca or Rome of countless pilgrims from all corners of the earth. And finally there was Athens; although in Paul's time its glory had faded, it was still the 'city of philosophers', though in fact at the time it was a half-dead, snobbish city which lived on its greatest – indeed monumental – memories. Did Paul see this as not being a sensible point of contact, where he might found a community? Or did his attempt to found a community fail completely? Luke, in Acts, has given his own masterful description of why no community could be founded here (Acts 17.15-34). Perhaps Paul learnt his own lesson, in view of what he wrote later to the Corinthians (I Cor.1.18-25; 2.1-5).

When we look at all this, we might say that Paul almost prepared for his missionary journeys with the Michelin guide to late antiquity in his hand. Of course at that time there were itineraries which had already been worked out, and often these were used as the frameworks for all kinds of travel accounts.[64]

True as all this may be, we may certainly ask what led Paul to bring the gospel to the remote and rough people of Galatia (Celts) in the hinterland of Ancyra (present-day Ankara). This was not along the lines of his missionary tactics, though he did carry on a mission here and later wrote an important letter to these simple people (he does not mention any cities in it). However, we discover from Acts 16.6-7 that it was evidently not his intention to Christianize the hinterland. His aim seems to have been to travel via Galatia and Phrygia to Bithynia, on the coast of the Black Sea, with its many ports, which were important for his apostolate. One might even say that formally the ports, rather than the capitals, were Paul's objective: from ports his news of Christ, the risen Crucified one, would automatically become known all over the world. However, Paul himself gives the real reason for this more 'chance' Christianization of Galatia. 'Sickness was the reason why I proclaimed the gospel to you (the Galatians) at that time' (Gal.4.13). On his journey through Galatia, illness compelled him to spend some time there, and that got in the way of his planned journey. He made a virtue of necessity and preached the gospel.

So it is certain that Paul did not bring the gospel to all kinds of cities by travelling criss-cross over the world. He deliberately limited his personal mission and activity to the obvious strategic places, above all ports, the junctions of the international trade of the time. Paul was in no way just concerned with individual conversions (he himself seldom baptized anyone), but with building up the church. Once he had successfully founded a community he knew that he was leaving a new mission centre behind. Thus the whole Lycus valley was Christianized from the community in Ephesus which he founded (Col.4.12-13): 'The churches of Asia send you greetings',Paul writes from Ephesus to Corinth (I Cor.16.19): these are Laodicea, Hierapolis and Colossae (founded by Epaphras, Col.1.6-8; 4.13). And a whole series of new communities were founded throughout Achaea from the community in Corinth. 'To the church in Corinth and to all the saints throughout Achaea' (II Cor.1.1). This was also true of Thessalonica: 'From Thessalonica the word of the Lord has resounded, and not just in Macedonia and Achaea' (I Thess.1.8).

This pastoral method indicates that Paul must have stayed longer in the main cities, where he founded a nucleus which was at the same time a new mission centre, than is indicated by the schematic account in Acts. Paul was not concerned with an irrational eschatological haste, however near he thought the coming of the Lord to be, but with a very carefully considered plan of forming churches in cities which would hand on the news further. 'So I have finished preaching the gospel of Christ from Jerusalem and round about to the coast of Dalmatia' (Rom.15.19b), Paul wrote when he had devised the plan of going on to Spain because 'his work' in the eastern part of the empire seemed to be complete (whereas he had in fact only visited the most important cities). At that time, moreover, Pauline Christianity was a 'city' Christianity, not a country religion.

Moreover, Paul's missionary journeys are governed by a particular code of mission. On principle he never carried on a mission in places where others – Christians of a different tradition from the Pauline one – had already founded a Christian community: 'But it was a point of honour with me never to proclaim (the gospel) where the name of Christ had already been named. I do not want to build on a foundation laid by others' (Rom.15.20). Of course in certain cities where Paul began his mission there were sometimes already some Christians (who formed a house community,but not yet a community); and on his missionary journeys Paul was concerned with laying the foundations for a solid Christian community.

Anyone who compares Acts, against this background, with the authentic letters of Paul and his vision of forming a church, will come to realize that while Paul's so-called two or three apostolic journeys as Luke describes them indeed correspond with Paul's own recollections of them, nevertheless Acts gives a schematic presentation (which also extends to the chronology). It reveals all kinds of gaps, and moreover reinterprets the journeys in the light of a clear Lucan salvation-historical view of the history of the origin of Christian churches, a history which is concentrated on Rome in the West.

Acts presents Paul's journeys as though he had always had Rome in mind as his final destination and as the culminating point of his world-wide apostolic activity. However, nothing is further from the truth. First of all, this would run counter to Paul's code of mission mentioned above, for Rome already had a flourishing Christian community before Paul arrived there; perhaps primarily, though by no means exclusively, made up of Christians from Judaism. When Paul writes a letter to the Christian community of Rome before his last journey to Jerusalem as the conclusion to all his pastoral activity in Asia and Greece, this is simply to tell them that he wanted to carry on a mission in Spain and to travel there via Rome. His planned stay in Rome is merely one on the journey there; he is not travelling to Rome to preach the gospel: 'Now I have no more work in this area, and for years I have had an ardent desire to visit you as I am going to Spain. I hope to see you on my journey through, and with your support to continue my journey to Spain, once I have enjoyed your

company for a while' (Rom.15.23-24); 'When I have finsihed this
task (bringing the collection from the communities of Macedonia
and Achaea to Jerusalem) and put the offering in their hands, I
shall travel to Spain by Rome' (Rom.15.28). For Paul, Rome is not
the goal of his apostolic journey but much more a kind of 'apostolic
vacation' in a sister community, before travelling on to reach his
own pastoral goal, Spain, the uttermost limit of the Western world
of the time.

However, when he arrives in Jerusalem, Paul finds himself in
difficulties which culminate in his arrest (Acts 21.27-38) and finally
in his appeal to the emperor in Rome (Acts 25.11-12). The journey
to Rome takes place as a result of this in quite a different way from
that planned by Paul. After a turbulent journey, with a shipwreck
off Malta, where he had to spend the winter, he was placed under
house arrest in Rome for two whole years (Acts 27-29.31). After
that he was freed, but we know nothing about his fate except that
he was finally beheaded outside Rome – officially, or by an
assassin (in line with the 'ghetto vengeance' of antiquity?). At all
events, a historical consensus is growing that Paul was not
murdered under Nero but some years earlier. That he did in fact
go on to make a journey to Spain is a pure, sometimes pious,
speculative guess without any historical basis. Paul proposes, but
God disposes!

Despite Luke's interpretation of Paul's journeys in terms of
salvation history, Acts 16.6-10 nevertheless stresses very strongly
that Paul regarded his mission as being complete in the Eastern
half of the Roman empire with the foundation of the Christian
community in Ephesus (Rom.15.9). From this time on his further
activity, as Acts narrates it, is also documented by comparable
information from Paul's own letters. However, Luke, who directs
the whole of Paul's activity towards Rome, clarifies this basic
intention (of Rome as the goal – by Acts attributed to Paul himself)
by two further mysterious events, from which it must seem that
Paul is snatched away from the eastern part of the empire to the
West by the Spirit of God: according to Luke he is moving steadily
nearer to Rome. On the one hand Acts 16.6 says, 'After that they
went through Phrygia and the district of Galatia because the Holy
Spirit prevented them from proclaiming the word in Asia', and
'having arrived in Mysia they arranged to travel to Bithynia, but
the Spirit did not allow them' (Acts 16.7). So they went to Troas,
the threshold of the West. Moreover, Paul had a vision in the
night: 'A man of Macedonia stood before him who entreated him,

"come over to Macedonia to help us'"(Acts 16.9). This 'divine transportation' of Paul from Asia to the West, beginning with Macedonia and Greece, which is indicated in Acts, is clearly dominated by Luke's Christian interpretation of church history. For Paul himself, this was the well-considered gradual implementation of his mission to the whole of the world of the time: first the eastern and then the western part of the Roman empire, which at that time made up the whole world. And in fact the first community which Paul founded in Europe, the community of Philippi in Macedonia, gave him special delight in the Spirit. This community was and remained Paul's favourite community. Did he feel himself a Roman among the Romans? Although Greek Philippi was a colony of Roman veterans (as far as they relate to Philippi, Paul's greetings are to Christians all of whom have Latin names), Philippi was mainly a Gentile Christian community (Phil.4.15; Thess.2.2; Acts 16.12-40) and the Philippians who were converted to Christianity usually had a well-to-do background. Or was he delighted to have taken the first great step in the direction of his final proclamation in the West?

There is a further cliché in Acts which does not coincide completely with Paul's own view. According to Acts Paul always first preaches in the synagogue: only when the Jews reject his preaching does he go to the Gentiles. This is a Lucan interpretation of what is nevertheless an authentic Pauline view: salvation is first for the Jew and then for the Greek or non-Jew (Rom.9-11). For Paul, this is incontrovertible. However, after the apostolic council there was a clear agreement, and Paul is keeping to it: 'He who worked through Peter for the mission to the circumcised worked through me also for the Gentiles, and when they perceived the grace that was given to me, James and Cephas and John, who were reputed to be pillars, gave to me and Barnabas the right hand of fellowship, that we should go to the Gentiles and they to the circumcised' (Gal.2.8-9). This demonstrates Paul's authenticity as a human and a Christian, despite his apparent difficulties. However, historically it is not incorrect to say that Paul in fact began preaching in the synagogue, for on the one hand he behaves in the synagogue as a Jew who proclaims Christ and therefore also obeys Jewish disciplinary rules (II Cor.11.24); on the other hand, in the Diaspora synagogues the people he met were the 'godfearers', i.e. Gentiles who were sympathetic to Judaism. (Already in Paul's days that was a fashion in many Hellenistic cities.) For Paul the synagogue was in fact the most

obvious way of making contacts with *Gentiles*, through these
godfearing proselytes who led him to other Gentiles. So this in
no way means that Paul first preached to the Jews and only went
to the Gentiles when they rejected him: that would indeed have
been an infringement of the agreement he had made. For Paul,
the crucifixion of Jesus is itself already also a call to the Gentiles
(Gal.3.13-14).

Furthermore, in Acts there are a great many gaps in the presentation of Paul's apostolic journeys, which is already a schematic
one. Only some of them are significant for this outline. Here,
moreover, we must realize that all the authentic letters of Paul
were written after the apostolic council. For his part, in Acts Luke
concentrates the spread of the church after the apostolic council
almost exclusively on the person of Paul. On the one hand this
gives the impression that the Pauline communities formed the
real substance of the early church, whereas already at that time
the bulk of Christianity was to be found in the East, in Palestine
and East and West Syria, not to mention Christianity in Egypt, of
which we have less historical knowledge. On the other hand Acts
makes it look as if within the Pauline missionary communities
Paul's fellow workers – Barnabas, Silvanus, Luke, Timothy and
so on (Titus, the Gentile Christian, is not mentioned once in Acts,
despite his strategic role in solving difficulties in the Christian
community of Corinth) – were so to speak merely travelling
companions of Paul, without any independent responsibility,
initiative and influence on Paul.

However, historically it is certain that Barnabas rather than
Paul was the formal leader during the first missionary journey
from Antioch to Cyprus and Cilicia (Acts 13.1-2). Evidently Paul
was inclined to take the lead spontaneously wherever something
had to be done, even in everyday matters (see the shipwreck on
Malta, Acts 18.3). Paul first mentioned his Roman citizenship to
the Roman governor of Paphos on Cyprus, with the result that
the governor in turn began to regard Paul as the foremost of
the three travelling companions (Barnabas, Paul and Barnabas'
nephew John Mark). This subtle change in relationships did not
escape John Mark; disillusioned, he did not become involved in
any further collaboration; he went home, to the great anger of the
emotional Paul (Acts 13.13; cf. Acts 15.37-39).

Acts obviously underplayed the role of Barnabas in the earliest
communities, which were also Pauline. This diaspora Jew from

Cyprus must already have become a Christian in Jerusalem at a very early stage (he hands over all his possessions to the Jerusalem community, Acts 4.36f.). Barnabas was not only older than Paul but had also been a Christian longer than he had. Acts 14.4,14 even calls him an 'apostle', which in view of Luke's concept of apostleship (the Twelve) is remarkable, and can only be explained by the fact that he is using an earlier source. According to Acts 11.22 Barnabas came to Antioch on behalf of the Jerusalem community. It was also Barnabas who brought Paul from Tarsus to Antioch (Acts 11.25-26) and so was to accompany him on the great missions from there. Paul himself does not conceal his debt to Barnabas in Christian terms (I Cor.9), even when their ways parted as a result of a bitter conflict. Barnabas also seems to have taken the initiative for the first missionary journey from the community at Antioch; at any rate, he is mentioned first among Antioch's leading 'prophets and teachers' (Acts 13.1). Barnabas also joins Paul in bringing the collection from the community in Antioch to Jerusalem (Acts 11.30) and he is again the one to introduce Paul in Jerusalem and argue for him in that exalted setting, where there is some suspicion of Paul (the former persecutor of Christians). With Paul, Barnabas represents the community of Antioch at the apostolic council. Barnabas respects the doctrine that the Gentiles who become Christians are free from the Law, and Barnabas and Paul also respect the same view that in their apostolic work they should as far as possible be financially independent of the communities by earning their own living (I Cor.9.6). Of course, after the apostolic council Barnabas becomes somewhat more sensitive to the objections of the Jewish Christians. After a new conflict Paul says dejectedly, 'even Barnabas allowed himself to be won over by their sophistry' (Gal.2.13b).

What had happened here? People were faced with a new situation which the apostolic council had not foreseen. Spheres of work had evidently been divided at this council: Paul and Barnabas for the uncircumcised, Peter and his followers for the circumcised. After that, Paul and Barnabas could express and put into practice the principle of 'Jew to the Jews and Greek to the Greeks'. However, this administrative principle was in no way sufficient. What was to be done when Jewish Christians and Gentile Christians came together? Above all, eating together presented an insuperable difficulty, given the Jewish standpoint. Here the principle of peaceful co-existence could not provide any solution in Christian terms: it went against the principle of the one *ekklesia* made up of Jews and Gentiles. This was the new element in the conflict, and for Paul it was a test case: for from a Christian perspective it implied that the Christians from Judaism had to relativize their Jewish laws and accept table fellowship with Gentile Christians. The agreement at the council (which was based on different spheres of work) had not provided for this. Jew to Jews and Greek to Greeks, a principle that Barnabas and even Peter respected, went by default the moment that Jew and Greek came together as Christians: 'For before certain men came from James, Peter ate with the Gentiles, but when they came he drew back and separated himself, fearing the circumcision party' (Gal.2.12-13). Because of this conflict Paul and Barnabas parted company – a development that Acts 15.36-39 innocently reduces to the somewhat episodic conflict over not taking John Mark with them a second time, since he had earlier left Paul in the lurch (Acts 15.37-39). Paul's attitude does not seem to have convinced the others, but it does seem that Barnabas and Paul maintained their position, which did not improve Paul's reputation among certain Jewish Christians. Even in the second century, Jewish Christianity rejects Paulinism.

The great authority of Barnabas in the early church emerges finally from the fact that a particular Christian tradition (to which Tertullian bears witness) attributes the Letter to the Hebrews to him and another tradition atttributes to him the 'Letter of Barnabas'.

Finally, Acts presents the communities founded by Paul as sound, internally coherent communities without any deeper conflicts worth mentioning. In Acts, the fact that Paul repeatedly has to give way is connected with episodic events. According to Acts (20.29-30), really serious internal crises were only to break out in the Pauline communities after Paul had finally departed. However, Galatians and Corinthians, and also what II Cor.1.8-9 says about Ephesus, and even Phil.3.2-3, give us a very different picture: Paul endured a good deal in all the communities which he himself had founded. Later, Deutero-Pauline letters were even to make Paul say, 'You know that everyone in Asia left me in the lurch' (II Tim.1.15). Historically this seems a more accurate picture.

With the completion of the founding of the community in the important city of Ephesus (which he did not in fact achieve), Paul regarded his sphere of work in the eastern part of the Roman empire as complete. His intention was next to travel to Jerusalem in order to hand over the financial gifts of his new communities to the community leaders there. However, on the eve of his journey he was confronted with the most serious crisis in his pastoral life: in the communities of Galatia, in Corinth and in Ephesus. Reports had reached him that 'strange missionaries' there were attacking his own gospel. Just as Paul himself strictly kept to the missionary code to the effect that he would not involve himself in Christian communities which had been founded by non-Pauline missionaries, so too he was almost aggresively intolerant over the involvement of others in Pauline communities. Here he could be sharp as a razor and hard as iron, not out of personal jealousy (see Phil.1.13-18), but because he had received the gospel which he proclaimed from God himself. No one, even an angel from heaven, could change this.

The fact that on the threshold of his planned departure from Asia Minor and Greece, hitherto his field of work, Paul was confronted for the first time with what he calls the beginning of schisms in the great community (still in fact one, I Cor.1.11), made him acutely aware for the first time of what a schism can mean in the church. Although he had always had to contend with a large number of difficulties in founding his communities, the recent events were a new threat even to this apostle, for all the trials that he had constantly endured. Although the substance of the difficulties differed, they all seem to have come to a head at the same time: in Galatia, in Corinth and finally in Ephesus. Paul writes of them: 'You must know, brothers, that serious difficulties overwhelmed us here in Asia' (II Cor.1.8-9).

It was precisely in this difficult period that Paul wrote his great letters from Ephesus: at least four to Corinth (perhaps incorporated by the later collectors of Paul's letters into I and II Corinthians); his letter to the Galatians; and in all probability also the letter to the Philippians and perhaps also the letter to Philemon. Somewhat later, when the difficulties in Corinth had been resolved, Paul travelled from Troas, full of joy, to the city from which he wrote his letter to the Romans.

Paul's letter to the Galatians is tough as nails, though we do not know whether it helped him to win his case. At all events, a similar harshness towards the situation in Corinth seems to have failed completely (see II Cor.2.1). Thereupon Paul wrote a 'tearful' letter (II Cor.2.4) to the Corinthians (which is perhaps included in II Cor.10-13). At that time he sent the apparently more flexible

Gentile Christian Titus to Corinth (II Cor.7.5-6, 13-14; 8.6, 16-19, 23; 12.18). In the meanwhile he himself had had to leave Ephesus and sadly awaited Titus in Macedonia; finally Titus could tell him that his mission in Corinth had been successful (II Cor.2.6; 7.5-16). Paul was overjoyed at this course of events, as is evident from a fourth letter to Corinth (fragments, at least, of which are perhaps included in II Cor.2.1-13; 7.5-16). Paul therefore travelled joyfully to Corinth.

Quite apart from the remaining difficulties in Ephesus, he could look back in Corinth on the course he had covered. The letter written from Corinth to Rome, a Christian community which he did not found (though perhaps it was influenced by his teaching – we have no historical knowledge) bears witness to this. This letter is a preparation for what for Paul himself had to present in the second phase of his apostolate: a thematization of the gospel which he had brought to the eastern half of the Roman empire – his first sphere of work, which he had now covered (Rom.15.23-24). In it he takes into account in a serene and thematic way the recent problems in belief as he now plans to preach *this* gospel in the extreme western part of the empire, Spain (Rom.15.24,28).

In this short survey we get a picture of what the founder of a community did and at the same time what he had to endure. But what conclusions can we draw from this for ministry in the foundation of new communities? Some theologians conclude that the foundation of churches happened 'hierarchically', so that a degree of complementarity would emerge in the view of ministry: communities were founded 'from above', but the building up of communities happened 'from below'. However, things were not as simple as that. In the view of the New Testament 'the apostles' are the eschatological community of God, modelled on the twelve tribes and twelve patriarchs of the Jewish people. The account of Paul's missionary journeys shows us that the communities founded by Paul in turn sent out their own missionaries. Community is itself mission. It is obvious that communities sent out tried members of their own team, like Epaphras, for this purpose. However, an inspired member of the church could equally well be sent out, who then became *de facto* a leader (minister) in the community which was to be founded, by virtue of his mission from the mother community. Along with the gospel, of course the new community accepted the person who had been sent out. How else could a community be founded in an area which hitherto had not been Christian? The basic point is that even in the foundation of a new community, an apostolic community delegated someone to a mission among outsiders and to that end gave him a special blessing (the laying on of hands?). Despite different accents, depending on the nature of the case, there is no essential difference between the founding of a church and its building up. Of course in a sphere which had still to be Christianized the message had to be brought before a community, attracted by it, could become a living Christian community. Sociologically this goes without saying. However, the hearing of the new message by those who were originally not Christians is the consequence of the 'ecclesial' awareness of a community that it must carry out God's own message – that of Jesus the Messiah. The history of the founding of new communities by Paul (about which we have the best historical information, as also about the first sending out of Barnabas and Paul by the community in Antioch), does not rob this of its force, but confirms the view of community and ministry which these chapters have attempted to clarify.

4. The theological content of ministry in the New Testament

(a) The four dimensions of 'apostolicity'

The early church was conscious of being an 'apostolic church', a consciousness which was later incorporated into the 'Apostles' creed'.

In his interpretation of what I say in *Ministry* about the apostolic content of the churches, my critic Pierre Grelot (whom I take most seriously), interpreted my book very one-sidedly and mistakenly, clearly dominated by his emotions. As an example, where I speak in a matter-of-fact and objective way of the 'official church', he attributes to me (for what reason, in the light of my book?) 'une nuance de dédain' (e.g. p.141). Clearly the same method is used as in the anti-modernist affair: everything that is said by believers here and there, and perhaps is not even said at all, is projected on to a few authors who in fact did not say anything of what perhaps was said here and there. This produces a picture of what has to be called heresy. A personal and friendly letter from the author (after the appearance of the book), in which he tells me that on re-reading it he himself is shocked by the sharp criticism in his own book, may reconcile me to him, but it leaves my readers, *believers*, out in the cold.

According to Grelot I derive apostleship from following Jesus, the praxis of the kingdom of God as a disciple of Jesus (to think that this rich concept could already be thought of as a reduction!). He says that I have omitted essential ingredients of that concept.[65] Nothing is further from the truth. Therefore I shall begin by setting out the four aspects or dimensions of what I already meant by apostolicity in *Ministry*.

(i) I regard as the fundamental dimension of the apostolicity of the churches the fact that these churches are founded or built up 'on the apostles and prophets' (Eph.2.20; 4.7-16, see already *Ministry*, p.14).

(ii) There is above all the apostolic content of 'tradition', *paratheke*, the gospel of the pledge entrusted, in other words the apostolic tradition. Here the New Testament writings are a permanent foundation document (see already *Ministry*, p.17).

(iii) There is also the apostolicity of the Christian communities of believers themselves, as called to life by the apostles and prophets on the criteria of the apostolic content of faith, what is handed down (see (i) and (ii)). The *sequela Jesu* or the praxis of the kingdom of God is an essential part of this, i.e. following Jesus in his message, his teaching and his actions (see already *Ministry*, pp.13f.).

(iv) Finally, there is the apostolicity of the church ministries, the so-called apostolic succession (see already *Ministry*, pp.17-18).

However, Grelot devotes all his attention to the last dimension which I recognize. He himself sees the concept of apostolicity exclusively in terms of structures and inter-personal relationships.

For me, 'apostolicity' is a richly variegated term that in no sense can simply be reduced to just one of these four dimensions. By means of this term (which is itself post-biblical), the New Testament (with the content of that concept) seeks to connect the phenomenon of Jesus of Nazareth with the reactions of the first disciples to his appearance. In fact the apostolicity of the communities of Christian believers and their character governed by the gospel, in the light of Jesus confessed as the Christ, means one and the same thing, though the accent is different. One could of course equally well speak of the 'prophetic character' of the Christian churches, which is what e.g. Ignatius of Antioch is to do (see below). For the New Testament, apostolicity points in the first place to the gospel of Jesus Christ as it has been 'mediated' to us by the apostles and prophets. Within all kinds of questions about boundaries (which can still be seen in the polemic over the proto- and deutero-canonical books) or about why this or that early Christian writing did not find a place in the Bible, the apostolicity of the church therefore goes back to what we call the New Testament as a book of the church, the account of a living, early Christian process of tradition.

The Christian communities came into being as a fellowship of people who stood in the tradition of Israel and above all of Jesus of Nazareth, confessed as Christ, Son of God, the Lord. On the basis of this (within divergent frameworks of thought and experience) they confessed the same faith. This fellowship also celebrated, and finally allowed its behaviour to be determined by, the guideline of the praxis of the kingdom of God – a kingdom of righteousness and love, in which Jesus had gone before them. In a gradual process of tradition, these communities were structurally built up inwardly by Christians themselves. Before and also during the period of the origin of the books of the New Testament, the communities of faith are still in search of the most appropriate structures; they do not create these *ex nihilo*, but within a particular social and historical context. Many factors play a role in this process of tradition: the confession of faith or *regula fidei*; the praxis of believers, and really the whole life of the communities of faith, above all baptism and eucharist; and finally also all kinds of specific ministries of different natures, differentiated in confrontation with social, cultural and also ecclesial contexts. In different ways, specific forms of church organization can be seen in these different situations, first very divergent and later, as the churches became established, in the direction of a greater uniformity. However, we cannot project the church order which grew up later back on the New Testament. Grelot defends a system, not the gospel.

Within this whole process of tradition, ministry is important, but it is only one of many authorities which are concerned to preserve and keep alive and intact the gospel of Jesus Christ and therefore of apostolicity. So we cannot reduce the apostolicity of the church to the one dimension of the apostolic succession. Moreover, the four dimensions of apostolicity stand in permanent reciprocal relationship. The *successio apostolica* is not to be isolated from the rich reality nor must it be formalized, with all the un-ecumenical consequences which ensue. If there are already accents, then in the New Testament they are clearly on the apostolic content of faith: 'The teaching which you have heard from me in the presence of many witnesses, hand on through reliable men, who are able in their turn to instruct others' (II Tim.2.2). The *apostolicum* is at heart this Christian confession of faith and the community which is founded on it. Ministers, and thus also the apostolic succession, are here a service of the churches built on the foundation of apostles and prophets and (along with other factors) ministry at the same time keeps the communities of believers on course, in line with the gospel and the apostles, albeit with their ups and downs, because they are human.

Paul in particular taught that competence and authority in the church is part of a more extensive move towards God and man, experienced beforehand by Jesus and put into force in his death. The root and foundation of gospel authority is in the last resort 'taking pity on the flock' (Matt.9.36). Performing the ministry is part of and also an expression of following Jesus. The *sequela Jesu* is thus an integral part of what is called mission (often in a very legalistic way). For Paul this following of Jesus was itself the criterion on the basis of which he distinguished authentic church authority from the authority of his opponents, though they were Christians too.

Ministry is essential for any church community, though of course it is only one of many factors which maintain the story of and about Jesus, in his significance for the future of all men (see Eph.4.11). The community of believers itself has a right, by grace, to ministerial support, just as it also has the right to the celebration of the eucharist. Thomas Aquinas would say later that all Christians 'have a right to the eucharist' (those are not my words: *habent ius ad mensam Domini accedendi*).[66] However, the specific differentiation in structural forms of ministerial service within the apostolic churches which are founded by the apostles and prophets and have a right to ministry takes place in a historical and contingent process which is not intrinsically necessary; it could have gone otherwise. In the actual process Christians may rightly (though not successfully) experience a response of the church to the leadership of the Holy Spirit.

Forms of a theology of ministry never arise in a void, but usually in a dispute over competence, in a process of forming roles in a group and here as part of a differentiation of a system – ultimately also as a later theological justification of positions of authority which have been arrived at historically. Thus in the first centuries there was a dispute between the presbyters and the deacons, which followed a struggle between men and women in the ministry; in the Middle Ages there was a dispute over competence between diocesan pastoral care and the abbatial pastorate, which later became a struggle between the monks and the regular canons and finally between the supra-diocesan pastorate of the Mendicants and traditional pastoral care. And so this process goes on. At the moment we can see here and there tensions between traditional priests and pastoral workers.

(b) Pioneers in the community, and those who inspired it and served as models by which the community could identify the gospel

Throughout the development of ministry in the New Testament one striking fact is that ministry did not develop from and around the eucharist or the liturgy, but from the apostolic building up of the community through preaching, admonition and leadership.[67] No matter what different forms it takes, ministry is concerned with the leadership of the community: ministers are pioneers, those who inspire the community and serve as models by which the whole community can identify the gospel. For the New Testament, there is evidently no special problem as to who should preside at the eucharist: we are told nothing directly in this connection. Furthermore, Paul does not call the eucharist an 'apostolic tradition' but 'a tradition of the Lord himself' (I Cor.11.23), to which, therefore, even the apostles are bound. The eucharist is Jesus' parting gift to the whole community, which therefore has the right to it – the right by grace – regardless of all kinds of complicated problems over the ministry: 'Do this in remembrance of me.' Nowhere in the New Testament is the explicit connection made betwen the ministry of the church and presiding at the eucharist (except perhaps in Acts 13.1f.). However, that does not mean that any believer whatsoever could preside at the eucharist. In the house churches of Corinth it was the hosts who presided at the eucharistic meal, but these were at the same time leaders of the house churches. Thus this does not in any way imply that the eucharist was detached from the ministry.[68] On the other hand, there are no biblical grounds anywhere for a sacral and mystical foundation to the ministry in the eucharist. If we remember that the early eucharist was structured after the pattern of Jewish grace at meals – the *birkat hamazon* – at which just anyone could preside,[69] it is evident that the leaders of house communities *ipso facto* also presided at the eucharist, and this is also evident from the texts written at the same time as the last part of the New Testament. In the earliest stratum of the Didache the "prophets and teachers' preside at the eucharist; in a later stratum they are joined by presbyters and deacons who do so by virtue of their office.[70] In I Clement the president is the *episkopos*-presbyter. Thus the general conception is that anyone who is competent to lead the community in one way or another is *ipso facto* also president at the eucharist (and in this sense presiding at the eucharist does not need any separate authorization). The New Testament does not tell us any more than this.

According to the New Testament understanding, ministry is a constituent part of the church (apart from the question whether one bases this on the baptism of the Spirit or on another rite which bestows charisma, and also apart from the question how this last takes on different structures depending on the different needs of the church in changing circumstances). Ministry is necessary for building up the church along apostolic lines, viz., as the 'community of God'. Here the apostolic community with its apostolic heritage, viz., the gospel, takes a central place. The ministry is a service to this apostolicity and for these reasons can also itself be called apostolic, especially as a service to the apostolic community living from its apostolic gospel. Thus it is apostolic not so much in the sense of an unbroken chain of apostolic succession in the ministry (which in view of the post-apostolic *ordinatio* has become *de facto* the actual form of church order), but first of all and in principle in the sense of the apostolicity of the gospel of the community baptized in the Spirit, which also has the right to authoritative leaders who make sure that it remains in line with this apostolic origin. Therefore the minister is not merely a mouthpiece of the life of the community, but occasionally can also reprimand it, just as on the other hand the community can also call its ministers to order. Precisely because the ministers are leaders and pioneers in the comunity, as 'the greatest' they must in fact be the least in the community: the principal servant of all (Mark 10.43-44). In this sense, the particular character of ministry is set against the background of many different services in the church. In the earliest understanding ministry is not a status but in fact a function, though in this sense it is rightly called 'a gift of the Spirit' by the community *qua* assembly of God. For the New Testament, the essential apostolic structure of the community and therefore of the ministry of its leaders has nothing to do with what, also under the influence of Pseudo-Dionysius, is called the 'hierarchical' structure of the church (on the basis of later Roman models in the Roman empire, and even later of feudal structures), except in a very inauthentic sense. It derives its own functions within the whole from what needs to happen within the church community. Ministry is not a status or *ordo* in the sense of the Roman senatorial *ordo* or status (although later, people began to put it this way, and in particular to structure it accordingly). Because, on the other hand, the church is not concerned with civil ministry, but with service to 'a community of God', the ministry of the church requires above all of its ministers leadership in the true discipleship of Jesus, with all the spirituality which this 'discipleship of Jesus' involves in New Testament terms. It is later said that the priest is *forma gregis*, the figure with whom the community identifies (see already I Peter 5.3).

5. Conclusion: Service on the basis of the baptism of the Spirit and official ministry on the basis of a distinctive sacramental rite

1. The development of ministry in the early Christian churches was not so much, as is sometimes claimed, a historical shift from charisma to institution but a shift from the charisma of many to a specialized charisma of just a few. Above all in the post-Pauline churches, although it was not yet swallowed up by, but concentrated in, a specific ministry, the charisma of all kinds of ministries in the church, that found its first basis in the baptism of the Spirit of the community members who lived by the Spirit, was connected with a distinctive rite which bestowed the charisma, the laying on of hands coupled with prophetic prayer – later epiclesis. This is no contrast between earlier charisma and now ministry, but points rather to a specific concentration and focussing of the charisma of the Spirit on ministry. The theological importance of this is that it emerges from it that the baptism of the Spirit also remains the matrix of ministry. We shall analyse this more closely later in this book.

Specialization by individuals of what belongs communally to everyone is from a sociological perspective and, in the case of a

church group, from an ecclesial perspective, an obvious development in any group formation. If there is no specialized concentration of what is important to everyone, in the long run the
community suffers as a result. That was the correct intuition of
Ambrosiaster when he saw the difference between the turbulent
first century and the later institutional ministries. The danger of
such a development is, however, that the particularized ministerial charisma of the Spirit, which also blows elsewhere in the
community, begins to be swallowed up and so 'the Spirit is
quenched' (I Thess.5.19) in the community. The charismatic
and pneumatic ecclesial dimension cannot be derived from the
ministerial church, but this last must be understood as rooted in
the baptism in the Spirit of all Christians. If that is not the case,
then the believers become the sheer object of ministerial or priestly
concern, and not the subject of faith and expressions of faith.

In this process of official, specialized concretization we see that
the prophetic function is gradually bound up with or drawn
nearer to the *presbyteros*; it is concentrated even more in the
president of the presbyteral council and ultimately in the mono-
episcopate. What is also involved here is the expansion of the
church and therefore also some fading of the first enthusiastic
pneuma christology and of the general experience in the church
of the power of baptism in the Spirit, the foundation of prophetic,
pneumatic and even ecstatic phenomena. However, it emerges
from the whole of this development that what is later rightly
called *sacramentum ordinis* is a specific, viz. diaconal or ministerial
heightening or crystallization of the baptismal gift of the Spirit.
This has theological consequences, as we shall see.

2. In the course of the centuries this gradual centralization of
ministry at the expense of the baptism of the Spirit was to produce
all kinds of side effects. From it arose the pattern of (*a*) teaching
(which is done by the church hierarchy), (*b*) explaining (which is
done by the theologians), (*c*) listening to the teaching of the church
– as explained by the theologians (which is done by the believers,
called laity). This paradigm in fact makes the believers subject-
less. Vatican II already contributed in some degree to the break-
up of this ideological scheme.

In Part Three we must pursue the further development of this
tendency which had already begun and yet at the same time had
tendencies to the contrary within the church. Here we shall bear
in mind the social context in which the church is involved at any
time: the world of late antiquity; the feudal patterns of Frankish,

Celtic and German society; from the sixteenth century the states in society (peasants, citizens, nobility); while in our present democratic societies, characterized by professionalism and functionality and oriented on information, we see the rise of all kinds of new desiderata in respect of ministry and its theology.

Part Three

Organization and Spirituality of Ministry in the Course of Church History

Section 1: **From the second century to the beginning of the early Middle Ages**

The forms taken by ministry in the second century cannot be brought together under one denominator. In literature about it the mistake is often made (and in *Ministry* I made it myself) of citing one after the other authors from Asia Minor or Syria, Egypt, Latin Africa or Rome. But that is to suggest that as early as the second century there was already a unified world church, which was certainly not the case. We must put the different authors within their regional contexts in order to become clear about the significance of their texts; this approach in fact produces a more accurate picture.

1. Specific concentration of the charisma of the Spirit given to all on the ministerial charisma of deacons, presbyters and *episkopoi* with its diaconal emphasis

(a) Ministries in the second century

(i) Ministries in the churches of Greece, Asia Minor and Syria

Already towards the end of the period in which the New Testament was completed Asia Minor had long been the centre of the young church. Different texts about ministry in the church from this area need to be considered. That is also true of Greece, where we hear a similar note.

First of all there is a letter from Clement to the church of Corinth. While it was written from Rome, it has clear knowledge of the situation of those to whom it is addressed. The occasion for the letter was a series of complaints which had come to Clement's notice about a conflict in Corinth between the party of the 'elders', or presbyters, who were the leaders, and 'youngers'. This conflict had reached the point that the younger men wanted to displace their presbyters, or had already done so. Clement's answer is that the presbyters are in fact responsible for the leadership and therefore have the last word. We can discover a good deal from this about the ministerial structure of the Christian community. The presbyters are called the leaders (*hegoumenoi*) of the community,[1] a term which Clement also uses for civic officials in the city.[2] The letter contrasts presbyters, 'elders', with 'youngers',[3] who clearly do not want to learn lessons from the presbyters.[4] The letter argues that the existing church order, the presbyteral leadership, must be respected, because the presbyters have the *episkope*, oversight, responsibility to see that things go well in the community.[5] Conflicts of this kind also arose in cities among civic officials; there, alongside a leading council of elders (*gerousia*, consisting of presbyters),[6] there was an official college of 'youngers' (*neoi*) who often had to defend other interests. The use of 'elders' and 'youngers' already seems to indicate that the Christian community had the same sort of structure as the civic community (although here we can perhaps understand the term to refer to the newly converted or even to deacons). In the civic community, colleges were kept together by a common president, the 'gymnasiarch'.[7] In the Christian community of Corinth, alongside the leading presbyters there was something like a council of youngers, who had come into conflict with their presbyteral leaders. Clement advises the church community to keep the peace and affirms that the task of the presbyteral college is to provide oversight (*episkope*) and leadership or service (*leitourgia*).[8]

Clement responds in the following way: the presbyters are rightly appointed as *episkopoi* and deacons in the Christian community:[9] *episkopoi* is put in the plural, so this is not the later 'bishop'; as presbyters, they are the leaders (*hegoumenoi*). It is striking that these presbyters seem to have a double function, 'episcopal' and 'diaconal'. Clement clarifies this terminology, which we find unusable, as follows: in so far as the presbyters 'practise righteousness', which clearly means 'govern well', they have the 'episcopal' function of correctly exercising leadership, care and oversight; in so far as they 'practise faith' they have a diaconal function.[10] This can only mean that on the one hand they exercise authority, but at the same time in so doing they are the servants (*diakoneo* = serve) of the community: there is thus no master-servant relationship, but authority in service. It lies quite outside the scope of Clement's argument to ask whether these two functions of presbyteral tasks are exercised by two different categories of ministers.[11]

At all events, in Clement the terminology for the ministry is clearly based on that used for civic government in the cities.[12] In the cities of Greece and Asia Minor any decision is taken by the assembled *ekklesia*, i.e. in civic terminology a popular assembly. Here, of course, a degree of relaxation could be noted: the role of the popular assembly, and that of the *gerousia* (the city presbyters), was weakened in favour of the authority of the governor. In decisions and elections the popular assembly only had the 'right of applause' or assent;[13] the 'council' or 'men of note' (an expression which Paul also uses) exercised greater power.[14] There is a parallel development in church and society.

It used to be supposed that the title 'presbyter' for minister was usual only in the Jewish-Christian communities (as it was in fact in Jerusalem from the very beginning), whereas the Hellenistic Christian communities used the term *episkopos* for the same function. However, historically the term presbyter seems to be equally well known for civic functions in the Hellenistic cities: there was a council of presbyters there, and in addition pagan temples were under the supervision of presbyters. Paul never uses the term in his own letters, but in the Hellenistic communities after Paul there is soon talk of presbyteral leadership.[15] On the other hand, the diaspora Jews in the first period of Christianity clearly avoided the term, and it was only taken up by Jews much later.[16] At all events, the Christian use of the title 'presbyter' for minister is based on the use of the term for a civic functionary in the Romano-Hellenistic empire, and was taken over by Jews and Christians.

The Letter of Polycarp to the Christian community of Philippi (possibly a compilation of two letters) is also relevant as a source in the case of Greece. We know little with any certainty about the author, and even the dating is uncertain (presumably round about 135).[17] The picture given by the letter of the structure of ministry in the church is reminiscent of that of Clement. This emerges most clearly from the opening of the letter, addressed to the 'presbyters and deacons', the leaders of the church in Philippi.[18] Here too there are no bishops: the *episkope* is an indication of what the presbyters in fact do: supervision, care and leadership.

The Didache, which probably comes from somewhere in Syria-Palestine, gives a similar picture: we never find *episkopos* in the singular; *episkope* is a function of the presbyters. Alongside them we find the older charismatic terms for leaders, 'prophets and teachers' (see above, Part One).[19]

It is also striking that 'suddenly' in the same territory quite a different structure of ministry emerges, in the letters of Ignatius, though there seems to be historical 'preparation' for his view. There we find a pattern reflected which can be detected generally only at a very late stage of the second half of the second century in local churches. Here too, of course, there is a college of presbyters, but they are led by one head who is called an *episkopos* and is so clearly distinct from the presbyters that he may be called bishop.[20] In addition to both of them, there are also deacons.[21] Thus here the leadership is in the hands of a bishop who has a college of presbyters under him, with whom he forms a unity,[22] though he is markedly superior to the presbyters.[23] It remains unclear how this development from *episkopos* (presbyters) to bishop took place. Some historians regard the fact that in Ignatius the *episkopos* is burdened with the *oikonomia* of the community, the task of the deacons, as an argument that the single *episkope* originated out of the diaconate.[24] Other historians[25] point out that for a long time the bishops still continued to be called fellow-presbyters; this is thought to indicate that in the long run one member of the presbyteral college became *the* man and that government under a single head began in this way.[26] This problem cannot be solved from the letters of Ignatius. Here too shifts in the sector of civil ministry shed some light. In the second half of the second century we find in certain places in Asia Minor a 'council of elders' with two leaders, and sometimes with a single leader or 'archon';[27] here too we also find the terms *oikonomos* and *episkopos* used for an administrative supervisor who at least in the richer cities is the treasurer of the council, though not its head. In the cultic communities or free associations of Asia Minor, too, this official could attract more power to himself because of his separate function. Of course this does not indicate how the difference between presbyter and bishop came into being, but it does illuminate the context in which the church worked in these areas. In the long run, in the council of the church, too, one of the presbyters became the 'first archon'.[28]

In this way a new model ministry emerged in comparison with the earlier phase: no community (*ekklesia*) assembled without the bishop, and only with him did it make up an *ekklesia*.[29] In a new phase of church order, with more stress on canon law, what was earlier the unity of community and ministry, which clearly stressed the ecclesial significance of ministry, became the unity of community and bishop. The dogmatic nucleus is the unity of community and ministry; the unity of community and bishop is the historical realization of this, a legitimate but not necessary development. The model of civic office in Asia Minor could be dogmatized in a different way! In modified structures the *biblical* conception of ministry returns: without a bishop and his presbyters the ordinary people are a *plethos*, i.e. a disordered crowd, and not an *ekklesia*.[30] Within his model of ministry, Ignatius stands for what Jerome is later to express as: 'no church community without priests'. This is the basic position of my book: no community without ministry, but also no ministry without community.[31] The content and structuring of this ministry is a matter of ecclesial involvement, led by the Spirit, in a specific situation of the community of believers. The previous section gives an example of this: the mono-episcopate followed a social and cultural trend in Roman Asia Minor.[32]

(ii) Ministry in Rome

In Rome, too, in the second century, as in the earlier phase in Asia Minor and Syria, we find a presbyteral college at the head of the community. This becomes clear from the letters of Hermas. He too speaks only in the plural of *episkopoi*[33] and presbyters[34] whom he calls leaders or presidents (*prohegoumenoi*);[35] he also mentions deacons[36] alongside the older forms of apostles, prophets and teachers.[37] It is said of these *episkopoi* in Rome that they perform 'diaconal services' and the *leitourgia* for the Lord,[38] in precisely the same way as Clement says. All this indicates that presbyters and *episkopoi* are the same persons, and their oversight points to their authority,[39] which at the same time is a 'diakonia' or service.[40] One may conclude from this that as originally in Asia Minor and Jerusalem, especially in the first half of the second century, there was a presbyteral church order in Rome with the remnants of old models of minstry. Perhaps here too the collegial character of magistrature and senate was influential in preserving the old presbyteral model of ministry longer, when the later episcopal structure became established.[41]

(iii) Ministry in Egypt, with Alexandria as a centre

This region is a good instance of how doggedly a presbyteral model of ministry could survive in the church of the second century.

The Roman province of Egypt had a 'college of elders' which held civil office and presbyters to lead the liturgy in temple service, all with equal status. The *city* administration, however, had one head, called the 'exegete'. In 202 the emperor Septimius Severus instituted a city council (*boule*) in Alexandria under the leadership of a *prytanis*. So here, too, there was first a collegial government by presbyters which in the end, under the pressure of the times, developed into a government under a single head, although this took longer than elsewhere. We can see the same development in church structures, although the origin of Christianity in Egypt is very obscure. In Alexandria a collegial presbyteral leadership was followed by government strictly under a single head, which was unparalleled elsewhere in the church. For once Alexandria had a bishop, for a long time he remained the only bishop in the whole of Egypt and was thus not only head of the great Christian community and the presbyteral college in the city, but also head of all the church communities in Egypt. The Bishop of Alexandria was able to make this *de facto* situation permanent at the Council of Nicaea.[42] This development is all the more striking since only towards 190, i.e. at the end of the second century, is there very suddenly mention of a bishop in Egypt as head of any presbyteral college.[43] At that time Alexandria already had a mono-episcopate, but in all the other cities of Egypt a presbyteral college was at the head of the Christian community.[44] Only after Bishop Demetrius (188-231) were bishops appointed in all the great cities (*metropoleis*) of Egypt, as it were *en masse*,[45] a process which was complete at the beginning of the fourth century. The strong position of the presbyteral college in the second century was thus later completely undermined, first through a bishop in Alexandria (who had still emerged from the college),[46] and after that by the extension of the episcopal system. Athanasius still says of Arius, who was simply a presbyter and made a great impression in Egypt with his teaching, that the presbyters have a strong position there.[47]

An old dispute beween the presbyteral college and the presbyter president, who in fact elevated himself to a position with mono-episcopal authority, is difficult to deny as a feature in the second century, though one cannot yet find hard historical evidence for this situation.

Thus both in the first and the second phases of the structuring of ministry, in the church of Egypt, too, the civic pattern served as a model, though more unconsciously than consciously. The mutual relationship between the bishoprics, once they had come into being, also runs parallel to the administrative division of the provinces;[48] as soon as the country areas became dependent on the big cities, a hierarchy came into being among the bishops, who ultimately were all dependent on the patriarch in Alexandria. This episcopalizing of church government robbed the presbyters of their original function;[49] in this the church followed a social and cultural trend towards government under a single head.

(iv) Ministry in the Roman proconsulate of Africa

In the Roman proconsulate of Africa, what elsewhere developed for the most part imperceptibly and unconsciously in fact developed very consciously: people opted to model the church structures on those of civil offices. We read something about Christian communities in Africa round about 180 in the ancient texts; the history before that remains obscure. Shortly afterwards, however, a Roman lawyer, Tertullian, comes to the fore with a clear programme for theology and church politics: he wants to prove to the emperor that in the legal sense Christianity is a permitted association (*collegium licitum*),[50] with all that is necessary for Rome to be able to recognize it as an *ordo*.[51] He also approaches the Christian life of faith as a Roman lawyer: according to him the baptized person is bound by an oath of allegiance (*sacramentum*), something like a civic action, to the basic law of the church, the *lex fidei*.[52]

In the middle of the third century, when the proconsulate of Africa and also Numidia had already been strongly Christianized, Cyprian, as Bishop of Carthage, continued the tradition of Tertullian. His church structure is very 'democratic', according to the Roman model (*Senatus populusque Romanus*). This emerges from the procedure for the appointment of a bishop: the candidate is presented to the assembled people, and they approve him,[53] since they have the power to elect him or to depose him.[54] The rite of *ordinatio* of a bishop consists in the election by the people, [55] i.e. either through 'the people and the clergy' or through 'the whole brotherhood'.[56] This is followed by the laying on of hands by the neighbouring bishops, which confirms the *ordinatio*. Only after all this is the appointment legally complete (*ordinatio iure perfecta*). The church structure reflects civil regulations in the Roman province of Africa. Here *ordinare* is the technical term for a firm appointment to imperial service.[57] The people has the right to vote (*suffragium*), but only the emperor can pronounce a final verdict (*iudicium*).[58] In a deliberate adaptation to this, Cyprian says of an episcopal appointment, *Factus est episcopus de Dei et Christi iudicio, de clericorum testimonio, de plebis suffragio*:[59] the clergy approves the candidate on good grounds, but the people itself chooses, and in the end God alone has the final verdict. Thus God appears to be analogous to the emperor, who can make a nomination valid or invalid. Later it will transpire what consequences this has for a bishop who is in serious dereliction of duties: according to Cyprian and Tertullian he has in fact never become a bishop, despite the whole *ordinatio*, or the people has made a mistake in choosing him.

Among historians there are disputes as to whether Cyprian meant a real choice by the people (and clergy) or just an *acclamatio*, and whether the neighbouring bishops formed the legal electoral college proper. This discussion loses sight of the particular situation in Africa: originally the community of believers had a real right of choice, which only in the fourth century was weakened to become a 'formal right' (acclamation). Civil law shows the same shift: there, too, in the end the people could only give their *acclamatio* to the candidates, who were assembled by the local authorities (*ordo decuriorum*).[60] However, the codex of Theodosius still alludes to privileges which had been maintained in Africa, including the *suffragium populi*. This must also have been the case in the sphere of the church, otherwise Cyprian's polemic about the lack of validity of a certain *ordinatio* would not make any sense.[61] In both the civil and the ecclesial sphere, in Africa the people retained for the longest time the authentic right of choice.[62] Later, by analogy with the civil *ordo decuriorum*, the clergy (and not just the church as a whole) also became an *ordo*, which in fact made the sole decision on the candidates.[63] This shift need not be explained in terms of later developments in connection with 'hierarchical church structures'; it usually follows a new trend in the social life of a locality.

In the third century, we already find in connection with the choice of presbyters what became established practice in the fourth century in connection with the election of bishops.[64] The *ordo clericorum* increasingly detached itself from the ordinary people, i.e. Tertullian's *ordo ecclesiae*; here too the same thing happens in church and society. This can also be noted at another point, the mutual relationship of bishoprics. Whereas elsewhere a mutual interdependence of bishoprics became established depending on the significance of particular cities, in the proconsulate of Africa each bishopric had the same significance. This also applied to the legal position of the cities: each city was its own *respublica* with its own *ordo*, independent of others. So the figure of the bishop could also take on considerable significance, as is evident, for example, from the case of Augustine, bishop of the little town of Hippo. In Africa the *sacerdotalis potestas* is so great that a bishop can act with or without the assent of his presbyteral council.

(b) Conclusion: Ministry in the second century

It should be sufficiently clear from the developments which have been described schematically that as it becomes institutionalized, the church increasingly clearly takes over the imperial structures in its environment, though in each case in a distinctive way. If there are shifts in the civil administration, we see the same kind of thing in the church.[65] In broad outline, the structure of the church's ministry thus develops as follows: along the lines of the New Testament 'brotherhood', to begin with there is still everywhere a very 'democratic', collegial government by presbyters; later, embedded in this college, there is leadership by one individual, after which the joint government by the presbyters gradually loses importance. In some areas a hierarchy of bishops, metropolitans and patriarchs comes into being. By analogy with diets in the empire, synods of all bishops in a particular region come into being, and finally ecumenical councils of all bishops in the empire. Even later, one of the patriarchs – at the end of the fourth century there were five great patriarchates, Jerusalem, Alexandria, Antioch, Constantinople and Rome – became the supreme leader of all bishops and patriarchs in the whole of the church: the Bishop of Rome, patriarch of the West. He was later called Pope, and in him what in the New Testament is the function of Peter is expressed in historical form.

Thus in the second century (and the period following it), what became visible in a later phase of the New Testament was increasingly focussed on a hierarchy in an upward direction. Whereas at first the prophetic charisma is concentrated on the the charisma of ministry in the presbyteral college, in terms of diaconal ministry, in the second half of the second century this presbyteral charisma of office is further concentrated in one person, the bishop. Moreover, in this 'order of bishops', metropolitans and patriarchs came into being, often in parallel to civic and provincial structures and, from the perspective of the church, on the basis of the relationship of mother churches to the daughter churches which were founded through them. This was an understandable sociological group development or historical choice, which was also a legitimate, though not a necessary, development in the church.

2. A link in liturgical witness: the first half of the third century

(a) The *Traditio* of Hippolytus

We have a liturgical document from the first half of the third century which points to the ongoing canonical and liturgical institutionalizing of ministry in the church, the so-called *Traditio Apostolica* of Hippolytus (which from then on influenced a whole liturgical tradition, above all the *Apostolic Constitutions* and the *Testamentum Domini*). The writings of patristic theologians at the time confirm this liturgical evidence,[66] as also do abundant polemical statements about it.

Of course some questions have to be raised about Hippolytus, although his *Traditio* is an important link within a long historical chain. Hippolytus had his own view of the church and its ministries which in his time was traditional, in reaction to the 'modernism' of Zephyrinus and Callistus and their followers. It was these very opponents of Hippolytus who were elected bishops of Rome. Precisely because according to Hippolytus they were not chosen by the whole community, as ancient traditions required, he raised questions about their consecration. This ecclesiological polemic can be found in some parts of the *Traditio Apostolica*. The *Traditio* says: 'Now... we have come to the essential part of the tradition which befits the churches, so that those who are well instructed should preserve this tradition, which has remained down to the present day, in accordance with the interpretation of it which I have given, and so that, having taken note of it, they should be established – with regard to the lapse or error which has recently come about through their ignorance – through the Holy Spirit which gives complete grace to members of the community with a right belief, so that those who are at the head of the church should know how we must teach these things and respect them without any omission.'[67] For all the essential elements of tradition in this *Traditio*, we find, above all in connection with the election of the bishop by the people, clear polemical accents against the rise of a new church order. This points to the tension between earlier traditions and new tradition in church order. Precisely for that reason the *Traditio* is theologically relevant.

In this *Traditio*, *ordinatio* (i.e. *cheirotonia* or appointment by ministers) of a bishop, priest or deacon, comprises different aspects.[68]

We begin with the appointment of a bishop in a local community.[69]

1. All the local community with its clergy chooses its own bishop, and the person who is called must in principle accept the choice of his own free will. We know from other documents that the one who was called was really expected to obey this call from the community, even against his own will. This happened, for example, to Ambrose and Augustine.[70] At all events, ministry is a necessary function for the community and therefore the community has the right to ministers. Furthermore, the local church tests the apostolic faith of the candidate and bears witness to it.[71] This is an expression of the ancient conviction that primarily the community itself is apostolic; but because in turn the bishop takes on a specific responsibility for the community and thus for its apostolicity,[72] the community which receives him first examines the apostolic foundation of his faith.

2. Episcopal laying on of hands with epiclesis, or the prayer of the whole community to the Spirit: although the local church chooses an episcopal minister of its own, it does not autonomously provide itself with a minister. Because he has been chosen by a 'community of Christ', his choice is experienced as a gift of the Holy Spirit. In the early church, as in the New Testament, the minister, the new bishop, is seen as a gift of the Spirit of Jesus. This was expressed sacramentally in the liturgy by the laying on of hands by bishops (later, according to the Council of Nicaea, at least three bishops), from neighbouring churches. This is an expression of the communion of all the Christian communities

with one another. No local church has the monopoly of the gospel or of the apostolicity which derives from the gospel; it, too, is subject to criticism from the other apostolic churches. The presence of the leaders of other churches in the liturgy is primarily a witness which confirms the identity of the faith of this community with that of the others. There is therefore no local introversion; in this way there is a creative expression of the collegiality among the local churches. The (three) bishops lay their hands on the candidate, silently assisted by the whole of the council of presbyters, while the whole congregation prays in silence to God (as the president asks out loud), for the power of the *pneuma hegemonikon* and the *pneuma archieratikon*: the power of the spirit of leadership as pastor and leader, and the spirit of high priesthood. Before this, it is said that God 'gave leaders (*archontes*) and priests (*hiereis*) to the generation of the righteous, the descendants of Abraham, i.e. the church': Moses and Aaron (in the Old Testament, the embodiments of theocratic secular and religious authority, Ezra 8.69; Neh.12.12; Jer.10.3; 31.7; Amos 1.15). It is said of the 'spiritual power of leadership' that God gave it to his Son (at his baptism in the Jordan), while he in turn gave it to the apostles, the founders of the churches, as a gift at Pentecost. Now this same 'spirit of leadership' (*spiritus principalis*, according to the Vulgate translation of Ps.50.14), is called down upon the new candidate. In the strength of this charisma of leadership he will 'feed the flock' (a messianic term: Isa.40.11; see Acts 20.28; I Peter 5.2).

The one who bears office (the bishop) receives the prophetic mission to proclaim 'the word of grace' (a reference to Luke 4.22; Acts 14.3; 20.32), i.e. the good news of Jesus, which has been handed down by the apostles. In addition, 'the power of the high-priestly charisma of the Spirit' (*pneuma archieratikon; spiritum primatus sacerdotii*) is called down upon the candidate. God also gave this charisma of the Spirit to his Son, who gave it to the apostles: now the community asks God to pour out the same spirit of priesthood upon the new candidate. It is characteristic that this charisma is focussed on the authority to forgive sins. In early penitential practice the bishop brought about the reconciliation of the church. Nevertheless, the bishop also has other tasks: (*a*) constantly to speak for his community to the best of his ability before God (cf.Heb.7.25; 9.24), above all asking for the forgiveness of sins; (*b*) the episcopal leader must also be a *sacerdos* in the sense of being president at the eucharist (*prospherein ta dora*); (*c*) he apportions and co-ordinates the *kleroi* (i.e. the duties of the ministers, above all those of the presbyterate and the diaconate); (d) finally, he exercises the power to bind and to loose (cf. Matt.18.18; impose a ban or lift a ban). He is to do all this 'humbly and with a pure heart' (see Matt. 5.5,8; II Tim.2.25). As earlier, in I Clement 42.1-4, here in the *Traditio Apostolica* there is a clear emphasis on one and the same power of the Spirit which goes from the Father to the Son, from the Son to the apostles, and which within the community built on the apostles, together with its leaders, is now called down upon the one whom the community has chosen here and now to be its leader. The *ordinatio* is liturgically a matter of course because church leadership was experienced as a gift of the Spirit: participation in the prophetic and priestly[73] spiritual charisma of Jesus himself.

The *ordinatio* of a presbyter[74] is performed through the laying on of hands by the bishop, but in this case fellow presbyters also lay their hands on the candidate who has been put forward by the community. The variation in the spiritual charisma is clear from the epiclesis: '... give him the spirit of grace and counsel of the college of presbyters, so that he can help your people and lead them with a pure heart.'[75] Presbyters are compared with 'the elders whom Moses had chosen' (Num.11.17-25). In the pre-Nicene church, presbyters as such might not preside at the eucharist (they formed the corona round the presiding bishop). Therefore nothing is said about charisma for this in the liturgical *ordinatio* according to the *Traditio* of Hippolytus. However, with the bishop's permission, the presbyter might also replace the *sacerdos*, i.e. the bishop, here (without a supplementary 'ordination' being thought necessary). At that time there were still no 'parishes': there were only dioceses consisting of towns. As the church spread, in smaller communities presbyters in fact took over the episcopal 'leadership and priesthood' within their communities. From that stage on – differing from one area to another – presbyters too gradually came to be called *sacerdotes*.[76] As a result, sacramentally, the difference between bishop and priest really became problematical; a pastor is in fact as it were bishop of a parish, just as many bishops in Italy now do what in Holland is assigned to a rural dean. Such historical differences demonstrate that the direct relationship of the community determines the concept of *sacerdos*.

The *ordinatio* of a chosen deacon was performed in roughly the same way, with the difference that the college of presbyters was not involved, because at that time a deacon was exclusively at the disposal of the bishop and not of the presbyters. So he does not receive the spiritual charisma in which the council of presbyters shares because he is not a member of it.[77] His charisma remains 'open'; he receives his spiritual charism 'on the authority of the bishop': thus he can and may do all that the bishop specifically requires him to do.

In these three instances of *ordinatio*, Hippolytus does not set out to prescribe invariable formulae. Rather, his *Traditio* is meant as an aid towards the improvisation of presidents: 'provided that the prayer be orthodox'.[78] At that time no liturgical appointment or *ordinatio* was necessary for other church ministries, e.g. those of lectors and subdeacons.[79]

This evidence from the *Traditio Apostolica* and the *Apostolic Constitutions* is also important because it is a recognizable parallel to the later canon 6 of Chalcedon. As in Chalcedon, there is a clear expression of the ecclesial and pneumatological conception of the ministry in the early church: ministry comes fom below, but this is experienced as a 'gift of the Spirit' and therefore 'from above'. The charismata imparted derive from the fullness of the Spirit with which Jesus himself was filled and with which he fills the church. After Vatican II, in 1969, this tradition from Hippolytus was taken up in the new *Pontificale Romanum*, which explicitly seeks once again to bring present-day tradition into line with the early church – by no means a small achievement (above all thanks to B.Botte, who edited the Hippolytus text).

In this liturgy the decisive element is the gift of the power of the Spirit (no distinction is made between 'grace' and 'character'; in this respect it is a charisma of the Spirit). This is further underlined by what the *Traditio* says about the *confessores-martyres*, Christians who have been arrested and have suffered for the cause of Christ, but who for fortuitous reasons have not been put to death. Because of suffering as a witness to the faith, any such person has the charisma of the Spirit. Whenever a community subsequently chooses him as a minister (deacon or priest, at any rate), no hands need to be laid upon him (this is, however, necessary if he is to be made a bishop).[80] At any rate he has the necessary power of the Spirit. Historically we know that these confessors had a particular activity, namely, the forgiveness of sins, although they were not appointed *per se* by the community. As often, we do not know much about martyrs who survived; they too probably sought to gain authority in the church as a result of their previous situation. Moreover, the early church respected them, even if it could not give them an official place in the church system. The church often does not know what to do with difficult saints!

From all this there emerges the twofold dimension of the old *ordinatio*: on the one hand appointment by the church (its ecclesial aspect in the context of church order) and on the other hand the charisma of the Spirit (the pneumatological and christological aspect). It must be said that what was later called the power of ordination and its character is simply the appointment of a minister to a particular community along with the gift of the Spirit, differentiated in accordance with different duties. Moreover (after a tip from a patrologist) I cannot avoid the impression that Hippolytus, with some degree of clumsiness, still has to defend the mono-episcopate (at the beginning of the third century) against other views which seem to be traditional in the church. However, this would call for a separate study. Still, such a study should be able to confirm that only in the second half of the second century did the earlier *episkopos* definitively take on the form of a 'bishop'.

(b) *Cheirotonia* and *cheirothesia: ordinatio* – appointment to ministry

The laying on of hands began to play an essential role liturgically in the whole ecclesiastical recognition of the candidate who had been called to the ministry. However, the history of the relationship between *ordinatio* or appointment to the ministry and the laying on of hands is, of course, very complicated, although history here is often interpreted ideologically.

In the Latin church the term laying on of hands (*impositio manuum*) renders both the Greek *cheirotonia* and *cheirothesia*. However, *cheirotonia* does not denote laying on of hands *per se*, but 'appointment' (indicating or appointing someone with the hand), while *cheirothesia* clearly means laying on of hands. Now it is evident in the texts of the Eastern churches, above all before the eighth century, that *cheirotonia* and *cheirothesia* are used interchangeably without any deliberate theological difference.[81] Only after the Second Council of Nicaea (787) does the difference between the two terms become sharper, and from the twelfth century onwards in the Eastern churches *cheirothesia* is used exclusively for the institution or *ordinatio* of bishops, presbyters and deacons, whereas *cheirotonia* is reserved for appointment to other church ministries. Even then, however, no special theo-logical value seems to be attached to this distinction.

In the Western church, as well as *ordinatio* we find simply the term *impositio manuum* as a translation of both *cheirotonia* and *cheirothesia*. It appears from Jerome[82] that the bishops are always chosen from the college of presbyters, without a new laying on of hands being given (at least we have no clear information about this); the choice of the bishop by the presbyteral college (always with the approval of the people) was enough (the analogy with the choice of a Roman consul is striking), although this was in no way a general custom. On the other hand, in the earliest Latin ritual of consecration (*Ordo* 34, Andrieu), from the eighth century, at the *ordinatio* of ministers of the church there is no mention of a laying on of hands, though Andrieu (in contrast to C.Vogel) presupposes this. At the beginning of the fifteenth century Macarius of Ancyra can still write that the choice of a community makes someone a bishop; here the laying on of hands is secondary.[83] Thus although the laying on of hands at *ordinatio* is a clear fact of the tradition, it is not regarded as the most important thing; what is essential is the church's mandate or the church's sending of the minister, not the specific form in which the calling and sending takes shape. For this reason, too, the liturgical laying on of hands at the *ordinatio* of ministers was to some degree relativized:[84] recognition and sending by the church is the really decisive element. This sending is essentially an act of the sacra-mental church; because it is self-evident, it is therefore also given specific form in a particular liturgical act consisting in the laying on of hands.

Above all the Eastern practice of the *oikonomia* in connection with the laying on of hands in heterodox churches is a clear indication that the all-decisive element is not the liturgical rite as such but the sending and acceptance by the church, though in practice the sending was always carried out in and through the specific liturgy of the laying on of hands.

Thus it emerges from the analysis of terms like *ordinatio*, *cheirotonia* and *cheirothesia* that the basic principle is that the minister of the church is one who is recognized as such by the whole of the church community (the people and its leaders), and is sent out to a particular community. As Pope Leo I put it: if the candidate is chosen by the clergy and wanted by the people;[85] in Leo's time this recognition, which was essential, was implemented by the laying on of hands by the candidate's own bishop with the assent of the metropolitan. Outside this ecclesial context the liturgical laying on of hands is is devoid of all meaning.

3. A new phenomenon, the *visitator*: from presbyter to priest

Towards the end of the second century the pattern described above had become established almost everywhere: the leadership of a church rests with one bishop, surrounded by his presbyteral council. After the distinction between bishop and presbyter which arose in this way, another shift takes place in the image of the presbyter, from which a new term, the familiar 'priest', originates. A first cause of this was the 'country priest' who appeared alongside the presbyters in the cities.

This only becomes completely clear in the documents in the fourth century. We find a sign of the development in the Council of Laodicea in Phrygia (second half of the fourth century). Its canon 57 lays down that no bishop may be chosen outside the cities but only a *periodeutes*,[86] a Greek term from the medical world of the time which means 'one who travels around'. Latin translations of this document did not know what to make of the term at first, but later they found *visitator* as an equivalent for it, i.e. someone who was sent into the country, for example to celebrate the eucharist in a farmstead. We find a similar canonical diposition in the councils of Sardica (342) and Antioch (341).[87] These country priests had quite a different function from the presbyters in the cities, and they also led quite a different life: they were no longer a college round the bishop, although they did have some connection with him. This is really the first beginning of what we now call diocesan or parish priests, and also of a new model, 'the priest', although other factors contributed to its profile.

A first consequence of this development was a greater stress on relationships between the priest and the eucharist. In the cities the presbyters 'concelebrated' with the bishop as a sign of collegial leadership; in addition, there now appeared the phenomenon of the 'mass-reading priest' as a separate development, and a 'priest' (as compared with the city presbyters) became someone who goes into the country to celebrate the eucharist. If in the second half of the second century in many places a relationship had already been established between the bishop and the eucharist, from now on the function of the priest was gradually to be defined in relationship to the eucharist. In turn, as a consequence of this, the prophetic or proclamatory function and the pastoral or 'royal' function of the ministry was increasingly reserved for the bishop and even taken away from the priest. Irenaeus (died about 202) already says that proclamation must remain the exclusive task of the bishops.[88] Here we must remember that in the first three and a half centuries priests were still not trained; candidates were chosen from pious believers who had shown signs of charisma, being moved by the Spirit in the gospel.[89] John Chrysostom (died 407) was later to say that administering the sacraments can be entrusted to uneducated priests, but that the proclamation of the word had to be restricted to 'wise and educated clergy'.[90]

4. The change under Emperor Theodosius

(a) Christianity becomes a state religion

People usually talk about the fourth century as the time of change, under Constantine.[91] What they mean by that would be better described as the change under Theodosius. The quite marked change that this represents for church life is thus shifted from the beginning of the third to the end of the fourth century, to the time of the Emperor Theodosius. What happened with the ministry under Constantine was largely already prepared for; what happened under Theodosius is a deeper break with the past.

Under the Emperor Diocletian the church was persecuted, the persecution coming to a climax in 303-304, while in the pagan empire crass polytheism had given place to a refined henotheism inspired by Neoplatonism. The imperial family of Constantine which came after this was well disposed to Christianity. Of course at an earlier stage the patristic theologians had already done their best to present Christian belief after the model of a *religio*, indeed the one true religion. Moreover in 311, one of the sub-emperors, Galerius, had promulgated the first edict of tolerance under which Christianity became a 'licit religion' with equal rights to other religions and the possibility of the free celebration of worship.[92] So this was no surprise. Tertullian had already called for it. After his victory over Maxentius in 312, Constantine the Great enacted new measures relating to the Christian church, in the first instance only relating to the church in Africa. The emperor felt himself responsible for the rise of the Donatist controversy, which in fact worked to the advantage of the official or Great Church. From then on Christianity became a religion which was protected by the empire in a special way. In the same year, all property which had been confiscated was restored to the church.[93] In 321 the Christian Sunday became a public day of rest throughout the empire.

The new situation in which Christianity thus found itself meant that the pagan conception of religion in late antiquity was transferred and adapted to Christianity. This implies an essential bond between the veneration of the supreme being (in cultic worship) and the welfare of the empire (*salus populi*).[94] *Religio* as worship is an expression of the first civic virtue. The consequence of the recognition of Christianity was that *clerici* were equated with the pagan colleges of priests and exempted from all duties in the empire; Christianity became one with the interests of the empire, and as ministers of the Christian cult, the clergy then became of central importance for the empire. The ordinary believer was thus forced well into the background, and Christianity was narrowed down to a cultic community under the leadership of *clerici* – at least in the eyes of the pagans, though this cannot have failed to have affected the way in which Christians understood themselves. As *religio*, the Christian cultic community stood surety for the civic ethos of Rome. The Christian church became a pillar of society, with the result that after the fall of the empire, in political respects, too, it remained the leading authority in society. It is notable that on the basis of the ancient cultic concept of religion, the buildings for worship were also from then on called *ecclesia*, church. An imperial decree in 324 then commanded that at the expense of the empire churches were to be built higher, broader and larger.[95]

Nevertheless, the real break in continuity with the Christian past only came with the Emperor Theodosius. In 380 he made Christianity, including belief in the Triune God who has become man in the Son, the imperial law. As a result Christianity became the 'state religion',[96] not just, as in the earlier Edict of Milan, with equal rights to other religions. This decision was clearly directed against Arianism, and although it was a one-sided imperial decision, it was certainly not taken without consultation with the church authorities. Because Christianity as a trinitarian confession of faith was the state religion, the theological term *ecclesia* could no longer be applied to those communities of believers which diverged from it, e.g. the Arians. Therefore Augustine had to resort to intellectual stratagems, for example to make a rational distinction between a 'valid' and a 'fruitful' or 'unfruitful' sacrament, in order, given this legalistically restricted concept of the church, to be able to uphold the traditional view of the sacrament of baptism over against the Donatists. What had been a historically conditioned contextual difference later took on universal significance for the church, without any critical thought about the legalistic narrowing on which this distinction rested.

The fact that from now on Christian belief had been prescribed by imperial law irrefutably amounted to a misunderstanding of the gospel and had profound consequences. In this way Christianity became an ideology in the unfavourable sense of the word, and from then on it embodied a political and ontological claim to totality and exclusiveness. This did not amount to an attack on the content of Christian belief *per se*, but the political privileges did bring with them a tendency towards intolerance and imperialism. This development of Christianity, first into a 'permitted religion' and after that into an imperial religion in the sense, current in late antiquity, of a cultic community, is a second factor – after the rise of the country priest – which to an increasing degree connected ministry solely with the cult; as a result the priesthood itself was connected one-sidedly with the eucharist as the highpoint of the cult. The difference from the picture of the priest in the first and second centuries is striking.

Moreover, within Christianity understood as *religio*, theology, making use of Old Testament themes, gradually began to move the function of the priest into the sphere of the sacral *tremendum*. At the end of the fourth century John Chrysostom writes that the priestly life is a 'terrifying existence, full of fear and trembling.' If the earlier Jewish temple worship also prompted religious awe, how much more the eucharist of which the priest is the minister? Like Elijah of old, the priest calls fire from heaven on earth, but now not to set a bundle of wood on fire; it is 'to inflame the hearts of believers'.[97] The priestly function is also awesome, though to a lesser degree, as power to absolve sins.[98] In contrast to former times the church fathers had less difficulty in equating the religious awe of the mystery religions – which in the meantime had fallen into decay – with the Christian mysteries or sacraments; this was correct, but not also without danger.[99] The work of reconciliation proclaimed by the priest nevertheless remains redemption through Christ, celebrated in the eucharist as dramatic proclamation of this mystery of Christ.[100]

(b) A brief account of the sacerdotalizing of ministry

However, the Theodosian sacerdotalizing of the ministry already had a long prehistory. Although even the New Testament knows only the priestly character of Christ and the Messianic people of God and in opposition to Judaism and paganism knows nothing of priests in the church, this ministry in the name of the priestly Christ is a service for the benefit of the priestly people of God. Thus the service lies embedded in the priestly community around the high priest Christ and is in fact a *diakonia* focussing on that. Moreover, it was only natural that in the long run people also began to talk about the *priestly* service of ministers. We find indirect tendencies in this direction even in the New Testament (see Rom.1.9; 12.1; 15.16; Phil.2.17). However, there the church ministries are still firmly founded on the mystical depth of the baptism of all Christians in the Spirit and thus on the universal priestly character of the people of God. Nevertheless, in the light of the New Testament one can see and accept the 'priestly model' of ministry, although it is only one possible view – a legitimate, albeit perhaps one-sided choice (here I am also thinking ecumenically).

Cyprian (and already Tertullian before him) had a clear predilection for the Old Testament priestly sacrifical terminology, to which he compared the Christian eucharist. In this way the sacerdotalizing of the vocabulary of the church's ministry in fact deveoloped gradually,[101] though this was at first in an allegorical sense. Furthermore, Cyprian is also the first who says of the *sacerdos*, i.e. at that time the bishop who presides over the community and therefore at the eucharist, that he does this *vice Christi*, in Jesus's place.[102] By contrast, Augustine continues to refuse to call bishops and presbyters 'priests' in the real sense, in the sense of being mediators between Christ and the community.[103] In his *Traditio*, Hippolytus is in a transitional period. In his epiclesis there is outright mention of the 'power of the high priestly charisma', a power which falls to the part of the bishop who presides, but on the other hand Hippolytus repeatedly says that the bishop is like a high priest (*Traditio* 3 and 34); the Old Testament allegorical usage is still played on. However, these comparisons are not made in the case of presbyters, who thus are clearly non-priestly (not a *sacerdos* or leader), although as time goes on (varying according to different local communities) they increasingly replace the bishop as presidents at the eucharist, as they already did automatically in the post-New Testament period (without needing a new 'consecration' for this). In the pre-Nicene period it is therefore difficult to speak of priests in connection with both bishops and presbyters. For the early church, *sacerdos* (as an Old Testament name for the Jewish priest) was applied allegorically, and to begin with only to the bishop,[104] who was then the figure with whom the city community really identified and in whom it found its unity. Because in the long run, within the 'episcopal' church order presbyters also normally presided at the eucharist (because they in fact were the local leaders of smaller communities), they too were finally called priests (*sacerdotes*), albeit *secundi meriti*, i.e. subordinate to the episcopal president.[105] Thus a first sacerdotalizing, at least of the vocabulary connected with ministers, came about.

The development which I have just outlined seems to suggest a link in the early church between 'priesthood' and the eucharist. However, this is not the case, or at least it is not the whole truth. In the early church there was really an essential link between the community and its leader, and therefore between the community leader and the community celebrating the eucharist. This nuance is important. It was essentially a matter of who presided over the community (as an individual or in a team): 'We do not receive the sacrament of the eucharist... from anyone other than the president of the community,' says Tertullian during his catholic period.[106] In fact at that time the bishop was the real leader of the community. In that case no eucharist could be celebrated against the will of the bishop.[107] The purpose of this rule (for both Ignatius and Cyprian) was that of preserving the unity of the community. The figure who gives unity to the community also presides in 'the sacrament of church unity',[108] the eucharist. Although the problem of ministry is involved here, nevertheless the prime factor is the apostolicity and the unity of the church: 'outside the church community there is no eucharist'.[109] In the first instance this means that a 'heretical community' has no right to the eucharist; the question of the ministry in connection with the president at the eucharist is subordinate to this.[110]

Furthermore, in the ancient church the whole of the community of believers concelebrated, albeit under the leadership of the one who presided over the community; the eucharist is a celebration by the community. A later, but still early *Liber Pontificalis* writes: *tota aetas concelebrat*:[111] the whole of the community, young and old, concelebrates. Some readers may already be asking whether 'concelebrate' then had the precise meaning which it has acquired now that it has become a twentieth-century technical term. The critical question to ask in reply is, on what grounds can one give a kind of theological priority to a narrowed-down technical meaning? This can just as much be a narrowing of perspective. In the early church, presiding at the eucharist was simply the liturgical dimension of the many-sided ministerial pattern of presiding (in many functions) in the Christian community. The one who is recognized by the church as leader of the community also presides at the eucharist.

Of course, for the early church the community itself is the active subject of the *offerimus panem et calicem*, of the offering of the bread and wine.[112] We may not define the specific function of the *sacerdos* who presides at the eucharist in terms of the later interpolations into liturgical books (such as e.g. *accipe potestatem offerre sacrificium* and *sacerdos oportet offerre*, which already presupposes a later *potestas sacra* in the priest, isolated from the church community and thus absolute). In the solemn *eucharistia* (which to begin with, of course, was improvised), the prayer of praise and thanksgiving, or *anaphora*, spoken by the president, in early times above all by the prophetic teacher, this figure speaks primarily as the prophetic leader of the community with pastoral responsibility, who proclaims the history of salvation, and therefore praises, lauds and thanks God, thus proclaiming the presence of salvation for the assembled company in the eucharist. The active subject of the eucharist was the community. It was for this reason that the president accepted the offertory from the whole of the community, gifts which through the Spirit were transformed into the gift of the body and blood of Jesus, i.e. the man Jesus. Y.Congar, D.Droste, R.Schultze, K.J.Becker, R.Berger and many others have shown quite clearly how in the early church the *ecclesia* itself is the integral subject of liturgical, including euchar-istic, action. The 'I' of the president never solely, or predomi-nantly, indicated the subject of the celebrant of the eucharist.[113] So at that time concelebration was not limited to a common celebration of the eucharist by concelebrating priests, but was the term for the concelebration of the whole of the believing people who were present.[114] The people celebrates, and the priest presides simply as the servant of all. Even where the reference is expressly made to concelebrating priests, there was only one president; the others concelebrated 'silently'. There is no question of a *recitatio communis* of the canon (said to be necessary for a valid 'concelebration') in the early church.[115]

(c) Nominations of bishops in the early church

From the fourth century, the time of Constantine, we see that the local organization of the church deliberately followed civil models of the empire.

At a very early stage, for many reasons the canons of many councils were silent about, or ignored, the essential role played by the people in the choice of a bishop, though nevertheless this was recognized by the church and by theologians.[116] The literature of the bishop-theologians of the time clearly shows the importance for the church of the contribution of the people. For Latin Africa this was taken for granted; in this respect this particular church followed the structures of the civil proconsulate. Elsewhere, however, bishops and the city clergy tended to exclude the people from the nomination of bishops because they were often riotous and sometimes divided. However, on the occasion of riots over the nomination of Bishop Caecilianus and Bishop Athanasius it was explicitly established that the presence of seven neighbouring bishops was in no sense adequate: the suffrage of the whole people was also necessary.[117] This requirement is confirmed by all kinds of documents and goes back to the traditions of the early church. On the basis of the *Traditio* of Hippolytus (itself a testimony to an earlier tradition), the *Constitutiones Apostolicae* VIII,4,3-4[118] point to the right of the believers to make their own contribution. Here Basil[119] and Augustine, who of course could allow the new custom, according to which a bishop already provided for a successor during his lifetime, nevertheless require the approval of the people; otherwise they regard the choice as basically wrong.[120]

At this time Christianity was mainly a city Christianity and in no way agrarian. The city population was deeply, and often emotionally, interested in any choice of bishop. Given the misery of those days (see below), the bishop was the only resort in cases of need, above all for the poor and those on the margins. Who in fact became bishop was therefore an important political matter for the population of the city, regardless of the ecclesiological dimensions. The turbulence in the choice of bishops like Athanasius,[121] Ambrose[122] and Martin of Tours[123] is a clear indication of this. Even John Chrysostom recognizes the right of the people to be involved, but because the people can be badly or wrongly informed or even manipulated, his own position is that there must be a prior discussion of the possible candidates among the clergy of the city before the people can – and moreover must – be involved.[124]

Despite this tradition in the early church, the official church nevertheless gradually followed the civil trend in which the voice of the people was gradually stifled when it came to decisions about city government. Authority, always frightened and anxious about the unpredictable behaviour and the pressure of the people, tried to limit or neutralize popular involvement as far as possible.[125] Moreover, we see the rise of a new custom: towards the end of their careers bishops begin to nominate their successors, as Augustine already tells us. He thinks this best, though on condition that the people give their assent to it.[126] The old ecclesial dimension of ministry continues stubbornly to work against new customs, as we already saw in the *Traditio* of Hippolytus.

By analogy with letters of commendation, from the emperor or influential people, in favour of a particular candidate for one or other city office, at this time we find the same usage in the case of the nomination of bishops. Tactically, the people also tried to provide itself with similar letters of commendation.[127] These letters were often sent, spontaneously or on request, both to the city clergy and the people.[128] Of course the clergy had all kinds of ways of protecting themselves against pressure from the people, which they did not always welcome. At any rate, the city clergy could considerably exceed the number of co-bishops prescribed in the canons as necesary for the election and consecration of a bishop;[129]; they could also refer to one or other bishop who was high in the people's favour,[130] and sometimes even involve the city magistrates.[131] Above all, if the choice of a bishop in a particular city was of more than local political significance (which was usually the case with the metropolitan churches), the city prefect could intervene - as he did in the turbulent election of Bishop Damasus in Rome.[132] In this sense the believers, despite their old ecclesial rights, were in fact almost powerless in the absence of support from bishops and notables in the city. At any rate in the ancient church there was no formal rule about the participation of the believing people in the choice of a bishop, although the whole of patristic literature presupposes this participation as an ecclesial requirement and usually also formulates it expressly.[133] Nor was there any rule about how this was to be carried out legally.

So far as there were any rules at all about the involvement of the people, these were vague and diverse. Thus to begin with in the East people and clergy drew up lists of candidates; later, however, only the clergy did this, with the help of the notables in the city;[134] the people were left outside. On a political level the population of the city had already been insignificant for a long time (always with the exception of Latin Africa).

However, despite this trend in civic life and later also in the church, the community of believers never gave up its ecclesial rights. Every nomination of a bishop also had a social effect on the daily life of the people. From a historical perspective the whole of the tumult between Ursinus and Damasus in Rome was connected with the many revolts sparked off by famine in late antiquity,[135] a situation against which little or no measures were taken by the civil authorities: here only the bishops took the side of the hungry people. This brings us to the question of the social and historical position of a Christian community leader in a city, the bishop, in the third and above all the fourth century.

(d) The *de facto* power of the bishop, born of necessity, and its subsequent official formalization

In the third and fourth century the bishop was the only recourse for the impoverished and oppressed people in the city. Only he could do anything for them. This care for the poor on the part of the church goes back to the *diakonia* of the church in accordance with the gospel, which from the second century on was seen as one of the main tasks of the bishops. At a very early stage, therefore, in the Roman empire the bishop was called *pater pauperum*, father of the poor, even by non-Christians.[136] It was precisely this that lent prestige to Christianity among the Gentiles. Stimulated by impulses from the New Testament, from the second century onwards all leaders in the church found the care of the poor one of their duties. In the long run this also required economic skills from the bishops.[137] Early in the third century, by efficient organization and as a result of what it had been given, the Christian church was already in the possession of a great deal of real estate, from the revenue of which it could also help the poor. When in the fourth century, as the imperial religion, the church was also paid, it turned into being a great landowner and was therefore the only authority which could in any way help the poor and the oppressed. So we hear from sources of this time that in Rome Fabian fed and gave shelter to about 1500 needy people;

in the time of John Chrysostom the church of Antioch looked after
about 3000 poor, foreigners and outcast at its own expense, and
in Alexandria the patriarch John, called 'the Merciful', fed and
gave shelter to about 7500 marginal people and foreigners.[138]
Although a kind of ombudsman, the *defensor civitatis*, appeared
in the empire, especially in Egypt after the third century, generally
speaking it was not the empire but only the Christians of the time
who were concerned for the fate of the poor and the socially
outcast. Even before Constantine, the bishops were called *pater
populi*, father of the people, because of their support for the poor
and the socially alienated, in the light of the gospel.[139]

Here we must not forget that the fourth century – the turning
point under Constantine – was socially and economically a nadir
in late antiquity. City culture, on which everything depended at
that time, had become decadent, and the people suffered under
the corruption of civic authorities who exploited them by excessive
taxation. In this situation the bishop was the only resort for the
enslaved populace. This *de facto* position of authority enjoyed by
the church in the person of the bishop in the eyes of the poor and
the oppressed also received legal sanction when Christianity
became an imperial religion. Thus from the sixth century onwards
the bishop also shared in the control of the finances of the city
with the endorsement of the civic authorities.[140] Fact became law.
After the barbarian invasions the bishops were the only authorities
anywhere in the land who seemed to be in a position to rebuild
and reorganize the cities. The city magistrature had disappeared
and there was a complete power vacuum. The bishops became
city builders and city organizers; episcopacy became socially
relevant. Episcopal power, born *de facto* out of need and this
power vacuum, was ratified by Justinian as imperial law.[141]

The historical consequences of this judicial sanctioning of what
was originally an emergency are certainly not to be overlooked.
It weighed on the church, both East and West, as a great burden.
The emergency implied that the bishops also had to defend
and protect the people militarily. So bishops also became army
commanders. Constantine's aim to integrate the church, which
since the third centruy had become powerful, into the empire that
he controlled in fact rebounded: the Roman empire went under,
and the church took over the insignia and power of the *imperium*.

At that time it all seemed natural; so much so that there does
not seem to have been any critical awareness, among Christians,
of these fundamental changes which had taken place since the

fourth century. Moreover, the people felt more secure with this change of power, and could give adequate reasons for it, going back to the second century: only the church was the protector of the poor and oppressed – as it had been for a long time.

The end-result of this whole historical shift in power was that the figure of the bishop, known for a few centuries as one who brought men and women freedom through the gospel, now began to take on quite a different aspect. Once in power, the mediaeval church began to practise political theology in an ideological sense, in theory and in its actions. Thus in the fourth and fifth centuries the Patriarch of Alexandria had control of a fleet of thirty ships, with which he could control the whole of the grain trade with Constantinople.[142]

It is very evident that there were enormous dangers for the church here, stemming from the tradition of care for the poor. Having become great through care of the poor, in the Middle Ages the church was to take over the role of pagan Rome. In all honesty it must be said that the early church did not strive for possessions (there is much to tell against that), but as a result of its spiritual preponderance in Rome it was at least one of the causes of the fall of the decadent Roman empire of late antiquity, while the barbarian invasion left a vacuum which only the church could fill. Historically this in fact brought the church 'to power'. After that, however, the church found a theological legitimation for the power which circumstances had brought it, and even took up arms to defend it.

5.Retrospect: typical differences between the first, second and fourth centuries

In the first-century view, the possession of the gift of the Spirit was decisive for all ministerial services, however they came into being. We heard Cyprian say that alongside the good witness of the local clergy, the assent of fellow-bishops and the choice of the people, God's verdict is decisive for the correctness of the appointment of a bishop.[1] Therefore R.P.C.Hanson and others assert – as do I in *Ministry* – that when in the second century a bishop was seriously in default, it had to be assumed that God's verdict had not recognized him;[2] subsequently it had to be said, certainly for the African church, that he had never been a bishop. In the second century the loss of the charisma of the Spirit reduced a minister to being a layman, just as in another instance a martyr confessor, having borne witness to the possession of the Spirit by the fact of his martyrdom, did not need laying on of hands if he was accepted as president in a community of believers.[3] This was based on the conviction that if a minister no longer possessed the Holy Spirit, he could no longer communicate it to others in the grace of the sacraments or the word that arouses faith;[4] in that case he could no longer claim for himself priesthood from God.[5] In the light of later developments we can of course establish that this conviction indicates a still undeveloped theology in connection with the relationship between priestly sanctity and the efficacy of sacramental grace. On this basis, however, one cannot fail to note that in the second century a different view of ministry held sway; when views about the effects of the sacraments were later made more precise, there was no need for a different view of ministry from that held, for example, by Tertullian and Cyprian. In the second century ministry is not an 'ontological quality' that is bestowed by the laying on of hands and which nothing can later erase, at least, certainly not in the church in Latin Africa.[6]

Things change in the fourth and fifth century. The difference cannot be better illustrated than with some quotations from sermons of Narsai, bishop of Nisibe, in the fifth century. What the priest is and does is summed up as follows; 'The priest has received the power of the Spirit by the laying on of hands. Through him all the mysteries in the church are performed. The priest consecrates the font with the water for baptism, and the Spirit gives the baptized person adoptive childhood. Without a priest, no woman would be given to be married to a man; without a priest their marriage obligations are not completed. Without a priest the water would not be blessed and the house would remain impure. Those who do not possess the *ordines* cannot celebrate the eucharist, however pious they may be. For through their purity the righteous cannot bring down the Spirit, but a sinful man (what is meant is a sinful priest) cannot prevent the descent of the Spirit through his sinfulness'; and elsewhere, 'As priests they perform on earth the mystery of the inauguration of the kingdom of heaven... To this end the high priest (=bishop) gave the priesthood to new priests, so that people could be made priests and forgive sins on earth.'[7] It should be clear that here there is a different picture of the priest from that in the first and second century.

In the Latin church, accents are placed more soberly. Let me quote a typical example from Ambrosiaster. In connection with Eph.4.11, he gives a commentary on the different ministries in the church; the text is also interesting because of the manuscript complications: 'All *ordines* are in the bishop, who is the prince over the priest, the prophet, the evangelist and so on, to do the work of the church in the service of the believers. After the bishop he is to be called the greatest who may be called prophet because of his disclosure of the hidden meaning of scripture, above all when he speaks words which open up hope for the future. This order now (*nunc*) belongs to the priests.'[8] The last sentence of the text appears in both the majority and the earliest of the mediaeval manuscripts in another version, with 'not (*non*)' instead of 'now' (*nunc*): 'this order does not belong to the priest'. Only in the fourteenth century do we find a codex which has *nunc*, though this version must be the right one. After the bishop, 'from of old' come the priest and the deacon. However, Ambrosiaster is well known as someone who was not well disposed to deacons, one reason for not seeing the deacon in the 'prophet'. And in his time it was precisely an ordinary priest, the exegete Jerome, who 'disclosed the hidden meaning of scripture'. The many mediaeval manuscripts with the other version do, however, bear witness to the general conviction of the time that priests do not have any part in the proclamatory, prophetic function of the church's ministry; they were then seen as 'mass-readers'. Ambrosiaster has evidently reacted against that, albeit with an eye to the deacon.

A third factor which led to the narrowing of the priesthood to 'presiding at the eucharist' was the law of continence for priests, who had canonical obligations in that direction for the first time precisely towards the end of the fourth century. This happened under the pressure of the new Neoplatonist spirit of the fourth century, which in pagan religions, too, put sexual continence above marriage and urged this above all on those who handled the sacred vessels in the liturgy (I shall discuss this further in a later chapter). Moreover, we should not forget that Christian monasticism also came into being in the second half of the fourth century.

6. Canon 6 of Chalcedon

Canon 6 of the Council of Chalcedon (451) condemned any form
of 'absolute consecration', viz., the consecration of a candidate
who had no connection with a particular community: 'No one
may be "ordained" priest or deacon in an absolute manner
(*apolelymnenos*)... unless an *ecclesia* is clearly assigned to him,
whether in the city or in the country, whether in a martyrdom (a
burial place where a martyr was venerated) or in a monastery';
then 'the holy council resolves that their *cheirotonia* (*ordinatio* or
appointment) is null and void... and that they may not therefore
perform functions on any occasion.'[9] This text displays a clearly
defined view of ministry in the church. Only someone who has
been called by a particular community (the people and its leaders)
to be its pastor and leader authentically receives *ordinatio* (I am
deliberately not translating this term by consecration). *Ordinatio*
is an appointment or 'incorporation' as minister to a community
which calls a particular fellow Christian and indicates him as its
leader (or, above all in the earlier period, which accepts the actual
charismatic emergence of one of its members and gives it official
confirmation). Here absolute consecrations are *ipso facto* regarded
as null and void, though the bishop who makes such consecrations
must bear the financial consequences. This rule, although it is
disciplinary, still expresses the old essentially ecclesial significance
of the ministry. The measure at the same time breathes the
spirit of the time after Theodosius. It is a matter of the canonical
disposition of 'wandering priests'; the bishop may lay hands on
a priest only if he can do service in a city or in the country, in a
monastery or in a place where martyrs are revered. Without such
an appointment, priests, though consecrated by the bishop, have
no right to salary from the empire in the context of the ancient
Roman *religio*. These are the travelling priests without any function
in the church; by ancient conviction this is in conflict with
the nature of the church and the ministry: absolute consecrations
are rejected. The bishop who performs them must himself provide
for expenses in the maintenance of those who have been consecrated,
at his own cost. This last implication, the financial one,
escaped me in *Ministry*; historical colleagues in the Nijmegen
faculty put me wise to it. Thus in financial respects Chalcedon is
really putting forward the same regulation as the Third and Fourth
Lateran Council did later. However, this does not do away with
the ecclesial significance of the rejection of absolute consecrations.

I myself would want to add this nuance. From the text of the
canon it seems clear that, as I said above, at this period church
(*ecclesia*) had a twofold significance: an actual community of faith
(already in the narrow sense, i.e those who meet for worship)
and the building where the meeting takes place. Both meanings
occur here, a community of faith and a building, viz., a sanctuary,
whether this is in a city or in the country, a monastery or a place
where martyrs are worshipped (see the section below on the
veneration of relics). A sanctuary where believers meet, an *ecclesia*,
needs a priest: he is a priest for the community of faith and
therefore belongs where the community meets. The living
community was only to be found in such a sanctuary, a church
building. By rejecting 'absolute consecrations' the canon is a
recollection of earlier conceptions of the ministry; it indicates a
break between ministry and *ecclesia* (in the double meaning of that
word). Of course the narrowing of the community of faith to a
cultic community is already clear, a trend which was to continue
further in the Carolingian period.

Above all in the pre-Nicene period, the Christian community
was aware of being a priestly people of God, though at that time
this priestly name applied less to individual Christians and more
to the community of faith as a whole.[10] Therefore the community
played an essential part in the appointment of ministers – although
the part played by believers was merely a formality (a move which
ran parallel to what was happening in civic society; this presented
practical difficulties). The *Traditio* of Hippolytus nevertheless
already protested strongly against this modernism which was
introduced at the time, also for practical reasons, and which was
later practised above all against the power of emperors and kings
in the nomination of bishops. In the meantime, however, the
believing people were also excluded.

In connection with the new trend, Cyprian already demanded
over against Pope Stephen the right of the community to have a
say in the appointment of bishops.[11] According to him this right
is even of divine origin and thus is part of the nature of a
'community of God'. 'No bishop is to be imposed on the people
whom they do not want.'[12] Leo the Great also puts the matter
succinctly: 'He who must preside over all must be chosen by all.'[13]
At the same time all this implies that the ministry is a public matter
and that therefore no one can appropriate the ministry of his own
accord. The mutual relationship between the community and the
ministry also points in this direction. The ministry is defined

essentially in ecclesial terms, and not as an ontological qualification of the person of the minister, apart from the specific context
of the church. The story of Paulinus of Nola is characteristic here.
He says that he was in fact ordained in absolute form in Barcelona;
he writes about this in an mock-pious way, to this effect: 'There
was I, orphaned, shamefaced, priest, as it were, only to our dear
Lord, but without a community: *in sacerdotium tantum Domini, non
etiam in locum Ecclesiae dedicatus*'.[14] Later, Isidore of Seville calls
those who are consecrated in an absolute way headless people,
'neither man nor beast'.[15] We know from the outsider Jerome that
he reluctantly bowed to the pressure on him to be ordained
presbyter, but only on condition that he did not have to perform
any ministerial functions.[16] Consecration also becomes status.

The prohibition of Chalcedon against absolute consecrations
was known not only in the East but also in the West and also held
there (for church lawyers and theologians) down to Trent. Pope
Leo,[17] famous lawyers like Burchard of Worms, Ivo of Chartres,
and the *Decretum Gratiani*, and theologians too refer to this
prohibition.[18]

7. The end of late antiquity and the transition to the early Middle Ages

(a) Church hierarchy: Pseudo-Dionysius

Since Yves Congar's *Lay People in the Church* appeared in 1953, a
good deal has happened in the church and in its many forms of
theology.[19] Congar wrote this book at that time in order to break
down the then current identification of the church with the
hierarchy. Some of the basic ideas of the book had an effect on
the final redaction of the Vatican II dogmatic constitution *Lumen
Gentium*. At the end of that constitution, a chapter about the
people of God, the church, was inserted even before there was
mention of ministry in this context. The church – the people of
God – is called 'priestly, pastoral and prophetic' and therefore is
said to share as a whole in the threefold ministry of Jesus as the
Christ. Linked with Jesus, leader of the messianic people filled
with the Spirit, the 'community of Christ' is itself the subject of
prophetic, pastoral and priestly action. By contrast ministries,
within this totality – and presupposing this priestly substance of
the people of God – are a diaconal or ministerial focussing of what
is common to all. They are a service to this churchly, priestly

people of God. Since they are derived from the priestly character of Jesus Christ and his messianic community, the Roman Catholic Church could therefore not unjustly also call the ministerial services for the priestly community of Christ 'prophetic, pastoral and priestly' – perhaps a one-sided development, but nevertheless legitimate both historically and theologically.

Before, during and for a time after Vatican II, there was talk everywhere of a 'theology of the laity'. But on closer inspection it emerged that many forms of this theology of the laity continued to take 'hierarchological premises' as their unconscious starting point. They wanted to provide a positive content to the concept of the laity, but these were still seen as 'not clergy'. Here it was often forgotten that this positive content is already provided by the Christian content of the word *christifidelis*. The characteristic feature of the laity began to be explained as their relation to the world, while the characteristic of the clergy was their relationship to the church. Here both sides failed to do justice to the ecclesial dimension of any *christifidelis* and his or her relationship to the world. The clergy become the apolitical men of the church; the laity are the less ecclesially committed, politically involved 'men of the world'. In this view, the ontological status of the 'new humanity' reborn with the baptism of the Spirit was not recognized in his or her own individual worth, but only from the standpoint of the status of the clergy. However, that is not a status or state, but a ministry with a function in the church. The ontological status obtained through the baptism of the Spirit was in practice misunderstood, whereas the ministry was reckoned to be a status, with heavy ontological connotations.

The connotations of the mediaeval concept of the non-clergy, laity, continued to be an influence here. The layman was identified with the *idiota*, the unlettered, the poor and fleshly man, the *vir secularis*: the man of the world (for at that time there was no thought of women in this connection, either in church or in society). Apart from the powerful laity (emperors and princes, who were hardly regarded as the laity – and indeed they were themselves sacrally anointed) the laity were the obedient dumb subjects, those under the control of the ones 'in the know', the *maiores*. Theological support was also provided for this social situation. Lawyers and also theologians of the time divided the community of the church up into two states, *duo genera* or *duo ordines*, the *ordo clericorum* (to which to some degree the *ordo monachorum* was assimilated) and the *ordo laicorum*. Moreover this division into states had a serious social and even ethical consequence: *duo ordines, clericorum et laicorum: duae vitae, spiritualis et carnalis*,[20] or as we can read elsewhere, the basis of the church consisted 'of fleshly men and married men' and the top 'of consecrated (celibate) clergy and religious'.[21] I know that here, too, the descriptions need to be taken with a pinch of salt. But this pyramidal hierarchical structure of the church community, also inspired by the social status-symbols of the existing Graeco-Roman *imperium*, is influenced very strongly from the sixth century by the Neoplatonist works of Pseudo-Dionysius.[22] Differentiations in the pastoral work and the sociology of the church are given theological support by this Neoplatonist view of the world; the various ministries in the church are put in a hierarchy, descending by steps to less high 'statuses'. Here the higher stage possesses to an eminent degree what the lower stage has only to a small degree and with limited power. The competence of ministry – of all the lower forms of service – is to be found in absolute fullness at the highest stage; from ancient times this was historically the episcopate. Thus all power began to come 'from above', in accordance with the authentic Neoplatonist view. This Pseudo-Dionysian principle of substitution devalued the many-sided specialized ministries in the church thought to be pastorally necessary as a result of historical needs in the church. In the end the so-called 'lower consecrations' were one step towards the 'higher consecrations'. Moreover, this hierarchy focussed on the top of the church devalued the laity at the base of the pyramid, so that they became merely the object of priestly pastoral concern. In principle the clergy (among whom the episcopacy had the highest *status perfectionis*) realized completely a religious pattern of life and unity with God which the ordinary believer could experience only indirectly and in an incomplete way – in obedience to the *maiores*, the people of note.

(b) Signs of a changed conception of the eucharist in the sixth and seventh centuries

In the sixth and seventh centuries the narrowing down of ministry to the celebration of the eucharist was further focussed by a marked shift in the theological interpretation of the eucharist, which again was to have far-reaching consequences. The clearest indication of this is a famous text from the *Leonianum*, a collection of liturgical prayers which goes back to the time of Leo the Great; experts even think that the text in question probably goes back to

Pope Leo himself. The text runs: 'As often as the remembrance of the sacrifice (*hostia*) which is well-pleasing to You is celebrated, the work of our redemption is made present (*exeritur*).'[23] The word *exeritur*, which is certainly correct, is rare and was not understood by later copyists. Therefore in the *Vetus Gelasianum*, a collection which was current round about 750, but which was made up of earlier material, the term was changed to *exercitum* and later still to *exercetur*, which means, 'the work of our redemption is completed'. It was then evidently supposed that the eucharist is a sacrifice (of the mass); indeed, the quotation is still used in this way in *Lumen Gentium* from Vatican II (no.3), but, after a protest from experts, without any reference to the *Leonianum*, though the incorrect version is retained. So what in the original text was a happy statement about the relationship between the eucharist and the offering of the cross, viz. that the sacramental celebration makes the sacrifice of the cross present, was regarded in the early Middle Ages as a *renewal* of the sacrifice of the cross in the sacrifice of the mass and thus was substantially distorted. This is a clear sign of a shift which still later would lead to the statement that the sacrifice of the mass is a bloodless repetition of the bloody sacrifice of the cross – which provoked great protest of the Christian Reformation.

(c) The origin of private masses, the veneration of relics and the cult of the dead

New historical studies of the origin of the private mass have appeared in recent years which to some degree confirm, but also challenge, the usual interpretation, stemming above all from O.Nussbaum.[24] As I have said, the remote origin of this phenomenon lies in the practice of the 'country priests'. However, there it is simply a question of a eucharist by one president, without concelebrating presbyters; the eucharist itself remained a community event. After the fifth century different new theological factors began to play a part and for the first time there arose the concept of the private mass with quite a different content.

The first factor which led to the multiplication of mass-readings was the veneration of relics. As an expression of this, from a certain time we can see a number of side altars in cathedrals in addition to the main altar, often in two rows of seven. The background to this is the ecclesiological value which was attached at this time, above all under the influence of Ireland and England (especially Columbanus), to the sacred number seven (*septen-*

arium): beginning from the seven churches of the Book of Revelation there arose the saying that 'seven churches' make up one church, and therefore within the church building as well, seven, or twice seven, altars appear. Another indication is that at the beginning of the sixth century a series of decisions by councils in Gaul lay down penalties for priests who on Christmas Day and Easter Day celebrated the eucharist in private oratories.[25] Canon 25 of the Council of Epaone (517) makes the aim of this mysterious ordinance clear: it is not a protest against the reading of private masses *per se*, but relates to an altar which has no reliquaries. The text reads: 'Where reliquaries are revered, a clergyman must be provided.'[26] This is a kind of echo of Canon 6 of Chalcedon. In that case the priests can give a lead in veneration 'through much singing of psalms', which in all probability includes the celebration of the eucharist. The veneration of relics had already begun at the end of the fourth century, but enjoyed a spectacular heyday above all in the sixth century. A typical illustration of this is a letter of Gregory the Great, towards the end of the sixth century, to Bishop Palladius of Saintes.[27] He had asked the Pope for relics to lend distinction to his basilica; there were already provisions for nine altars (where masses could be read) and four altars had not yet been provided for; no veneration could be given there and therefore no mass could be read. So the church choir seems to consist of a high altar and thirteen side altars, two rows of seven.

In historical terms the veneration of relics is the first and decisive factor in the multiplication of private masses, long before there was any question of masses for the dead or all kinds of votive masses, which according to Nussbaum mark the origin of the practice. This development encouraged the idea that only the priest was essential for the celebration of the eucharist. This gradually led increasingly to the conviction that he must have a very mysterious power. But here we have already found ourselves well into the early Middle Ages.

Section 2: **The priest from the eighth to the thirteenth century**

Introduction

From a social and economic perspective, but also in the sphere of Christian spirituality, the period from the eighth to the thirteenth century can, generally speaking, be divided into three clear, but nevertheless overlapping, periods.[28]

1. From the eighth to the tenth century: the ritualistic priest

The Carolingian and Ottonian period of the early Middle Ages[29] shows us a society in which the liturgy increasingly becomes the work of privileged specialists. The ecclesial dimension of the eucharist fades right into the background and a typically ritualistic interest comes to the fore. As a result the spirituality becomes markedly individualistic. Private masses and votive masses 'for particular intentions' became established in the ninth century. One might say that the gulf which had already come into being between clergy and people was almost deliberately emphasized: at the eucharist the priest from then on turned his back on the people and the believers no longer received communion in their hands but on their tongues; a *schola cantorum* of specialists took over the singing. The Carolingian idea of the transplanting (*translatio*) of the Roman empire (Aix as the new Rome) put the clergy under the spell of everything which came from Roman culture: the liturgical language, Latin, became the monopoly of those who at that time were the only intellectuals, the clergy.

In the eucharist the emphasis was no longer on the witness of praise and thanks to God but on the distinctive sacrifice of the eucharist as a renewal of the sacrifice of the cross: a gift of God to believers through the exclusive mediation of the priest. From then on the main eucharistic prayer, the canon, was prayed silently: the eucharist is no longer a proclamation of salvation in grateful homage for Christ's sacrifice on the cross; the central feature is now the mysterious event of the changing of bread and wine, surrounded by sacral mystery. Only the priest celebrates; the people look on.[30] In the *De ecclesiasticis officiis* of Amalarius of Metz the liturgy of the mass is explained down to the smallest detail as an allegory in which Jesus' life is depicted; although this book was condemned in 838 at the Council of Quierzy,[31] it accurately reflects the ritualistic and almost magical spirituality of Carolingian believers. Of course it must not be forgotten that these people had been transplanted collectively, *en masse*, at a stroke, from Frankish, Saxon or Celtic paganism to Christianity. For example in Brittany we can now see how figures from Old Breton religion were taken over by Christians under a new name. The old religious roots also explain something of the changed attitude towards the eucharist, with increasing emphasis on the mysterious change of the bread and wine and above all the consecrated host. Believers in fact ceased to communicate at the eucharist; even St Boniface limited himself to advising believers to communicate at least at Christmas, Easter and Pentecost. Down to the eleventh century, consecrated hosts were buried in fields in order to ensure a good harvest. Almost everything took on a sacral dimension and there was a clear distinction between the sacraments proper and all kinds of other sacral signs and projects. Nature and grace overlapped; people lived in a symbolic world.

Moreover in these centuries, even as early as the seventh century, the Irish penitential books circulated through Europe.[32] As a result, in addition to the old canonical penitential practice for serious public sins, oral confession came into vogue, a penitential process which followed the laws of 'weregeld', in which the right penance was established by complicated methods of compensation and calculation. To begin with, some bishops were resolutely opposed to this, but without success. The system of 'weregeld' gradually gained acceptance and in turn led to the system of indulgences.[33] In the long run an attempt was made to replace this penitential practice (conversion and penitence) by a stipendium for the reading of masses, a new reason for the multiplication of private masses. Because there was a gulf between cultic priesthood and the people, the latter began to seek satisfaction for their religious needs elsewhere. An extensive para-liturgy developed with a great many popular devotions. During the course of the ninth century the feast of All Saints was inaugurated because of a lively veneration. The cult of angels, above all of Michael, Raphael and Gabriel, was extremely popular. Saints were also venerated for all kinds of ills; each had his or her own speciality, e.g. for toothache, measles or childlessness. We still come across survivals of this attitude.

The image of the priest in the early Middle Ages reflects the difficult times which were being experienced in Europe, in which people had barely enough to live on and the gulf between the rich and the mass of the poor was enormous. In this world the priest was regarded as a magical person: he performed the mystery of changing bread and wine into the body and blood of Jesus Christ; only through him did God's grace come down on earth. It is already a privilege for the people to be able to see him on Sundays, as the tax-collector behind the church, from then on apprehensive of and subject to the 'feudal lords' in the church.

2. From the end of the tenth to the end of the eleventh century: the monastic priest

The monastic ideal may be said to be the characteristic of this period: it was also presented as a model to priests and of course to all believers.[34] At the end of the ninth and the beginning of the tenth century the reputation of the priesthood may be said to have reached its nadir. The bishops themselves came from noble families and behaved as great lords, church potentates who were preoccupied with their careers and were concerned more with political and financial interests than with religious ones. The country clergy consisted of freed bondmen who were consecrated to perform services in the private churches of the nobility; for the most part they were left almost (or even entirely) to their own devices and only read mass on Sundays in the neighbouring villages, without knowing what they were doing. Such were the times!

In the first half of the tenth century there was a reaction against this. Monastic life began to flourish again. Cluny was founded in 909, soon followed by other abbeys, so that after the year 1000 a whole series of centres of religious renewal had come into being in Central Europe. In accordance with the ideology of this time society was thought to consist of three categories of people: those who prayed (*oratores*), those who waged war (*bellatores*: the lay aristocracy of feudal lords and knights) and the 'workers' (*laboratores*, the people). This cataloguing was intended for feudal society and was meant to express the usefulness of prayer, war and the work of the feudal servants for the general welfare of feudal society. However, the priests were no longer regarded as men of prayer; this function was taken over by the monks and also by the laity. The monasteries were the centres of feudal spirituality, and all kinds of new religious orders emerged precisely at this time.

Thus Christian spirituality took on a monastic and feudal colouring. Christians began to pray to God like vassals promising fidelity to 'their lord', with folded hands; piety became a relationship of the subject to the feudal lord. Consecration as bishop and abbot (there was hardly any difference between the two) was at the same time a feudal commitment between the master and the liege man. The religious in the great abbeys were as much great landowners as the bishops and laity, dispensed from manual work. Of course the choir monks were mostly drawn from noble families, who would send one of their children to an abbey at a very young age as an oblate, just as they sent their other sons to a castle to be trained for a military careeer. As a result of this close connection between the abbeys and the world of the nobility, feudal-monastic spirituality developed; it was to remain the general mentality down to the beginning of the thirteenth century. Its main features were liturgical choral prayer (*opus Dei*) and the 'angelic life', characterized by a contempt for the world (*contemptus mundi, contemptus sui*). Monks put stress on choral prayer, not in the rule of Benedict but only from the Carolingian period onwards (when it became longer and longer); its centre was the 'monastic mass', twice a day, early in the morning for the departed; the feast of All Souls originated at the end of the tenth century. The monks who were priests – at that time (in contrast to the past) they were in the majority – also read private masses at the side altars. These were further encouraged by 'foundations', in which a fixed contribution was put at the disposal of the clergy to read masses for the departed.

The breeding ground of feudal spirituality was not the New Testament – which only came to occupy a central position in the twelfth century – but the Old. The monks felt themselves to be the firstfruits of the people of God. Those who 'lived in the world' were regarded as second-class Christians, and felt that they were. The monastic profession (so called by analogy with the feudal oath of fidelity) was regarded as a second baptism, even as the real baptism, since it was 'conversion' as a farewell to the world. This negative attitude towards the world of creation is to be regarded as a criticism of the rough and barbarian society of those days: in the world of the time there was constant experience of injustice, violence and plundering. However, here, on the rebound, people also had a negative attitude towards the good gifts of creation. Holiness was thought to be impossible in the married state unless the married persons maintained the ideal of the monks. We should also see in this light the practice of promising to become a monk as a response to extreme situations of need: for a lay person this was an extreme remedy.

The ordinary priests were the first to feel the repercussions of the new spirituality, or in fact to embark on it. At this period it was established more sharply that the ideal of the priesthood is intrinsically incompatible with living with a woman. Priests were still allowed to marry at that time and even live together in love with their wives, but they had to refrain from the marriage relationship. But there was protest against this, especially from the laity: priests had to remain unmarried, like monks. Masses said by married priests and those living with a woman were boycotted: about 1010 Bishop Burchard of Worms had to pronounce strict penalties on lay-people who did not want to come to a eucharist presided over by a married priest.

Monastic feudal life was held up to the priest as a model, above all as a result of the Gregorian reform at the end of the eleventh century.[35] At that time there developed a threefold profile of the priesthood: even secular priests had to live in community, were obliged to engage in choral prayer and to live without a wife, in complete abstinence. The majority of priests rebelled against these plans, but many others opted for another form of life with monastic features: the first forms of 'canonical life' (in contrast to those of the twelfth century, these were certainly influenced by monasticism). Other priests withdrew from their parishes and became hermits. The rule that priests should 'live in community' was clearly also connected with the aim of withdrawing the clergy from the power of the feudal lords and bringing them more directly under episcopal control. However, many priests found this form of life too difficult and rebelled, which ultimately led to the failure of the Gregorian reform. A synod of Rome ultimately required simply that the income from property owned by the church should be held in common, even if the priests did not live together. In fact only a minority of priests came to live together as 'regular canons', eating and sleeping communally.

In the pastoral sphere the Gregorian Reform produced much improvement, in spirituality as well, but a consequence of this was that the believing laity were increasingly left in the cold, both religiously and culturally. Laity were excluded from both the sacral and the intellectual world. An obvious sign of this is that precisely in this period the choir of the church was closed off with heavy screens from the nave where 'the laity' were; other factors were involved here, including keeping the clergy warm, but the spread of this form of church building at the time was connected with the 'separation of the sacral' which was becoming established, one of many convergences of spirituality and architecture in the Middle Ages.

The different, now truly feudal situation also provided another categorizing of the hierarchy in society. The most typical description is this: (*a*) The *continentes*, viz., monks and regular canons; (*b*) the *praedicatores*, the ordinary priests, no longer seen as mass readers but as popular preachers, a development of what the image of the priest was to become in the twelfth century as a result of the Gregorian reform; (*c*) the *coniugati* or married. Abbon of Fleury described the three categories of feudal times as follows: the life-style of the laity is good, that of the clergy is better and that of the monks and canons is excellent.[36] The criterion is evidently detachment fom the sexual sphere.

This was the time when the pattern of the three monastic vows also came into being. Here people sought to follow the way of salvation through three negations, the negation of power, of possessions and of sexuality, the three areas which determined the whole of society; in this perspective the three promises also expressed an unmistakable criticism of society. On the other hand it is striking that the first 'great heresies' after the year 1000 were connected with the same areas: (*a*) a repudiation of the world and its power; (*b*) mistrust of the physical and the sexual; (*c*) rejection of church structures and even of the sacraments. In contrast to the Carolingian period many people now regarded these last as almost magical, materialistic and therefore too easy remedies. These heresies expressed to the most radical degree what was kept within reasonable proportions in monastic life, through a certain 'discerning of the spirits'.

The laity did not want to be imposed on by the monks and looked for forms of compensation. This century was marked by the spiritual combat, the *militia Christi*. For want of persecutors, people chastized themselves; flagellants went on the streets, others became hermits. At this time holiness was thought to lie in the extraordinary and the heroic: people felt they had to do something, especially physical. Sacraments were too easy a way. Forms of compensation for monastic life were, for example, hard pilgrimages, above all to the tomb of James in Compostella, to

Jerusalem or Rome. For feudal people, only a painful penance could provide forgiveness of sins. Moreover various religious orders of chivalry came into being; the violence of the time was sublimated in the *militia Christi*, unconsciously, through social and culturally mixed aims. The spirituality of the first crusaders towards the end of the eleventh century (Clermont 1095) did not arise by chance: for the first time the way was open to attain eternal life without having to forsake a military (knightly) career – a replacement for the monastic ideal.

As far as the priesthood is concerned, the feudal period is thus to some degree characterized by an ascetic trend: priests who took refuge from parish life or priestly service behaved as quasi-monks; on the other hand we can see a counter trend, which rediscovered the proclamation of the word apart from the monastic and even the canonical life. This was to be typical of the next century.

3. From the end of the eleventh to the beginning of the thirteenth century: the evangelical priest within a world-affirming spirituality

Socially and economically, the period between 1080 and 1220 is a period of spectacular progress in all areas, the 'renaissance of the twelfth century'.[37] There was a demographic explosion,[38] and all kinds of 'technological discoveries' (often of foreign origin) affected the processes of production and led in agriculture and trade and industry to an unprecedently increased yield. The main accent was still on the country, but the cities began to flourish, and there a new class of tradespeople and craftsmen came into being: armourers, lawyers and notaries, 'bankers' and many others, the mediaeval middle class. Thus above all in Italy, Southern France and Flanders there was something like an industrial revolution, by some historians compared with that in the nineteenth century; and even then the conservatives called it 'devilish' because of the new technology. Of course the feudal framework with its landholdings continued to be the dominant factor, but the great lords had to adapt themselves to economic developments and concede many kinds of freedoms, which were laid down in charters. 'Welfare states' came into being and with them also a concern to pursue profit, to which the church was unaccustomed. As a result of the Gregorian reform many priests and monks became individually poorer, but the collective possessions of churches and abbeys had become considerably greater as a result of this poverty; the opposite side of the interiorization it had introduced into spiritual life was that the church had never been so rich and powerful. Of course the feudal spirit required that each higher degree of authority and power should be matched by equivalent outward signs: brilliance, splendour and riches were regarded as a sign of God's election. In the texts of the time, in addition to the old criticism of the moral behaviour of the priests we now also find criticism of the riches and power of the church. Earlier, arrogance was regarded as the worst sin, but in the twelfth century that suddenly became covetousness and a desire for gain. The resentment of the middle class towards the church got even worse when the rich church laid down a great many canonical measures in order to set bounds to the greed of the new middle class.

To begin with, the church reacted cautiously to the flourishing trade. Moreover there was no lack of theologians who fiercely challenged the modern developments of the twelfth century which also found expression in theology: they included Rupert of Deutz, who was vigorously opposed to the movement in the cities. The most striking thing in this time of prosperity was that the gulf between rich and poor became still greater, so that a split arose in the category of the *laboratores*: in addition to a group of 'rich farmers' there was the mass of the population, who became unemployed, poorer than ever and reduced to the life of a vagrant or vagabond. This situation was the breeding ground for the great movement of voluntary poverty in the twelfth century, one of the first forms of a completely new non-monastic spirituality from which finally the Orders of Francis and Dominic were to emerge. For Carolingian Christians, who hardly had the minimum to live on, the ideal of voluntary poverty made little sense; paradoxically enough it only began to make sense when in a time of prosperity the gulf between rich and poor achieved proportions which cried out to heaven.

The four great crusades between 1096 and 1204 also left their mark on the spirituality of the twelfth century. After them people had to go back to the order of the day; the religious solemnity of knights and people suddenly lost its object. A kind of anti-clericalism perceptibly developed: those who returned called for a poorer and above all more apostolic clergy. Forms of popular evangelism arose all over the place, in which orthodoxy and 'deviation' were mixed. In Rome towards the end of the eleventh century a curial centralization set in which sought to get more of a grip on the whole of Christianity.

Now that Europe was developing at an accelerated tempo and mobility was high, the old monastic ideal of being bound to the abbey (*stabilitas loci*) came under pressure. Forsaking the world also became theologically problematical. Between 1120 and 1140 the canonical school of Chartres formulated the first beginnings of a theology of creation in which the new spirit of the time was expressed. The sphere of magic was dissociated from the sacral Christian sphere and the nature of the sacraments was clearly described in a theory of the 'seven sacraments'. Here the sacrament of ordination was more sharply thematized; it was said to consist of seven orders.[39] Above all, however, the real value of the secular was recognized: this is not just a reflection of God but has a value of its own. To begin with, these ideals were confined to an élite, but they formulated the new sense of life which had come into being in the twelfth century. We find a clear sign of this at the end of this period, when at the fourth Lateran Council (1215) divine ordeals were declared worthless and forbidden; this was the rejection of something that had been fundamental to the spirituality of previous ages. Whereas for the Carolingian Christian the world was a vale of tears, the twelfth century was more well-disposed to the earth, and the world began to look more attractive – at least for an élite. Courtly love was solemnly celebrated in Southern France, whereas the North preferred to celebrate the heroic deeds of the Frankish knights in the crusades (Gilbert de Nogent, *gesta Dei per Francos*). Bernard was to challenge this new spirit of the age fiercely, but he was already fighting a rearguard action.

However, the twelfth century is not to be described as modernism, but as renaissance. The 'new' feature of this century is that on the basis of a better economic substructure it is reaching back to 'the old', not just in classical Roman culture but also in the 'gospel', viz., the 'apostolic life' and the 'life of the fathers', i.e., of apostles and martyrs. On the one hand old Roman law was discovered in Bologna and many classical writings (above all Ovid) began to be circulated: perfection lies 'in the classical past'. On the other hand, in reaction to the gulf between rich and poor, which was growing larger, the 'perfection of the old days' was rediscovered, and the new spirituality of the twelfth century arose, which sought new sources in the earliest church (*ecclesiae primitiva forma*). This was already expressed when in 1098 the

Cistercians left Cluny, although it was experiencing a period of prosperity: people wanted to go back to the old *vita patrum* and the original rule of Benedict, which from Carolingian times had been loaded with all kinds of accretions; for, it was said, the *regula Evangelii* was more perfect. Manual work, which had had to give way to lengthy choral offices, was restored to honour and the *opus Dei* was reduced to more sober proportions. 'Evangelical life' made traditional monastic observances secondary in the twelfth century.

Priests, too, embarked on this 'return to the sources'. Many of them had been opposed to the earlier Gregorian reform, while others found that it did not go far enough; now many people came under the spell of the apostolic life with its two elements, life in community and the *cura animarum*, pastoral care with proclamation of the gospel (*cura animarum* and no longer *vita angelica* became the watchword of the renewal). In fact the old idea of building up the community was also restored to favour: parish life was taken very seriously, and new parishes were established all over the place. This new twelfth-century form of canonical priesthood found many echoes especially in Italy and Southern France, and also in Spain, but the majority of priests, particularly in the Rhineland and in Northern France, stood aside and kept to the original regulations of the Carolinian Council of Aix (816) on canonical life, without monastic features. The new canonical priests, as I have said, had founded a large number of new parish churches in addition to their own collegial churches, which contributed a great deal towards a general evangelical revival. The new feature of these priests was that from then on they opted for the rule of Augustine, in which the 'care of souls' was primary. In 1090, Pope Urban II recognized this priestly way of life in which, for the first time in history, the canonical priestly life itself was officially recognized as a 'state of perfection'.

However, these 'regular canons' formed a very varied society. Two directions can clearly be recognized in it. The first, which is sometimes called *ordo antiquus*, is the more progressive: it has a marked apostolic orientation and is extremely flexible in laying down observances (as was the rule of Augustine itself). The more rigoristic trend seeks to take over much of the old monastic ideal (paradoxically it is called the *ordo novus*) and was in fact soon to turn into the monastic life. At all events, in this period it was no longer the monastic life but the canonical life, above all that of the Praemonstratensians, that became the model for priestly spirituality; the concern was not to make the priests monks, but to raise their pastoral life to a higher level and develop a spirituality for active pastors. What was earlier an exclusive accent on celebrating the eucharist was relativized by being incorporated into a more comprehensive project of evangelical proclamation; the eucharist becomes the centre of life in the community of 'popular preachers'. Here the old primacy of the contemplative life for the first time began to slip, and this also led to vigorous discussions between monks and regular canons. Nevertheless the old monastic ideal remained so strong that the typical canonical spirituality did not persist for long. And the priests who found the canonical life unsuitable for their pastoral work found themselves out in the cold without any really appropriate spirituality.

Alongside this there was also a search for a completely new form of eremitical life, e.g. coupled with a community life, like that formulated by the Carthusians at the end of the eleventh century under the impulse of Bruno. We see city people leaving the rich cities to live in caves and woods in the country, from there proclaiming the gospel to the people as travelling preachers. They were often followed by crowds. They deliberately dressed in a slovenly way, and had long hair and beards to show their refusal to conform. They also parted company with the sacramental life of the church. The emergence of a Cistercian monk from Calabria, Joachim of Fiore, was characteristic of this. He preached an eternal gospel: the time of the Spirit would dawn and a pure, merely contemplative and spiritual, church would arise. He was clearly a critic of the monasticism of the time, and perhaps also of the canonical life of the priests. But he was no outsider at this time: as a result of the crusades a wave of messianism swept Europe that proclaimed the coming of the gospel to the poor. Joachim was the interpreter of something that was a driving force for the whole of this century.

Thanks to the improved pastoral care and the multiplying of parishes in city and country, the twelfth century clearly brought a religious revival among the laity. In taverns and mills there were disputes over difficult theological questions, and from the end of the eleventh century the laity wanted to have direct access to the Bible. Many also thought that they had the right to preach the gospel on the basis of their life in accordance with it. This evangelism has to be distinguished from that of the canonical priests; in the twelfth century there was a dispute between the clergy and the laity who began to preach; the clergy looked askance at this. The laity based their right to proclamation on their sacrificial life in the discipleship of the apostles. However, they did not have permission from the bishop; later many of them received permission from the Pope. The *Decretum Gratiani* states, in a quotation from a pre-mediaeval text, that laity may indeed preach in the absence of priests, but if they do so they must obtain permission from them.[40]

Also connected with this theme is the general rise of a great many movements, typical of the twelfth century, which have a common basis, though two trends must be distinguished, one fundamentally orthodox and the other heterodox. On the one hand there is a lay movement of 'poor' who stress the practical realization of the gospel. In reaction against a rich and worldly church, all kinds of groups of fervent Christians mobilized who were not attacking the institutional church as such but its actual structures. In 1184 such a lay group of poor was condemned because some of them were preaching the gospel without the bishop's permission. On the other hand there is a dualistic heterodox trend after 1140 the views of which we know more precisely only from the writings of their opponents.[41] They are called Cathari, and they brought dualistic views from the East to the West via the Bogomils of Bosnia and Bulgaria through trade contacts: on the basis of a view which sees the world as the scene for a conflict between two supreme principles, one of good and the other of evil, they called for a revision of all Christian doctrine and all structures of the church.[42]

One question is how the trend, which clearly contains elements alien to Christianity, could gain such great influence in the twelfth century, which was very Christian. There are certainly different reasons for this. Despite its distinction between the perfect and ordinary believers, Catharism had a message of the equality of all men, so that social outcasts, like women, felt attracted to it. We can also ask whether the dualism of the Cathari would have had such a power of attraction had it not at least unconsciously been seen as a reflection of the dualism betwen poor and rich in society. At all events, both trends had in common their critical attitude to the principle that salvation is dependent on the mediation of the church and priests, or rejected this principle – an understandable but one-sided form of Spiritualism at the time. Both also criticized the riches and splendour of the church, above all of the papal curia. This led the preacher reformer Arnold of Brescia and his followers, the poor of Lombardy, to rebel against the church hierarchy and stress the universal priesthood of all believers on the basis of baptism. This was a direct attack on ministry in the church: only personal trust in the gospel is the basis for preaching, and reciprocal confession of sin replaces penance in the presence of a priest.

All these tendencies can only be understood against the background of the general 'spiritual movement' of the twelfth century. In reaction against the prosperity in the cities, then as now neo-religious trends arose which show the same paradox: while Christianity experienced critical detachment from the monastic ideal and people began to experiment with new forms of religious life, others returned to the old monastic life in a more extreme form than Christian monasticism had yet known. The evangelical movement which had argued for the right to preach gained this right just before the thirteenth century. Pope Innocent III solved the problem by making a distinction in scripture – which in the last half of the century began to appear in the vernacular – between 'clear passages' (*aperta*, the narrative and ethical parts) and difficult passages (*profunda*, the kerygmatic and systematic passages, e.g. the book of Revelation and the Gospel of John); these last were reserved for the clergy. In principle papal approval had thus been given to the proclamation of the gospel by the laity;[43] groups like the Waldensians, Humiliates and poor gratefully took in hand revivalist preaching in which in fact they could express what they saw as the nature of the gospel.

A last characteristic of the spirituality of the twelfth century to colour the picture of the 'evangelical priest' is a new emphasis on the manhood of Jesus Christ. Already noticeable in the middle of the eleventh century, this trend was expressed at the end of the century in Anselm's *Cur Deus homo*, though only the twelfth century enjoyed the fruits. Here we still do not find the devotion to the person of Jesus which broke through in the thirteenth century. Anselm addresses himself – albeit from a feudal context – to the Jesus of history as the Gospels represent him, in other words to the manifestation of the glory of God (the feudal Lord) in the man Jesus. This concern for Jesus being the man for others gave rise in the twelfth century to a wave of solidarity with fellow human beings. Not just the 'voluntary poor' but all the poor from then on were called *pauperes Christi*. This produced many kinds of caritative initiatives: no longer riches, not even 'penance', but poverty is the sign of God's election. Hostels, hospitals and houses for vagrants mushroomed and a variety of religious orders came into being for this purpose, e.g. the order of Trinitarians, founded in 1198 to free prisoners and to redeem Christian slaves from Islamic countries.[44] People even sought out the poor and the vagrants. Here the understanding of fasting in the church also underwent a change; from then on people fasted to give their savings to the poor in a spirit of 'brotherly sharing'. Theologians began to regard almsgiving less as an act of penance than as an act of justice towards the poor. Some said that the poor might 'steal' beause they were taking what rightly belonged to them, just as Bernard makes a poor man say to a rich man, 'our poverty is your riches'. This twelfth-century mysticism of poverty, clearly only possible in prosperous cities, was based on the feeling that the poor represent the suffering Christ to us and also share in his function as redeemer. The poor are also called *vicarii Christi* or 'our lords the poor', clearly not without a dig at both the nobility and the church.

This development and this spirituality were the breeding ground for the ideal of poverty which was to take shape in the thirteenth century in the movements of Francis and Dominic, each with a distinctive stress. Francis' kissing the leper was thus an exemplary summary of the evangelical movement which also characterized the image of the priest in the previous period.

4. Priestly pastorate (*cura animarum*) and lay preaching in the Middle Ages

(a) Conflicts between diocesan-parochial and abbatial centres of the church's pastorate

Above all from the ninth century onwards, proclamation and pastoral care were functions of the local parish priest or local leaders of communities. Whereas in the early church catechesis (the catechumenate) was in the hands of both priests and deacons as well as the laity, in the Middle Ages, as time went on, preaching and catechesis was increasingly bound up both with the church building and the celebration of the Sunday eucharist, and thus with the pastoral clergy who had care of the local parish. Proclamation gradually became synonymous with preaching which was tied to the priest and even to the diocese. A first threat to this traditional mediaeval diocesan and parochial pastoral care was the enormous expansion of the monastic abbeys. Even those abbeys which had no parishes became centres of pastoral care.

This gave rise to all kinds of clashes between the parochial and the abbatial centres of the pastorate. It is a fact that to begin with all the local councils and synods of the time defended the parochial pastoral structure; monastic pastoral care had to be integrated into the diocesan and parochial context.[45]

A long polemic preceded these church regulations. In fact at that time most of the monks were not priests, and in this sense were laity. And these monks now began to preach and attracted a large number of believers to a new life in the gospel. From a historical perspective the aim of the eventual prohibition by the church of preaching by monks who were not priests was simply to protect the parochial and diocesan structure; it was an expression of opposition on the part of the church to the emancipation of monastic pastoral care from the diocesan context. The consequence of this opposition was, moreover, that in the tenth and eleventh centuries all the great abbeys abandoned any pastoral care in the surrounding district; this was reserved for the diocesan clergy. Above all Gregory the Great, in his day, in 591, had already laid the foundation for this system in his famous *Liber regulae pastoralis*.[46] This book was to determine the whole of the mediaeval spirituality of the ministry of proclamation and pastoral care.

This pope began from the presupposition that preaching is the sole right of the bishops who possess the pastoral office to the full; the bishops form the *ordo praedicatorum*, the order or the body of preachers. This system was based on the hierarchical difference between the higher and the lower, between leadership and obedience. Communication at that time went one-sidedly, from above downwards. The social and political models of authority in the Roman cultural sphere (which at that time was in decay) were taken over by the church, which had now become powerful; they were the model for the whole organization of church life. So the believers were subject to the *imperium praedicatorum* in the sense that preaching became a form of rule, *praedicatio* and *praelatio*, i.e. preacher and prelate. Leaders (including the prince) were essentially interconnected.

Because even in these beginnings of a feudal structure the woman was subjected to the man, she was above all excluded from the ministry of proclamation. However, the fact that this was not a restriction on the woman as woman but an expression of her *de facto* subordinate position is evident from the fact that an abbess, in so far as she was a Superior, the head of a community, of course had the right to proclaim the word of God to her 'subjects' (even if these included men). As the 'order of preachers', the bishops were regarded as the successors of the twelve apostles. The parochial clergy, by contrast, were regarded as the successors of the seventy-two disciples whom Jesus sent out. This led to a quasi-episcopal spirituality of the parish priest who only have the right to preach as those who have been sent out by their bishop, and are responsible to him. Their pastoral ministry is connected with an episcopal feof or estate in fee (a *beneficium*), so that between the bishop and the parochial clergy a kind of feudal relationship of liegeman to liegelord arose: a knightly oath of fidelity; and from the side of the bishop came protection for his priestly subjects. Only the pastors – bishops and parochial clergy – are 'the light of the world'; the believers are mere underlings, the object of priestly pastoral care, really not the subjects of creativity in faith.

This traditional mediaeval church organization was severely shaken by all kinds of new phenomena in the eleventh century. A great many new religious orders came into being: lay people – said to be heretics – travelled round the whole country preaching. Parish clergy also began to live together in community as 'regular canons'. The investiture struggle between *sacerdotium* and *imperium*, between the pope and the emperor, came to a head. In this period all the preaching seemed to become detached from the traditional type of pastoral ministry with its territorial organization. The Gregorian Reform sought to bring back above all the secularized diocesan clergy to a way of life in accord with the gospel.

As a result of this, preaching also came within the scope of church reform. Everywhere believers were vigorously opposed to unworthy priests, above all to administration of the sacraments by them. Monks, too, preached against the corruption of the diocesan clergy. So popes forbade the monks, who at the time were all still laity, to preach.[47] If earlier the laity were not allowed to preach because they were in fact unlettered, and often endangered the faith because of their ignorance, now it was said that only priests could preach and not monks and laity, 'however educated they might be'.[48] This was in fact a reaction to the sharp criticism directed by laity and monks against the worldly parochial clergy; it was not really a theological reaction to lay preaching but a defence of the existing structure of church pastoral care.

Nevertheless, there were popes who protected lay preaching

because these monks and laity supported their papal programmes of reform against unwilling diocesan clergy and bishops. These popes saw lay preaching as a welcome ally for their politics of reform which at the same time centralized church politics, a development which was thwarted by many bishops. This led to a kind of emancipation of the people from the traditional church structures with the support of popes who through this tactic tried to strengthen their rights of primacy over the bishops. Contrary aims strengthened each other.

During the course of this polemic it was Gregory VII above all who gave papal permission to individual priests and also groups of priests for supra-diocesan preaching, as it were a kind of exemption of preachers from the oversight of local bishops. (The first papal permission to preach without the permission of local bishops dates from 1122 and was given to a Flemish monk from the Abbey of St Peter in Ghent.) These monks 'happened to' support the pope against imperial policy and bishops calling for autonomy.

Nevertheless, there was no departure from the principle that preaching is a priestly function. However, now the preaching was carried on with papal approval as an instrument in the hands of monastic priests against territorial priestly pastoral care, which often negated the papal reform decrees. This gave rise to a new kind of preacher, the *praedicator publicus*, public preacher, i.e. priests who obtained permission to preach from Rome, regardless of what local bishops thought of this. So religious were the shock troops of the pope against bishops who ignored his reforming decrees.

(*b*) Polemic between abbatial pastoral centres and new centres of 'regular canons' who were disposed towards reform

The dispute between the monks and the regular canons disposed towards reform, who attacked the authority to preach given to priestly monks who had no parochial pastoral care, was finally resolved when both parties came to an agreement that the basis of the authority to preach did not lie in a papal or episcopal sending or mission but in the sacrament of ordination as such. This was a complete shift in the theology of the ministry of preaching.

The arguments which are used in support of the right to preach at this period are, moreover, extremely significant:

1. Some claimed, on the basis of the New Testament, that the

right to proclaim the gospel lies in the *vita apostolica*, i.e. in real discipleship of Jesus through a life-style in accordance with the gospel; this gives the right to bear witness to it.

2. Others explained this right with a reference to the mission either of the local bishop or of the Pope, which was supra-diocesan.

3. Yet others saw the foundation of this as lying in the *ordo clericorum*, i.e. in incorporation into the status of clergy, at least through the tonsure; not in baptismal 'living by the Spirit' but in a specific gift of the Spirit bound up with the sacrament of ordination.

4. Finally, yet others saw the right to preach as being based solely on consecration to the priesthood as such.

To begin with, both the monks and the canons appealed to the *vita apostolica* as the basis of all authority to preach.

Thus in the twelfth century the traditional bond between pastoral care (*cura animarum*, with prebendal rights) and preaching was loosened in favour of the new bond between consecration as priest and preaching: this was the consequence of the compromise in the dispute betwen monks and canons. The monks otherwise saw no chance of legitimating their actual proclamation over against the canons. The 'clericalizing' of the ministry of proclamation was the consequence of this historical compromise.

In the twelfth century, the authority to preach, which through pastoral care was still connected with a particular parish, became an abstract privilege of one who was consecrated (quite apart from a particular community); more than ever it became a dividing line between laity and priests. At the same time the authority to preach became detached from pastoral care. The immediate result of this was that someone who was not consecrated, a lay person, was declared *per se* incompetent to preach.

In this way, as a result of polemic among the clergy, there was a break with the old charismatic and missionary tradition to which the whole of Europe owed its Christianization, viz. thanks to the proclamation of Irish and Scottish monks, many of whom were not priests. The monks went against the old charismatic foundation of their function of preaching, forced by the polemic with the canons to base their function of proclamation in future on consecration as priest. From then on the principle was *mitti est ordinari*,[49] i.e. that consecration as priest is itself the *missio canonica* and the competence to preach.

The dispute between monks and canons was essentially not

about the laity as such but about an emancipation of the secular clergy from the early mediaeval supremacy of the monks and thus about a pluralism of forms of life in the organization of the church. The historical coupling of authority to preach with the clerical status (the standpoint above all of the Benedictine monks) was the result of a rivalry among the clergy. Consequently, in the future the scope of what was theologically possible and legitimate in preaching was essentially limited. For when in the second half of the twelfth century laity again referred to the *Statuta Ecclesiae Antiqua* (according to which laity may preach with the permission of a priest) this appeal no longer had any effect: from then on it was laid down in the canons that preaching is a matter for priests alone. The monks who could have defended the rights of the laity in the light of their age-old charisma left them in the lurch. The truce which they made with the canons, on the basis of their common priesthood, led to a heightened delimitation of the ministry of preaching over against the activities of the laity. From then on, lay preaching was seen as an illegitimate appropriation of clerical authority.

Theologically, we can already come to a first conclusion. The refusal of the mediaeval church to allow laity to preach publicly did not in fact have any theological foundation, in that it was not founded on the nature of the Christian community with its multiplicity of ministries but was rather:

(*a*) the consequence of a rivalry over the preaching ministry among the clergy;

(*b*) also the consequence of general unrest caused by heretical propaganda which was above all circulated by sometimes unlettered laity who were nevertheless committed to the gospel;

(*c*) also the consequence of the view, general in the Middle Ages, of the laity as unlettered and as *vir saecularis*, i.e. as being only concerned with worldly matters and not with church matters, and finally as being no more than underlings in the whole Christian world (*Christianitas*).

(*c*) Conflicts between the pastorate of the Mendicants (Beggars), which was outside the dioceses and the parishes, and the traditional pastorate

A new polemic emerged in the thirteenth century. The main protagonists, fiercely engaged in it, were on the one hand the Franciscan Bonaventure and the Dominican Thomas Aquinas, and on the other a diocesan priest, William of Saint-Amour. As background, we need to look at the situation in the thirteenth century.

(i) A new development: the pastoral activity of the Mendicants

The *Praedicatio Jesu Christi*, as the Dominican movement *qua* priestly movement was originally called, is particularly relevant here, because originally the Franciscan movement was not a priestly movement but a lay movement (although it soon allowed itself to be clericalized). A number of even radical innovations were to be found in this new, primarily Dominican model of the priest, though what to begin with was an order of preachers at more than parochial level, though nevertheless bound to the bishop, later became a supra-diocesan movement. A measure had been passed shortly beforehand by the Council of Avignon that all priestly service, including supra-parochial priestly service, remained in the last resort under the local bishop.[50] Therefore at least to begin with, the *ordo praedicatorum* saw itself as a helper of the local bishops, albeit with no parochial connection. It was sent by the bishop as a religious order and also paid by him from tithes of the diocese. Here preaching is detached from the leaders of the parish community. The new development is above all that an order as such (and not individuals) becomes the subject of authority for supra-parochial preaching of the gospel.

In the meantime, however, the Fourth Lateran Council took place (1215). At it Pope Innocent III presented his twenty-year-long policy for church reform to the council of bishops and abbots for their evaluation. This council reaffirmed the traditional view that the ministry of proclamation is in the first place the prerogative of the bishops; but (because in fact many bishops at that time often neglected this task) the council laid on bishops the binding obligation that they were to provide a body of preachers to be responsible for the proclamation in their place. For their part the bishops were to arrange for the support of these preachers.[51] Thus at Lateran IV, in principle the model of preaching brothers set up by Dominic in Toulouse was urged on all bishoprics: it was a kind of functional mission aimed at pastoral care and carried out by specialized preachers at a diocesan (or supra-parochial) level. What was envisaged here was a mobile group of preachers recruited above all from the canonical clergy of the cathedrals and chapter churches. Because preaching, including that relating to heretics, at the same time called for penance, only priests were

potential members of this supra-parochial body of preachers. It
is clear that the basic Toulouse document relating to the first
foundation of the Dominicans, i.e. six months before the Fourth
Lateran Council, was the mid-point between the decree of
Avignon and that of the Fourth Lateran Council. Wherever the
Council goes further in substance than the local synod of Avignon
it corresponds almost literally with the Dominican foundation
document of Toulouse, viz., with the idea of an *ordo praedicatorum*
as an aid to the bishop in a wholly diocesan connection. The new
element here is also that the recruiting is principally sought from
the 'regular canons' (a line from which Dominic originally came),
i.e. clergy with a religious rule of life (to which Dominic had also
committed the Dominicans). Another new factor is the granting
of permission to preach and also to administer the sacrament
of penance; the Dominican Toulouse document *Praedicatio Jesu
Christi* and its activity of reconciliation was a model for this. Thus
the sacrament of confession or penance was not connected with
the permission to preach in an abstract way, but historically and
specifically: preaching for conversion is by the nature of things
essentially bound up with the ministry of reconciliation and thus
with the sacrament of penance.[52]

However, evidently as a result of the unwillingness and lack of
interest on the part of the local bishops, this Council did not have
any immediate consequences. Moreover, neither the Dominicans
nor the Minorites understood the council as a challenge to
extend and organize themselves at a diocesan level. Rather, their
development went more in the direction of a supra-diocesan
organization.

In its *constitutio* 13, the Fourth Lateran Council had still ruled
that no new monastic orders were to be founded unless an already
existing rule was taken over.[53] At a diocesan level the Dominican
Order had already been approved.[54] There were no problems
here. Historically, this prohibition seems to be the personal
contribution of the bishops, who on this point dissociated themselves from papal politics in Lateran IV. The abbots in particular
were critical at the council of the new Dominican and Franciscan
movements, while many bishops did not agree with the pope's
attempt to reconcile the heretics and lay preachers. However,
Innocent III was able to protect the Franciscans from this conciliar
verdict against new religious orders by approving the rule of St
Francis before the decrees of the council came into force.[55] On this
point the Lateran decree was directed against the pope, who on

the basis of the difference between *exhortatio* or *disputatio* and *praedicatio* wanted to give room within the church to the reconciled groups (Humiliates and Waldensians). Nevertheless, the canonical tradition was to weaken the general statement 'no one but priests may preach' (from a letter of Leo the Great) with an old gloss from the *Statuta Ecclesiae Antiqua*, adding 'except with the permission of the priest'. Moreover, the canon lawyers pointed out that laity from the order of Templars and Hospitallers were allowed to preach on the basis of a privilege.[56]

The general tendency of the Western church was clear: there was a desire to integrate the supra-diocesan groups of preachers who acted by virtue of papal authority into the traditional pastoral structures of the bishoprics. Only under the pontificate of a subsequent pope was Dominic to develop his original plan further.

In 1227 Gregory IX gave the Dominicans and Franciscans (who in the meantime had become clericalized) a supra-diocesan, territorially unlimited authority to preach and provide pastoral care. This had been preceded by a long history.

When Dominic returned to Rome in 1216, a year after the Fourth Lateran Council, the successor of Pope Innocent III, viz. Honorius III, confirmed (on 22 December 1216) the foundation of the brotherhood of Saint-Romains in Toulouse, still 'as a community of regular Augustine brothers'. However, some weeks later, with the help of Cardinal Hugolino, Dominic secured approval for his original idea: protected by the façade of the foundation of an order of preachers as 'Augustine canons', the pope approved the new order as *Praedicatio Jesu Christi*.[57]

Moreover, in a letter of 21 January 1217 Dominic secured the support of the pope against the successor of the Bishop of Toulouse. In 1217 Dominic had a conversation in Rome with the Bishop of Lund. After this meeting, against the advice of this bishop and also of some of his companions, Dominic abolished the monastery of Saint Romains: he sent his followers out two by two, to Paris, Spain, Rome and Bologna. A small remnant, however, remained behind in Prouille and Saint Romains.[58] Clearly Dominic wanted to give his order a supra-diocesan status. On a subsequent journey to Rome he achieved his aim, again with the help of Cardinal Hugolino. On 11 February 1218 the pope asked all bishops and abbots to support the brothers of the *Ordo Praedicatorum*, to accept them and stand by them out of respect for papal authority; these preaching brothers, says the papal letter, bear the honourable title of a poor life-style and they proclaim the gospel without any request for financial support.[59] Although this is only a recommendation, it is already clear in this letter that Dominic does not see his Order as a 'community of canons' but as a supradiocesan religious order of preaching brothers, directly under papal authority: a brotherhood of apostolic poverty at the service of preaching the gospel throughout the church. This is a new development over against the canonical authorization, in which the pope asks the bishop for free access wherever the preaching brothers present themselves.[60] Instead of being originally a diocesan body of specialized preachers, the Dominican Order now becomes supra-diocesan. That these papal commendations stopped suddenly at the death of Dominic, while they were repeated abundantly under the pontificate of Dominic's friend Cardinal Hugolino, when he was elected pope in 1227 under the name of Gregory IX, indicates that the initiative did not lie with the previous pope but with Dominic and his guardian Hugolino. On 26 April 1218 Honorius III wrote to all bishops that they had the duty to receive the preaching brethren and 'to let them exercise the preaching ministry to which they had been declared to be authorized'.[61]

In this way the Order received papal authority to preach throughout the church as an Order. Strengthened by this authority, Dominic now travelled throughout Europe and chose as centres from which the supra-diocesan Dominican preaching was to go out the university cities of Paris and Bologna, at that time the two great centres of European spiritual life. Sober Christian common sense made Dominic always have his appearance backed up by papal commendations. The import of these letters varied. We can distinguish three different types in them. Some of them stress the poverty of the preaching brothers and are aimed at furthering the foundation of new Dominican communities in different areas. The bishops are asked to encourage their faithful to listen to the 'Dominican preaching'.[62] Other letters stress Dominican pastoral care; here Dominic, through papal letters, and moreover with reference to the Fourth Lateran Council, tries to make it clear to the bishops that they must regard the Dominicans as the necessary preachers which canon 10 of the Fourth Lateran Council envisaged. Thus Dominic mobilized both the council and the authority of the pope to back up 'Dominican preaching'.[63] At the same time, papal bulls condemned the misuse of the name *praedicator* by some. In a third type of papal letter to protect Dominic's programme, Dominican preaching was seen as a 'providential gift from heaven against the heretics' (perhaps this formulation is more that of Gregory IX than of Dominic himself).[64]

In 1220 the Dominicans held their first General Chapter, in Bologna. There they codified the actual development of the Order in the post-conciliar period after Lateran IV: it was an order of preaching brothers, by virtue of papal authority with a supra-territorial commission to preach, exempt from the bishops. This Chapter dealt very pragmatically with religious observances: the fathers of the Chapter took the constitutions of the Premonstraten-sians as their basic model: they developed these flexibly with an eye to free preaching, which was Dominic's real concern. They allowed all kinds of dispensations in favour of the preaching, a complete novelty in religious law. The distinctive character of the Dominicans is clear above all from the formulation of the aim of the Dominican Order, above all in the chapters about the General Chapter, about study and in defining the proclamation of the gospel.[65]

Stress is laid on the apostolic life-style of travelling preachers. Despite all the papal church politics, which sought to strengthen papal authority over the bishops by means of the new Orders, the Order nevertheless remained sensitive to the authority of the local bishops. The exemption could not be an excuse for the first Dominicans to break down the traditional frameworks of diocese and parish. As a result of Dominic's experiences in southern France, however, the Dominicans wanted 'freedom to preach the gospel'.[66] Here Dominic was largely inspired by the gospel freedom of the first Waldensian preachers, but in contrast to these, he wanted to achieve a symbiosis between Dominican preaching and the diocesan and parochial structures. These first constitutions declare that on their first entry into a diocese, the Dominicans must pay a visit to the local bishop.[67]

However, despite this readiness to collaborate with the local clergy, the constitutions make it clear that the *Ordo Praedicatorum* does not derive its commission to proclaim the gospel from the local bishops, but has its mission as an Order, approved by the pope. Therefore the Order itself is to test in its General Chapter who of the individual members is in fact competent to preach the gospel.[68] This is a canonical innovation: a free brotherhood of Christians, priests, sees itself as an independent group of preachers, independent of the local episcopate. Within it the norm is the candidate's virtue, conformity to the gospel and competence to preach.

Given this innovation, the use of the term 'regular canons' for the preaching brothers was an anachronism. In the General Chapter of Trier in 1249 the Order dropped the term *canonicus* which had still been pressed in the Paris Chapter of 1246 (on this basis the Order was approved by the pope).

(ii) The opposition of William of Saint-Amour and his condemnation

Just as in the eleventh and twelfth century new circumstances in the church and the world had produced a dispute between the old monastic Orders and the new institutions of regular canons, so the second half of the thirteenth century produced a dispute between the Dominican and the Franciscan movement (which in the meantime had become clericalized) on the one hand, and the reaction on the other of the diocesan clergy (who saw much of their financial income flow into the new Orders). Here we are interested only in the polemic over competence to preach.

In 1255, a theologian, a diocesan priest, launched a basic attack on the whole emergence of the Mendicants, who were undermining the church's traditional pastoral system, conceived in terms of the parish and the diocese. This theologian, William of Saint-Amour, was spokesman here for many who saw the rights of the local clergy being fundamentally attacked by the papal privileges accorded to Dominicans and Franciscans. Here two different views of the church clashed: one a view based on the autonomy of the local churches, and the other a view of the church based on the primatial privilege of the pope. In fact Rome also made use of the Mendicants to impose the Roman policy of papal primacy on the whole of the world episcopate. Moreover, the begging rights of the Mendicants thoroughly undermined the whole financial basis of the mediaeval church, which was based feudally on prebends. As a result of these attacks, Dominicans and Franciscans were compelled to express their own authority to preach in sharper theological terms. There grew out of this in fact a new theology of ministry.

William of Saint-Amour introduced *auctoritates*, authoritative arguments from the *Decretum Gratiani* and Pseudo-Dionysius, as proof texts against the practice of the Mendicants. In his view the Mendicants were false prophets who wrongly claimed the authority of preachers. He began from the church's mediation or necessary *missio canonica* to preach. He rejected in principle a charismatic mission of the people of God on the basis of life in accordance with the gospel. Coming from God, preaching is the sole right of the bishops and, under their supervision, of the parish clergy, who are seen as successors of the 'seventy-two disciples' whom Jesus sent out. Thus the actual mediaeval organization of pastoral care is seen as a divine right by which even the pope is bound. 'Priesthood' is identified as it were with the term *pastor*, the parochial clergy, whereas the Franciscans and Dominicans are regarded as monks in the old style. In the meantime canon law had said of monks that they had no authority to preach unless they were priests. Thus in their opposition to the Mendicants the secular clergy identified ministry with territorial limited ministry; for them the church was a kind of federation of dioceses and parochial local churches. In their view the pope was also bound by this structure, and he was wrong in bestowing privileges on the extra-diocesan and extra-parochial Mendicants.

Here what was essentially a principle of the early church, that of the inner bond between community and ministry, was territorially narrowed and identified with historical and contingent forms of church order. But at the same time one can note opposition here from the diocesan clergy to the centralizing influences stemming from the Roman Curia. They stress increasingly smaller church units as autarkic subjects which are then sanctioned by divine right. For them, preaching is the monopoly of the leaders of the community: the principle of a supra-diocesan, specialized body of preachers is resolutely rejected. Moreover the doctrine is justified theologically by a reference to the teaching of 'Dionysius' on the hierarchy and is thus given an ontological basis. According to this, both heavenly and earthly 'hierarchical thinking', each effective activity goes from above downwards; the grass roots of the church is denied any church activity of its own. It is not the consecration but the *electio* or *missio canonica* which is the foundation of any competence to preach. The new theology of the twelfth century which gave a sacramental basis to the authority to preach was thus once again abandoned: authority is based on jurisdiction.

The tactical error of the Mendicants was that, given the spirit of the time, they began to adopt the same jurisdictional perspective and in their slogans failed to refer to the experience of their own charisma, which they could have defended with a reference to the *statuta ecclesiae antiqua*. To defend their authority as preachers they drew a distinction between general papal jurisdiction and the locally limited jurisdiction of bishops. Historically they came out on top and the works of William of Saint-Amour were banned by the pope. However, because the Mendicants had taken over certain starting points from their opponents, the mediaeval principle of the link between the *praedicatio* and the *praelatio* was continued in the church, so that here too the laity again became the victims of polemic among the clergy. Thomas Aquinas in fact had hesitations about this rigid hierarchical thought. In his view people 'lower' in the hierarchy could also teach those with higher status.[69] Here Thomas opens up, at least in principle, the possibility of lay preaching, but he himself does not draw this conclusion in any way. His historical concern was not with the question of the theological possibility of lay preaching but, given the needs of the time, only with emancipation for the clergy, giving them authority to preach outside the traditional framework of the organization of the church: the diocese and the parish.

The gain from all this polemic is the insight that the proclamation of the word could again be seen as a qualified and specialized ministry within the totality of different ministries necessary for the building up of a Christian community. Proclamation need not be bound up *per se* with the leadership of a community in a particular territory. Proclamation is detached from its twelfth-century ontological basis and is functionalized, albeit within the church. However, thirteenth-century theologians did not also take into account the possibility of preaching as being based on the charismatic witness of a life according to the gospel, the baptism of the Spirit, and thus let slip a historical opportunity. This applies above all to the Franciscans, who clearly began as a lay movement and very soon allowed themselves to become clericalized, while from the beginning the Dominicans clearly kept in view that priestly preaching had to be in line with the gospel. The Mendicants did not break down the bond between *praedicatio* and *praelatio*. In the end it was a matter of the authority of the pope on the one hand and the bishops on the other and not (at least in this polemic) of the actual substance of preaching in accordance with the gospel and thus of human salvation.

(*d*) Lay preaching, meanwhile forgotten

It is clear that in accordance with the canon law in force at the time, lay preaching was forbidden. However, whether this is connected with the very nature of the church is quite a different question. In fact we see that the prohibition of lay preaching had quite different causes and motives and was connected with historical demarcations of authority determining who was set in office over the church. Historically it was a matter of maintaining inherited positions, which then began to be defended ideologically, with theological arguments. The paradoxical element in all this is that the thirteenth-century theology, which reduced the whole of preaching the gospel to a question of jurisdiction, in principle made lay preaching possible. But at the same time Gregory IX (1227-1241),[70] by his prohibition of lay preaching, had seen preaching as the exclusive prerogative of the *ordo clericorum*. Up to the present day there are still bishops who claim that proclamation by a priest is qualitatively different from lay preaching! I find it a riddle to know on what mysterious factor such an assertion could be based. In fact during the mediaeval disputes over authority to preach there was never any discussion of the theological competence of the laity also to speak amongst the brothers and sisters with the authority of the content of the gospel: other questions and interests were at stake.

Of course in the *Decretum Gratiani* canons were taken over from the *Statuta Ecclesiae Antiqua*. These date from the second half of the fifth century and come from southern Gaul.[71] There it is said: *laicus autem praesentibus clericis, nisi ipsis rogantibus, docere non audeat*: (male) laity may only preach in the presence of the clergy with their assent. Origen and Jerome had already said that earlier.

According to the 'classical' conception in the church, the basis of all proclamation in the church is rightly interpreted as sending by Christ, but historically this sending is reserved for the apostles and bishops, priests and deacons.

However, this interpretation is open to a different exposition. The term 'mission' is always understood in a purely legalistic sense; what is involved here, then, is an institutional conception of authority or competence. This legalistic conception is in turn connected with a period in which there was a surplus of candidates; it was therefore important to clarify who could hand on the message of Jesus in the name of the church. Nowadays, however, our problem is not who *may* hand on the gospel but who *can* hand it on. Even the most attractive ecclesiological legitimation cannot make good the fact that at present it is no longer the ministry which supports the proclaimer but that on the contrary the individual proclaimer must give credence to the ministry by his own personal commitment and the inspiration he receives from the gospel. The biblical concept of mission comprises more than what a legalistic narrowing has made of it.

Note: Lay proclamation in the new Codex of 1983

Although the new Codex of the Roman Catholic Church avoids the term 'ministry' for pastoral workers who have not been ordained, this lawbook implicitly has repealed the mediaeval prohibition of lay preaching. From now on laity may preach in the church (canon 759) and there is even mention of 'ministerial' preaching by the laity (canons 766, 767.1). In the new Codex there is ample room for the participation of the 'laity' in the church's jurisdiction (see canon 1421.2). It is expressly said, 'Where the need of the church requires it because of the lack of ministers, laity can perform certain of their tasks, especially in exercising the ministry of the word, presiding in liturgical prayers, administering baptism and giving holy communion' (canon 130.3). Even the pastoral care of a parish can be entrusted to the laity (canon 517.2). If the usual minister is prevented, the catechist may baptize (canon 861.2) and a lay person may also be an official witness at a marriage (canon 1112).

On the one hand we must welcome all this, but on the other this canonical view is weak in two contrasting theological concepts. The new dispositions again mark a break between jurisdiction and ordination, while the great gain of Vatican II has been to establish that the power of jurisdiction has a sacramental basis, in other words that the power of ordination is the basis of all jurisdictional authority. However, ordination is denied to those laity (who are in fact married). The good thing, which was perhaps unintentional, in these new regulations is that there is an implicit concession that both jurisdiction and ordination have their deepest sacramental foundation in the baptism of the Spirit in which all believers share, though all this must all be interpreted on the basis of a positivistic hierarchical authority which can decide as the sovereign wills.

5. Causes of the changed image of the priest in the Middle Ages

We can see from this survey of the spirituality of the early Middle Ages, stamped by feudalism and monasticism and ultimately both canonical and evangelical, that the image of the priest is much more varied than some canons of the Third and Fourth Lateran Councils might suggest. Of course in other places these councils also stress the duty of bishops to consecrate suitable men as fellow workers with the bishop to see to the ministry of the word and the hearing of confessions.[72] The new keyword of the twelfth century, *cura animarum*, was taken over in this connection. I must concede to critics that the measures of the Lateran Councils which I quoted in *Ministry* do not of themselves make a contribution towards locating the mediaeval conception of the priest.

Although the function of the priest in proclamation was reassessed in the twelfth century, this element remained outside the definition of the sacrament of ordination as presented by the theological syntheses in the thirteenth century. Thus Thomas sees the mark of consecration (which is sevenfold) as a participation in the priesthood of Christ, not in his pastoral or prophetic functions.[73] The sacrament of ordination is defined wholly in relation to the cult. Moreover, in respect of sacramental priesthood or the power of ordination Thomas does not see any difference between pope, bishop and priest. They differ only in jurisdiction, which is participation in the royal power of Christ that is his on the basis of his divine nature, although he only exercises this in his humanity.[74]

There is mention of 'priestly spirituality' in the Middle Ages only in terms of the monastic or canonical model; there seems to be no distinctive spirituality for priests who are not involved in pastoral care according to this model, and that is the majority. Only in the twentieth century were voices to be raised to formulate such a 'spirituality of the diocesan clergy'. At the beginning of the sixteenth century Clichtove tried to work out a distinctive spirituality for the priest, but that was only for 'mass-readers', men with few or no pastoral duties.[75]

It may well be asked how this mediaeval change in the church's view of its ministers could have taken place historically. Some historians and other writers put the whole of the blame on the fact that precisely at the time of the Third and Fourth Lateran Councils, the theory emerged of a mysterious sacramental character, the basis of the whole *sacramentum ordinis*.[76] I think that this is quite wrong, above all because the so-called major scholastic theologians, that is, Bonaventura, Albertus Magnus and Thomas Aquinas, interpreted the very vague theory of the character (which dated from the end of the twelfth century), however modern it then was, in continuity with the early church. Despite their diverging interpretations, for them character points to the visible link between 'ministry' and 'church'.[77] Furthermore, this character was given at all ordinations, from bishop to acolyte and sacristan. The term *mancipatio* – to be called to and accepted by the community for a particular service in the church – was the most tangible point of this character in the Middle Ages; and in essentials this followed the conception of ministry in the early church.

Nevertheless this scholastic doctrine contained elements which, much later, would contribute to an even magical sacer-dotalizing of the priesthood. The germs of this are also present in the Middle Ages, but they were only projected on to the mediaeval theory of the character from late contexts. What are these other contextual factors?

From the sixth century on, the Popes had become the pawns of the emperors with their still influential Byzantine Caesaro-papism. The spiritual renewal which the Irish missionaries brought to the continent of Europe had a completely different spirit from that to which 'Germanic' and 'Gallic' Christians had become accustomed. We can follow many historians in saying that with the conversion of the 'barbarians' the church was made barbarian! Bishops who formerly had been independent and free now became the servants of powerful seigneurs, secular lords, who to enhance their status built private churches and secured clergy for them at whim. The Carolingian renaissance indeed brought a reaction against this, but at the same time it consolidated the whole feudal system of foundations and donations. Even the Council of Aix-la-Chapelle (818-819), which wanted a spiritual renewal of the clergy,[78] primarily occupied itself with foundations (of churches) and donations, with an eye to the beginnings of feudalism, although an attempt was made to withdraw the nomination of priests from the meddling of secular seigneurs. As part of this feudal system, spiritual autonomy was restored to the bishops. Nevertheless, under the incipient feudal system, kings, counts and dukes had priests and even bishops under their control.

At that time *ecclesia* was no longer a living community as before, but often simply a status symbol of secular rulers with 'private churches'. The involvement of the church in feudalism gave rise to prince bishops, who were hardly well versed in the great church tradition. It has to be acknowledged that in this confused situation the reform of Gregory VII was nothing short of a downright revolution. At the end of the eleventh century Gregory sought to extricate the church from its feudal entanglements. The Gregorian reform marked the beginning of a constantly recurring 'evangelical movement' – in spite of everything – which kept cropping up in the Middle Ages.

However, towards the end of the eleventh century and the beginning of the twelfth there was also a renaissance of Roman law. Its influence seems to me to have been decisive, above all in ecclesiology and therefore also in connection with the church's view of the ministry. This particular legal view, also through the feudal context, detached the power of leadership (in whatever sphere) from the concept of 'territoriality' and therefore, in the religious sphere, from the concept of the 'local church' – territoriality and local church must be seen above all as a 'human sphere' (not purely geographical). At the end of the thirteenth century this would lead to the famous remark of Vincent de Beauvais, *quodque principi placuit, legis habet vigorum*:[79] the principle of the 'fullness of power' (*plenitudo potestatis*); authority as value-in-itself apart from the community, in the civic and the ecclesiastical spheres.

Thus non-theological factors (feudal and legal) made the mediaeval 'theological shift' possible. Before that, for Christians the boundary between the 'spirit of Christ' and the 'spirit of the world' lay in their baptism: their sense of being accepted into the elect community of God's *ecclesia*; now with the massive expansion of the church, this boundary came to lie above all at the point of the 'second baptism', that of monastic life. However, in the earliest period monks were laymen, not priests. The Christian community saw them as the deepest realization of their ideal Christian model. This perspective was shifted, to some degree through the Carolingian Council of Aix-la-Chapelle, but above all after the Gregorian reform. At a time when virtually everyone was baptized, the boundary between 'the spirit of Christ' and 'the spirit of the world' came to lie with the clergy. As a result the priesthood was seen more as 'a personal state of life', a *status*, than as a service to the community; it was personalized and privatized.[80] In particular, the new conceptions of law, *ius*, and thus of jurisdiction, brought about a division between the power of ordination and the power of jurisdiction,[81] in my view one of the most fundamental factors which marks off the second Christian millennium from the first. At any rate, here lawyers developed the idea of 'sacred power' (*sacra potestis*), strongly influenced by the context in which they lived. *Potestas* is the stake in the whole of the investiture controversy between *imperium* and *sacerdotium*, emperor and pope, and the sphere of their authority. For the theology of the church, however, the division between the power of ordination and the power of jurisdiction meant the opening of the door to absolute ordinations. For although the ordained man might not be assigned a Christian community (i.e., legally speaking, had no *potestas iurisdictionis*), by virtue of *ordinatio* he had all priestly power in his own person. Only now did *ordinatio* in fact become a sacred rite (*Weihe*): a man is a priest quite apart from a particular *ecclesia* (in other words, the definition of what Chalcedon had called an invalid 'absolute ordination'). This view opens up the way to practices which would have been unthinkable to Christians earlier, above all the private mass.[82] If a man has been personally ordained priest, he has the 'power of the eucharist' and can therefore celebrate it on his own. For the early church this was inconceivable.[83]

This was the origin of a theology of the ministry with another orientation. This is already evident from the new church documents, in which it is explicitly said that if the rite of the laying on of hands is performed in due order, albeit in the context of an 'absolute consecration', this consecration of the minister is valid and in force. This is connected with the developing conception of the *opus operatum* of the sacrament through which the ecclesial context is forced into the background. This is particularly evident in documents of Pope Innocent III (1198-1216). At that time in the West, after the revival of Roman law, the old principle of *oikonomia* was widely adapted to become the so-called principle of dispensation. Innocent III practised this principle in such sovereign fashion that in effect all consecrations became 'absolute' and were nevertheless valid.[84]

The consequence of all this is that the old relationship between *ministerium* and *ecclesia*, between ministry and church, now shifts to a relationship between *potestas* and *eucharistia*, the power of consecration and the eucharist. Moreover, this change is brought about in what is by no means a fortuitous semantic shift, i.e. the mediaeval semantic shift between *corpus verum Christi* and *corpus mysticum Christi*.[85] In the ancient church the theological and liturgical documents had constantly said that it is necessary to hold an ecclesial office to preside in the church, i.e. in the *corpus verum Christi*: leadership of the community. However, after the dispute over the eucharist between Rhatramnus and Lanfranc this terminology had begun to be confused. In the ancient church, *corpus mysticum Christi* did not mean the *ecclesia* but the eucharistic body of Christ. In the Middle Ages, however, things were different. Polemic altered the significance of the words. Thus whereas formerly it had been said that a minister needed to be ordained to preside over the church community (= *corpus verum*), the terminology now became that of presiding over the *corpus mysticum*, i.e. of celebrating the eucharist. The *mediaeva sacra potestas* which had grown up in the meantime began to influence this situation: ordination then became the bestowal of special power to be able to perform the consecration of the eucharist. As a logical consequence of this, the Fourth Lateran Council went on to say that only a validly ordained priest can speak the words of consecration. Thomas later produced a sharp formulation of what had developed since the twelfth century: 'Actions can be directed immediately to God in a twofold way. On the one hand, they can proceed from an individual person, like saying prayers, and so on; all those who are baptized are in a position to perform such an action. On the other hand, they can be performed by the whole church; and in this respect only the priest is capable of performing actions which are directed immediately to God, since the action of the whole church can be performed only by the person who consecrates the eucharist, which is the sacrament of the whole church.'[86] In comparison with the ancient church, circumstances here have taken a markedly different direction: a priest is ordained in order to be able to celebrate the eucharist. In the ancient church it is said that he is 'appointed' as minister in order to be able to appear as leader of the community; in other words, the community called him as leader to build up the community, and for this reason he was also the obvious person to preside at the eucharist. This shift is at all events a narrower legalistic version of what the early church intended.

Section 3: **The 'modern' picture of the priest**

Introduction

Above all in the Ancien Régime of absolute monarchy, consecrations with a view to, and the practice of, ministries in the
church which were also conditioned by feudalism led to the
picture of the church which was initially formulated by Josse
Clichtove.[87] His picture of the priest to some degree influenced
the Council of Trent, but this Council rightly protected itself
against the one-sidedness of his view. In the seventeenth century
the picture of the priest was worked out with unmistakable
religious verve by de Bérulle, Jean Eudes, Olier, and further by
the Oratory and Saint Sulpice, the so-called Ecole Française. They
made some fine statements, but also with rhetorical supernaturalist exaggeration.

The picture that they sketch of the priest forms the background
to all clerical literature about the priesthood from the nineteenth
century down to Vatican II.

Of course it must be added here that images of the priest worked
out by pious scholars do not coincide with what priests in the
field actually did, confronted with the needs of the people, and
how they lived. They too daily experienced the tension between
practice and theology. A study of the actual life of priests at the
grass roots in the past four centuries would therefore not be
superfluous.

Nevertheless it has to be said that since the establishment of
Great Seminaries after Trent, candidates for the priesthood were
brought up in a very special world of priesthood. The fact is that
in the first half of the twentieth century a whole series of books
have been published in the ethos of the priestly spirituality of the
French school, and some of them have also been translated.

What was the basic tendency here?

1. Prehistory: Josse Clichtove (1472-1543)

Clichtove combined biblical, patristic and mediaeval ideas with
the situation of the 'modern society' which was beginning in his
time. In itself this was a proper thing to do. However, in a
hierarchical Christian society, governed by a power founded on
divine law, the result was that by virtue of his state of life, the

priest is detached from the world, even from the world of the Christian laity. The idea of 'being taken out of the world', i.e. escape from the world, completely determines this image of the priest. The Levitical priestly laws from the Old Testament as well as the tradition of monastic life determined Clichtove's image of the priesthood. Priesthood is essentially defined by its relation with the cult (and not with the community), though this is the cult of the community. A priest, even a pastor, may have as little contact as possible even with his own parishioners, except for the necessary administration of the sacraments. To be a priest is to be a 'cultic priest'. Precisely on the basis of this relation to the cult, the priest is the one who is set apart from the people, and priestly celibacy is the only adequate expression of this essential separation. Therefore in his last works Clichtove even says that priestly celibacy goes back to the natural law and 'divine law', and that the legislation of the church alone can sanction this divine law. The consequence of this is that even the pope cannot dispense with the law of celibacy. This is equivalent to the religious 'solemn vows' of an enclosed monk. Celibacy, regarded solely as restraint from what Clichtove calls fleshly impurity (*spurcitia*), is the *claustrum* that cuts off the priest from the world and segregates him. To give permission to the priest to marry would be equivalent to blurring the distinction between layman and priest. The whole of Clichtove's view is based on the supremely sacred power of the priest to offer sacrifice. Therefore 'religion', worship, *par excellence* belongs to the caste of the priests and monks, who are far above the ordinary believers. Precisely on the basis of this power to offer sacrifice the priest is the mediator between God and believers.

Clichtove was concerned to work out a special 'priestly spirituality' for the large number of priests who had been consecrated at the beginning of the sixteenth century but had not been given any pastoral responsibility. In itself, this was a very dubious starting point, so that in addition, albeit for other reasons than for the religious life, he gives priestly spirituality more and more monastic features as time goes on. The basis of this 'modern spirituality of the priesthood' is the priestly 'state of grace'; this is essentially 'sacrificial' and is experienced in society in the priestly state; priesthood is less an office than a state, grounded in cultic activity. So it is understandable that Clichtove breaks with the conceptions of, for example, Thomas Aquinas, who sees the celibacy of the priesthood purely as a disciplinary measure of the church,[88] and makes a sharp distinction between the celibacy of the minister and the celibacy of religious and monks. For Clichtove, celibacy is an essential part of the cultic separation of the priest from the believing people. Only at this time does the image of the priest become completely hierarchical and monastic. The priest-theologian Clichtove wanted to present himself as the great, strict reformer of spirituality in the face of the collapse of priestly morality in the late Middle Ages, against which both Luther and Erasmus had fulminated (he already did this before the break-through of the Reformation, which made him even more rigorous on some points). He wanted a new spirituality of the priesthood, but on the basis of a very narrow theological view of the church's ministry (which is not really a ministry but simply a state). Unfortunately he cast this already one-sided spirituality in juridical forms. Also, above all under his influence, the Catholic image of the priest came to be seen in the light of an absolutizing of the law, for which the mediaeval image of the priest had laid only a very few foundations. Furthermore, the image of the priest as the solitary private reader of 'masses', without further pastoral responsibilities, took on a certain divine aura. The Council of Trent, faithful to its standpoint of not taking up any positions in theological controversies within Catholicism, refrained from sanctioning the basic views of Clichtove, although something of his spirit can already be felt in the actual canons of Trent.

2. The Council of Trent on ministry

It is in no way my purpose to discuss the Tridentine doctrine of the 'sacrament of ordination', except in connection with the differences in conceptions of ministry down the ages.[89]

At the beginning of my account of the second millennium I already said that the church definitely did not intend a break with the church of the first millennium. On the contrary. People were convinced, rather, that they remained in line with the ancient church, despite actual marked divergences caused by new situations in the church and the world. Both the continuity and the break clearly come to the fore in the Acts, and somewhat less in the final reaction of the Canons, of the Council of Trent.

The statements made at the Council of Trent, like those of any council, have a quite specific historical setting; furthermore, at Trent possible correction from the Eastern churches was absent. In its final statements, according to its own words this Council only wanted to express what, according to its own understanding and estimation, had been denied by the Reformers. In the meantime the further course of history meant that the fathers of the Council of Trent simply had a summary and sometimes misguided conception of what really happened at the Reformation. Thus – in accordance with the actual aim of this assembly of the Western church – the resolutions of this Council were only counter-positions; they are silent at the points over which the fathers of the Council were at one with Reformation positions. So we cannot look to Trent for a complete doctrine of the Catholic conception of ministry, not even as it was current at that time. The resolutions are deliberately one-sided with respect to what the fathers of the Council themselves thought about ministry. To give just one example: in its canons on the sacrament of ordination this Council connects the ministry of the church ('priesthood', as what presbyters and bishops have in common) almost exclusively with presiding at the eucharist (the power of consecrating and performing other sacramental actions), whereas on the other hand in the reforming decrees (which were concerned more with reforming the clergy than directly challenging the Reformation) pastoral direction and proclamation were seen as the primary task of the priestly episcopate.[90] This apparent inconsistency can only be understood in the light of the strict intention of the canons of Trent, viz., of simply formulating opposing positions where in the view of the church fathers the Reformation either denies certain primal Christian traditions connected with the ministry or allows them to become obscured.

Conciliar authority lies in the final text of the Council of Trent as it has come down to us, and not what the fathers engaged in the Council may have thought personally, and may even in fact have stated in the two sessions preceding the solemn session. Of course we cannot estimate the historical and theological significance of a particular council without critical study of the Acts of the three sessions in which the sacrament of ordination was discussed. However, it would be unrealistic to ignore the inluence and after-effects of the Tridentine *doctrina* and *canones* as they appeared in their final version in the period following the Council of Trent. For these canons, too, made a specific contribution to a one-sided hardening of the conception of the ministry in the second millennium. It was these canons which made history, and not (or rather not yet) what critical historical hermeneutics over the last twenty years has discovered about the real purposes of the Council of Trent. Anyone who is familiar with the Acts of this Council can say that despite differences which are nevertheless real, and cannot be brushed aside, as a purely Latin Council, Trent nevertheless in many repects both honoured views from the first millennium and equally anticipated views from the later Second Vatican Council. However, this justifiable historical view of Trent is markedly different from the actual historical consequences of the Council. Anyone who wants to evaluate the historical relevance of a Council must take account of both sides of the coin if they are not to be naive or unrealistic, or to reduce dogmatic theology to apologetics.

Furthermore, in its canons on the ministry, the Council of Trent did not want to adopt any position in connection with themes over which the Scotists, the Thomists and the Augustinians - the three great Catholic movements in the Council – were in mutual disagreement. Now these differences related not only to the substance of the sacrament of ordination and the relationship of presbyters to bishops, but also to the role of the believing people in the mandate of the church or the calling of candidates to the priesthood; they also related to the significance, the content and the extent of the so-called 'priestly character' - to mention just a few controversial matters! Thus very little was left that could actually be defined. In other words, given the fundamental task which the Council had set itself, the final result was inevitably going to seem 'poor' over against the rich and varied ideas (albeit narrowed down by their mediaeval context) which were current among the fathers of the Council. This poor final result is noticeable if we compare the canons of Trent, from the third session (15 July 1563), with what theologians and bishops had said about the ministry in the first session devoted to it (1557), in which Luther's views on the ministry were the chief subject for study, and in the second session (1551-1552), in which Calvin's views also came up. Only once was a bishop heard to lament that what was regarded by everyone 'as heresy' would be better countered by a positive, synthetic account of the Catholic view of the ministry than by fragmentary positions taken up against the Reformation.[91]

It is wrong to say that the way in which the Canons of Trent are directed against the Reformation has been the reason why since then the 'priesthood' has almost exclusively been seen in connection with presiding at the eucharist (the power of consecration). That was already an earlier, mediaeval position (see above), against which the Reformation was in part a right reaction. In the Tridentine counter-reaction, this mediaeval view in fact gained one-sided importance, and that was the way in which this Council later began to function. Furthermore, I have already explained how in early mediaeval theology the meaning of *corpus verum* (the church) and *corpus mysticum* (the eucharistic body of Christ) were seen as being opposed, a fact over which this Council (in so far as any of this semantic shift was perceived at Trent) was evidently at its wits' end. The relationship of the ministry to Christ on the one hand and to the church on the other was kept very vague by the Council, in a disappointing way; at the time of this session there was still no worked-out 'ecclesiology', while the experience of the community at that time (see the reforming decrees) left a good deal to be desired. Furthermore, the fact that Trent rightly also had to combat the attempts of the nobility – at that time the laity were the ones who had the power – to nominate bishops and priest led the Council (sometimes under the protests of a number of theologians) to reduce the role of the community of believing people to nothing in the nominating of ministers, though we already note a Tridentine reaction to the Reformation which stressed the role of the community in the nomination of its ministers, following the line of the early church (but within new 'bourgeois' experiences). This historical background to the Council of Trent does not do away with the fact that the view of the church held by this Council, deriving from feudal times, was very strongly hierarchical (pope, bishops, priests, deacons and then, a long way away, the believing people).

Finally, the eight canons concerning the sacrament of ordination[92] are a reaction against a view which reduces the priest to a preacher, spokesman and proclaimer (with the result that at least in defining the functions of the priest the canons only stress his cultic activity and so do not say anything about the tasks of preaching and teaching, which were stressed so strongly by scripture and the early church as the task of ministers of the church). In their final version the canons are also silent on the universal priesthood of believers, about which theologians and bishops had spoken so much in the first two sessions, evidently because mention of it could only play into the hands of the Reformation; however, the fathers of the Council in no sense denied this datum of scripture and the early church. Not once does Trent define what is the precise nature of the church's ministry or the sacrament of ordination, because Thomists and Scotists and fathers at the Council with a different orientation held divergent views on the matter. The Scotists believed the sacramental character of consecration to lie in the 'rite of consecration' (in fact the laying on of hands with anointing); the Thomists stressed, rather, the impression of the 'permanent sacrament': the state of being ordained, on the basis of the character and the powers which were acquired. These powers could be withdrawn, but not the character. In the final version, the hierarchical structure of the church (bishops, presbyters and deacons), first formulated as a divine institution (*divina institutione*), is reduced to a divine ordinance (*divina ordinatione*: in his providence God allowed historical developments to take this course).[93]

In most instances the Council defended the actual structures of the ministry as they had developed in the tradition and were then advocated by church authorities as church order. Here it defended directly less the developed structures in themselves (now and then the Council fathers show signs of being aware of historical changes in the structures of the ministry) than the authority of the church to define its own church order (which is now accepted ecumenically by all churches).[94] Thus the Tridentine decree on the ministry is less dogmatic than it seems; it defends the *de facto* church order and the right to establish church authority over this order. The historical consequences of this defence by the Council of the church order in force at the time, and the absence of a real theology of the ministry, was that in actual fact the Council simply took over the deviation in the conception and practice of the ministry and fundamentally strengthened and sanctioned this, though not deliberately. Furthermore, the sharp distinction between the power of consecration and the power of jurisdiction made it difficult for the fathers of the Council of Trent to gain a clear view of ministry. Here the absence of the Eastern churches also made its effect, to the detriment of the Council. The legalistic narrowing down of the (mediaeval) view of the priest is in fact the result of all this. In the twentieth century, in particular Pius X, Pius XI and Pius XII contributed a great deal towards the popularizing of this narrow view of the priest,[95] which for many Christians down to the present day is a determining factor in their view of the priest.

3. The nucleus of the post-Tridentine view of ministry: the danger-point in the spirituality of ministry in the 'Ecole Française'

At the Council of Trent, the chapter on the sacrament of ordination was finished very quickly under the pressure of political circumstances. The canons, are of course, anti-positions, directed against the Reformation. As a result, in canon 1 all the emphasis came to lie on the power of the priest in consecration and absolution; his function in proclamation is fading into the background. In the reforming decrees of the same council the proclamation of the word and the cure of souls were also mentioned. However, at the great seminaries, themselves a consequence of the Tridentine reforming degrees, the dogmatic canons above all had an almost exclusive role and from that perspective influenced later history. Thus a narrowed theological priestly image was extended into coming generations. When this came into contact with the typically seventeenth-century spirituality, above all of the 'French school',[96] of which the pious Pierre de Bérulle was the head, there came into being what one might call the modern image of the priest. Theologically, this is determined by the idea – for which de Bérulle and his historian pupil Thomassinus appealed to Origen, that Christ is not a priest on the basis of his humanity but on the basis of his divinity. Through ministry the priests therefore share in a very mysterious, highly mystical power. Thomas himself had in no way envisaged this with his doctrine of the 'sacramental character'. We also find statements opposed to this in Cyril of Alexandria.[97]

In this context belongs the long-standing question whether the priest is a mediator between God and humanity. However, Augustine, who recognizes the specific character of the *sacerdotium* in the church and defends it fiercely, was opposed to the conception that the priest (bishop or presbyter) might be mediator between God and the people.[98] Nevertheless, in modern times this priestly mediatorship received unexpected support on the basis of a mistaken interpretation of a text of Origen.

Despite the attractive things which the French School of spirituality wrote about the priesthood, I find dangerous accents in it which at the same time have given shape to the modern image of the priest. Thus for example Jean Eudes writes that 'the Son of God... makes you (= priests) participate in his quality of being mediator between God and man, in his worth as sovereign judge of the world, in his name and ministry as "redeemer of the world" and in many other excellencies of which he is the image.'[99] The basis of this mystical elevation of the priestly ministry lies in the fact that it sees the priesthood of Jesus based, not on his humanity but on his deity. Newman had already vigorously opposed this view in the nineteenth century in connection with a publication by Manning.[100] If the mediatorship of Jesus is located in his humanity, the priesthood of the church indeed takes on a different significance, but this is no less a truly Christian sacramental significance.

In the meantime, since this polemic, Origen's *Dialektos* has been discovered, the work that indirectly was in part the source of this historical confusion. However, the text shows that in the eucharistic sacrifice of the church, *the man Jesus* is the *propheros* (sacrificing priest) but that on the basis of his divinity, this sacrifice was acceptable to God.[101] So its content is rather different.

Vatican II made a first, still hesitant attempt – in fact it was a compromise – by on the one hand stressing the full riches of the charisma of the spirit of baptism, and on the other hand describing ministry not just in priestly but also in prophetic and pastoral terms: leadership of the community (pastoral function), liturgical worship (priestly function) and proclamation of the gospel (prophetic function).[102]

Section 4: Continuity and significant breaks in the history of the theology and practice of ministry

To begin with, the communities of God who had received from Jesus' first disciples the message of the executed but living and glorified Jesus Christ and accepted baptism in Jesus' name, lived a life 'filled with the Spirit'. All had pneumatic power, but this manifested itself more or differently in some Christians than in others. The community of faith was a *koinonia*, an assembly and gathering of equal partners, with no difference between slave and free, between male and female, between Jewish Christians and Gentile Christians. They had all been freed, free in and through the Spirit of God – in freedom bound to the message, the doctrine and the praxis of the kingdom of God, as all this had become visible in the career of Jesus. However, this equality of all in no way excluded leadership and authority in the community. But all the Gospels are fiercely opposed to a hierarchical leadership 'in the way of the world'. Authority lies in love which serves the church, a service; it is not social, let alone ontological, status. This is really the essential feature of what the New Testament has to say about ministry and leadership in the church.

The later tendency, which is already perceptible in the Pastoral Epistles and after the New Testament even more clearly in the letters of Clement and Ignatius, goes in the direction of the fact that *pneuma*, prophetic authority, in which all believers share on the basis of the baptism of the Spirit (although this became evident to different degrees depending on the individual's capacity to receive it) is at the same time specifically focussed on and concentrated in a ministerial charisma of the Spirit which was connected with a different rite from that of baptism, although baptism remains the basis and matrix of this ministerial concentration of the universal charisma of the Spirit. The universal can never come into its own without specialization and concentration in individuals who make their faith their work. This also applies in the church.

When the universal prophetic charisma of the Spirit is appropriated at a first stage of institutionalization by the college of presbyters in ministerial concentration, we soon see that within this college the presbyter-president (perhaps originally a rotating function within that college) in turn began to concentrate the spiritual charisma of prophecy (along with the apostolate, the main principle of leadership in the early church) in the ministerial function of the *episkopos*, a function which later gained the significance of what we historically call the bishop. From this there then developed, over against and together with his presbyters and deacons, the figure of the bishop, who concentrated the fullness of the charisma of the Spirit in the episcopal function and had this fullness shared by his personal deacons and his presbyteral council.

Above all after Constantine and Theodosius, moreover, the clergy began to encourage the attitude of hierarchical behaviour in authority, now that Christianity was recognized throughout the empire as a state religon. The senior clergy in particular began gradually to take over the insignia of the emperor and of princes (they often came from noble families). In this way the church became clericalized, a development which from the perspective of the New Testament is clearly one against which the gospel warns.

Believers (who from then on began to be called 'laity') ceased to be the subjects of faith, in the Spirit, and were reduced to being the object of priestly care.

The result of the later development of this tendency in the Middle Ages was that the concentration (sometimes even exclusive) of all the charisma of the Spirit in the specific ministerial charisma of the Spirit, which had already come about in the patristic period, was now also legalistically narrowed and firmly established. What was a ministerial service in the New Testament period, a service and a serving love, was from then on expressed in terms of power (*potestas*), which was in turn divided into power of consecration and power of jurisdiction.[103]

Above all from the seventeenth century onwards, people ceased to base the priesthood of Jesus on his manhood but sought it directly in his divinity, and as a result the whole of this development was sacralized. Thus the priesthood of the church also began to participate in deeply sacred mysteries and was set on a new ontological level, above the new creation which is baptism with the Spirit. This development obscured the fact that the reality of baptism is itself the ontological matrix and root of the sacrament of ordination, relating to a function in the church, and gives ordination its substance.

The conceptions which developed in this way express a view of the church which looks at everything in the church in terms of 'from above to below', and in practice identifies the church with the church's hierarchy, despite the splendid things which e.g. Vatican II said about the people of God. In *Lumen Gentium* this Council dropped the term *potestas* (power) as far as possible (though not always!) and spoke above all in terms of *ministeria* and *munera*, the work of service, in the church. Moreover, it made at least a beginning of breaking through the legalism surrounding the ministry as a result of the earlier clear division into the power of ordination and the power of jurisdiction, with the nuance that the jurisdiction (which from an ecclesial perspective is also connected with the intrinsic bond between the ministry and the community of believers) and its essential foundation is already given with ordination itself (this was at the same time an attempt to rule out 'absolute ordinations' and declare them irrelevant).

Vatican II nevertheless sometimes still locates the 'representation of Christ' by the priest in the minister as a person and not formally in the act of the exercising of his office;[104] this points to a confusion between two levels, the ontological level of the baptism of the Spirit and the functional level of the ministry, which essentially presupposes precisely this first level in order to be able to be what it in fact is. At all events, the representation of Christ comes about not purely on the basis of ministry, which is simply a typological ministerial focussing of the universal charisma of the Spirit at the level of ministerial service as mandated by the church. It goes without saying that this diaconal service is coupled with a Christian ethic and spirituality. That is almost the only thing about which the New Testament speaks in connection with the ministry. However, this spirituality must be sought in the first place in the mystical depths of the baptismal anointing of the newborn Christian and therefore in the consequences of belief in the gospel and the *sequela Jesu*.

The continuity between Jesus Christ and the church is fundamentally based on the Spirit. The ministry is a specific sign of this, and not the substance itself. Whereas in the early church ministry was seen rather in the sign of the Spirit which fills the church, later, people began to see the ministry in terms of the ecclesiology which regards the church as the extension of the incarnation. People moved from a pneuma-christological view of ministry to a theology of ministry based directly on christology. In fact the two need not be in contradiction and can be supplementary. However, the danger of taking the Spirit into one's own hands becomes great in a direct christological view.

Both views retain the realization, which is both old and also very modern, that no Christian community can say that it is autonomously the ultimate source of its ministers. But the view of a direct christological foundation of ministry is a theology of ministry with a suppressed and even concealed ecclesiology, with no foundation in the living reality of the community of believers who live by the Spirit. Although Thomas still always spoke of the sacraments as *sacramenta ecclesiae*, celebrations on the part of the whole community of the church, later on they were usually defined as the action of a consecrated person as a *signum efficax gratiae*, an effective sign of grace, in which the ecclesial dimension was no longer perceived.

In the fourth and the beginning of the fifth century Jerome, the exegete, gave pointed expression to the self-understanding of the Christian churches as 'communities of believers', in connection with ministries in the church: *Ecclesia non est quae non habet sacerdotes*,[105] the church is not a church without ministers – priests. The church itself is the womb of the ministry, which is itself in the service of the community of believers and draws on its mystical depths. In this view the 'shortage of priests' is really an ecclesiological impossibility – unless the Spirit is 'quenched' in the community of believers. And for anyone who can see what is happening, this is certainly not the case!

Now the longer parishes are without priests in the ancient Christian countries, while in other continents Christian communities flourish without local ministers, communities which are only visited by a priest once or twice a year, authorized to preside at the eucharist (the heart of the community of believers), the more something seems to be wrong. That is why I have been in search of the attractive history which shows us – for better or for worse – how living churches, supported by the Spirit of Christ, have looked for particular forms of organization in the ministry, sometimes in different ways, depending on religious needs and on the needs of the church communities. Throughout this history I therefore recognize on the one hand the normative significance of the New Testament model and on the other hand the inspiring force of the whole of church history for faith and theology (therefore ruling out mere biblicism).

I was and am essentially concerned with theological criteria, with the theological significance of the church's practice of the ministry, on each occasion in very precise historical settings. These criteria are provided by the living life of the communities which take initiatives; the theologian can do no more than reflect on them. The critical point – in every sense of the phrase – is whether the practice of the ministry (albeit on each occasion in a very precise historical setting) is shaped primarily by theological criteria, or on the basis of non-theological factors. Or more precisely, whether it is formed from theological reflection on new human and cultural situations in which Christian believers are involved.

One of the tasks of the theologian is to confront the church and its living practice on occasion with the whole of the tradition of the faith. He or she must present this tradition, with all its historically changing contexts, and the theological or non-theological models which are invested in them, whether consciously or unconsciously. For all its importance, even the Council of Trent is only one of the many regulating factors in the correct interpretation of scripture. Thus it in no way expresses the many-sided totality of Christian faith; it is only a segment of that, and is so in a very limited historical situation, which is exclusively that of Western churches. Although this council, too, expressed 'Christian truth', it did so at all events in a particular context, i.e. in a specific way relating to a very definite Western situation, and within a distinctive view of it. The result of all this is that the statements of all councils, and particularly other, non-conciliar statements made by the church, must be interpreted not only within their own historical context but also with the whole of the Christian tradition of faith, as this gave orientation and inspiration to the further history of the church in the light of the biblical and apostolic faith. This is essential if we are to understand their significance for people now. For better or worse, then and now, this ongoing history of the church regularly gives renewed expression to inspiration in constantly new existential contexts. There the Christian churches have sometimes done well, and sometimes less well, leading to disillusionment. We can regard all this as a generally accepted consensus among contemporary theologians, though the instruments of the church's teaching authority often have a tendecy to dwell on 'the letter' of earlier statements and to underestimate their historical and hermeneutical dimensions.

Part Four

Listening to the 'Complaints of the People'

Introduction

At the 1971 Synod of Bishops, in a discussion of the present shortage of priests and what has been called the crisis of identity among priests, a bishop said that a particular – traditional – theology of the ministry was partially the cause of this crisis. There seems to be discontent about the practice and above all the theology of the ministry as it is presented in the classical 'modern image of the priest', while candidates for the ministry who are believers cannot recognize themselves in it. Therefore we must listen to and analyse the 'complaints of the people', the discontent among priests and even bishops about ministry, in order to note rather more precisely the negative experiences over the ministry and see what their content is. In terms of pastoral theology, negative experiences of contrast have a power to lead to criticism of ideologies, the formation of diagnoses and the provision of dynamic inventions for the future. They disclose the need in the church for a theology of ministry which does not mystify, for an appropriate form of organization in ministry and for some pastorally inevitable shifts in present-day canon law which is itself new.

It emerges from the historical and theological sketch which I have given that the constant element in the church's ministry is always to be found only in specific, historically changing forms. Church order, with its changes, is a very great benefit for Christian communities. In one form or another church order is part of the specific and essential manifestation of the 'communities of God', the church. However, this church order is not an end in itself.

Like ministry, it too is at the service of the apostolic communities built on the gospel and may not be made an end in itself or be absolutized. That is all the more the case because it is evident that at all periods of the church it is utterly bound up with a specific, conditioned history. At a particular point in history, moreover, certain forms of church order (and thus also criteria for the admission of ministers), called into being by earlier situations in the church and in society, come up against their limitations; this can also be demonstrated in sociological terms, even in a 'church of God'. These limitations can clearly be shown in terms of specific experiences of their shortcomings and faults, in other words, from negative experiences with a particular church order in changed circumstances. With a shift in the dominant picture of man and the world, with social and economic changes and a new social and cultural sensiblilty and set of emotions, a church order which has grown up through history can in fact hinder and obstruct precisely what in earlier times it was intended to ensure: the building up of a Christian community. Experiences of contrast then give rise to spontaneous experiments in possibilities of new forms of life for Christianity and the church (which also happened in New Testament Christianity). Experiences of defects in a given system in fact have a regulative force. Of course even a largely unanimous experience of what has gone wrong with a valid system which has grown up through history by no means amounts to agreement over the positive steps which must be taken. Here I too am questing and hesitant. The specific direction in which things can change can only emerge from tests made through a large number of models, some of which will succeed and some fail. These can and may also go wrong; they are precise experiments with that possibility in view. Failure is nothing to be ashamed of, but a phase within the quest for a new discovery of Christianity. In these manifold attempts, the binding character of the new possibilities for Christian life and the life of the church, which have been brought to life but stil not given a completely specific form, will gradually become evident. This will happen in the case of ministry also.

On the other hand, it is also a sociological fact that in changed times there is a danger that the existing church order will become a fixed ideology, above all by reason of the inertia of an established system which is therefore often concerned for self-preservation. This is true, even sociologically, of any system in society, but perhaps in a special way of the institutional church which, rightly understanding itself as a 'community of God', often wrongly shows a tendency to identify even old and venerable traditions with unchangeable divine ordinances. This is not a judgment on persons, but on the inherent tendencies of a system. Here Vatican II was more careful than people perhaps thought at the time. Whereas at the Council of Trent (see above) there was at least a suggestion that the tripartite division of ministry into episcopate, presbyterate and diaconate went back to divine law, the Second Vatican Council replaced the *ordinatio divina* ('through divine dispensation'), which had already been weakened at Trent, with the still more relativistic formula: 'it was like this from antiquity.'[1]

Here I shall analyse a variety of symptoms from which it is evident that in terms of ministry in the church the present church order at some points does more to hinder than to help the building up of the church in the gospel.

1. Discontent among the bishops: the 1971 Synod of Bishops on the priesthood: the crisis of the apolitical, celibate priesthood

(a) An analysis of speeches in the debate

In the period after the Second Vatican Council, the process started in the Council began to go further, both at the level of exegetical and dogmatic studies and also at the level of the living practice of church communities.

From both sides it has become clear that a more empirical approach to the problem of the ministry and the practice of official ministry has begun to prevail in the church. This has wrongly, but understandably, given the impression that the pneuma-christological character of the ministry is on the way out and that ministry is seen purely as delegation by the community, without further theological implications. Although this sociological 'professionalization' may be the intention here and there, i.e. that the priest should ultimately be seen as a kind of social worker, this is by no means the basic tenor of these new practical and theoretical approaches, whether among theologians or among priests. Although it was largely based on a misunderstanding, or to a small degree on one or two disparaging interpretations of ministry, a reaction began to develop. In turn, others spoke more strongly about ministry in supernaturalist terms than before. A certain polarization became inevitable. It is against this background of two powerful extremes, 'supernaturalism' (and 'fideism') on the one hand, and 'horizontalism' on the other, that we need to see the second 'ordinary synod'[2] of October 1971. This synod did not propose any kind of solution, because it still thought ecclesiologically in a dualistic way and therefore could not provide any meaningful correction on the one hand to supernaturalist conceptions and on the other to conceptions which saw the ministry simply as a profession and which did not express its real religious depth, or passed it over.

Even before the synod, the conferences of bishops could inform Rome about their reactions to the synod working paper which was sent to all the bishops. A résumé of these reactions was sent to members of the synod by the synod secretariat. Here the sense of all the bishops that their priests were caught up in a crisis of identity came clearly to the fore. In addition, on the basis of these written reactions from bishops, Bishop Enrico Bartoletti, Apostolic Administrator of Lucca, gave a panoramic survey of present problems connected with the priesthood, at the beginning of the synod debate. Of course this survey, with both positive and negative aspects, was incomplete, and was not always clear and accurate in its analysis or explanations; generally speaking, however, it gave an adequate background against which the synod could reflect on the pastoral demands of the moment. Nevertheless, factors within the church causing disquiet to priests were played down, and in a somewhat supernaturalistic way the survey pointed out that priests have virtually stopped praying and are one-sidedly involved in social and political affairs. No analysis was made of the so-called loss of a sense of transcendence, so that the survey gave the impresssion that, given a revival of prayer, all could be well again. This unmistakably carried with it the connotation that no alterations to the *status quo* in the church were necessary. It is here that we find the supernaturalism of this attitude. Furthermore, it made the call to prayer lose credibility.

This approach to the problem of the priesthood was expressed in harsher terms in the actual synod working paper, so that its positive aspects were robbed of all credibility by the issues that were not mentioned in it. After the general speeches in the plenary sessions, the bishops were also given topics to discuss in the *circuli minores*, i.e. the twelve discussion groups in which the bishops could take part, depending on the language that they could speak. These topics were determined by the agenda of the synod and the speeches given in the debate. The groups' answers on the topics were to provide the basic material for the definitive version of the synod's view of the priestly ministry.

By way of a survey, I shall sum up the points discussed, from both the doctrinal and the pastoral (the official term was 'practical') parts of the synod working paper. This survey already gives a direct perspective on the actual course of the synod, for which it would finally decide.

The key points in the doctrinal section were questions over which doubts had arisen in the minds of many priests. These were: the specificity or the 'distinctiveness' of the official priesthood as compared with the universal priesthood of believers; a more than purely functional conception of the church's ministry; and the ministry as a representation of the one priesthood of Christ over against the Christian community (there was a clear tendency to focus this contrast on the priest as the official president at the celebration of the eucharist, as happened at the Council of Trent). There was also a concern not to suggest any opposition between purely charismatic churches and churches with an official organization. However, the ministry of the church must nevertheless be seen within the whole context of the one mission of the entire church for ministry: the official ministry is a specific form of this mission. The ministry does not come 'from below', but 'from above', just as salvation itself is given to us from above. In other words, a position is adopted here against those who would claim – and this is the way in which 'from below' is interpreted – that the ministry of the church is 'purely a social ministry of leadership by way of a mandate from the community' (*Relatio* by Cardinal Höffner, 5 October 1971).

Along with Cardinal Höffner's second *Relatio* (from which the key points quoted above have been taken), another list of six key points was sent through the secretariat of the synod. These had been compiled on behalf of the synod by the International Theological Commission.[3] There was also a list with eight key points which had come from the conference of German bishops. By and large these three lists were concerned with the same problems, though the accents were different. Nevertheless, the discussion groups were left free to do as they liked with these 'prefabricated resolutions', since officially the question put to the discussion groups was: 'In your view, what are the key doctrinal questions on which the synod must pronounce in its major proposals?' (*Relatio* of Cardinal Höffner). The individual points here were: some doubt about the priestly character, and priest-

hood 'for a specific period'; doubt about the direct institution of
the presbyterate by Christ; the opposition seen by some between
Trent and Vatican II; and, once more and most emphatically, the
connection and the difference between the priesthood of the
community (the universal priesthood) and the official priesthood.
(Shortly before the synod the International Theological
Commission met again to study these doubts, which were also
evident from the written reactions of the bishops to the agenda
of the synod.)

Although the 'Report of the Priesthood' by the Pastoral Council
of the Netherlands need not necessarily have been in mind, it is
nevertheless clear that all the problems posed there are directly
connected with the key points indicated in the synod and
presented to the synod. It is evident from the speeches at the
debate that the Dutch approach was not just typical of Holland,
but reflects a world-wide view of many bishops, priests and
theologians.

Seven clear questions were presented as points for discussion in
connection with the second, pastoral section, and the discussion
groups had to give answers to them. What is the relationship
between the evangelizing activities of the priest (preaching,
catechetics and building up the community, or the work of
formation, welfare and development, etc.), and his liturgical and
sacramental, i.e. sacral activity? What is the relationship between
the activities of the priest as minister and the secular calling or
'temporary job' which may well be carried on by the priest? What
is the shared responsibility of the priest in the whole of the
pastoral undertaking, given on the one hand priestly participation
in the concerns of the bishop and on the other participation by
the whole of the local church? In connection with the celibacy of
the priesthood: on the one hand there is the matter of the
preservation of the discipline of celibacy in the Latin church; on
the other hand, what is to be said about the desirability of
ordaining as priests those who are already married? What should
be the spiritual life of the priest? What financial provisions need
to be made to arrive at a fairer remuneration for all priests (within
a diocese, a province of the church, or the world church)? What
guidelines can be given for training for the priesthood and for
post-ordination training and continued education? This was the
whole complex of issues on which the synod had to make some
meaningful pronouncement. To whom? To the Pope? Or directly
to the priests? This question was never answered. However, if

one is saying anything, it is vitally important to know to whom one is saying it.

First of all, it should be pointed out that some bishops were unhappy about the division between doctrinal and pastoral sections. The French bishops, in particular, pointed out that this division is disastrous, and that one can only make a pastoral approach to the church's ministry in modern times, in fidelity to the gospel and the apostolic tradition, on the basis of contemporary 'signs of the times', i.e. the specific questions and problems raised by priests, and by reflecting on what they do. Furthermore, this seems to be to be a hermeneutical necessity: one cannot give an *a priori* definition of what a priest needs to be 'in himself'; his relationship to the present is part of the very nature of priesthood. Here the past is necessary, as a warning to remind us that we should not have a blind fixation on the present. Human life is the place where the past defines and opens up the possibilities of the future. The synod did not discover the art of listening to the past as the question which the future puts to us now, in circumstances which are different from the past. On the other hand, without a decision for the present, remembrance of the past remains a repetition of how priests in their time (our past) have been devoted to the gospel: it does not call for an encounter with the needs of the present. Because of our repetition of old traditions, we do not seem to be in a position to produce new ones, as happened as a result of the activity of the past. Without the experiment of historical experience, neither we nor a synod can tell what ought to be the significance of the church's ministry in our own time.

However, the majority of the members of the synod resorted to the 'deductive method': they began from doctrinal positions in the past in their attempt to find a practical solution for today. Of course they were all agreed that in the last resort a synod does not need to do what a Council does; indeed, this is impossible. In fact it was resolved that because of 'the uncertainty of younger men as a result of contemporary theological ideas' (*Relatio* of Cardinal Höffner), the synod needed to establish, with some force, a number of unassailable principles for the priesthood. These were to be expressed in quite short basic statements. Because the task was expressed in this way, there was every chance that the twelve groups would begin their discussions in a conservative or even reactionary atmosphere. For when priests embark on experiments, in the first stages, of course, there is always chaff with the corn. But when there is a tendency towards conservatism, the accent tends to lie on the shadow side of the experiment and not on those insights within it which provide hope for the church. Mgr Ramòn Echarren Isturriz, auxiliary bishop of Madrid, had already seen this clearly when he remarked in a speech during the debate: 'The ways of faith are always and necessarily ways of creativity... We should keep firmly before our eyes the fact that the present crisis in the priesthood cannot be solved only through this theology, which itself partially bears the guilt for the crisis.'[4] This Spaniard said that earlier theology was one of the causes of the crisis of identity among priests. On the other hand, however, Bishop Anthony Padiyara of Kerala was a spokesman for precisely the opposite point of view. 'The present crisis, I am afraid, is in part at least due to the unrestrained activity of those theological writers who come out with dogmatic pronouncements with scant regard for the *magisterium* and the age-long ecclesiastical tradition. In some of their statements one hardly notices a reverence for the sacred or a sense of faith.' The polarization or hardening of the different views which arise within the church was reflected in the synod. Diametrically opposed statements could be heard in the debate. Just a few examples, taken from many, should be enough. On the one hand: there is a clear tendency among our priests to engage in purely social and political questions on the pretext of preaching the gospel (Bishop R.F.Primatesta, Argentina); on the other hand: 'The crisis among priests lies in the fact that they cannot recognize the integration of the human and social liberation movement in the gospel' (Bishop E. Pironio, Argentina). On the one hand: 'Sociology and psychology have taken the place of grace and prayer, and in place of profound purity there comes the pseudo-scientific impurity of psychoanalysis' (Cardinal A.dell'Acqua, in a speech greeted with applause, reading out a passage from a letter written by a teacher in an Italian grammar school); on the other hand, many speeches from bishops criticized the agenda of the synod because it spoke disparagingly about the contribution of the humane sciences in pastoral approaches to the problem of the priesthood. On the one hand: 'Are not we bishops also responsible for the crisis of identity experienced by our priests?' (Bishop A. Lorscheider, Brazil; Cardinal Alfrink); on the other hand, arguments put forward by priests make it impossible to fulfil the role of a bishop (Bishop A. Baroni, Sudan). On the one hand: one individual criticized Pope Paul VI, with a reference to canon 131 par.1 and canon 1072, for wanting to give too many dispensations to priests who wanted to marry (Bishop Y. Ijjas, Hungary), while on the other hand: one person (in passing) criticized the Pope for calling priests who marry 'apostates and faithless' (*inter alia*, the Superior General of the White Fathers, P.T.van Asten), instead of regarding them, with love and righteousness, at least as completely integrated members of the Christian community (the Canadian and French bishops, and a number of others); it was important for everyone to make a personal study of how far these priests could again be involved in some pastoral work on the grounds of their earlier priestly experience (above all the Canadian bishops).

This short survey may be enough to indicate the polarization in the synod. Its consequences for the final proposals of the synod were far-reaching, at least given that the synod, which in accordance with domestic rules offers advice to the Pope, was intrinsically inclined to arrive at as much unanimity as possible. That in fact seemed to be the purpose. An advisory resolution from the synod carries so much moral weight in public that although the Pope can in fact dissociate himself from it, it is not easy for him to do so. A large degree of unanimity of course makes it easier for the Pope to show his approval of the decision of a synod. However, given the existing polarization, the result of this mechanism was that it was only possible to arrive at a degree of unanimity at the cost of failing to make courageous pastoral decisions. As a result, from an institutional point of view the synod was, of course, inconclusive, a lowest common denominator which on one point – *mirabile dictu* – at least in the discussion groups proved even more minimalist than the Pope himself (reluctantly, but with justification) had felt to be possible in principle (in his letter of February 1970 to Cardinal Villot). Thus this synod became more Roman than the Pope.

The synod was unable to achieve its goal, that of reaching unanimity at least in a central, uniform perspective, i.e. of attempting to give a universal, uniform answer to problems which presented themselves in quite different ways in the different local churches. A very different possibility, namely that, given the great local differences and polarization and conflicting opinions, a unanimous decision could have been made to recognize the pastoral competence of local churches, with their conferences of bishops, as being the most urgent pastoral need of our time, was raised only by a minority at the synod.[5] This, regardless of the fact that in the previous, extraordinary synod the way had been opened for the possibility of a pluriform solution and for an adaptation of the principle of subsidiarity to the pastoral sphere. At any rate, this synod said more hopeful things about the local church than had emerged from Vatican II. Furthermore, this pastoral possibility is theologically justified on the basis of the consecration which in principle gives the bishop all necessary authority for the pastoral support of the community which is in fact entrusted to him. The only limitation that can be placed on this authority is the need for collegial solidarity with the welfare of the whole church. (While this idea is correct in itself, it must not lead to the victimization of particular local churches in favour of an abstract 'general well-being'.) The fact that the synod was not brave enough to take account of this possibility may perhaps be described in subsequent history as the 'great refusal' which explains its failure. Perhaps Bishop Damert Bellido (Peru) felt this when in a speech in a debate on the priesthood he said, 'Any attempt at changing an infrastructure (in this case the priesthood) within a greater structure (the church) without changing this greater structure is a utopia':[6] he could have said, putting it more precisely, 'an ideology'. This statement did not attract any attention either in the debate or in the press, but the speaker hit the nail on the head and at the same time condemned in anticipation the dubious outcome of the synod. Thus R.Weakland, Abbas Primus of the Benedictine Confederation, already seemed to be too late with his appeal finally to stop any attempt at *aggiornamento* and instead of adapting the church to the world, now to take 'the lead' as the church and adopt a critical attitude to the world.[7] The synod had already resolved in fact not even to continue Pope John's programme of *aggiornamento*, and as an institution was doomed to pre-conciliar conservatism. Let me make this clearer by highlighting some other points from the synod.

It is significant that some conservatively-minded representatives found even the synod working paper too modern and theologically unsound. They referred to the Council of Trent to demonstrate that this agenda did not adequately express the ontological, sacral character of the priesthood. The consequence of this ontological interest was a call for an exact definition of the 'essential difference' (Vatican II) between the universal priesthood and the official priesthood. This interest became almost an obsession with many bishops, above all when it seemed that other members of the synod thought that a functional distinction was enough to underline the view of Vatican II. The fact that this functional distinction was denied here and there in some critical grass-roots communities, in theory or in practice, made some bishops take refuge, out of fright, in pre-conciliar conceptions. The general result of this was a return to the one-sided approach of the Council of Trent, understandable at that time, which ultimately associates the distinctive character of the official priesthood almost exclusively with the eucharist and the hearing of confession. Thus the wider perspective in which Vatican II had seen the priesthood was completely abandoned.

Despite this narrowing, one cannot miss a complete shift in the problem of the priesthood at the synod, as compared with a revaluation of the priest primarily as one who preaches the word and, as leader, provides a stimulus, or is the pioneer who builds up the community. This contrasts with Trent's exclusive accent on the sacral, i.e. sacramental, cultic activity of the priest. In the synod, on the other hand, the activity of the church (proclamation and the formation and leadership of the community, along with the ministry of the sacraments) is called the sacral activity of the priest, but now in contrast to the social and political involvement of the priest, and also in contrast to his possible secular profession. The context of the synod is of course quite different from that of Vatican II and is a reflection of developments in the exercising of the priesthood, above all in critical and grass-roots communities, and by many individual priests.

In fact this new practice among priests dominated all the debates on the priesthood in the synod, whether or not this was expressly stated. Among some bishops a clear understanding of these new accents can be detected; among the others, in reaction to 'refractory priests, globe-trotting theologians and the communication media' – according to some bishops the three causes of the crisis over the priesthood – a clearly conservative, pre-conciliar tendency can be detected. For many bishops the actual situation of priests today therefore makes the question of the essential difference between priest and laity the key issue at the synod, while the New Testament obviously is little concerned with drawing any clear dividing lines, though it recognizes the particularity of each member's charisma and service. In fact many members of the synod wanted an *a priori* definition, a sharp delimitation, so that they could solve all problems with a convenient rule of thumb: the problem of political involvement, the question of secular professions, the problem of celibacy and so on.

Anyone who makes a careful study of the tone of the speeches in the debates will sense that the same group of problems lurks everywhere: fear of identifying the message of the gospel with social and political, critical and even revolutionary trends towards liberation. There is a fear of connecting Christian identity with human integrity and liberation. In fact to reduce the gospel and the liberation of purely Christian salvation to the problem of changing social and political structures is an unmistakable temptation of our time. However, anxiety-reactions are seldom healthy, and threaten to form an excuse for ignoring the evident need for these changes. It is in fact difficult to divide the two problems of the synod – priesthood and righteousness in the world – in the minds of its members. So if no meaningful pastoral approach could be achieved to either the first or the second group of problems, one could hardly expect a meaningful conclusion to both of them. Bishops who do not want to give up the social *status quo* in their country argue for an apolitical church, and oppose the active politicization of the task of the priest. On the other hand, bishops who oppose personal dictatorships and institutional force, in their own country and elsewhere, point emphatically to the political relevance of the faith. In my view, these are the contrasts which, whether consciously or unconsciously, governed the conflicting views of the priesthood in the synod. The trend towards conservatism, the apolitical trend, was given strong support when, to the surprise of many other representatives, Cardinal Höffner argued that it has not been established that the liberation of man from social and political alienation can be said to be an integral part of Christian salvation. But in plain language, this means either that the church cannot be bothered with the suffering endured by human beings as a result of institutions and structures (that cannot be the concern of a Christian), or that the church has a social, therapeutic function in respect of people who suffer in this way but that precisely because it is Christian it does not need to concern itself further with these structures. Without doubt it is difficult to make a precise definition, or to locate exactly the relationship between salvation or Christian redemption and human liberation. But salvation and redemption which does not take any tangible form in our historical dimension seems to me to be tantamount to supernaturalism and ideology. *Gaudium et Spes* had already said that both a renewal of the mind and a reformation of social structures were demands on Christians (no.26); and many fathers at the Council were so opposed to any division between the process of humanization and the growth of the kingdom of God that a key text in *Gaudium et Spes* was ultimately changed. In so far as this process is an instance of concern for our fellow human beings, an expression of *caritas*, one can never make an adequate distinction between dedication to a better and more righteous earthly future for mankind and dedication to the one thing that is necessary: God's honour shown forth in living man (see no.39).[8] It is clear how the speech by Cardinal Höffner falls below the level already attained by Vatican II and betrays a conservative approach. I could point to more of these pre-conciliar signs in the synod.

They show that even Vatican II has not yet been assimilated. By this kind of speech and others in the same direction, some members of the synod dissociated themselves from those causes with which younger priests in particular identify themselves on the basis of their concern for mankind and their prophetic priestly function. It is hardly possible to imagine a clearer break between the tendencies noticeable in the synod and what can be found in the experience of many priests. An uncertain theology, lagging behind Vatican II, here got the better of a pastoral concern which, while seeing dangers, does not fearfully cut itself off from hopeful possibilities for the future.

This sacrificing of pastoral intentions to 'abstract principles' emerged most clearly in the discussion of the ordination of already married men as priests. From the speeches of those who represented the conferences of bishops it clearly emerged that, of the bishops spread out over the world, half, if not more, regarded the ordination of married men as a pastoral necessity (though their reasons for this might differ). However, when for the first time Cardinal Conway (Ireland) pointed to the danger of escalation – the ordination of married men would make a breach in the Latin law of celibacy and is in fact 'the beginning of the end' of the law – many bishops seemed to be seized with cramp. After this the principle of escalation was brought up dozens of times. Above all when Cardinal Seper suggested that this escalation was in fact envisaged and that for many bishops the 'ordination of married men' was simply a pretext for finding a way to *de facto* facultative celibacy after a generation, many people were not prepared to entertain even this minimal openness. In the name of a whole conference of bishops, some bishops made a passionate plea which in fact was taken as a pastoral *cri de coeur*. They said that they would be caught in a pastoral impasse if they had no possibility of ordaining married 'spontaneous leaders' of a community as priests. However, they fell silent under the threat of the principle of escalation. Furthermore, the fact that about nine members of the synod (in the name of their bishops' conferences) asked in so many words for the separation of ministry and celibacy and thus made a plea for facultative celibacy or for the possibility of two kinds of priests – married and unmarried – was the reason why the initial readiness also to ordain married men as priests by virtue of pastoral necessity, in countries where this seemed to be a pastoral imperative for the church, came to a standstill among some members with their *non possumus*: that cannot be. Cardinal Alfrink had seen through this social psychological mechanism beforehand, and therefore remained modest in his pastoral demands. However, even these modest demands in respect of his own church province sounded impossibly exorbitant. One bishop, who was apparently concerned only with Cardinal Alfrink's contribution, out of all the other speeches, said: 'One father, referring to collegiality, asked that this door should not be closed. For the sake of this same collegiality I ask that it should not be opened.'[9]

It is important to establish that no one in the synod attacked the intrinsic value of celibacy as a charisma. On the contrary. Although two members of the synod had questioned the law of celibacy simply on the grounds of human freedom (Patriarch Merouchi and the representative of the Bishops' Conference of Paraguay defended the most progressive standpoint in the synod),[10] even the so-called pastorally progressive bishops did not go so far. Instead of 'the law of celibacy' they preferred the expression: celibacy as a principle of selection for normal admission to the priesthood.[11] Although in actual practice this does not introduce any external change, a 'principle of selection' is nevertheless less liable to criticism than a law of celibacy associated with the official priesthood. However, given at least this general principle of selection (on the basis of an intrinsic affinity between ministry and celibacy) some people wanted the ordination of married men as well, not so much as a dispensation from this rule or purely because it was pastorally necessary or desirable, but explicitly on grounds of substance, i.e. because of the particular value of the pastoral work of married priests and the fact that particular pastorates ask explicitly for married priests ('student pastorates' were given as an example of this by the Canadian bishops: speeches in the name of the Scandinavian

episcopate by Mgr J.Gran, the Austrian episcopate by Mgr
Johannes Weber, and the episcopate of Zaire [Congo-Kinshasa]
by Cardinal Maloela, the episcopate of the Antilles in a shrewd
speech by Mgr Sam Carter SJ, all pointed in the same direction).
Disregarding their more prudent presentation, this was also the
virtual drift of speeches like those of Cardinal Suenens, Cardinal
Alfrink and Vicar General W. Goossens. By contrast, from the
beginning the German episcopate adopted the standpoint that
the (married) deacons were the appropriate leaders of the smaller
grass-roots communities and that male and female pastoral lay
helpers could provide for pastoral needs, at least in the present
situation. Only when there had been thorough experimentation
in this respect, a revision of the present priestly state and a
transition to a differentiated pastoral ministry of men and women,
could one consider the ordination of married men as presbyters
– and that only if in the last resort all other expedients were of no
avail. This is the thesis which was also accepted by the majority
in the discussion groups.

One cannot deny a certain meaningfulness in all this. However,
it is a meaningfulness within an *a priori* principle which was not
discussed: cost what it might, no breach was to be made in the
traditional discipline of celibacy in the West. Here the 'sign' was
formalistically manipulated as a 'sign' (even when in practice it
no longer functioned as a sign). Mgr Sam Carter of Jamaica rightly
said in the name of the Bishops' Conference of the Antilles that
in the present situation married priests must stand alongside
unmarried priests if in the eyes of the world the celibate priesthood
is in fact to be a real sign. Despite all kinds of theoretical sophistry
(especially the argument that the church does not compel anyone
to become a priest), in the eyes of the world an obligatory coupling
of celibacy with the priesthood is from a psychological perspective
compulsory celibacy, as a result of which it loses its authentic
force as a sign.[12] Bishop J. Gran of Oslo went even further and
said: 'To close this subject allow me to say this: if we have the
choice between having a sign and having priests, then let us have
priests.' A sign which does not in fact function specifically and
psychologically as a sign seems to these bishops to be an ideology:
a suspect sign.

Thus this synod produces a precarious result. It is clear from
the speeches of the bishops who formally represented their
conferences of bishops that, given the particular needs and the
particular cultural patterns of their local churches, the problem of

celibacy cannot be solved uniformly and centrally in a single direction, whereas people wanted the synod to produce a unanimous judgment despite this. All the facts laid on the table point in the direction of a collegiate recognition of one another's needs and particular cultural patterns, and therefore in the direction of a prudential pastoral responsibility on the part of the bishops (in agreement with the Pope) within a homogeneous cultural sphere. There is a particularly apt illustration of this in two social and cultural patterns which take different directions: East Asia, and Ghana in Africa. In the name of the Ghanaian bishops, Mgr P.K.Sarong said that in accordance with the social ideas of his people a (spiritual) leader of a community needed to be married, because among them marriage was the sign of adulthood and potential leadership. This was so obvious that after a round trip another African bishop found that when he said goodbye to those whom he had visited they spontaneously sent greetings to his wife and children. He added, 'Only the catechists smiled. For the others, there was nothing unusual about it' (speech by Mgr J.Ndayen, Central Africa). On the other hand Cardinal Parecattil (Kerala), Mgr P. Nguyen-kim-Dien (South Vietnam) and others testified from the Eastern Asian cultural pattern with its already pre-Christian Buddhist evaluation of celibacy that a spiritual leader, a man of God, who was not *unmarried*, was tantamount to a squared circle. It was clear that a pluralistic solution to the problem of celibacy in the priesthood was a pastoral requirement.

However, the majority of the members of the synod were not convinced by this pastoral evidence. Why? If we analyse the tenor of the speeches that were made in the debates we can distil from them four basic reasons why the synod rejected the ordination of married priests, despite the wishes of a majority of the world's bishops.

1. The principle of escalation, in two senses: first, despite pastoral necessity ('we sympathize deeply with the heartache of some bishops', the Italian discussion group remarked in its report on the discussions that were held), the ordination of married men is nevertheless a breach in the Western discipline of celibacy and a first step towards facultative or freely-chosen celibacy; on the other hand, the concession of the consecration of married men in some provinces of the church would work as an 'oil slick' on other provinces – an 'infection', as some people put it; furthermore it would become a kind of social and psychological pressure on those priests who were still celibate.

2. The principle that at a time of crisis no fundamental changes should be introduced was invoked by many people after Cardinal Cooray of Ceylon had said, 'The hurricane is not the time to renovate the roof.'

3. The leadership of the church would make fools of themselves if five years after they had unanimously and solemnly renewed and reestablished a full obligation to celibacy, they were to go back on this principle at a synod (the same Cardinal Cooray).

4. The principle of the total availability of celibates, which was emphasized in most of the speeches (though the speakers were careful to keep quiet about the 'element of power' which is so bound up with this concept).

There is much truth in all this. And Cardinal Samore could support it with facts about the escalation of the married diaconate. The Dogmatic Constitution *Lumen Gentium* opened up the possibility of married deacons (no.29) on condition that they had been examined and were 'of mature years'. Although in 1971 only twenty-five conferences of bishops had asked for permission to ordain married people as deacons, Cardinal Samore pointed out that requests were being made for the ordination of men who were thirty years of age and even younger. Furthermore, he added, there were already demands for dispensations for the remarriage of a deacon whose wife had died. However, the real question is why there should be such panic fear of escalation. Without doubt it is humbug to praise the free charisma of celibacy verbally if in the last resort no one wants to pledge themselves to an apostolic celibacy. This makes talk about the value of the charisma of celibacy incredible. On the other hand, however, there would seem to be little confidence in what is called the ideal of the unmarried priestly life, if escalation can only be or will only be prevented by a legal prohibition. This absolute, rigid reliance on the law became all the more incredible in the eyes of many representatives because those who insisted on this law did not couple it with the reality of the availability required by the gospel, which involves poverty, the renunciation of power and titles of honour, and giving oneself away for fellow human beings, the features of religious celibacy which Superior General T.van Asten and some discussion groups in the synod after him, rightly noted. What is the sense of celibacy in a church in which members strive for honours, possessions and a comfortable middle-class life? Certainly, the official church may not approve of these things, but they are widely tolerated, and those whose life is marked by such privileges are not obliged to resign from the ministry as a result. 'What witness is given by a celibate priest, consecrated to God, if he has not renounced riches, ambition or honours? Would the care of children and the love of a woman be more dangerous for a priest than the care of riches or the smoke of incense? Why this strange lenience towards ambition, honour or riches... and this strictness over marriage?' (Superior General T.van Asten in his speech). In fact, failure to observe the law of celibacy is the only action which incurs an obligation to resign from the ministry, not the jockeying of priests and bishops for comfortable positions. Why? In other words, why this desperate attempt to hold back an escalation which to some extent - for anyone who retains their common sense – may in fact be a consequence of the ordination of married men as priests? Why not take account also of the positive aspect of some degree of escalation, as Mgr Sam Carter of Jamaica said? In the eyes of the world all priests are under suspicion of secretly 'wanting to marry, but not being able to', and in this way the sign that celibacy in accord with the gospel is a true possibility for living vanishes completely from the world.

An analysis of the speeches as they took place chronologically, one after the other, demonstrates quite clearly that the above-mentioned four themes in fact moved the synod in a conservative direction which did not match up to pastoral demands. Anxiety and rigidity – rather than pastoral concern, indeed even rather than concern for religious celibacy – made the majority of the synod, in contrast to at least half the bishops of the world, close their eyes to pastoral imperatives.

A certain ideology can be seen in all this. First of all, it must be remembered that some of those who in their speeches supported unqualified retention of celibacy for priests conceded that the motives for priestly celibacy presented so far did not carry any conviction, above all with younger men. Even those who believed in maintaining celibacy without qualification, *a priori* above discussion, thus advocating an 'unmotivated' principle of celibacy, beseeched the theologians to think of new and better motives for priestly celibacy. Another member of the synod said without further ado: if we do not impose the charisma of celibacy by law, it will not be put into practice;[13] here we can see the bankruptcy of the ideal which disguises other concerns. This ideological factor also played a part in another sense. When the doctrinal section was being discussed, as has already been said, many bishops were obsessed by the question how to draw an essential distinction between the activities of a priest and the pastoral work that the laity can and may do. Some even protested against the appearance of the laity in the pulpit. Nevertheless, when celibacy was discussed in the pastoral section, the same bishops often – in order to maintain unqualified observance of the law of celibacy, made a passionate plea that pastoral authority should be given to laymen, and suddenly even laywomen, in order to let as many pastoral services be carried out in the context of a shortage of unmarried priests. A cardinal, who (in the doctrinal section) had been concerned to limit preaching only to priests, suddenly said in the practical discussion: 'In the last resort it was the laity, and not the priests, who carried Islam over a great part of the world.' Furthermore, it seemed that the married laity (who would already have a job of their own) suddenly had to have total availability and would in fact have it, when of course this possibility had been ruled out in the case of married priests. All this robs the synod of credibility. And even now I have still not said anything about the rather naive ideas about sex held by some members of the synod. One bishop took no trouble to disguise his ideology. A whole chorus of fathers at the synod began to argue in favour of relaxing the obligation to celibacy and ordaining married men, vying with one another in stressing the intrinsic and existential but not essential relationship between celibacy and priesthood. Whereupon this bishop pleaded with the others in God's name not to insist so fiercely on this relationship. For, he said, 'that may give some people the idea of looking for an affinity between marriage and the priesthood' (Mgr V.Mensah from Dahomey). Another bishop at the synod had meanwhile done that long before (Mgr M.Hermaniuk).

There was even mention of at least objective insincerity, both among some conservative bishops who kept quiet about the real situation in their dioceses, and among bishops open to pastoral needs. Cardinal Conway of Ireland cleverly pointed to this when he said, 'There are bishops who argue for a degree of separation of celibacy from the priesthood, but *non nobis, Domine, non nobis*; that is for other countries where it is necessary.' For some this was in fact an expression of collegial concern for the situation in other provinces; for others at the same time – given the situation as known from elsewhere – it was (in objective terms, at least) an act of insincerity, for fear of cutting a bad figure in front of the whites. That is understandable. Cardinal Seper, who by virtue of his office is well up with the situation in various parts of the world, said with sobering realism: 'I am not at all optimistic that celibacy is in fact being observed', and added, 'still less that marriage is', whereupon the conclusion followed quite logically: 'therefore celibacy must be maintained in full force'.[14]

It is obvious that in an age which is obsessed with sex, people must also be aware of the commercial exploitation of sex and love and of the pressure this brings to bear on candidates for the priesthood. The synod did in fact have a sensible and critical word to say in this connection. But many members of the synod clearly looked on marriage in pre-Vatican II terms: as procreation and sheer sex.[15] They said things about married ministers which were a slap in the face for many married, Reformed pastors. Some gave as a reason for not proceeding with too much haste to the ordination of married men: 'In the West we have no experience with married priests.' First of all, even within the context of the Western Catholic church this statement is incorrect: there is already some experience with married priests (above all Protestant ministers who have been consecrated priest with the Pope's permission). Furthermore, we have had centuries of experience of Protestant ministers.[16] If the concern was really to arrive at a well-thought-out, pastorally responsible decision on this practice, whether positive or negative, in connection with the question of the ordination of married men as priests (as the agenda of the synod envisaged), why were no observers invited from the Reformed churches (as they were to the Second Vatican Council)? Whatever the outcome of the synod, at least it would have been more credible. So we are compelled to say that there was no openness after the discussion because *a priori* – in whatever way - people did not *want* to change anything.[17] This makes a considerable amount of the open talk in the synod unbelievable, though we should not underestimate the consequences of this openness. Before the forum of the world it emerged that it was objectively desirable to have married priests. At least this openness towards the media is to the credit of this synod.

I have discussed the question of celibacy at some length, but this is completely in accord with the actual situation at the synod. Celibacy was in fact a test in which the synod had to choose whether it was uninfluenced by ideology, had pastoral concerns and wanted to illuminate the theological and theoretical implications of pastoral practice, or whether it had a contrary understanding, narrow 'orthodoxy' and a timid attitude which prevented brave pastoral involvement. An African bishop said,

'God's act of creation was also full of risks' (Mgr J.Ndayer); he added somewhat grimly: if we do not have the courage to take risks now, 'Let us give up celebrating the eucharist and baptizing, and tomorrow I will go and plant cabbages.' Later he was to say that he had not travelled thousands of miles to join in the dancing in Rome.

Despite all this, we should not minimize the valuable contributions made by bishops in speeches at this synod. Thus for example the Canadian episcopate, by virtue of its privileged position in being represented by four bishops – in contrast to e.g. Holland and Belgium, whose sole representatives could each make only one speech on one theme – was able collectively to present a coherent view of a *pastorale d'ensemble* by spreading the speeches over four people. In pastoral terms this was far superior to anything that the synod produced by way of documents or mere archives.

Nevertheless, in the question of celibacy the synod debates marked quite clear progress from Vatican II in two ways: officially and psychologically. When there was a concern to reaffirm the law of celibacy at the Second Vatican Council, in the first instance about 400 bishops proposed the insertion, 'at least in the present circumstances of the church'. This amendment was rejected. Now this very same amendment was accepted by the synod, at least in the discussion groups. The first proposition which was accepted by the discussion groups with a two-thirds majority ran as follows: 'On the ordination of married men. Although this solution is theologically possible, it is neither useful nor necessary at the present moment in the Latin church.' The reason why it was not opportune at the present moment was explained in these terms: 'First there must be a redistribution of the clergy; the possibilities of the permanent diaconate must be explored; and finally, thought must be given to a possible division of ministries and their differentiation through lay participation.' Although a small minority wanted to vote against the clause 'at the present moment in the Latin church', in its discussion groups the synod thus in fact simply accepted the continuation of the law of celibacy in full force for the moment. Vatican II did not in fact go as far as this. Escalation, however minimal, has begun officially here. Thus the pastoral concerns expressed in the speeches in fact had some effect.

Furthermore, this was a social and psychological effect. First of all the bishops could speak out freely about the problems of celibacy, and at greater length than the agenda really allowed. Celibacy was not in fact on the agenda, but only the question of the ordination of married men as priests. It was not the Pope, but Cardinal Samore, who criticized the synod for going outside its brief.[18] The Pope, who was present, tacitly allowed the bishops to go beyond the limit that had been prescribed (because in the last result nine conferences of bishops asked in so many words for 'facultative celibacy'). In this way, in terms of social psychology the Rubicon was indeed crossed. Without doubt this is an escalation. The only question is how it is to be evaluated: in trust in the Spirit of God, as a pastoral escalation, or in fear and pessimism at the evil world, as an escalation in the loss of norms and values. Although in our broken situation no motivation is completely pure and is always mixed, in real redemption Christian faith takes in both restricted motives and is therefore bold.

Meanwhile it can be regretted that by concentrating on the problem of the 'ordination of married men to the priesthood', members of the synod lost interest in all the procedural problems which still exist in connection with applications for dispensation from priestly celibacy. Only a few bishops called attention to the excessive and tedious bureaucracy here, and to the needless centralization for the settlement of this question. Almost mournfully and incomprehendingly Mgr F.Cheng-Ping Hsu, Bishop of Hong Kong, gave a long account of this sorry procedure, ending, with Asiatic realism: 'If a man's priesthood no longer makes sense to him, or if he knows that he is unsuitable to continue as a priest and has resolved to resign, what point is there in continuing for a single day longer?' The question of the use of defamatory language in this connection also came up on several occasions. Many priests have no intention of 'resigning their ministry'; they want to marry. If they do that, they are 'deprived' of exercising their ministry. That is the legal position, and to many people that is also psychologically the case. A few really want to resign, but many are actually given dispensations – these are two completely different things. None of this was adequately discussed at the synod.

In its final form, the synod's concept of the priest was expressed in nineteen propositions, of which only fourteen were accepted by the synod with the required majority (two-thirds of the votes). It is clear that both the final text on social and political involvement and that on the ordination of married men as priests did not satisfy either the majority or the minority, and therefore did not get the required majority. Furthermore, the first version of the final text on the ordination of married men as priests was so ambiguous that it was opposed both by the conservatives and by the pastorally more progressive. Against the practice of the Second Vatican Council, the list of amendments in the first instance was not communicated to the members of the synod; this only happened later, after a good deal of protest. I myself was no longer in Rome during the last week of the synod, but this week reminded me of the same situation at the end of the last session of the Second Vatican Council: some people wanted to prevent the formulation of a particular tendency, which at that time was strong. The same clear lack of clarity predominated during the last week of the synod. The responsibility for the ambiguous final text was shifted by one side on to the other. The *relator* responsible for the pastoral section of the concept of the priesthood himself had to say: 'I'm sitting uselessly in the middle.' The disagreement was so great that one bishop, Mgr Santos Ascarza (Chile), is said to have remarked that the one thing needed was a free discussion on facultative celibacy. In fact, tacitly this was the issue for the whole of the synod – whether the law of celibacy should be reaffirmed or 'opened up'. In the end, with Cardinal Munoz Vega as spokesman, the presidency conceded that the proposed final text was ambiguous. For clarification, therefore, the proposed proposition was to be divided into two separate final propositions, which were to be put to the vote:

1. 'It is proposed, subject to the consent of the Holy Father, that the ordination of married men to the priesthood shall not be allowed even in special cases.'

2. 'Only the Holy Father has the right, in special cases, out of pastoral necessity and for the general well-being of the whole church, to allow the priesthood to married men of mature years and a proven way of life.'

The first proposition did not succeed in getting a two-thirds majority (only 107 for, out of 198 present who were entitled to vote); the second was even less successful (87 for, the others against, with two abstentions and two invalid votes). The ambiguity did not seem to be removed in these two propositions. The third proposition which was presented to the discussion groups is also typical: 'Given the shortage of priests in some communities and also for other pastoral and theological reasons, which make this new form of priestly ministry in some ways convenient, it seems opportune to recognize that conferences of bishops, with the approval of the Holy Father, should accede to the ordination of married men.'

Nevertheless, Mgr Lorscheider, a member of the amendments committee, explained the two-part proposition by saying that the expression 'in special cases' in the first proposition needed to be understood as applying to exceptional people (this is remarkable since the Pope had already been doing this for a long time 'in special cases'), whereas the expression 'in special cases' in the second proposition meant cases of local churches, so that the third proposition put to the discussion groups was obliquely implied in the final propositions one and two made by the synod, albeit in a more centralistic direction.

What seems to me to be even more illuminating is the fact that the insertion 'at the present moment in the Latin church', which was included in the first proposition approved in the discussion groups, despite the opposition of a small conservative minority, disappeared completely from the final version. This is clearly the work of the committee which produced the final drafts, against the trend of the synod itself. We might say that in the final version of the statements about the ordination of married men as priests, as a result of the final redaction, on this occasion we are confronted with an 'inbuilt' *nota praevia*: through simple omission. But despite its re-affirmation of the law of celibacy endorsed by Vatican II, in its final resolutions the synod simply expressed officially a malaise over the full enforcement of the Western obligation to celibacy. The result is meagre, but all the more significant for that reason: despite a general declaration of principle, only 54% of the members of the synod did not want any change in the unqualified continuation of this obligation to celibacy.

At the conclusion of the synod, Pope Paul VI said, 'We should give appropriate weight to the conclusions of the bishops when decisions have to be taken for the well-being of the universal church.'

The Synod of the Dutch Bishops in January 1980 simply confirmed the final conclusions of the Synod of Bishops of 1971.

(b) An evaluation of the 1971 Synod

Where it was a matter of the priesthood, the 1971 Synod was in fact obstructed by a burdensome heritage: not by the original doctrine of the Council of Trent on the priestly character, but by the way in which this doctrine in fact began to function after Trent in the church life of the West. As a result of a mistaken interpretation of Tridentine doctrine, the character became the feature which isolated the priest from the church community. The Second Vatican Council was extremely matter-of-fact in its reference to this character. It began from the priestly ministry which the Christian community itself requires (*Lumen Gentium*); it soberly adds: 'the sacerdotal office of priests is conformed by that special sacrament through which priests, by the anointing of the Holy Spirit, are marked with a special character' (*Presbyterorum Ordinis*, no.2). Given the fact that in the time after the Council the functioning of the priest in the community came to occupy a central place in the specific experience of the priest, the post-Tridentine exaggeration of the character was as it were automatically 'displaced' by practice. The synod was a certain reaction against this.

This reaction seemed, however, to be ambiguous, because of the ambiguity of the conceptions surrounding this character. Since Trent, the character had also been made the key concept of the priestly ministry. The character became as it were the 'ideology' of the priesthood.

At the synod, many bishops understood in the light of their pastoral practice that an ideology had grown up around the priestly character. But they also had sufficient Christian feeling to understand, without knowing precisely what this implied, that Trent must have meant something significant. Hence the uncertainty among the 'pastorally progressive'. Other bishops saw the only solution to the present-day problem over the priesthood to be a return to what they understood by the true teaching of Trent. This background obstructed the whole of the synod. Three bishops complained at the synod: Do people have to ask us for a judgment on the precise significance of the character now, and on what the ministry must have been like in the early church?

Seen against the background of the universal tradition of the church in both the East and the West, what is the character of the priesthood but the 'charisma of the ministry' itself, which is called down on a believer who wants to commit himself to the official ministry of the church with the laying on of hands and *epiclesis* to the Holy Spirit in the name of the whole church community? Cardinal Suenens rightly stressed in the synod the pneumatological character of the ministry in the church, as many Eastern patriarchs who (in so far as they have not been Latinized) do not recognize the Western 'character'. And in that case it seems clear that the charisma of ministry is given as a function of a service to the community, a service which in fact requires complete personal dedication from the one who is called through 'the community of God'. Many priests who are dedicated to a believing community and are not burdened with a 'doctrine of the priestly character' thus show that in practice they have a deeper sense of what the traditional faith understands by 'character' than others who, making the most of a kind of *ordinatio absoluta*, defend the 'ontological character' verbally as the heart of the priesthood and do not know what it really comprises. This is where all the blockages arose in the debates in the synod. The priest is in fact 'bound to service' in the church community for his brothers and sisters, i.e. to the Christian community in its mission in the world, not simply through a personal will but through the Christian community and a charismatic gift of God, both of which transcend the priest as person. And once we realize that God and man, Christ and the Christian community – the 'body of the Lord' and the 'temple of the Holy Spirit' – while not identical, are nevertheless not diametrically opposed to each other, we shall not see professionalism and charisma as dilemmas, or, over and above all this, feel obliged to postulate an even deeper mysterious reality which is thought to make the priest a priest. That is to look for the mystery where it is not to be found, and to fail to see how the mystery of God is revealed precisely in the very lowly and profoundly human affairs of the church as a community and of the priest. In other words, in that case we fail to see the depth of the mystery and replace it with an ideology. Furthermore, this ideology is elevated to be the expresssion of orthodox Christianity. In this way polarization among believers is inevitably hardened.

In that case, must we not rather rejoice when young priests more than ever want to stand in solidarity with their fellow human beings in the church and in the world? Is this secularization? Or, despite the risks, is it not an insight into the true understanding of the priesthood, which arises through practice itself? The synod could have given so many priests encouragement, and could even have outlined a picture of the priesthood which younger men could again feel to be a real challenge. By missing this chance it inevitably provoked reactions which take up a good deal of time and energy that as a result are not available for the needs of pastoral work.

The procedure at the synod also made impossible a breakthrough

in Christian pastoral work. Although it is not easy to devise
another method of working, the procedure followed at the synod
makes everything a matter of numbers. There is no discussion.
Arguments are put on the table, but they are never discussed,
nor is their strength tested. An argument which is advanced a
great many times wins through in the end, no matter what its
intrinsic value. An argument of high intrinsic value which is only
presented once immediately gets discounted. The result of all this
is that the editorial committee is given a position of virtual
omnipotence. Although they are bound by the speeches in debate,
they can influence the final version quite fundamentally, above
all depending on whether or not they take account of minority
views. One feature of this synod in comparison with Vatican
II was the almost striking difference in dealing with minority
positions, depending on whether they were conservative or
progressive.

The fact that arguments produced in a discussion are not
analysed or tested as to their value is fatal in a gathering of
two hundred persons. Thus dozens of times an argument was
produced in terms of the 'general welfare of the church'. But
what do we make of the fact that the pastoral needs of different
local churches are sacrificed to this abstract term? Thus in the
long run an accumulation of arguments which have not been
analysed critically gives the impression of a massive witness,
when perhaps not one of them actually holds water. Finally,
leaving aside the arguments, a proposition is put forward which
generally speaking reproduces something of what the quantative
majority has proposed: this quantitative result is then put to the
vote.

While the result of the synod may thus have been negative,
nevertheless the synod itself shows some division between the
members of the synod and the conferences of bishops. At least
half of the bishops spread over the world, if not more (as emerges
from the speeches in the names of the great conferences of
bishops), have a broader outlook and think in more progressive
pastoral terms than the synod, at which their views were
represented by a minority (albeit a strong one). That means that
in at least half of its hierarchy the church wants to take a different
course from that sanctioned by the synod. That is something in
itself. On that basis it is difficult to attribute the new pastoral
tendencies which were given modest expression in the synod
simply to a few hot-headed priests or theologians, as often

happens, without bringing at least half the episcopate of the Roman Catholic church into discredit. This makes one remark by Cardinal Seper very ambiguous, to say the least: 'Let me say clearly, that the pressure which is gradually becoming stronger and which comes only from a limited number of priests, in no way seems to me to be a sign of the times through which God is speaking to his church.'[19]

In addition to the division between the synod and the conferences of bishops there is a second division: that between some conferences of bishops and the priests who stand behind them. This was expressed above all in the remarks made by the conference of bishops in the United States, where the point was explicitly made. After giving a series of figures from which it seemed that a considerable majority of their priests thought in progressive pastoral terms, it was said that 'our conference of bishops does not share this view and had a different view of things'. This division seems to me to be more dangerous.

Nevertheless, anxiety and rigidity are forcing the church in the direction of a doubtful 'holy remnant' with a strongly-developed hierarchical top, whereas the real life of the Christian church flows elsewhere or is removed to the grass roots. In this sense the result of the synod was that the formation of grass-roots communities not only continued but became more intensive. In this way, against its will the synod gave new strength to the new trend which has been manifesting itself throughout the world for several years. The lack of interest in the synod and in problems which arise 'at the top' among many priests is striking in comparison with the first two synods. Many priests are finding their identity again in small Christian communities where they want to give a new form, authentic to the church, to the concept of priesthood, working it out in actual practice and sharing their responsibility with others. They are truly concerned with building up the church. Thus orthodoxy is given its best form in priestly orthopraxy.

2. Discontent among women

At present, discontent in the church is fiercest among women. Moreover, it is no longer just discontent as a result of the negative experiences of women with the institutionalized churches but a very conscious accusation. Above all in North America this discontent is organized into a deliberate 'Women's Church', a

movement which intentionally accuses the patriarchal, masculine
character of the church and its leaders, as indeed of society. This
Women's Church seeks to 'weave' sisterhood between all the
women in the world who are oppressed in one way or another
by society and the church. Concentrated in this feminism is the
awareness of all the situations of injustice which emerge from a
particular social and economic system. It is not so much a matter
of men oppressing women; the problem is structural violence,
which moreover is given an ideological legitimation by philosophy
and theology. Women and slaves, the old Roman Hellenistic
house code had it, are possessions of males, and therefore they
are subject to them and less than them 'in all things'. Against the
basic tendency of the earliest Christian inspiration, Christianity
took over this pagan house code, brought it within the church
and, moreover, gave it theological legitimation (see above, Part
One, Section 2).

I shall quote literally the suppressed complaint of women –
finding expression in the consciousness, in faith, that they too
are *subjects* of faith and being-the-church. This consciousness
emerges in a liturgical prayer written by women and for women
(it is a modest manifesto expressed in prayer):

Spirit of Life, we remember today the women, named and
nameless, who through the ages have used the power and the
gifts which you gave them to change the world.

We refer to these mothers who went before us to help us
discover in ourselves this power, and how to use it in such a
way that we help to advance a kingdom of justice and peace.

We remember Sarah, who with Abraham responded to God's
call to leave the land in which she was born and to put her trust
in a covenant with God.
We pray for her strength in faith.

We remember Esther and Deborah, who saved their people
through acts of personal courage.
We pray for their strength to be bold, to act in the interest of
the greatest good.

We remember Mary Magdalene and the other women who
followed Jesus and were not believed when they proclaimed
the resurrection.

We pray for their strength to believe against the temptation to doubt.

We remember Phoebe, Priscilla and the other feminine leaders of the early church.
We pray for their strength to spread the gospel and inspire communities.

We remember the abbesses of the Middle Ages who kept faith and knowledge alive.
We pray for their strength of leadership.

We remember Teresa of Avila and Catherine of Siena, who strongly opposed the corruption of the church at the time of the Renaissance.
We pray for their power of insight and bravery.

We remember our own mothers and grandmothers, whose lives shaped us.
We pray for the special power with which they try to hand things on to us.

We pray for the women who are victims of violence in their own homes,
that power will be given them to overcome their anxiety and look for solutions.

We pray for the women who stand face to face with a life of poverty and undernourishment,
that power be given them to hold fast and open possibilities for all women.

We pray for our daughters and granddaughters, that power may be given them to seek their own lives.

(Add here any woman whom you want to remember and for whom you want to pray.)

We have stood silently in the power of many women from the past and present. Now it is time to stand by ourselves. In each of us there is the same life, light and love, and within us lie the seeds of power and glory. Our bodies can feel love, our hearts can heal, our spirits can go in search of faith, truth and justice.

Spirit of life, be with us in our quest.
Amen.[20]

The exegete Elizabeth Schüssler Fiorenza puts into words the discontent of women, which has become a deliberate self-definition, in the following way:

> For the first time in Christian history we women no longer seek to express our experience of God's Spirit within the frameworks of an androcentric spirituality but to attempt to articulate that we have found God in our soul in such a way that this experience of her presence can transform and break through the traditional framework of androcentric theology and patriarchal church.'[21]

That this feminism has found expression in a confession of faith primarily in North America is a result of the sufficient economic and institutional independence that women have achieved there. They also have sufficient theological training not 'to be just the object of men's theologizing and to be the initiating subjects of theology and spirituality'.[22] They fight against patriarchalism as a political, social and cultural system of domination which pervades all levels of life to differing degrees and has made women subject and deprived them of a voice.

However, now those without a voice have achieved independence; the silence is broken and evidently for good.

Christian feminism painfully feels the dualism between the liberating hope given by the gospel on the one hand and, on the other hand, the enslaving patriarchal structures of the hierarchical church which keeps us to that gospel. Therefore many feminists no longer argue directly for the admission of women to the ministry.[23] In their eyes this would be the integration of women into patriarchal church structures. They demand their Christian birthright (in the power of the baptism of the Spirit), their right also to be the church *qua* women, fully endowed and responsible subjects of faith, of the expression of faith and of the reflection of faith. This also implies that as a matter of course they too can take a leading position in the church and also in the ministry.

This discontent of women is no longer just a complaint; it has become a sharp accusation. As long as women in the church are completely excluded from all the authorities which make decisions, there can be no question of the true liberation of women in and through the church. Perhaps the criticism expressed by women (more than half of the church community) is at present the most fundamental charge levelled at the churches, and one that they cannot avoid. Such a massive, and now overwhelming, call for liberation which cannot be stifled, from the other half of the whole church, can no longer be held back; in the long run it will change the face of the church, and its structures of ministry as well.

3. Discontent connected with the deployment of married priests away from pastoral work

Since Vatican II, thousands of priests have ceased to be able to exercise their ministry because they have married, while on the other hand in many places there is talk of a shortage of priests and most of these married priests at heart want to continue their priestly apostolate. They can do even less than Christian 'laity'; as far as the church is concerned (and in some countries in social terms as well), they are shunted off into a siding, treated as lepers.

(a) Abstinence and celibacy

The law of celibacy, at first implicit in the Latin church at the First Lateran Council (1123) and then promulgated explicitly in canons 6 and 7 of the Second Lateran Council in 1139, was the conclusion of a long history in which there was simply a law of abstinence, applying to married priests. This earlier history extends from the end of the fourth century until the twelfth century. This history shows that the fundamental matter was a law of abstinence: the law of celibacy has grown out of a law of abstinence promulgated with the intention of making the law of abstinence effective.

In the New Testament period and in the early church there were from the start both married and unmarried ministers. The reasons why some of them remained unmarried might be personal, social or religious. Of course in the biblical post-apostolic period it is constantly stressed that ministers must be 'the husband of one wife' (I Tim.3.2; 3.12; Titus 3.6), i.e. that they must love their wives devotedly. But there is no mention here of the impossibility of remarrying. At that time we often find on epitaphs, 'he was the husband of one wife', i.e. he loved his wife.

However, in the first centuries there was an increase in the number of priests who remained unmarried of their own free will, inspired by the same motives as monks. Only towards the end of the fourth century did there appear in the West completely new, ecclesiastical legislation concerned with married ministers (here bishops, presbyters and deacons). However, we have to wait until the Second Vatican Council before the church mentions Matt.19.11f. in one of its canonical documents (which, to begin with, discuss a temporary law of abstinence and later a permanent law of abstinence and finally the law of celibacy, in connection with the clergy). This passage talks of 'religious celibacy', i.e. 'for the sake of the kingdom of God', without any reference to ritual laws of purity (which were, of course, completely alien to Jesus).

Until a few years ago, this beginning of the law of abstinence was generally put at the beginning of the third century. Both the Council of Elvira (the beginning of the third century) and the Council of Nicaea, along with certain *Canones synodum Romanorum ad Gallos*, played a part here. However, since then historical criticism has definitively shown that canon 33 of the Spanish Council of Elvira, along with other parts of this assembly, has nothing to do with the Council. This canon goes further back to a collection from the end of the fourth century. Furthermore, we also have historical proof that an alleged discussion about the abstinence of priests never took place at the Council of Nicaea: this is a legend which came into being in the middle of the fifth century as a reaction from the East against the law of abstinence which had meanwhile been introduced in the West.[24] Further-more, the collection of the *Canones ad Gallos* is so problematical that for the moment, because of doubts about chronology, we cannot draw any conclusions at all from them.

Thus the origin of the law of abstinence for married priests unmistakably lies in Rome at the end of the fourth century: the only question is whether it happened under Pope Damasus (366-384) or Pope Siricius (384-399).

It appears from these official documents that the dominant reason for the introduction of a law of abstinence is 'ritual purity'. In ancient times the Eastern and Western churches of the first ten centuries never thought of making celibacy a condition of entering the ministry: both married and unmarried men were welcome as ministers. Originally, i.e. from the end of the fourth century on, church law, which was at that time new, contained a *lex continentiae*.[25] This was a liturgical law, forbidding sexual inter-course in the night before communicating at the eucharist. Furthermore, this custom had long been observed. However, when, in contrast to the Eastern churches, from the end of the fourth century the Western churches began to celebrate the eucharist daily, in practice this abstinence became a permanent condition for married priests.[26] A law to this effect became necessary for the first time at the end of the fourth century, and there was canonical legislation accordingly. What we have, then, is not a law of celibacy, but a law of abstinence connected with ritual purity, focussed above all on the eucharist. Despite this obligation to abstinence, married priests were forbidden to send away their wives; not only abstinence but also living together in love with his wife was an obligation for the priest under canon law.[27]

The critical question posed by the New Testament is: how could Christians again allow the force of ancient laws of purity, when Jesus and the New Testament writers revoked the ritual precepts of the Old Testament and declared them void? For it is a fact that all church documents, down to and including the encyclical *Sacra Virginitas* of Pius XII (1954),[28] always refer to the Levitical laws of purity in connection with priestly celibacy (the main passages quoted are: Ex.19.15; I Sam.21.5-7; Lev.15.16f.; 22.4).

We saw above that in the first centuries, as time went on, the ministry was increasingly compared with the Old Testament priesthood, so that the church's vocabulary of ministry became 'sacerdotalized'. However, while the allusion to Old Testament laws of purity could certainly evoke this, it could not make it acceptable to Christians. This acceptance can only be understood in the light of the general cultural climate of antiquity, above all in areas round the Mediterranean. In this Hellenistic area, which was also influenced by Eastern thought, laws of purity for pagan priests were very prominent: 'Anyone who approaches the altar must not have enjoyed the pleasures of Venus the night before',[29] a rule which can later be found in all Catholic liturgical books (though put in a more modest form). We can understand these ancient liturgical laws of abstinence in the light of the Stoic ideal of 'equanimity', which was widespread at that time (in antiquity sexual intercourse was called a 'little epilepsy', above all by the Stoics; it robs people of their senses and therefore is not 'in accord with reason'). Neo-Pythagoreanism and later, above all, Neo-Platonic dualism also played a part: the Neo-Platonist pagan Porphyry wrote a book entitled *On Abstinence*,[30] which enjoyed great popularity at the time. Christians, too, were children of their age, although they were critical of their pagan surroundings. In addition, we should not forget that to begin with there were Christian churches which regarded sexual abstinence as a baptismal obligation, which was therefore binding on all Christians.[31] And although the official church constantly and emphatically defended marriage against such views as being good and holy and a gift by God at creation, pressure from its pagan environment led it to be more reserved towards what was referred to as the 'use of marriage': this was only permissible for the purposes of procreation and even then any pleasure associated with it was regarded as being not quite right.

Thus at the origin of the law of abstinence and later the law of celibacy we find an antiquated anthropology and an ancient view of sexuality. *Omnis coitus immundus* was the way in which Jerome expressed the then universal view of pagans and Christians: 'sexual intercourse is impure'.[32]

Furthermore, when in the twelfth century the ritual law of abstinence was turned into a law of celibacy, this theme continued to remain the chief reason behind the actual law of the celibacy of ministers. The Second Lateran Council, in which this law is officially promulgated, puts the emphasis here: '*so that* the *lex continentiae* and the purity which is well-pleasing to God may extend among clergy, and those who are ordained, we decree...':[33] the law of celibacy is explicitly seen as the drastic means of finally making the law of abstinence effective. It emerges clearly from the Councils between the fifth and the tenth centuries that the law of abstinence was observed only very superficially by married priests. The church authorities were aware of this.[34] After a variety of vain attempts to make it more strict by sanctions and 'economic' penalties they resorted to the most drastic means of all: a prohibition against marriage. Only from that time (1139) does marriage become a bar to the priesthood, so that only the unmarried could become priests.

I said above that in the first ten centuries many Christians were called upon to preside by the community against their inclination. Once complete abstinence was enjoined on priests in the West towards the end of the fourth century, we can see to what degree this extra burden led many priests into deplorable situations: these ancient councils bear abundant witness to this. In many cases at that time there was no question of abstinence freely accepted, certainly not as long as it was law that anyone could be called – and often was called – to preside over a community against his will.[35]

Even after the Second Lateran Council, the law of abstinence, and thus ritual purity, therefore remained the all-decisive and sole motive in the question of the 'obligatory celibacy' of priests. There is all the less mention here of a 'religious celibacy for the sake of the kingdom of God'. 'One does not approach the altar and the consecrated vessels "with soiled hands"': so went the pagan view which had now been taken over by the Christians.

Historically speaking, it can therefore no longer be denied that even the relatively recent law of celibacy is governed by the antiquated and ancient conviction that there is something unclean and slightly sinful about sexual intercourse (even in the context of sacramental marriage). This is not to deny that in the first ten centuries there were many priests who practised celibacy much more 'as monks', viz., for the sake of the kingdom of God (even Thomas makes a sharp distinction between the celibacy of the religious and that of the clergy 'because of considerations of purity').

Again historically, it seems to be of very secondary importance that other motives also played a role in the mediaeval law of celibacy; at all events, they do not seem to have exercised any deomonstrable historical influence. For example, there was the mediaeval confiscation of the goods of 'priests' sons', through which the church fought itself clear of the tutelage of secular powers. In fact celibacy considerably increased the church's resources (and thus the independence of the church over against princes and emperors).[36] However, the ritual law of abstinence is the only decisive and the only determinative element in ecclesiastical legislation. It is therefore historically incorrect, and ideological, to regard the law of celibacy as a means used by the church to acquire power, at least in antiquity and in the Middle Ages. In later times, once the law was established, it began to function in the context of a struggle for power; but this has nothing to do with the reasons why it came into being.

It was only at the Second Vatican Council (at least in the canonical documents), for the first time in the whole of church history, that the traditional motivation for the law of celibacy was seen to have become untenable in modern times. For the first time, too, reference was made to Matt.19.11f., so-called 'religious celibacy' for the sake of the kingdom of God, in connection with the celibacy of the ministry. Furthermore, this Council carefully avoided going over all the old reasons; it deliberately refrained from speaking of *perfecta castitas* (so as not to belittle those who are married), talking rather of *perfecta continentia*, in which context (though only because of strong pressure from Cardinal Bea) there was also praiseworthy commemoration of the non-celibate lifestyle of the priests of the Eastern church (something the Council of Trent explicitly did not want).[37] Beyond question, since the Second Vatican Council the law of celibacy has been put on quite a different basis from that which it had in the earlier history of the church. In fact this presents the problem in a new way, though in this connection one cannot evade the problematical origin of this law. It must, however, be said that to lay open the history of the origin of a phenomenon does not imply anything either for or against its validity or truth. Methodologically speaking, these are two completely different questions. A reconstruction of the history of the origin of a phenomenon can, however, indicate the ideological elements involved in it.

On the other hand, it is impossible to say of a celibacy which has been voluntarily accepted, and experienced as a charisma, what one could justifiably say of the old law of abstinence, namely, that it goes back to an antiquated and mistaken anthropology. Although this raises another set of new problems (which I shall discuss below), it is impossible to dismiss celibacy (provided that there is no disdain for sexual or human relations), on the basis of religious or other noteworthy reasons (sometimes even fortu-itous), with the slogan 'an antiquated anthropology'.

However, this does not solve all the problems. The new motivation for the celibacy of the ministry given by Vatican II also raises new questions. What is the precise meaning of 'religious celibacy', i.e. celibacy for the sake of the kingdom of God? This can have two meanings which, with some theological justification, for the sake of convenience I shall call 'mystical' and 'pastoral' (or apostolic), without being able to distinguish the two aspects adequately. The mystical and apostolic (and also the political) aspects are the two intrinsically connected aspects or dimensions of the one Christian life of faith. It is indeed justifiable and legitimate that someone should remain unmarried in order to be completely free for the service of church work and thus for his fellow human beings, just as others also do not marry (although that does not in fact imply 'celibacy') in order to devote themselves wholly to science, to art, to the struggle for a juster world, and so on. Sometimes it amounts to an existential feeling that no other course is possible. In other words, not to marry is seldom, if ever, the object of a person's real choice. The real object of the choice is 'something else', and this something else preoccupies some people to such an extent that they leave marriage on one side. Not marrying is usually not a choice in and of itself, but one 'for the sake of...': in religious terms, for the sake of the kingdom of

God. As a result, we may not consider the negative and exclusive aspect of this choice, which is really for some other reason, in isolation and on its own. Of course in the life of any culture it so happens that a particular existential 'I cannot do otherwise' in the long run becomes ritualized. Thus, for example, the fact of 'not being able to eat' because of a death, or because, in a religious context, one is looking forward excitedly to the feast of the Passover, developed into a ritual: penitential fasting, or fasting for forty days. People then fast even though they may perhaps have a great longing to eat. We must not underestimate the ritualizing of life, though in every culture in the long run there is the threat of a formalized evacuation of the content of this ritualization. It becomes narrow and rigid, when it was originally meant to serve, or at least to evoke, an existential experience.

Thus although the theme of celibacy has become a pastoral and religious one, we must also be able to test the truth of the affirmation by the facts. Historically, it can be seen from the history of married leaders throughout the churches of the Reformation that in most cases the marriage of ministers has in no way hindered their utter dedication to the community; on the contrary, in many cases it has furthered this (in so far as we are able to judge on this question from a statistical investigation). One or the other depends purely on the person in question and cannot be established *a priori* in the abstract. The danger – and the facts – of egotism, unavailability and even boorishness on the part of celibates is not unknown, least of all among celibates themselves. Therefore the pastoral theme, even in its political dimension of the struggle for those who have been deprived of their rights, cannot become the decisive motive and argument for a universal law of celibacy. There remains, then, the 'mystical element' in celibacy for the sake of the kingdom of God, the service of mankind in the cause of the gospel, which can scarcely be distinguished from the 'pastoral element'.

Here the Second Vatican Council also introduced some important qualifications. Earlier, it was generally accepted that there was a kind of competition between love of God and married love, for reasons already given by Paul, namely, the need 'to please one's wife', which would detract from undivided love of God (I Cor.7.32-34). This alleged competition, too, can no longer be justified theologically. For this reason Vatican II explicitly rejected a prepared text which said that 'undivided love' and 'dedication to God alone' must be seen as the real characteristics of religious celibacy. This competitive opposition between love of God and love of a fellow human being (including sexual love) was deliberately rejected. The definitive text runs: 'That precious gift of divine grace which the Father gives to some men... so that by virginity, or celibacy, they can more easily devote their entire selves to God alone with undivided heart' (*Lumen Gentium*, no. 42). It was thus conceded that total and undivided dedication to God is the calling of all Christians; according to this text from the Council, celibacy simply makes it to some degree 'easier' to realize this spirituality, which is in fact enjoined upon all Christians. If we purify the law of celibacy from all antiquated and incorrect motivation, which is what this Council wants to do, some basis in fact does remain, but it is a very narrow one, viz., an abstract and theoretical 'greater ease'. I call this 'abstract and theoretical': that is because in practice it can be easier for one person to arrive at a greater and more real and undivided love of God in marriage, whereas for someone else this only happens through an unmarried life.

This, then, is the way in which the Tridentine view that unmarried life for the sake of the kingdom of God is a 'higher state' than the 'married state' has generally been interpreted in the theology of the last twenty years. The alleged superiority is dependent on the person in question, and cannot be established generally in purely abstract terms. What is better for one is less good and perhaps even oppressive for another, and vice versa. (In this connection a choice should be possible between 'a provisional celibacy in the service of the kingdom of God' and a celibacy intended to be 'perpetual', especially as in the course of a lifetime someone may arrive at the discovery that a perpetual celibacy undertaken as a convenience has in fact become a deep-rooted hindrance. However, we cannot discuss these problems here.)

If all of this is correct, a universal law of celibacy for all ministers would at least be a serious exaggeration, on the basis of an abstraction, and therefore without concrete pastoral dimensions. At all events, one cannot interpret 'the new law', by which I mean the new motivation which Vatican II has given to the old law of celibacy, as a principle of selection, in the sense that the church chooses its ministers exclusively from Christians who voluntarily embrace celibacy. Given the earlier history of the existing law and official custom of speaking of a law of celibacy,[38] despite new motivation, the canonical legislation persists in seeing the celibacy of the ministry as a kind of *statutory obligation* on the basis of an abstract and theoretical superiority of celibacy. Despite many affinities between ministry and celibacy, however, there are also unmistakable affinities between marriage and ministry, and the New Testament texts about 'the husband of one wife' point precisely in this direction.

However, many who argue for the detachment of priesthood from the ideal of celibacy do so primarily on the basis of an appeal to human rights. But anyone can in fact renounce his or her own rights (though not those of others)! Thus the question is whether here and there a liberal bourgeois conception of freedom does not sometimes take the place of gospel freedom. If – and this is clearly not the case, though since the Second Vatican Council it has increasingly become the practice from Rome – if voluntary celibacy is thus boosted as a principle of selection for the church's ministry, then in principle it is difficult to put forward decisive arguments against the 'celibacy of the ministry'. Any community has the right to impose principles of selection in the choice of its officials – in the case of the church, in the choice of its ministers. The New Testament also demonstrates this clearly (in the Pastoral Epistles). However, it must be conceded that this can often be the beginning of 'discrimination', though that need not necessarily be the case. Thus to my mind the only decisive argument for continuing to fight for the separation of ministry and celibacy (in other words, the only decisive argument against a law of celibacy) is twofold. On the one hand there is the credibility of the charisma of celibacy, freely chosen, in the eyes of the world and the person's own church (now, celibate priests are constantly under the suspicion of 'wanting to marry, but not being allowed to', as the common saying goes); on the other hand there is an argument from the theology of the church, viz., the right by grace for Christian communities to have presidents and to celebrate the eucharist. As a result of the present coupling of celibacy and ministry, at least in the Western church, in many places the apostolic vitality of the community and the celebration of the eucharist are endangered. In such a situation, church legislation, which can in any case be changed, must give way to the more urgent right to the apostolic and eucharistic building up the community. (Finally, it is obvious that the pastoral authorities in the church must also, and above all, make a decision here.) However, one would be naive to think that the so-called 'crisis situation' among priests will be of short duration, or is even over. That is to underestimate the force of the old spirituality which made many young men accept celibacy because they had in fact thought that marriage was indeed something of less value. This idealism, mistaken though it was, led many people in fact freely to accept the celibacy of the ministry. If marriage is given its full value (and it should be remembered that for Catholics, it is a sacrament), the vocations to a religious celibate life will of course decrease. One could say: earlier, people in fact chose not to marry because marriage was a lesser, indeed almost a mistaken 'good'. In that case celibacy can directly be an object of choice. Nowadays a direct choice of celibacy (apart from the real choice of some other good which proves utterly demanding) is in fact ambivalent. Often it is even suspect.

At this point I should also indicate the 'ideological element' that can be present in an appeal to 'prayer for vocation'. No Christian would deny the value and the force of prayer, even for vocations; but if the reason for the shortage of priests is 'church legislation' which can be changed and modified in the course of time for pastoral reasons, then a call to prayer can act as an excuse; in other words, it can be a reason for not changing this law.

(b) The so-called 'third way'

Finally, even after everything that the Second Vatican Council has said on the subject, the precise content of the official church view of celibacy as such still remains obscure and vague. This emerges from a new set of questions which (at least in their modern form and the practice to which they give rise) only arose after this council. Here I am referring to the problem of the so-called 'third way', at least understood as 'shared celibacy' (and including abstinence). From the whole of the earlier legislation of the church it is clear that the church has never pronounced against the love of a priest (although not married) for someone else (in fact a woman is meant). The church has always condemned exclusively genital sexuality, and what leads to that. This is evident even from the Second Lateran Council, in which the law of celibacy was formulated for the first time: the legal prohibition of marriage was only intended to safeguard observation of the law of abstinence more effectively.

With the Second Vatican Council, which wanted to exclude any disparagement of sexuality, the situation is to some extent different, although a certain ambiguity remains. The basic reason for religious celibacy is now in fact the 'greater ease' for universal, Christian undivided love of God, though this greater ease is given specific form as 'specific abstinence'. In other words, in essence, down to Vatican II the law of celibacy essentially remains a law of abstinence. Here a connection is established between complete abstinence and an easier undivided love of God, but not with presence or absence of love of a woman, which does not arise. The over-riding concern is the exclusion of sexuality, and not love. And in that case the urgent question arises whether the motivation of this Council is anthropologically so essentially different from the earlier motivation. Here we come to the real heart of the problem of celibacy in a modern context, a problem on which ecclesiastical legislation has still never pronounced – except in the Synod of Dutch Bishops at Rome in January 1980. (Here it remains uncertain precisely what the synod understood by 'the third way': what does one mean by a middle way 'between marriage and celibacy'?) If we interpret this Synod along the lines of 'shared celibacy' (with a view to complete abstinence), then for the first time in the history of the church, or at least in the church's legislation, we have a pronouncement which is completely new, viz., that it is of the nature of celibacy to exclude not only sexuality but also 'the love of a woman'. It would certainly be extreme for one 'particular synod' to make a decision on the nature of the charisma of celibacy which differed radically from anything that had happened before in church history! It is at all events impossible to appeal to Vatican II in connection with the Synod's decision (interpreted in the sense mentioned above).

The problem itself is by no means new in the literature of Christian spirituality. On the contrary. But it is completely new in the canonical legislation of the Catholic church (which is what I am concerned with now). Here the real problems connected with 'celibacy as such' are formulated in the most profound way... and left unanswered. At all events, what does the mystical and pastoral element of religious celibacy involve? What is at stake is the anthropologically inner relationship between sexuality and love. And precisely this anthropological question is left unanswered throughout the legislation of the church. This confronts us with a new dilemma. Either we are dealing purely with a law of abstinence, in which case the question is: does 'physical abstinence' as such, of itself, ever have a religious value? That is hard to affirm if we do not want to fall back into the old attitude which is opposed to sexuality. Or it is a matter of a degree of competition between love for God and love for a fellow human being – let me limit it here to love of a woman. And this, too, is

theologically unjustifiable. However, it is impossible, anthropologically, to separate the two problems unless one wants to
dehumanize sexuality and make it a purely physical
phenomenon.

Thus the subject under discussion is either a competing love or
a physical act. The one is theologically unjustifiable and the other
is anthropologically unjustifiable. It is obvious that here we need
renewed study of, and reflection on, human sexuality if we are
to acquire a clearer understanding of the nature of 'religious
celibacy'.

Within this short space, at any rate, I want merely to point to a
first attempt in this direction made above all by J. Pohier, who on
the one hand is opposed to the anti-sexual views of antiquated
anthropology and on the other has made a psychological analysis
of the 'ambiguity' of sexuality.[39] Sexuality is indeed a two-edged
sword which can also evoke dark powers. Over-sexualized society
and the misuse of sexuality in our culture are the clearest indication
of this. Sex has become a consumer article and a means to power.
Precisely here religious celibacy can in fact function as an acute
criticism of humanity and society, to the benefit of truly human
sexuality and to the advantage of mankind itself. As abstinence,
it is a religious protest both against 'liberalism' and against all
forms of subjugation and 'objectification'. A certain trend in
feminism bears witness to this. However, such abstinence does
not tell against sexuality as such in any way whatsoever; still less
does it tell against human love, which never competes with love
of God.

However, it cannot be demonstrated *a priori* whether, anthropologically speaking, despite human weakness, such deeper love
represented by a 'celibate protest' can, through complete abstinence, finally be turned into a realistic and truly human possibility. Experiments which at the moment are being carried on all
over the world will eventually give us better information about
this. Here naivety is not the best teacher, far less anxiety and
strictness! Nevertheless, in my view the debate about celibacy is
not closed; it has barely been opened. And that is where I will
leave the question for the moment.

(c) Married religious in the Middle Ages and modern experiments

Although this problem really lies outside the scope of this book,
which is concerned with ministry and not with the religious life,

the theme is really relevant in so far as many religious are also priests.

In the Roman Catholic Church the religious life (= monastic life) has always been regarded as irreconcilable with married life. Without celibacy, religious life (in the sense in which the church speaks of it as a state of perfection) would be impossible. Of course a married person can in fact be very religious, even holier than the religious, but in this case the person is not living in a state of perfection. There is a widespread discussion going on about this which falls outside the scope of this book. I simply want to point to a very remarkable statement by the church's *magisterium*, although this clearly departs from the traditional views which are held in the church.

Pope Alexander III, living at the time of the twelfth-century Renaissance with its warm humanity, had a high human estimation of marriage and sexuality. It was he who in 1175 declared that the old law which prohibited marriage relations at fast times must be regarded as advice and not as church law. However, what interests us here is his official approval of the order of chivalry of St James.[40] The traditional link between celibacy and religious life had already become somewhat problematical as a result of the religious life-style of e.g. married Humiliates. This was expressed in a quite revolutionary statement by Alexander III, who on the occasion of a discussion on the canonical status of the order of St James explicitly affirmed that the church's 'state of perfection' is not *per se* bound up with celibacy. The married knights could canonically regard themselves as true religious, on the basis of their promise of obedience to their superiors in the Order and their life in chivalrous sacrifice. Thus the traditional focal point was shifted to fidelity to the order (in the form of a feudal oath) and *paenitentia*, the term with which people in the twelfth century denoted repentance in the gospel (*metanoia*). The shift in the three promises of poverty, obedience and purity (in the sense of unmarried, continent life) which had taken place not long before is clear in the canonically approved Rule of this religious order: *paupertas, obedientia et castitas coniugalis*. Precisely because of this sensitive change the Roman Curia took three years to approve this Rule. *Castitas coniugalis* certainly did not mean continence. In this Rule (canon 12, op.cit.99) it is said that these religious were to refrain from intercourse only at fast times and on certain high days. Moreover, provisions were made for the children of the professed brothers. The introduction to the Rule says, with a reference to Paul, 'It is better to marry than to burn.' With the approval of the master of the Order, there was even a provision for the possibility of remarriage after the death of the wife (the language in fact remains androcentric: it was aimed above all at male knights). The pope also made this Order of chivalry exempt (or independent of the bishops). Of course there were also some unmarried priests in this Order, who looked after the spiritual life of these *freyles* or religious brothers.[41] The fact that there was long hesitation before this Rule was approved indicates that this was no superficial, light decision. The spirit of the time also made the decision possible. However, there is still less historical reason to blunt the point of this statement by acute theological distinctions, even if with it the pope did secure the military support of this religious Order for himself. For if only church politics was at stake, canon lawyers could well have approved this Order through the pope under quite a different title, as a corps or canonical group.

In earlier times, when society was 'Christian', the life of the religious had special symbolic value in respect of the life of Christians according to the gospel in the world. In a modern, secularized world, however, being a Christian is no longer a matter of course. In our world, the ordinary Christian life in the face of a non-Christian pluralistic society has largely taken over the role of being a token of religious presence, according to the gospel, in the world. This situation inevitably has consequences for the life of religious. We can also see the rise of all kinds of new forms of religious life.[42] One can say that this believing is deliberately dissociated from the model that was dominant in a Christian society. Nor is there a search for a canonically recognized state of perfection: people want to live an ordinary life in accordance with the gospel, with no distinction between married or unmarried, men or women. These believers form communities where there is a place for married people and also for those who deliberately choose the unmarried life. Here the preference is for small-scale structures, in which in addition to a degree of privacy for individuals and families, all the attention is focussed on the life of the community. Ecumenism here is almost a matter of course. One can find both Catholic and Protestant Christians in one and the same religious community. The central feature is ordinary Christian life in accordance with the gospel, a pattern of life which people hope may be a witness to others – attractive and credible.

We also see religious who belong to a traditional religious institution joining these new communities. Thus here a bridge is being built between old religious institutions and new religious inspiration. The link between all members, brothers and sisters, is nevertheless dominant, for all the recognition of difference in fucnctions and ministries in the church. There is a concern to break through the old model of 'states'. The married in the group feel themselves to be no less religious than the unmarried. Here gospel and humanity are not a duality, but all work in a growing Christian humanity which nevertheless always remains incomplete.

Whether the bond to the group is a lifelong commitment is not settled once and for all; it remains a horizon towards which everyone, according to his or her own inspiration and career, can grow, and in so doing may expect help from all.

Both the mediaeval canonical approval of the knights of St James as a full religious Order and the modern experiments with new forms of religious life, to which the married also feel themselves to be called, again cast their shadow on the canonically compulsory coupling of ministry and celibacy in the Catholic, Western or Latin church.

5. Discontent expressing itself in alternative practices of ministry

Apart from the categories of believers mentioned above who have expressed discontent in one way or another with the theology and practice of ministry, today we can note all kinds of forms of ministry which depart from the existing church order. It emerges most clearly from these alternative forms which are put into practice to an increasing degree, almost all over the world, that there is a gulf between dominant conceptions of ministry and the pastoral needs of men and women in Christian communities of believers.

Thus against the background of the existing church order, new and perhaps urgently necessary alternative possibilities can usually be seen only through the medium of what must provisionally be called 'illegality'. This is not a new phenomenon in the church; things have always been that way. Furthermore, the old mediaeval scholasticism, which was still very free (in contrast to later scholasticism, which ignored this fact), sometimes elevated this provisional illegality to the status of a theological principle, especially in its theory of the *non-acceptio legis*, the rejection of the law-from-above by opposition from the grass roots. Whatever the value of the law may be, in particular instances it is rejected by a great majority and in fact is irrelevant. It emerges from this that in the history of the church there is also a way in which Christians can develop a practice in the church from below, from the grass roots, which for a time can compete with the official practice recognized by the church, but which in its Christian alternative form can eventually nevertheless become the dominant practice of the church, and finally be sanctioned by the official church (whereupon the whole process can begin all over again, since time never stands still!). That is how things have always been!

What each of us hears about practices in the ministry which diverge from the official church order therefore: 1. has a diagnostic and dynamic effect, and serves to criticize ideology: and 2. itself has a normative power. This latter is not, of course, on the basis of sheer facticity, but as a Christian reflection on the facts, in which on the one hand there is an anticipation of future developments and on the other the expression of a Christian apostolic conviction, authentically in line with the gospel, which has to be tested by the whole history of Christian experience.

The normative force of facts as such – 'hard facts', as the sociologists say – reigns supreme in our secular, bourgeois society. But none of us would claim that facts or statistics in themselves have any normative authority. Such a position would in fact be a blunder, because it would also and even *a fortiori* have to attribute even more massive authority to the even greater factual dimension of the church order which exists at present. But just as the official church order must be justified in the face of the ups and downs of the historical experiences of Christians, and in our time in the face of the negative way in which Christians experience this church order, so too must the critical, new alternative forms of practice in the church and in the ministry also be justified over against our historical experiences and over against the great Catholic Christian tradition. An alternative, or the new for its own sake, is nothing. A particular practice of the Christian community, whether old or new, always has authority only in so

far as it is indwelt by the Christian 'Logos', that is, by what I have
called the apostolicity of the Christian community.

Historically, accounts of new, alternative practices in Christianity and the church are always connected with reminiscences
and experiences of what is faulty and sometimes even absurd in
the existing system: with the obstructions which are in fact there.
In assessing the authority of an alternative practice it is certainly
possible to begin from present-day experiences of the situation:
from demands made in the name of humanity, human rights and
so on. This is a legitimate and even obvious way. However,
because of the experiences I have been through, and in view of
the toughness of any system, I have preferred to adopt another
way which also seems to me to be a more strategic one, namely
to choose as my starting point what has been accepted and
defended by both sides of the church with a view to building up
the Christian community: both by representatives of the official
church order, which is still in force, and by the protagonists of
the critical, alternative practice. To put it briefly, this is the right
of the Christian community by itself to do everything necessary
to be a true community of Jesus and to be able to develop itself
intensively, albeit in connection with and in the light of mutual
criticism from all other Christian communities. This situation can,
of course, lead to restrictions from above or from below (Vatican
II). To make the same point in a more limited way: this is the right
of the community to the eucharist as the heart of the community
(Vatican II). Alternatively, it is the apostolic right of the community
to have leaders: i.e., a leader (male or female) or a 'significant
other figure', who on the basis of the fundamental values of
the group, clarifies, dynamizes and also is able to criticize the
community, and in so doing can also be subject to the criticism of
the community. Fundamentally, the official church also accepts
these New Testament affirmations, but at the same time in this
respect it begins from decisions which have already been made
at a prior stage of history (e.g. on criteria for admission to the
ministry). However, when circumstances change in the church
and the world, these can in fact obstruct this original right, by the
grace of the gospel, which belongs to the community. Thus, for
example, the present shortage of priests (which itself can partly
already be explained in terms of pre-existing historical conditions)
leads to all kinds of substitute forms of church ministries. Alongside an authentic multiplicity of ministries which have become
necessary because of the present-day situation of the community,

i.e. the more differentiated ministry in the church, there is also an inauthentic multiplicity – simply because specific consecration or appointment as a minister has in fact been withheld.

This approach serves to show more clearly the dilemma in which the so-called modern view of the priest now finds itself. On these grounds it will be clear to everyone that in modern conditions, for example the actual celebration of the eucharist has come up against fundamental difficulties; it is sometimes trivialized and often completely blocked. A whole series of accounts of negative experiences which have been brought about by the actual functioning of the 'service' priest within a sacral vision of the ministry shows that at the moment this view of the priesthood often makes the community and the eucharist look utterly ridiculous in the context of Christianity and the church. And this happens when there is an abundance of pastoral workers available, in some cases believers who sometimes have already spent many years in full-time work for the community. These negative experiences make it quite clear that the actual order of the church now threatens to become prematurely fixed as an ideology and itself hinders the original purpose of the church. And the reason for this problem over the sacraments is the absence of a male, celibate priest – both non-theological concepts. Many Christians can simply no longer take this. Consequently such negative experiences are an occasion for particular Christians and their ministers for the moment to take it into their own hands to begin an alternative practice for the sake of the salvation of the community. This is not a normal circumstance in the life of the churches.

Conclusion

All these complaints, and the alternative practices which have come into being as a result of negative experiences with the ministry, have in fact a diagnostic significance. They serve to diagnose symptoms of sickness in the existing system, and in addition function as a criticism of the ideology which is bound up with traditional practices. For many Christians it has become clear meanwhile that the alternative practice is a clear expression of the New Testament datum of the priority of the community over the ministry (and *a fortiori* over criteria for admission to the ministry which are not necessary in themselves). Furthermore, it is a sociological fact that existing ordinances in a particular society, even when that society is the church, remain intact as long as they carry intrinsic conviction, i.e. as long as no one doubts their (Christian) 'logos' or 'reason'. In itself, the fact that at a particular moment a wave of alternative practices is sweeping over the church throughout the world indicates that the existing church order has lost a structure of credibility and at some points is in urgent need of being revised. For many believers it no longer carries any conviction, so that spontaneously, and on all sides, we find the social and psychological mechanism of the *non-acceptatio legis*. This is what we now in fact see happening on a large scale. If despite this the church wants to maintain its existing church order, then from this point it can do so only in an authoritarian fashion (because it carries no conviction with a great many 'subjects'). This course would simply make the situation more precarious, because in turn the authoritarian way of exercising authority conflicts with the basic themes of the way in which life is experienced today, and is also experienced by Christians.

Finally, all these laments and this alternative practice also have a dynamizing effect. At any rate, particular Christians are gradually recognizing the new structure of credibility; further-more, as time goes on, they come to identify with it more and more. It is not the bare fact of these complaints and an alternative way of exercising ministry which has dynamic force, but the way in which, by virtue of the 'Christian reason' which can be found in them, Christians almost infallibly recognize a modern form of 'apostolicity' here. It is precisely because a new practice of this kind among Christians carries conviction that in the long run it acquires authority among them, and the power to attract. Nevertheless, we cannot claim that this experienced conviction, which now already inspires and determines the lives of many communities and ministers even before it has been recognized openly by the official church, does not possess an inherent Christian apostolicity, and can only acquire this when it is sanc-tioned by the church at a later stage. On the contrary, it is recognized later when, and in so far as, it already has in fact an innate Christian 'Logos' or apostolicity: when it in fact provides the possibility for a meaningful Christian life today in the light of the gospel.

Part Five

The Church with a Human Face

1. Roman Catholic problems with ministry, the Declaration of the Congregation for the Doctrine of Faith, and the ecumenical Lima Report

1. In this book I have deliberately been occupied with problems connected with ministry within the Roman Catholic church. The very impasse in which many people find themselves there in connection with the conception and practice of ministry also has ecumenical significance. Positive and negative experiences with ministry within a particular confessional tradition of faith at all events call for a confrontation with experiences of ministry from other traditions in the church in which distinctive stresses are also placed and in which another church order is predominant. These traditions also have their own origins, which I shall not analyse here. My starting point here will be the Lima Report, in which theologians from many traditions have arrived at an ecumenical working paper that they have presented for the judgment of the official churches.[1] Because this report is meant as a starting point and basis for a possible consensus within the church, no single Christian church will fully recognize its own perhaps legitimate accents in it. On the other hand it is not the greatest common denominator either, acceptable as it stands by all the churches without their coming a step nearer to one another.

The document begins from the early church, up to the Second Council of Nicaea (787), when it was not yet divided by the Eastern and the Western schisms. Thus the document begins from a tradition of faith which is common to all communities of Christian believers. This is anything but an abstraction, which of course would be ecumenically unproductive. It is the old, living tradition of faith of the *Catholica*, which did not yet need to add *Romana* in order to distinguish it from the *Catholica* as this is present in other churches. Here there is indeed a reference to at least one criterion which is valid for all Christian churches.

The present accents of a distinctive view of ministry and church are also measured by this old common tradition. This is doubtless one pole of a more comprehensive criterion (see below).

As it stands, the Lima Report is *a* (not the) legitimate and ecclesially responsible starting point for a conversation among the churches with a view to an official consensus.

As far as ministry is concerned – a problem which cannot be considered apart from a view of baptism and the eucharist, this report draws a distinction between the universal priesthood of all believers and the special or ministerial priesthood that from ancient times has undergone a tripartite division into oversight (*episkope*), presbyterate and diaconate, though this is not prescribed by the New Testament. This tripartite division is seen as the historical result of a development from the first century. In the report, *episkope* (oversight and care) is seen as a centre of unity which both church and ministry need. However, the report leaves open the question how this tripartite division is implemented historically in the various churches, as it also leaves open the question to what extent the Calvinist division into elder, preacher and deacon is a legitimate specialization of the old tripartite ministry. Churches which do not know the threefold ministry in any respect are asked to accept it. The episcopal churches are called to accept the apostolic content or the apostolicity of the ministry in non-episcopal churches and also the multiplicity of figures in which the ministry of *episkope* takes form in non-episcopal churches. On the other hand, non-episcopal churches are asked to accept the episcopal succession (which the Roman Catholic church above all calls the 'apostolic succession'), at least in the sense that this succession is seen as a sign (not a guarantee) of continuity in the apostolic tradition and that this sign can also strengthen and deepen this continuity.

The report does not describe *ordinatio* or 'installation' as an exclusive action by a particular group in the church but as an action of the whole community of believers. I myself wrote in *Ministry*: 'Here the validity of consecration is bound up not so much with one isolated sacramental action of the church, i.e. the liturgical laying on of hands seen in itself, as with the action of an apostolic church community as a whole' (p.71). Roman Catholics can best recognize themselves in the Lima text at this point, even if not all the accents are recognizable there.

Finally the report gives a recommendation, namely that the churches should appoint a bishop at a more than local level. In many churches of the Reformation the 'preacher' presides at the Supper in which word and sacrament go together, although the greater emphasis is usually on the word. Oversight or *episkope* in the church is exercised there by the church council (to which the preacher belongs). Oversight is on the one hand essential and necessary for the church, but on the other hand it is not tied to one person, but to a group, in the last resort to a gathering in the form of a *classis* or synod. In episcopal churches, like the Roman Catholic Church, the Orthodox Church, Anglicanism and Lutheranism, this oversight is bound up rather with the person of the bishop, though (also according to Vatican II) bishops must act collegially. In the recommendation of this report there is a great, albeit not insurpassable difficulty, above all for the Calvinist churches. Historically this tradition has been very hesitant about leadership by one person. Nor must we forget that episcopal leadership by one person (albeit at that time incorporated in a presbyteral council) followed a civil trend in the early church. Thus in the sixteenth century too, the Calvinist conception of the ministry came into being in a very particular social and historical context, viz., that of the rise of the middle class, with the greater involvement there of all citizens. Thus a bit of democratization became part of the Calvinist conception of the ministry. The unity of the church was not realized there by the ministry of one person so much as by the principle of collegiality (church council, classis, synod). I think that theologically or in terms of the gospel, both options are possibilities for the church. However, whether they are of equal value is perhaps another question. History teaches us that both possibilities also have their disturbing sides. Leadership by one individual, without inbuilt critical control – or some division of power – can lead to authoritarian exercise of authority which does not match the gospel, to personal power and compulsion. Synodal leadership, on the other hand, experiences the difficulties and weaknesses of any democracy in which a changing majority in fact decides over government and sometimes over 'truth'. A recommendation of rule by a single individual without the introduction of some controlling authority seems to me, in the circumstances of modern life, to be an unfortunate move within the churches.

However, what seems to me to be more important than the discussion of leadership by one person or synodal *episkope* is the intrinsic link of this ministry of *episkope* with the living church community and in this sense with the grass roots. The question of episcopal collegiality or anonymous synodality seem to me to be important, but the question of the standing of personal or synodal leaders in and in the midst of the community – the *ecclesial communio* – seems to me to be even more important. Otherwise we get the contrast between 'from above' and the living 'church grass roots' – the temple of the Holy Spirit, in whose service (also under the leading of the same Spirit) ministry is.

Here there emerges what in my view is the greatest deficiency of the Lima Report. This report has rightly brought forward one pole of the problem, viz. the old, still undivided church. However, it takes no account of the other pole, viz. the practice, even alternative practices, of ministry in the present, in connection with the many new forms of ministry instituted by pastoral workers, ecumenical ministries and so on. Must these forms be excluded from the ministry, or *per se* introduced within the tripartite division of episcopacy, presbyterate and diaconate? In that case does not this church order which, while very old, is nevertheless the result of a historical development, become so important that it can hinder the vitality of churches in the gospel?

Or is the *de facto existence* of a fourth kind of ministry which is now emerging the consequence of historical blockages to be found above all in connection with priesthood and episcopacy in the Roman Catholic Church?

The Lima Report is not a grass-roots working paper but a piece of theoretical theology – a working paper written in studies, not on the basis of practical experience. As such it certainly seems to me to be a good piece of work, in which, in self criticism, every church can to some degree find traces of itself. However, I doubt whether many ecumenical basic communities will recognize themselves in it. Nevertheless, the Lima Report is also a challenge for them, though on the other hand the basic communities are a challenge for the Lima Report.

This report cannot be called 'Catholicizing' in any sense; it is certainly 'high-church'. Baptists, Calvinists and other churches will have more difficulty with it than the episcopal churches.

On the other hand, this report can already bring many kinds of Christian churches closer together. And does not the ecumenical path in fact amount to a way of forming increasingly large clusters?

The ecumenical movement is concerned with the challenge of the adventure of allowing oneself to be confronted with the distinctive traditions of other Christian churches, placing other accents which, since the division of the churches, have perhaps been undervalued or overvalued in specific traditions. To speak of 'Protestantizing' or 'Catholicizing' of the ministry points to differences in experience, understandable in the light of historical divisions, but which often simply made possible the survival of the great tradition of the early church. The differences between the churches, whether theoretical or as matters of principle, in connection with conceptions of the ministry, are not as wide as many people think. However, given the great Christian tradition, it is difficult to accept a church 'without ministry'. Ministry is not only a sociological and theological necessity but also an ecclesial necessity. However, its forms are regulated by a church order which changes historically.

Moreover, there is a 'hierarchy of truths of faith'. In fact the celebration of baptism and eucharist or Lord's Supper as a community celebration is more basic than the ministerial service in it.

2. It is worth the trouble of comparing this provisional theological inter-church report with the Declaration of the Congregation of the Doctrine of Faith of the Roman Catholic Church.[2] In some broad outlines the two reports run parallel. However, it is striking that the Roman Catholic letter (a document from the Prefect of the Congregation of the Doctrine of the Faith, written by him in that capacity, albeit with the approval of the Pope), lays almost exclusive stress on one aspect of what all Christian churches call apostolicity, i.e. not so much on the horizontal apostolicity of the church communities themselves, which on the basis of the apostolic content of their doctrine and life go back to the original apostolic church, but rather on what is called the horizontal apostolicity of the succession in the ministry. In an early chapter I have said that this last is only one of the four essential dimensions of the apostolic content of the Christian churches – one aspect which may not be isolated from the three other aspects. Nevertheless, *sacerdotium ministeriale* shows a tendency to let this element dominate to such a degree that all the other elements of apostolicity (in their authentic distinctiveness) are completely dependent on it. But in that case there is no longer any talk of fruitful complementarity, but of sovereign priority of whatever or whoever. Here it is in no sense a matter of a

contrast between a functional and a sacramental conception of the ministry, a contrast (or dilemma) which in my view is a false one. It would be wrong to see the apostolicity of the church community simply in vertical terms, as an instrument of the effective presence of Christ's Spirit in the church, while the ministerial succession is meant to ensure the 'horizontal' link with the original apostolic church. At all events, for their apostolic content of doctrine and life, the apostolic communities of believers themselves also have a horizontal link with the original apostolic church of scripture. A contrast between a pneuma-christological and a direct-christo-logical basis of both community and ministry comes from the devil. These are complementary aspects of one and the same reality, as is already shown by the Johannine pneuma doctrine; the actual presence of the pneuma throughout the community of believers *recalls* (the anamnetic or horizontal bond) Jesus of Nazareth, the Risen One, and thus points to the original apostolic church.

If matters are looked at in this way, pastoral possibilities are opened up which are definitively ruled out in an ecclesiological view that in fact derives apostolicity exclusively from the apostolic succession. This last is clearly the standpoint of *Sacerdotium ministeriale*.

3. Apart from (and yet with a view to) the ecumenical world, some present-day developments in the Roman Catholic Church in connection iwth the exercise of the highest form of ministry nevertheless seem to lay a heavy burden on the coming ecumenical world. In my view rightly, the Roman Catholic Church cherishes the principle of both unity and catholicity (or inter-cultural plurality). The Spirit of God is the ultimate source of both principles, and he is the Spirit as he lives throughout the church, which is filled with him. Unity and Catholicity are therefore a task for every believer and for the whole of the believing community.

Nevertheless, here too *ministerial* service is necessary. The ministerial principle of unity is then embodied in the Petrine function in the church, while the ministerial principle of many-coloured and polycentric catholicity is embodied in the episcopal college, spread all over the world. This in no way means that the bishops are not also concerned for unity, much less that the ultimately binding Petrine principle of unity must not also be concerned for many-sided and polycentric Catholicity.

Of course a degree of tension will always arise from this structural unity between the principle of unity and the principle of catholicity. However, if the pope so becomes the centre of the whole of the church that the local episcopate simply has to nod assent (and indeed does this), something has gone wrong ecclesiologically. If on the other hand a local church did not tolerate any intervention by the pope, this would be equally irresponsible in ecclesiological terms. Apart perhaps from, for example, the church in China and other non-Western countries, however, nowhere in the church at present is there any danger of Gallicanism or national churches. Of course we see established among some bishops the conception that the pope is the only bishop in the whole of the church, as it were the super-ordinary in every bishopric. In that case the principle of catholicity (and thus also of inculturation of the one church in different cultural clusters) begins to suffer seriously and this suffering in the long run becomes a threat specifically to the unity of the church and the *Catholica*. If the different factors in the continuity of the apostolic tradition through the ages are robbed of their complementary counterbalance, both unity and many-sided catholicity suffer.

2. Problems surrounding the diaconate and the question of a fourth ministry

In the present-day blockage and impasse in which ministry finds itself, we can see the beginnings of disintegration everywhere (which is theologically to be regretted): 'the word' is detached from 'the sacrament', Bible teaching becomes a secular occupation, the liturgist is cut off from the community which celebrates the liturgy; those who have to accompany the sick to their deaths have abruptly to hand over the sacramental sealing of this whole process to a strange priest summoned from elsewhere – to the disillusionment of the dying person; above all, the eucharist, so highly praised in Vatican II as a place where the heart of the community beats, must now suddenly give place to other liturgical celebrations (praiseworthy and welcome though they may be in themselves) for want of a priest, and many believers have to be content with a longing for the eucharist; and so on. Here the church of Christ is indeed stood on its head. Above all, I find it difficult to place ecclesiologically situations in countries like Africa, where dedicated catechists inspire communities all their lives, while these communities can celebrate the eucharist only a few times a year (for want of an unmarried priest).

Some people see the solution in the consecration of 'pastoral workers' as deacons. In many local churches, however, precisely these pastoral workers are the ones who are opposed to their own inclusion in the diaconate. The reasons for this are understandable. The renewal of the diaconate as this has been carried through since Vatican II comes near to a part-time ministerial activity by older people who during the week are engaged in a secular profession; moreover, they are not so well trained theologically as the pastoral workers, who have mostly had a complete theological training and are moreover occupied full time in the life of the churches. In addition, according to new ecclesiastical legislation, in cases of need 'laity' can do precisely what in fact the deacons do by virtue of their ministry. So why be consecrated deacon?

So two possibilities remain open. Either the ministry of deacon should be given a completely new content which corresponds in a more appropriate way to what pastoral workers in fact do as those who inspire a community of believers; or there should be a fourth ministry, alongside the episcopate, presbyterate and diaconate, bestowed by the community of the church and its leaders on pastoral workers: by laying on of hands and an appropriate epiclesis, a prayer in which the task of these pastoral workers is precisely described. Then there would also be people appointed to intervene in cases of need so that in all circumstances the church community can be and remain a church community, also because it has ministers who are always present.

Or do all these pastoral problems emerge simply as a result of the fact that the presbyterate is not open to married as well as unmarried believers?

In my view this last factor certainly plays a role, but not the most decisive one, which many people attribute to it. In the circumstances of the life of churches in our present-day societies the building up of a community of faith calls for more differentiated ministerial tasks within a community through which, as time goes on, as many members as possible can be actively involved in building up the church.

Greater confidence from the leaders of the church in the Spirit of God which also plays an inscrutable role in the community of the church, and indeed outside it, in secular events, would help our Christian communities to show more vitality in the gospel, with the permanent but restrained oversight (*episkope*) of the pastoral ministry of the church's *magisterium*. It is in that hope that I have written this new book.

Abbreviations

AAS	*Acta Apostolicae Sedis*
BLE	*Bulletin de littérature ecclésiastique*
BTB	*Biblical Theology Bulletin*
BWANT	Beiträge zur Wissenschaft des Alten und Neuen Testament
BZNW	Beiheft zur Zeitschrift für Neutestamentliche Wissenschaft
CBQ	*Catholic Biblical Quarterly*
COD	Conciliorum Oecumenicorum Documenta
Conc.	*Sacrorum Conciliorum nova et amplissima collectio*
CSEL	Corpus Scriptorum Ecclesiasticorum Latinorum
FZPT	*Freiburger Zeitschrift für Theologie und Philosophie*
GCS	Griechische Christliche Schriftsteller
HJ	*Historisches Jahrbuch*
HTR	*Harvard Theological Review*
JAC	*Jahrbuch für Antike und Christentum*
JEH	*Journal of Ecclesiastical History*
JES	*Journal of Ecumenical Studies*
JQR	*Jewish Quarterly Review*
KuD	*Kerygma und Dogma*
LCC	Library of Christian Classics
MTZ	*Münchener Theologische Zeitschrift*
NRT	*Nouvelle revue théologique*
NTAbh	Neutestamentliche Abhandlungen
NTS	*New Testament Studies*
OCP	Orientalia Christiana Periodica
PG	J.P.Migne, *Patrologia Graeca*
PL	J.P.Migne, *Patrologia Latina*
QD	Quaestiones Disputatae
RAC	*Religion in Antike und Christentum*
RevAscMyst	*Revue d'ascétique et de mystique*
RGG	*Die Religion in Geschichte und Gegenwart*
RHE	*Revue d'histoire ecclésiastique*

RQ	*Revue de Qumran*
RSPT	*Revue des sciences philosophiques et théologiques*
RSR	*Recherches de science religieuse*
RTL	*Revue théologique de Louvain*
SBS	Stuttgarter Bibelstudien
SC	Sources chrétiennes
SdZ	*Stimme der Zeit*
TDNT	*Theological Dictionary of the New Testament*
TheolStud	*Theological Studies*
TQ	*Theologische Quartalschrift*
TRE	*Theologische Realenzyclopädie*
TTZ	*Trierer Theologische Zeitschrift*
TuG	*Theologie und Gemeinde*
TvT	*Tijdschrift voor Theologie*
VC	*Vigiliae Christianae*
WUNT	Wissenschaftliche Untersuchungen zum Neuen Testament
WuW	*Wort und Wahrheit*
ZKG	*Zeitschrift für Kirchengeschichte*
ZKT	*Zeitschrift für katholische Theologie*

Notes

Preface

1. *Ministry*, New York and London 1981.

Introduction and Part I

1. P.Grelot, *Eglise et ministères. Pour un dialogue critique avec Edward Schillebeeckx*, Paris 1983. Similarly unfair criticism can be found in W.Kasper and above all A.Vanhoye. Their criticisms and those of H.Crouzel have been edited in translation with an introduction by Mgr R.Malone under the auspices of the 'Committee on Doctrine' of the Bishops' Conference of the USA, *Review of Contemporary Perspectives on Ministry*, Washington 1983, and used as a dossier against me.

2. See E.Schürer, *Geschichte des Jüdischen Volkes*, Leipzig 1901, Part 1, 418-21.

3. Some literature on the subject is: R.Travers Herford, *The Pharisees*, Boston 1962; L.Finkelstein, *The Pharisees*, two vols., Philadelphia 1962; John T.Pawlikowski, *Christ in the Light of the Christian-Jewish Dialogue*, New York 1982; J.Neusner, *The Rabbinic Tradition about the Pharisees before 70*, three vols, Leiden 1971; id., *From Politics to Piety*, Englewood Cliffs 1973.

4. S.Brandon, *Jesus and the Zealots*, Manchester and New York 1967; J.Carmichael, *The Death of Jesus*, New York 1966; H.Maccoby, *Revolution in Judaea. Jesus and the Jewish Resistance*, New York 1980.

5. O.Cullmann, *Jesus and the Revolutionaries of His Time*, New York 1970; M.Hengel, *Was Jesus a Revolutionist?*, Philadelphia 1971; John Howard Yoder, *The Politics of Jesus*, Grand Rapids 1972.

6. See also Albert Nolan, *Jesus before Christianity. The Gospel of Liberation*, Cape Town 1977.

7. Elizabeth Schüssler Fiorenza, *In Memory of Her. A Feminist Reconstruction of Christian Origins*, New York and London 1983.

8. C.Thoma, *Christliche Theologie des Judentums*, Aschenburg 1978, sections 45-50.

9. A.Stock, *Einheit des Neuen Testaments*, Zürich 1969, is an older, but good, study.

10. B.van Iersel, 'Son of God in the New Testament', *Concilium* 153, 1982, 37-48.

11. S.M.Ogden, *The Point of Christology*, San Francisco and London 1982.

12. See G.Dautzenberg, in *Die Frau im Urchristentum*, QD 95, Freiburg 1983; E.Schüssler Fiorenza, *In Memory of Her*, 205-36.

Part Two, Section 1

1. C.Geertz, *The Interpretation of Cultures. Selected Essays*, New York 1973, 20f.

2. See the bibliography on this Part, 296f. below. Here I would refer to my Farewell Lecture, *Theologisch geloofsverstaan anno 1983*, Baarn 1983.

3. The *'ekklesiai* of the saints' (I Cor.14.33-34); 'each *ekklesia*' (I Cor.4.17); 'all the *ekklesiae*' (I Cor.7.17; II Cor.8.18; 11.28).

4. I Cor.6.4; 10.32; 12.28; 14.4,5,12; 15.9; Gal.1.13; Phil.3.6; Eph.1.22; 3.10,21; 5.23,24,25,27,29,32; Col.1.18,24.

5. Fliche-Martin III, 437-41; IV, 577-81; P. de Labriolle, 'Paroecia', *Bulletin du Cange* III, 1927, 196-205; R.Aigrain, 'Diocèse', *Catholicisme* III, 834-9; R.Mumm, 'Parochie und Gemeinde', *Monatsschrift für Pastoraltheologie* 47, 1958, 116-23; E.Stengel, 'Kirchenverfassung', *RGG³*, Tübingen 1959, 3, cols. 1549-64.

6. Clement, *ad Cor.* I,1; Eusebius, *HE* 4, 23.

7. *MGHConcilia* I, 20-1.

8. Op.cit., I, 79-80.

9. Op.cit.,II, 485-63.

10. *Decretalia*, lib.I, tit.VII, c.1, and tit.XXX, c.4.

11. Du Cange, *Glossarium Mediae et Infimae Latinitatis*, Paris 1845, s.v.*parochia*, 5, cols.102-4.

12. *Corpus Scriptorum Latinorum*, 6,9148 (cited by W.Meeks, *The First Urban Christians*, 222 n.17).

13. Cf. K.Kertelge, *Gemeinde und Amt im Neuen Testament*, Munich 1972; id., *Das kirchliche Amt im Neuen Testament*, Darmstadt 1977.

14. Cf. Josephus, *Antiquitates* 14, 259-61.

15. G.Schille, *Die Urchristliche Kollegialmission*, Zürich 1967.

16. However, the significance of this in I Thess. remains problematical, while Rom.12.8 more clearly means *patroni* (financial guardians). In the post-Pauline letters it is unmistakably a matter of 'presidents', whether the *paterfamilias* in the house communities (I Tim.3.4,5,12) or presiding *presbyteroi*, who deserve double honour (I Tim.5.17).

17. I have taken the list from W.Meeks (n.12 above), 135.

18. See Gerd Lüdemann, *Paulus der Heidenapostel*, 2, *Antipaulinismus im frühen Christentum*, Göttingen 1983.

19. J.Meier, 'Presbyteros in the Pastoral Epistles', *CBQ* 35, 1973, 323-45.

20. For *ordo* see below n.60.

21. See especially J.E.Crouch, *The Origin and Intention of the Colossian Haustafel*, Göttingen 1972; W.Schraege, 'Zur Ethik der Neutestamentlicher Haustafeln', *NTS* 21, 1974/75, 1-22; see the bibliography, 296f. below.

22. Tacitus, *Histories* V, 5.

23. C.C.Richardson, *Early Christian Fathers*, LCC, London and New York 1970; K.Beyschlag, *Clemens Romanus und der Frühkatholizismus*, Tübingen 1966.

24. G.Deusen, 'Weisen der Bischofswahl in 1.Clemensbrief und in der Didache', *TuG* 62, 1972, 125-35.

25. R.Padberg, 'Das Amtsverständnis der Ignatiusbriefe', *TuG* 62, 1972, 47-54; P.Stockmeier, 'Bischofsamt und Kircheneinheit bei den Apostolischen Vätern', *TTZ* 73, 1964, 321-35.

26. E.Dassmann, 'Zur Entstehung des Monepiskopats', *JAC* 17, 1974, 74-90.

27. F.Hahn, 'Der Apostolat im Urchristentum', *KuD* 20, 1974, 54-77.

28. Cf. J.Ash, 'The Decline of Ecstatic Prophecy in the Early Church', *TheolStud* 37, 1976, 227-52; E.Schüssler Fiorenza, *In Memory of Her*, 293f.

29. See J.Audet, *Le Didachè*, Paris 1958.

30. Ambrosiaster, *Litt.ad Eph.* 4,11-12, CSEL Ambrosiaster III, 81, 99.

31. M.E.Boring, *Sayings of the Risen Jesus. Christian Prophecy in the Synoptic Tradition*, Cambridge 1982.

32. I Thess.2.14; I Cor.1.2; 10.32; 11.16; 11.22; 15.9; II Thess.1.4; Acts 20.28.

33. Rom.16.16; cf. I Thess.1.1.

34. I Cor.3.16; 6.19.

35. The figure 'seven' has a symbolic significance in Jewish thought. However, we might suppose that 'the seven' was a technical term for the 'council of elders' made up of seven, in the Jewish synagogue. Perhaps now Greek-speaking presbyters in Jerusalem are mentioned alongside the Christian council of presbyters made up of Aramaic-speaking Jews.

36. It is striking that 'Philip the evangelist' (Acts 21.8), one of the Hellenistic 'seven' (see also Acts 6.5), organized the mission to Samaria (Acts 8.5,12,26-40) and other places on the Mediterranean coast among Greek-speaking Diaspora Jews, with Caesarea as a centre.

37. Acts 1.21f.; cf. Luke 24.36-39.

38. In the so-called 'Niceno-Constantinopolitan' creed; however, this is in fact an Eastern baptismal creed which later came into general currency. The qualification 'apostolic' was inserted into the description of the 'one, holy and catholic' church at a time when Christians were in danger of forgetting the historical origin of the Christian communities and were involving themselves too much in speculation. Emphasis was laid on this apostolicity even in the later New Testament period as a counter to excessive speculation (albeit in an incipient 'doctrinal' sense): Jude 3; II Tim.1.13, 14; 3.14; Titus 2.1; I Tim.3.13; 4.1,6; 6.3,12,20); II Tim.2.2, 5,18; 3.8ff.; Titus 1.13f.

39. In other New Testament texts also the leaders of the community still do not seem to have any official name, or are referred to by names which vary from community to community, which is why they are

generally called 'those who lead you', 'those who labour for you', etc. (II Thess.5.12; Rom.16.6,12; also Heb.13.7,24).

40. As is well known, the tripartite division into apostles, prophets and teachers (or wise men) is of Jewish inspiration. The apostles as it were lay the foundation for the 'law of the gospel' (see Matt.5.1ff.; II Cor.3.4-11; Luke 6.12ff.; Acts 15.21). Paul, who does not make a very convincing systematic theologian in this respect, tries to synthesize this into the triad: (*a*) varieties of charismata, deriving from one pneuma; (*b*) varieties of *diakoniai* or services, in the service of the one Lord; (*c*) varieties of *energemata* or activities, as the fruit of one and the same God (I Cor.12.4-6): 'each... for the common good' (I Cor.12.7). 'Prophets' played a considerable part in the first Christian communities (the details of which cannot now wholly be recovered). The writer of the book of Revelation still calls himself a 'prophet' (Rev.1.3; 10.7; 22.18f.) and ultimately writes 'prophetic letters' (Rev.2.1-3.22) and 'extraordinarily prophetic', i.e. specifically 'apocalyptic', letters (Rev.4.1-22). See also the role of the prophets in Luke's account of Paul's journey from Corinth to Jerusalem (Acts 20.3-21.17). The spirit of the prophets is the 'spirit of Jesus' (Acts 16.7; Phil.1.19), who was felt to be a prophet before he was recognized as Messiah.

41. 'Pastors' (Eph.4.11) probably has no specific significance for a differentiated ministry. It is an image of feeding the flock (John 21.15-17; Acts 20.28; 20.35a; I Peter 5.14). Jesus is called the arch-pastor (I Peter 5.4; see 2.25). Only in the post-apostolic period as represented by the New Testament does pastor – also directed against the heretics (Acts 20.28) – become a general term for all church officials (Eph.4.11; Acts 20.28; I Peter 5.1-4; see also Matt.16.18f.; 18.18; John 20.22f.).

42. See e.g. N.Brox, *Pseudepigraphie in der heidnischen und jüdisch-christlichen Antike*, Darmstadt 1977, and W.Speyer, 'Die literarische Fälschung im Altertum', in *Handbuch der Altertumswissenschaft* I-1, Munich 1971.

43. See F.Prast, *Presbyter und Evangelium in nachapostolischer Zeit*, Forschung zur Bibel 29, Stuttgart 1979; E.Nellessen, 'Die Einsetzung von Presbytern durch Barnabas und Paulus (Apg.14,23)', in *Begegnung mit dem Wort*, ed. J.Zmijewski and E.Nellessen, Festschrift H.Zimmermann, Bonn 1980, 175-94; J.Michl, 'Die Presbyter des ersten Petrusbrief', in *Ostkirche-Weltkirche*, Festschrift J.Kard. Döpfner, Würzburg 1973, 48-62.

44. R.Brown, *Priest and Bishop*, New York 1970, 33ff., 63ff.

45. R.Pesch, *Das Markusevangelium*, Freiburg 1977, II, 175.

46. E.S.Fiorenza, *In Memory of Her*, 316-23.

47. Even in the Middle Ages, all the great theologians rejected the idea that those who held office in the church should have any position of power (despite the dispute between *imperium* and *sacerdotium*). See e.g. Thomas: *Dicendum quod subiectio servitutis repugnat libertati: quae servitus est cum aliquis dominatur ad sui utilitatem subiectis utens. Talis autem subiectio non requiritur in ordine, per quem qui praesunt, salutem subditorum quaerere*

debent, non propriam utilitatem (*In IV Sent.* d.24 q.1, a.1 q1a, ad 1). This is put even more sharply by Bonaventura, *In IV Sent.* d.24, p.1, a.2, q.2.

48. *Traditio*, Botte 1963, 28-9. See C.Vogel, 'L'imposition des mains dans les rites d'ordination en Orient et en Occident', *La Maison Dieu* 102, 1970, 57-72. See M.Lods, *Confesseurs et martyrs, successeurs des prophètes dans l'Eglise des trois premiers siècles*, Paris-Neuchâtel 1950; D. van Damme, 'Martus, Christianos. Ueberlegungen zur ursprünglichen Martyrertitel', *FZPT* 23, 1976, 286-303.

49. See E.Schillebeeckx, *Christ*, London and New York 1980, 258-61.

50. See G.Richter, *Die Fusswaschung im Johannesevangelium*, Regensburg 1967.

51. E.Schweizer, *Church Order in the New Testament*, London 1961, 117ff.

52. See T.Lorenzen, *Der Lieblingsjünger im Johannesevangelium*, SBS 55, Stuttgart 1971; R.Brown, *The Community of the Beloved Disciple*, New York and London 1979.

53. K.Donfried, 'Ecclesiastical Authority in 2 and 3 John', in *L'Evangile de Jean* (ed. M.de Jonge), Gembloux 1977, 325-33.

54. W.C.van Unnik, 'The Authority of the Presbyters in Irenaeus' Works', in *God's Christ and His People*, Festschrift N.A.Dahl, ed. J.Jervell and W.A.Meeks, Oslo 1977, 248-60; J.Munck, 'Presbyters and Disciples of the Lord in Papias', *HTR* 52, 1959, 223-43.

55. H.Schlier, 'Der Hl.Geist als Interpret nach dem Joh-Evangelium', *Communio* 2, 1973, 97-108; R.A.Culpeper, *The Johannine School*, Missoula 1975, 265-70; R.Brown, *The Community of the Beloved Disciple*, New York 1979; M.de Jonge, *Jesus: Stranger from Heaven and Son of God*, Missoula 1977; D.M. Smith, 'Johannine Christianity', *NTS* 21, 1974-75, 228-48; H.Conzelmann, 'Was von Anfang war', *Neutestamentliche Studien für R.Bultmann*, BZNW 21, Berlin 1954, 194-201; J.O'Grady, 'Individualism and Johannine Christology', *BTB* 5, 1975, 227-61, and 'Johannine Ecclesiology. A Critical Evaluation', *BTB* 7, 1977, 36-44.

56. De Jonge, op.cit., 205.

57. R.Brown, *The Beloved Disciple*, 160.

58. See E.Ruckstuhl, 'Zur Aussage und Botschaft von Johannes 21', *Die Kirche des Anfangs*, Festschrift H.Schürmann, ed R.Schnackenburg, Leipzig 1977, 339-62, esp.360f.

59. See already Ignatius, Smyrn.8.1; 9.1; Eph.5.3; Trall.2.1.

60. *Ordinatio* or institution, later called consecration, is a Christian reinterpretation of the Jewish *ordinatio* of a rabbi. After he had been instructed by a rabbi, hands were laid on a rabbinic candidate by his teacher – in the presence of two rabbis as witnesses (following the model of the installation of Joshua by Moses, Num.27.21ff.: although we only find assured literary evidence for this consecration of a rabbi about AD 75, it is at all events before the Christian Pastoral Epistles). The purpose of the Jewish consecration of a rabbi was that the wisdom of the teacher should pass over to the rabbinic candidate, who from that point on might also call himself a rabbi (teacher); it guaranteed continuity with the Mosaic law-giving, though the rabbi could interpret this tradition independently (see E.Lohse, *Die Ordination im Spätjudentum und im Neuen*

Testament, Göttingen 1951; K.Hruby, 'La notion d'ordination dans la tradition juive', *La Maison-Dieu* 102, Paris 1970, 52-72; A.Ehrhardt, 'Jewish and Christian Ordination', *JEH* 5, 1954, 125-38; G.Kretschmar, 'Die Ordination im frühen Christentum', *FZPT* 22, 1975, 35-69.

61. From Acts 20.17, compared with 20.28, and I Peter 5.5, compared with 5.2, it seems that *episkopoi* and *presbyteroi* are the same people. Titus 1.6ff. also suddenly mentions an *episkopos* in a context which is concerned with *presbyteroi*. Furthermore, in I Clement 44.1, as compared with 44.5, the *episkopos* is obviously a *presbyteros*. However, the so-called 'monarchical episcopate' is not a biblical norm, although it is a legitimate form of church order.

62. Ignatius, Magn.2; 3.1; 4; 6.1; 7.1; Trall.2.2-3; 3.1; 7.2; Smyrn.8; Polyc.5.2; ad Phil.4. For years historians have tended to give a late date ot the model of the so-called monarchical episcopate, which it is difficult to place early. This is connected with the grave historical suspicions attached to an early dating of writings which had been attributed to Ignatius of Antioch. The longer they go on, the more convincing are the arguments that this monarchical episcopate should be dated much later. See a critical revue of various publications on this problem, A.Davids, ' "Frühkatholizismus" op de helling; rond de brieven van Ignatius', *TvT* 20, 1980, no.2, 188-91.

63. Since there are those who elevate the 'episcopate' and the 'presbyterate' to an apostolic norm because they occur in the New Testament (at the same time forgetting that both the distinction between them and their content is far from clear in the New Testament), why is there not also a remembrance that in the same way the Pastoral Epistles presuppose that the *episkopoi-presbyteroi* and deacons are always married? And in I Cor.9.4-6, Paul even talks about the right of the apostles to be married. There is no hermeneutical justification for such selectivity in the use of the Bible. The question is what the New Testament itself means to affirm as a norm, and in the Pastoral Epistles this is merely the principle of apostolicity and not the specific structuring of the ministries.

64. See M.Charlesworth, *Trade Routes and Commerce in the Roman Empire*, two vols., Cambridge 1926.

65. P.Grelot, *Eglise et ministères*, 18-41.

66. Thomas, *Summa Theologiae* III, q.67, a.2.

67. In this connection see a recent booklet, *Das Recht der Gemeinde auf Eucharistie. Die bedrohte Einheit vom Wort und Sakrament*, edited by the Solidaritätsgruppe katholischer Priester der Diözese Speyer, Trier 1978.

68. In *Das Recht*, J.Blank defends the position that from the perspective of the New Testament the eucharist is really 'outside the ministry'. I think he is wrong. The position is indeed that in the New Testament the ministry did not develop from and around the eucharist, but from and around the formation of the community. However, I would add that it did so from the way in which the apostolic communities took shape by a practical 'discipleship of Jesus', after the fashion of the apostles.

69. See K.Hruby, 'La "Birkat ha-mason"', in *Mélanges Liturgiques*, Louvain 1972, 205-22; L.Finkelstein, 'The Birkhat Ha-mazon', *JQR* 19,

1928-29, 211-62; T.Talley, 'De la "Berakah" à l'eucharistie', *La Maison-Dieu* 125, 1974, 199-219.

70. See J.Audet, *La Didachè*, Paris 1958.

Part Three, Section 1, 1-4

1. Clement, *Ad.Cor.* I,3, ed.J.A.Fischer, *Die Apostolischen Väter: Schriften des Urchristentums* 1, Darmstadt 1970, 24.

2. *Ad Cor.*, 5.7, ibid., 32.

3. *Ad Cor.*, 1,3, ibid., 24.

4. *Ad Cor.*, 44,1, ibid., 80.

5. Ibid.

6. E.Herrmann, *Ecclesia in re publica: Die Entwicklung der Kirche von pseudo-staatlicher zu staatlich inkorporierter Existenz*, Frankfurt 1980, 25-7. Cf. D.Magie, *Roman Rule in Asia Minor to the End of the Third Century after Christ*, two vols, Princeton 1950; S.Hirschfeld, *Die kaiserlichen Verwaltungsbeamten von Augustinus bis Diokletian*, Berlin 1905. On the basis of the historical situation which comes to the fore here I find it difficult to be convinced by the position of E.Dassmann ('Zur Enstehung des Monepiskopats', *JAC* 17, 1974, 74-90, esp.90), in which he denies any borrowing of structures of ministry from civil administrative structures. Moreover, his argument is essentially based on a certainty that the letters of Ignatius date from the beginning of the second century, which has now become at least problematical. In my view, Dassmann, who is an expert in this period, gives reasons how and why government by a single bishop, *once it had come into being*, was given theological support, above all by Ignatius himself. However, it seems to me historically far from certain that Ignatius could have pressed the monepiscopate, probably for the first time, on the basis of theological insights, above all with an appeal to monotheism, especially when one remembers that what took place unconsciously in the church at that time was implemented consciously by Tertullian and Cyprian, viz. by looking for points of contact with models from the Hellenistic Roman empire (see below). Of course I am not clear whether Dassmann would still want to maintain his 1974 view in his later studies.

7. Herrmann, op.cit., 26.

8. Clement, *Ad Cor.*, 44.1-3, p.80.

9. *Ad Cor.*, 42,4, p.78.

10. *Ad Cor.*, 42.5, p.78.

11. Herrmann (op.cit., 27) wrongly asks this question, which indicates that he seems not to have noted Clement's use of *episkope* to denote a function of authority, and of *diakonia* to denote the charcter of the same function of authority as service.

12. *Ad Cor.* 44.3, p.80.

13. L.Brandis, 'Ekklesia', in *Realenc.* V/2, cols.2163-2200.

14. Magie, *Roman Rule*, 649f.

15. *Ministry*, 21-22.

16. G.Bornkamm, *Presbys*, TDNT 6, 655-61.

17. The author refers to letters of a certain Ignatius which - if the reference is to Ignatius of Antioch – again raises problems in connection with recent shifts in the dating of these letters.

18. Polycarp, *Ad Phil.* 5.3; ed. Fischer, 254,256; see also SC 10, Paris 1951.

19. *Didache* 15.1 and 11.2,11.

20. Ignatius, *Ad Magn.* 6.1; ed. Fischer, 164; *Ad Trall.*3,1, ibid., 174; *Ad.Phil.*8.1, ibid., 198-200. For the dating of Ignatius' letters see n.6.

21. *Ad Magn.* 6.1, ibid., 164.

22. *Ad Eph.* 4.1, ibid. 144.

23. *Ad Eph.* 6.1, ibid., 146.

24. *Ad Magn.*3.1, ibid., 162; *Ad Eph.* 6.1, ibid., 146.

25. For a bibliography for this period see pp.298-300.

26. Eusebius, HE V, 16,5 (SC 31, 41, 55, 73).

27. Herrmann, op.cit., 28-9.

28. A.Adam, 'Bischof', *RGG*³ 1, 1957, 1301ff.

29. Ignatius, *Ad Magn.* 6.1, 164; *Ad Trall.* 3,1, 174.

30. *Ad Magn.*6.1, ibid., 164; *Ad Trall.* 3,1, ibid. 174; *Ad Smyrn.* 8,2, ibid., 210.

31. *Ministry*, 9.

32. It should be remembered that the term *ekklesia* only became an authentic canonical church term when the use of *ekklesia* in a civil context in the Hellenistic world and Asia Minor had ceased. See O.Linton, 'Ekklesia', *RAC* 4, 1959, 905-21; also Brandis, op.cit (n.13).

33. Hermas, *Sim.* 9,27,2: GCS *Apostolische Väter* I, 96; SC 53. The text comes from the middle of the second century. The visions of an 'old woman', the church, have to be read aloud 'in the presence of the presbyters who lead the church' (*Vis.* 2,4,3).

34. *Vis.* 2,4,2-3: GCS I,7.

35. *Vis.* 2,2,6: GCS 6; 3,9,7: GCS 16.

36. *Sim.* 9,26,2: GCS 95.

37. *Sim.* 9,15,4: GCS 89; 9,25,2: GCS 95.

38. *Sim.* 9,27: GCS 96.

39. Here too Herrmann (n.33) interprets the text wrongly: the question is not whether the functions are carried out by two different sorts of presbyters.

40. *Sim.* 9.26.2. Herrmann (op.cit.,33) wrongly sees here the possibility that *episkopoi* are a link between 'presbyters' and 'deacons'.

41. See Hirschfeld, op.cit. (n.6).

42. Nicaea, canon 6. See Hefele-Leclerq, *Histoire des conciles*, Paris 1907, I, 1: *Conc.Oec.Dec.*, p.8.

43. Eusebius, *HE* VI, 3,8, GCS IX, 2, 524f., 534ff.

44. Ibid., VII, 24; GCS 688.

45. Eutychius, *Annales*, PG 111, 982.

46. Jerome confirms this in his *Epist.* 146.1, CSEL 56,310.

47. Athanasius, *Apologia contra Arianos*, 6.

48. Eusebius, HE VI, 44-45. Cf. K.Lübeck, *Reichseinteilung und kirchliche Hierarchie*, Kirchengeschichtliche Studien V,4, Münster 1901; H.Grotz,

Die Hauptkirchen des Ostens: Von den Anfängen bis zum Konzil von Nikaia 325, Rome 1964.

49. It emerges from Jerome that in his time the right of the community to elect its presbyters was transferred to the neighbouring bishops (*Epist.* 146); see also O.Barlea, *Die Weihe der Bischöfs, Presbyter und Diakone in Vornizänische Zeit*, Munich 1969.

50. Tertullian, *Apol.* 38,1,39, CSEL 49,90.

51. *De corona* 13, CSEL 70, 181. See A.Beck, *Römisches Recht bei Tertullian und Cyprian*, Halle 1930, reprinted Aalen 1967; G.Krüger, *Die Rechtsstellung der vorkonstantinischen Kirchen*, Stuttgart 1935; J.Straub, 'Zur Ordination von Bischofen und Beamten in der christlichen Spätantike', *JAC Ergänzungsband 1*, Münster 1964, 336-45; P.Stockmeier, *Zum Verhältnis von Glaube und Religion bei Tertullian*, Berlin 1972.

52. Tertullian, *De praescr.haer.* 13, CSEL 70, 17.

53. Cyprianus, *Epist.* 67.4, CSEL III-2, 738.

54. Ibid., 67.3, 738.

55. *Epist.*67.5, ibid., 739.

56. Ibid. see also *Epist.* 51.1, CSEL 615; *Epist.* 76.6, ibid.741: *Fraternitas omnis* stands for community and clergy.

57. Suetonius, *Ad Vespasianum* 23. See the literature in n.51. Similarly R.Frei-Stolba, *Untersuchungen zu den Wählen in der römischen Kaiserzeit*, Zurich 1967.

58. Pliny, *Epist.* X, 86, a.87,3; see Frei-Stolba, op.cit.

59. Cyprian, *Epist.* 55.3, CSEL III-2, 625.

60. Herrmann, op.cit. (n.6), 47. See *Codex Theod.* XII,5,1.

61. Cyprian, *Epist.* 67.5, CSEL III-2, 739.

62. J.Gascou, *La politique municipale de l'Empire Romain en Afrique proconsulaire de Trajan à Septime Sévére*, Rome 1972.

63. Cyprian, *Epist.* 67, 6; ibid., 741.

64. Cyprian, *Epist.* 39, 1,4-5; ibid., 580,581,584; *Epist.* 38.2; ibid. 547.

65. My study from the second to the twelfth century has convinced me that all theologizing about the structures of ministry threatens to become ideology if it does not at the same time study the social structures in society. H.Marrou had already called attention to this in his *Histoire de l'Eglise*, 2, 27: 'The influence of civil administration is clear.'

66. *La tradition apostolique de saint Hippolyte*, Liturgiewissenschaftliche Quellen und Forschungen 39, ed. B.Botte, Münster 1963 (= SC 11 bis), 113-26; B.Botte, 'L'ordination de l'évêque', *La Maison-Dieu* 98, Paris 1969, 113-26; id., 'La formule d'ordination "la grace divine" dans les rites orientaux', *L'Orient Syrien* 2, 1957, 285-96; id., 'L'ordre d'après les prières d'ordination', in *Études sur le sacrament de l'ordre*, Paris 1957, 13-35; A.Rose, 'La prière de consécration par l'ordination épiscopale', *La Maison-Dieu* 98, Paris 1969, 127-42; C.Vogel, 'L'imposition des mains dans les rites d'ordination en Orient et en Occident', *La Maison-Dieu* 102, Paris 1970, 57-72; id., *Le ministère charismatique de l'eucharistie*, Studia Anselmiana 61, Rome 1973, 181-209; J.Lecuyer, 'Episcopat et presbytérat dans les écrits d'Hippolyte de Rome', *RSR* 41, 1953, 30-50; H.J.Schulz, 'Das liturgisch sakramental übertragene Hirtenamt in seiner eucharistischen

Selbstverwirklichung nach dem Zeugnis der liturgische Ueberlieferung',
P.Bläser et al., *Amt und Eucharistie*, Paderborn 1973, 208-55; id., 'Die
Grundstruktur des kirchlichen Amtes im Spiegel der Eucharistiefeier
und der Ordinationsliturgie des römischen und des byzantischen Ritus',
Catholica 29, 1975, 325-40; H.M.Legrand, 'Theology and the Election of
Bishops in the Early Church', *Concilium* 8, 1972, no. 7, 31-42;
J.H.Hanssens, 'Les oraisons sacramentelles des ordinations orientales',
OCP 18, 1952, 297-318; U.Brockhaus, *Charisma und Amt*, Wuppertal 1962,
674-6; V.Fuchs, *Der Ordinationstitel von seiner Enstehung bis auf Innocenz
III*, Bonn 1930; G.Pinto da Oliviera, 'Signification sacerdotale du ministère
de l'évêque dans la Tradition Apostolique d'Hippolyte de Rome', *FZPT*
25, 1978, 398-427.

67. *Traditio* 1, SC 11 bis, 40.

68. Hippolytus is a Christian author writing from Rome, leader
(presbyter? bishop?, even anti-pope?) of a Christian community which
had a controversy with Pope Pontianus (231-235). At this time the
liturgies had not yet been fixed; people improvised on a canvas which
was in one sense established. Hippolytus gives specific models which
more than probably reflect the Roman liturgy of the beginning of the
third century. This model is the earliest Christian liturgy known to us; it
also circulated in the patriarchates of Alexandria and Antioch. At that
time Greek was still the official language in Rome; only individual
fragments of the Greek have been preserved, but in addition we have
the complete very slavish Latin text (which suggests the individual Greek
even down to details), and also a number of other ancient translations.

69. *Traditio* 2: Botte (1963 ed.), 4-11. From Ps.-Dionysius onwards the
prayer to the Holy Spirit at the *ordinatio* was called *epiklesis* (*De Eccl.
Hierarchia* 5,2: PG 3,509).

70. Y.Congar, 'Ordinations "invitus", "coactus" de l'Eglise antique au
canon 214', *RSPT* 50, 1966, 169-97. The consequences of this pressure are
analysed in a detailed study, above all when from the end of the fourth
century the senior clergy in the West were obliged to be completely
celibate: P.H.Lafontaine, *Les conditions positives de l'accession aux ordres
dans la première législation ecclésiastique (300-492)*, Publications sériées de
l'Université d'Ottawa 71, Ottawa 1963, esp. 71-100. Moreover it emerges
from this study that even at this time the community still always chose
its presbyter itself (until often fights broke out when the wishes of the
believers were not honoured).

71. *Constitutiones Apostolorum* 8 (F.X.Funk, *Didascalia et Constitutiones
Apostolorum* 1, Paderborn 1905).

72. 'Apostolicity' in the sense of Part Two.

73. Nevertheless, it should be remembered that even in the third
century there was considerable caution about sacerdotalizing, in whatever form, of ministry: only Christ and the people of God are priestly.
Hippolytus himself therefore repeatedly says: the bishop (= *sacerdos*) is
like a high priest (*Traditio* 3 and 34). The presbyters are still not priests
(*sacerdotes*), although they may preside at the eucharist with the bishop's
permission (at least in many church provinces). This practice increases

as time goes on. In the ancient church, to begin with *sacerdos* was applied to the bishop purely in Old Testament and allegorical terms. After that it gradually came to be used in a real sense. Generally speaking, down to the fifth century *sacerdos* usually means the bishop. (See P.M.Gy, 'La théologie des prières anciennes pour l'ordination des évêques et des prêtres', *RSPT* 58, 1974, 599-617; Schillebeeckx, s.v.'Priesterschap', in *Theologisch Woordenbok* 3, esp. 3974f.). In the West, *sacerdotes secundi ordinis* is common from the fourth and fifth centuries onwards (see B.Botte, *'Secundi meriti munus'*, in *Questions Liturgiques et Paroissales* 21, 1936, 84-8); at the end of the fourth century and the beginning of the fifth bishops were also called *archiereis* and presbyters *hiereis* in the East. The *Traditio* of Hippolytus is still in a tradition which calls only the bishop 'priest'. In other words, before the time of Nicaea the term 'presbyter' may not in any instance be translated as 'priest'.

74. For the Jewish background to *ordinatio* see the literature in n.60 of the previous chapter.

75.*Traditio* 7, Botte, ed.1963, 20f. (See B.Botte, *'Presbyterium et ordo episcoporum'*, *Irenikon* 29, 1956, 3-27.)

76. Gy, 'La théologie des prières anciennes', n.73 above.

77. *Traditio* 8: Botte, op.cit., 22-7.

78. *Traditio* 9: ibid., 28f.

79. *Traditio* 11 and 13; ibid., 30 and 32. In the *Constitutiones Apostolorum* 8,21,2 and 8,22,2 (Funk I, 525), the sub-deacons and lectors also receive the laying on of hands (about the end of the fourth century). See also K. Rahner and H.Vorgrimler (eds.), *Diaconia in Christo*, QD 15/16, Freiburg im Breisgau 1962, 57-75.

80. *'Non imponetur manus super eum ad diaconatum vel presbyteratum. Habet enim honorem presbyteratus per suam confessionem. sin autem instituitur epsicopus, imponetur ei manus'* (*Traditio*: Botte, ed. 1963, 29f.). Botte denies that the suffering *confessio* takes the place of an ordination (however, a distinction should be made here: it is certainly liturgical institution, but without the laying on of hands); C.Vogel, 'L'imposition des mains dans les rites d'ordination en Orient et en Occident', *La Maison-Dieu* 102, 1970, 57-72, takes the same line as Botte. We do not find adequate explicit references outside the *Traditio*, but in antiquity what seems to Western men who grew up with later scholastic presuppositions to be liturgically impossible may itself have been taken for granted! In the ministry, the early church was primarly concerned with the gift of the charisma of the Spirit, which to begin with was itself purely charismatic, though here too (as also in the New Testament), the *receptio ecclesiae* was always a factor. Tertullian says, *'Christus in martyre est'*, (*De pudicitia* 22.6; cf. Cyprian, *Epist*.40). See M.Lods, *Confesseurs et Martyrs, successeurs des prophètes dans l'Eglise des trois premiers siècles*, Paris-Neuchâtel 1950; D.van Damme, 'Martus. Christianos. Überlegungen zur ursprünglichen Märtyrentitel', *FZPT* 23, 1976, 286-303. The laying on of hands is certainly necessary for the episcopacy of confessors (*Traditio* 9; Botte, op.cit., 28f.). It is of interest in this respect that the *doctores* or teachers in Hippolytus' *Traditio*, 15 and 19 (Botte, ed.1963, 32 and 40) – he is referring to the

leaders of the catechumenate – could be either clergy or laity (above all *Traditio* 19), and that at the end of the religious instruction both the lay teacher and any ordained teacher there could lay hands on the catechumens. Thus the *didaskaloi* are not ordained *per se*.

81. Cyrille Vogel, 'Chirotonie et Chirothesie', *Irenikon* 45, 1972, 207-35, and, 'Unité de l'Eglise et pluralité de formes historiques d'organisation ecclésiastique du IIIᵉ au Vᵉ siècle', in *Episcopat et l'eglise universelle*, Unam Sanctam 39, Paris 1964, 591-636.

82. Jerome, *Epist.146 ad presbyterum Evangelium*, CSEL 56, 310. Here we must remember that at least Jerome did not estimate the laying on of hands all that highly (*Comm.in Isaiam* 16.58, 10: PL 24, 569).

83. C.Vogel, 'Chirotonie', 20f.

84. An authoritative historian like C.Vogel can happily write: 'C'est la preuve, à n'en pas douter, que l'essentiel n'est pas le rite d'ordination, la chirotonie, mais le fait que l'Eglise reconnait, même sans impositions des mains, comme presbytres ceux qu'elle veut bien acceuillir: c'est la "reconnaissance" comme ministre de l'Eglise, le mandat que fait le clerc, non la chirotonie' (Vogel, op.cit., 21).

85. Leo I, *Ep. ad Rusticum*: PL 54, 1203.

86. Council of Laodicea, see E.Funk, *Kirchengeschichtliche Abhandlungen und Untersuchungen* 2, Paderborn 1899, 369f. The whole question of 'chora bishops' (bishops in the country) is discussed here. Finally the Gallican model was followed: no bishops, but country priests. The priests are dependent on the bishop of the nearest city – the origin of the later 'parochial system'.

87. Council of Sardica: see H.Hess, *The Canons of the Council of Sardica*, Oxford 1958; also Hefele-Leclerq II-1, 777-8, 782. Council of Antioch: Hefele-Leclercq, II-1, 717.

88. Irenaeus, *Adv.Haer.* I, 3: ed. Harvey, I, 94.

89. See P.Stockmeier, 'Aspekte zur Ausbildung des Klerus in der Spätantike', *MTZ* 27, 1976, 217-32.

90. John Chrysostom, *Hom.3.3 in Epist. ad Cor.*, PG 61, 26.

91. For this dispute see e.g. Hugo Rahner, 'Konstantinische Wende', *SdZ* 86, 1960/61, 419-28; P.Stockmeier, 'Konstantinische Wende und kirchengeschichtliche Kontinuität', *HJ* 82, 1963, 1-21; id., *Glaube und Religion in der frühen Kirche*, Freiburg 1973, 82-93.

92. See Eusebius, HE VIII, 17,9: GCS IX, 2,794.

93. Ibid., X, 5, 15-17; X, 5, 1-2: GCS 990.

94. Ibid., X, 7,2; ibid., 891. See A.Wlosok, 'Römische Religions- und Gottesbegriff in heidnischer und christlicher Zeit', *Antike und Abendland* 16, 1970, 39-53; J.Gaudemet, *L'Eglise dans l'empire romain*, Paris 1958; see also the literature at n.51.

95. *Vita Constantini* II, 45; GCS 7, 60.

96. *Codex.Theod.* XVI, 1,2 (Berlin 1905) Vol.1. The document really says *volumus*, but formally this need not mean imperial law. However, the decree was historically effective as an imperial law, though people were very tolerant to pagan religion. Moreover, in accordance with their concept of *religio*, the pagans interpreted the conquest of Rome in 410 as

a divine punishment, because the kingdom had abandoned 'the religion of the fathers'.

97. John Chrysostom, *De sacerdotio* III, 4, 19-33 (SC 262, 147). Nevertheless it should be noted that Chrysostom says nothing, at least directly, about a 'fiery change of bread and wine', of which he elsewhere speaks in realistic terms: here he is only concerned about the change of heart through the eucharist.

98. Ibid., 149.

99. E.Schillebeeckx, *De sacramentele heilseconomie*, Antwerp 1952, 22-106. This process already came about under Constantine.

100. According to the Preface to the 'Liturgy of Serapion', Bishop of Thmuis (who died after 359), the priestly president prays in the liturgy, 'Give us the Holy Spirit, that we may be in a state to tell forth and articulate these unspeakable mysteries' (see Funk, *Didaskalia* 2, Paderborn 1905, 158-95). In other words, 'mysteries' (laden with the *tremendum*) are here still clearly in line with the Pauline concept of mystery and not with the mystery religions: the eucharist is here still proclamation of the salvation achieved in Christ, in praise and thanksgiving – *sacrificium laudis' (eucharistia, euchologia)*. See also *De sacramentele heilseconomie*, 75ff.

101. See V.Saxer, *Vie liturgique et quotidienne à Carthage vers le milieu du IIIᵉ siècle*, Rome 1969, 194-202; A.Janssen, *Kultur und Sprache. Zur Geschichte der alten Kirche im Spiegel der Sprachentwicklung von Tertullian bis Cyprian*, Nijmegen 1938.

102. 'Sacerdos vice Christi vere fungitur' (Cyprian, *Litt.* 634, PL 4, 386). See B.D.Marliangeas, *Clés pour une théologie du ministère*, Paris 1979, 47.

103. Augustine, *Contra Ep. Parmeniani* II, 8,15 and 16: CSEL 51, 1908 (PL 43, 49-50).

104. See P.M.Gy, 'La théologie des prières anciennes pour l'ordination des évêques et des prêtres', *RSPT* 58, 1974, 599-617.

105. B.Botte, 'Secundi meriti munus', in *Questions Liturgiques et Paroissales* 21, 1936, 84-8.

106. Tertullian, *De Corona* 3. See also Justin, *Apology* I, 65, 3 and 67, 5; A.Quacquarelli, 'L'epiteto sacerdote (hiereis) ai crestiani in Giustino martire *Dial.* 116,3', *Vetera Christianorum* 7, 1971,5-19. See C.Vogel, 'Le ministère charismatique de l'eucharistie', in *Ministères et célébration de l'eucharistie*, 198-204; M.Bevenot, 'Tertullian's Thought about the Christian Priesthood', in *Corona Gratiarum* I, Bruges 1975.

107. See Ignatius, *Smyrn.* 8.1f.; M.Jourgon, 'La présidence de l'eucharistie chez Ignace d'Antioche', *Lumière et Vie* 16, 1967, 26-32; R.Padberg, 'Das Amtsverständnis der Ignatiusbriefe', *TuG* 62, 1972, 47-54; H.Legrand, 'La présidence de l'eucharistie selon la tradition ancienne', *Spiritus* 18, 1977, 409-31.

108. Cyprian, *Epist.* 45.

109. Cyprian, *Litt.* 69.9.3; 72.2.1; *De unitate Ecclesiae* 17.

110. This is a tradition which applied until the Middle Ages in both East and West. See e.g. Jerome, *Epist.*15.2; Innocent I, *Epist.* 24.3; Leo, *Epist.* 80.2; Pelagius I, *Epist.*24.14; Aphraates, *Dem.*12 *de Paschate* 9; *Decr.Gratiani* II, c.1. q.1, chs.73 and 78; Peter Lombard, *Sent.* IV, d.13.

111. To be found in *Vita Zephyrini* 2 (ed. L.Duchesne I, 139f.).

112. See D.Droste, *'Celebrare' in der Römischen Liturgiegesprache*, Munich 1963, above all 73-80; R. Schultze, *Die Messe als Opfer der Kirche*, Münster 1959; R.Raes, 'La concélébration eucharistique dans les rites orientaux', *La Maison-Dieu* 35, 1953, 24-47; R.Berger, *Die Wendung* offerre pro *in der römischen Liturgie*, Münster 1965; Y.Congar, 'L'Ecclesia ou communauté chrétienne sujet intégral de l'action liturgique', in *La liturgie d'après Vatican II*, Paris 1967, 241-82; E.Dekkers, 'La concélébration, tradition ou nouveauté?', in *Mélanges Liturgiques*, Louvain 1972, 99-120; B.Botte, 'Note historique sur la concélébration dans l'eglise ancienne', *La Maison-Dieu* 35, 1953, 9-23.

113. For an apparent exception see the *Gelasianum*, Droste, op.cit., 80.

114. Even at the end of the eleventh century, Guerricus of Igny writes: 'The priest does not consecrate by himself, he does not offer by himself, but the whole assembly of believers *consecrates and offers* along with him' (*Sermo* 5; PL 185,57).

115. See above all E.Dekkers, op.cit. (n.112), 110-12; R.Berger, op.cit., 246; R.Schultze, op.cit., 188.

116. Hefele I, 564ff.

117. Optatus, *Contra Donatistas* I, 18: CSEL 26,20; Athanasius, *Apologia c.Arianos* 6: PG 25, 257ff.

118. Ed. Funk, 472f.

119. Basil, *Epist.* 28.3: PG 32,310.

120. Augustine, *Epist.* 213, 1: CSEL 57,374; see F.Lotter, *Designation*, 129-39.

121. Athanasius, *Apologia c.Arianos* 6, PG 25, 257ff.

122. See Rufinus, HE II, 11: PL 21, 521ff.

123. Sulpicius Severus, *Mart.* 9,2-3: CSEL 1, 118f.

124. John Chrysostom, *De sacerdotio* (On the office of bishop) II, 4; IV, 2; Gregory of Nazianzen, *Orat.* 18, 35.

125. J.Colin, *Les villes* (see Bibliography, 299), 132ff.

126. Augustine, *Epist.* 213, 1.4; CSEL 57, 374; 376f.

127. Augustine, *Epist.* 78.3: CSEL 34, 1-2,334; see the Council of Orleans (549), can.11: MGHConc.I, 152.

128. Gregory of Nazianzus, *Epist.* 41.7,8,9; PG 37, 85.

129. Id., *Epist.* 40.2.

130. Augustine, *Epist.* 213,1; Gregory of Nazianzus, *Epist.* 42.5.

131. Sidonius Apoll., *Epist.* 7,9.

132. See E.Herrmann, *Ecclesia*, 301 n.104.

133. Fustel de Coulanges, *Histoire* 3, 533.

134. *Corpus Iuris Civilis* 2: *Codex Justinianus* (ed. Krüger), Berlin 1954, I,3,41 (*anno* 528).

135. E.Herrmann, *Ecclesia*, 302.

136. Jerome, *Epist.* 52.6: CSEL, 54,425.

137. See already Augustine, *Epist.*, 125.2; CSEL 44.4; also John Chrysostom, *De sacerdotio* III, 16: PG 48, 653.

138. Eusebius, HE VI, 43,11.

139. Fortunatus, *Carm.* 3,14.

284 Notes to pages 150–155

140. The Council of Arles, canon 7 (Hefele I, 208ff.) is a first sign of this.
141. *Codex Iustinianus* (ed. Krüger), I,4,26.
142. E.Herrmann, *Ecclesia*, 303.

Part Three, Section 1,5 – Section 4

1. See notes 50-64 in the previous section.
2. R.P.C.Hanson, 'Amt, Ämter, Amtsverständis I: Alte Kirche', *TRE* 2, 1978, 548; H.F.van Campenhausen, 'Die Anfänge des Priesterbegriffs in der alten Kirche', in *Tradition und Leben*, Tübingen 1960, 278-82; E.Dassmann, 'Ambt en autoriteit in het vroege christendom', *Communio* 5, 1980, 327-41; O.Perler, 'Der Bischof als Vertreter Christi nach den Dokumenten der ersten Jahrhunderte', in *Das Bischofsamt und die Weltkirche*, Stuttgart 1964; C.Vogel, '*Laica communione contentus*: Le retour du presbytre au rang des laics', *RSR* 47, 1973, 56-122.
3. See *Ministry*, 61f., and the bibliography; to be supplemented with B.Kötting, 'Die Stellung des Konfessors in der Alten Kirche', *JAC* 19, 1976, 16-22; T.Baumeister, 'Ordnungsgedenken und charismatische Geisterfahrung in der Alten Kirche', *RQ* 73, 1978, 150-5.
4. E.Dassmann, *Character indelebilis*, Cologne 1973, 12.
5. Cyprian, *Epist.* 65.2.4, CSEL III-2, 723-5. Leo the Great is still thinking along the same lines, *Epist.* 167, PL 54, 1203.
6. Dassmann, 'Ambt en autoriteit' (n.2 above), 337.
7. *The Liturgical Homilies of Narsai*, ed. R.Connolly, Oxford 1929, 21-2, 63.
8. Ambrosiaster, *Ad Eph.* 4.12, 1-4; CSEL Ambrosiaster III, 81,99.
9. PG 104, 558; commentary PG 104, 975-1218; 137, 406-10. There are editions in *Conciliorum Oecumenicorum Decreta* (ed. Bologna), Freiburg 1962, 66; P.P.Joannou, *Discipline générale antique I-1, Les canons des conciles oecuméniques*, Grottaferrata 1962, 74f. Latin translations: E.Schwartz, *Acta Conciliorum Oecumenicorum; Concilium generale Chalcedonense* II, 2,2, Berlin-Leipzig 1936. Explanatory literature: V.Fuchs, *Die Ordinationstitel von seiner Enstehung bis auf Innocenz III*, Bonn 1930; Cyrille Vogel, '*Vacua manus impositio*: L'inconsistance de la chirotonie en Occident', in *Mélanges Liturgiques* (offerts au R.P.Dom B.Botte), Louvain 1972, 511-24; J.Martin, *Die Genese des Amtspriestertums in der frühen Kirche*, QD 48, Freiburg 1972; A.Lemaire, *Les Ministères dans l'Eglise*, Paris 1974; id., *Les Ministres aux origines de l'Eglise*, Paris 1971.
10. See G.Otranto, 'Il sacerdozio comune del fideli nei reflessi della I Petr. 3.9', in *Vetera Christianorum* 7, 1970, 25-46. See J.Delorme, 'Sacerdoce du Christ et ministère (à propos de Jean 17)', *RSR* 62, 1974, 199-219; J.H.Elliott, *The Elect and the Holy. An Exegetical Examination of I Peter 2.4-10*, Leiden 1966 (the term 'priestly people of God' does not have any cultic significance; this expression indicates the election of the Christian community).
11. Cyprian, *Epist.* 67,4; 61.3; 73.7.
12. Cyprian, Epist.4,5: PL 50, 434. See F.Nikolasch, *Bischofswahl durch*

aller konkrete Vorschläge, Graz-Cologne 1973; K.Ganzer, *Papsttum und Bistumsbesetzungen in der Zeit von Gregor IX bis Bonifaz VIII*, Cologne 1968, from which it emerges how there was historically a break with the old church order.

13. Leo the Great, *Ad Anast.*, PL 54, 634. There we also find: 'No one may consecrate a man bishop against the wish of the Christians and without them having explicitly been asked.'

14. Paulinus, *Epist.I ad Severum*, c.10: CSEL 29.9.

15. Isidore, *De Ecclesiasticis officiis* II, 3: PL 83, 779.

16. *Vita Hieronymi*, XII, 3: PL 22,41.

17. Leo, *Epist.* 167: PL 54, 1003.

18. Burchard of Worms, *Decretum*, PL 140, 626; Ivo of Chartres, *Decretum* VI, 26: PL 161, 451; *Decretum Gratiani* I, d.70, c.1; ed. Friedberg I, 254; Council of Pavia (850), in Mansi, *Conc.* XIV, 936; Council of Piacenza (1095), in Mansi, *Conc.* XX, 806; Hugo of St Victor, *De sacramentis* II, p.3, c.2: PL 176,421.

19. Y.Congar, *Lay People in the Church*, London 1953.

20. Stephanus of Doornik, *Summa*, Prologue.

21. *Decretalia* VII, 12, q.1: ed. Friedberg I, 678.

22. A.Faivre, *Naissance d'une hiérarchie. Les premières étapes du cursus clérical*, Paris 1977.

23. *Sacramentum Veronense*, ed. L.Mohlberg, Rome 1956, p.13, marginal note 93: *Quia quotiens hostiae tibi placatae commemoratio celebratur, opus nostrae redemptionis exeritur.*

24. O.Nussbaum, *Kloster, Priestermönch und Privatmesse*, Bonn 1961, attributed the origin of the private mass to the monks who are said to have begun with votive masses and masses for the departed. That certainly accords with the ninth century but private masses are mentioned even earlier. See C.Vogel, 'Le passage de l'Eucharistie communautaire à la messe privée', *RSR* 4, 1980, 231-50, and, even more accurate historically, J.H.Crehan, *Priesthood, Kingship and Prophecy'*, *TheolStud.* 42, 1981, 216-31.

25. Canon 21 of the Council of Agde (506): Hefele-Leclerq (op.cit., II-2, 990); and Council of Orleans (511), ibid., 1014.

26.Council of Epaone (a town in Burgundy near Vienne, probably St Romain d'Albon, in 517): Mansi VIII, 556f. (*Mon.Germ.Conc.* I, 15-30). It is striking that his synod also abolished the consecration of deaconesses, i.e. only in the sixth century; this is often not mentioned in present-day disussions.

27. Gregory the Great, *Epist. ad Palladium: Monum.Greg.Epist.*, 422ff.; Hefele-Leclercq, III, 196f., 208-14.

28. For a bibliography of this period see pp.300f.

29. For a bibliography of the Ottonian period see p.300.

30. *Ministry*, 54-8.

31. Council of Quierzy (Carisiacum), Mansi 14, 741f. See the opponent of Amalarius, Florus the Deacon, in PL 80-81.

32. I.Bieler, *The Irish Penitentials*, Dublin 1963 (which contains two suggestive tables of commutations, 163-6; 277-83); G.LeBras, 'Les péni-

tentiels irlandais', in *Le miracle irlandais*, Paris 1956, 172-207; C.Vogel, *La Discipline* (see Bibliography).

33. See E.Schillebeeckx, 'The Spiritual Intent of Indulgences', *Lutheran World* 14, 1967, 11-32.

34. For literature for this period see Bibliography, p.300.

35. See A.Fliche, *La réforme grégorienne*, 3 vols, Louvain 1924/37; Fliche/Martin, *Histoire générale de l'Eglise*, 8, *Réforme grégorienne et la reconquête chrétienne (1057-1123)*, Paris 1940.

36. Abbon of Fleury, PL 130, 463.

37. For bibliography on the Middle Ages see p.300.

38. See Le Goff, *La civilisation médiévale*, Paris 1964, 249-318.

39. E.Reynolds, *The Ordinals of Christ from their Origins to the Twelfth Century*, Berlin and New York 1978; J.Crehan, 'The Seven Orders of Christ', *TheolStud* 19, 1958, 81-93.

40. *Decretum Gratiani* d.23, c.29: Friedberg I,86.

41. For heretical tendencies in the Middle Ages see e.g. H.Grundmann, *Ketzergeschichte im Mittelalter*, Göttingen 1963; G.Koch, *Frauenfrage und Ketzertum im Mittelalter*, Berlin 1962; R.Nelli, *Spiritualité de l'hérésie: Le catharisme*, Toulouse 1953. See also the historical portrait by E.Le Roy Ladurie, *Montaillou*, ET Harmondsworth 1980.

42. See the literature in n.41.

43. See R.Zerfass, *Der Streit um die Laienpredigt*, Freiburg 1974; on Innocent II see esp. 192-252.

44. See the magisterial work by M.Mollat and his team, *Etudes sur l'histoire de la pauvreté au Moyen Age*, Paris 1974; *Recherches sur les pauvres et la pauvreté dans l'Occident médiéval*, Paris 1974. Also E.Werner, *Pauperes Christi; Studien zu sozial-religiösen Bewegungen im Zeitalter der Reformpapsttums*, Leipzig 1956.

45. See R.Zerfass (n.43).

46. Gregory, *Liber Regulae Pastoralis*, PL 77, cols.13-128.

47. Friedberg, I, 764.

48. Loc.cit., 765.

49. Rupert of Deutz, PL 170, 533f.

50. Council of Avignon (1209), canon 1: Mansi 22, 785; see also P.Mandonnet, *St Dominique, L'idée, l'homme et l'oeuvre*, 2 vols, Paris 1937, I, 175; H.M.Vicaire, *Histoire de Saint-Dominique*, 2 vols, Paris 1957, I, 326.

51. *Conciliorum Oecumenicorum Decreta*, 615.

52. P.Mandonnet, *Saint Dominique*, I, 176.

53. COD, 218.

54. H.Grundmann, *Religiöse Bewegungen im Mittelalter*, Darmstadt ²1961, 141f.

55. Grundmann, op.cit., 142-52.

56. *Corpus Iuris Canonici*: Friedberg I, 1097-8.

57. M.H.Vicaire, op.cit., II, 63-9; H.S.Scheeben, *Der hl. Dominikus. Gründer des Predigerordens. Erneuerer der Seelsorge*, Essen 1961, 98, 125.

58. Vicaire, II, 86-99.

59. Laurent, *Monumenta historica S.P.N.Dominici I. Historia diplomatica S.Dominici*, MOP 15, Paris 1923, no.84.

60. Vicaire, II, ibid; I, 235-74.

61. Ed.Lauret, no.87; Vicaire II, 110f., 380f.

62. Ed.Lauret, 103.

63. Vicaire, II, 381.

64. Vicaire, II, 237; ed.Lauret, nos.112,127.

65. Vicaire, II, 214f.; Mandonnet, II, 273-92.

66. Vicaire, II, 226f.

67. Mandonnet II, 291.

68. Mandonnet II, 288; Vicaire II, 214f.

69. Thomas Aquinas, *Summa Theologiae*; I can see the text clearly but cannot place it.

70. Friedberg II, 789.

71. *Decretum Gratiani* 23,29: Friedberg I, 86. See C.Munier, *Les Statuta Ecclesiae Antiqua*, Paris 1959, 137.

72. Lateran IV, COD 215f. The *cura animarum* comes permanently to the fore in canon 3 of the third Lateran Council, see R.Foreville, *Latran I,II, III et IV*, Paris 1965.

73. *Summa Theologiae* III, q.63, a.3.

74. Ibid., q.59, n.2.

75. *Ministry*, 58-60. See below.

76. In fact for the first time in official church documents in 1201 there is mention of a 'character of baptism' (Pope Innocent III, Denzinger-Schönmetzer 781), and in 1231 of a priestly character (Pope Gregory IX, Denzinger-Schönmetzer 825). I very much doubt whether this had the sacral-mystical significance in the Middle Ages which was assigned to it in subsequent centuries. B.McSweeney ('The Priesthood in Sociological Theory', *Social Compass* 21, 1974, 5-25) may advance relevant sociological insights, but his historical appreciations seem to me to be very crude.

77. See E.Schillebeeckx, *Sacramentele heilseconomie*, Bilthoven/Antwerp 1952, 185-98, and s.v. 'Merkteken', in *Theologische Woordenboek* 2, 3231-7.

78. A.Poeschl, 'Die Entstehung des geistlichen Benefiziums', *Archiv für katholische Kirchenrecht* 106, 1926, 3-121, and 363-471; A.Werminghoff, in *Monumenta Historica Germanicae, Legum Sectio III, Concilia II, Concilia Aevi Karolini* I, Hanover/Leipzig 1908; see also F.Oedinger, *Über die Bildung der Geistlichen im Späten Mittelalter*, Leiden 1953.

79. *Speculum doctrinale* VIII,34. See G. de Lagarde, *La naissance de l'esprit laïque au déclin du Moyen-Age, I; Bilan du XIIIᵉ siècle*, Paris-Louvain 1956; the emergence of the juridical idea of *plenitudo potestatis*.

80. The emphasis on the clergy is already evident in the Carolingian period. The earlier ecclesial terminology, *conficere, consecrare, immolare* – actions of which earlier the whole of the community was the active subject- is gradually limited to the clergy's own actions. The earlier *tota aetas concelebrat* (*Vita Zephyrini*, 2: ed. L.Duchesne I, 139ff.), now becomes: what the priest does is simply done *in voto* by the whole of the believing people of God (Innocent III, *De sacro altaris mysterio* III, 6: PL 217, 845).

81. See R.J.Cox, *A Study of the Juridic Status of Laymen in the Writing of the Mediaeval Canonist*, Washington 1959; L.Hödl, *Die Geschichte der scholastichen Literatur und der Theologie der Schlüsselgewalt*, Münster 1960;

W.Plöchl, *Geschichte des Kirchenrechts*, Vienna ²1960, I, 224ff.; K.J.Becker, *Wesen und Vollmachten des Priestertums nach dem Lehramt*, QD 47, Freiburg 1970, 113-21; M. van de Kerkhove, 'La notion de jurisdiction dans la doctrine des Décrétistes et des premiers Décrétalistes, de Gratien (1140) à Bernard de Bottone', *Etudes Fransciscans* 29, 1937, 42-55; P.Krämer, *Dienst und Vollmacht in der Kirche: Eine rechtstheologische Untersuchung zur Sacra Potestas-Lehre des II.Vatikanischen Konzils*, Trier 1973; Y.Congar, *Sainte Eglise*, Paris 1963, 203-38; id., 'R.Sohm nous interroge encore', *RSPT* 57, 1973, 263-94; J.Ratzinger, 'Opfer, Sakramentum und Priesterum in der Entwicklung der Kirche', *Catholica* 26, 1972, 108-25, and id., *Das neue Volk Gottes*, Düsseldorf ²1970, 75-245.

82. For the consequences and above all the development of the private mass see *inter alia* O.Nussbaum, *Kloster, Priestermönch und Privatmesse*, Bonn 1961; A.Haussling, *Mönchskonvent und Eucharistiefeier*, Munich 1973; id., 'Ursprünge der Privatmesse', *Stimme der Zeit* 90, 1964-65, 21ff.

83. I am in no way denying the value of a private mass as deep personal prayer, much less its formative value for the priest who celebrates it; I am simply saying that in terms of the priestly ministry and the church, at the least it is very peripheral. A sacrament is the celebration of a local community (of whom a large number will be present), not of a community 'envisaged as being there'.

84. For the emergence of the mediaeval principle of dispensation, above all from Hinkmar of Rheims on, see E.Plazinski, *Mit Krummstab und Mitra*, Buisdorf 1970; M.A.Stiegler, *Dispensation, Dispensationswesen und Dispensationsrecht*, Mainz 1908; A.Schebler, *Die Reordinationen in den altkatholischen Kirche unter besonderer Berücksichtigung der Anschauungen Rudolphs Sohms*, Bonn 1936; L.Saltet, *Les réordinations*, Paris 1907; L.Buisson, *Potestas et Caritas. Die päpstliche Gewalt im Spätmittelalter*, Cologne-Graz 1958. The Western principle of dispensation differs on a number of points from the common Eastern *oikonomia* principle. See M.Widmann, *Der Begriff Oikonomia im Werk des Irenäus und seine Vorgeschichte*, Tübingen 1956; Mgr J.Kotsonis, *Problèmes de l'économie ecclésiastique*, Gembloux 1972; Mgr P.l'Huillier, 'Economie et Théologie Sacramentaire', *Istina* 17, 1972, 17-20; L.McDonnell, 'Ways of Validating Ministry', *JES* 7, 1970, 209-65; K.Duchatelez, 'De Geldigheid van de wijdingen in het licht der "economie"', *TvT* 1968, 277-401; P.Dumont, 'Economie ecclésiastique et réitération des sacraments', *Irenikon* 14, 1937, 228-47, 339-62; Y.Congar, 'Quelques Problèmes touchant les ministères', *NRT* 93, 1971, 785-800.

85. H.de Lubac, *Corpus mysticum: L'Eucharistie et l'Eglise au moyen-age*, Paris ²1949, esp.ch.5; also Y.Congar, *L'Eglise de saint Augustin à l'époque moderne*, Histoire des dogmes III/3, Paris 1970, 167-73 (= Handbuch der Dogmengeschichte III-3c, Freiburg 1971, 105-8).

86. *In Sent.*, d.24, q.2, a.2, ad 2. Like the whole of scholasticism, Thomas also says: *sacramentum ordinis ordinatur ad eucharistiae consecrationem* (*Summa Theologiae* III, 2,65 a.3). Although I have already said that above all in the first four centuries the ministry was primarily seen in relation to the building up of the community and in that to the eucharistic nucleus of any Christian community, we have to concede

that from the end of the fourth century, with the origin of the canonical law of abstinence, which was seen in terms of abstinence before the eucharist (see below), as time went on at least the emphasis came to be placed on the altar service of the priest, which also involved this far-reaching canonical legislation. See J.-P.Audet, *Mariage et Célibat dans le service pastoral de l'Eglise*, Paris 1967, 10f., 124-35.

87. See above all J.P.Massaut, *Josse Clichtove, l'humanisme et la réforme du clergé*, two vols, Paris 1969; id., 'Vers la Réforme catholique. Le célibat dans l'idéal sacerdotal de Josse Clichtove', in *Sacerdoce et célibat* (In memory of J.Coppens), Gembloux-Louvain 1971, 459-506; id., 'Théologie Universitaire et Requêtes spirituelles (un texte inédit de Josse Clichtove)', in *La Controverse Religieuse* (XVIᵉ-XIXᵉ siècles), Actes du Premier Colloque Jean Boisset, Montpellier 1980, 7-18. (I am grateful to J.P.Massaut, who drew my attention to these works after my contribution to *Minister?* '*Pastor? Prophet?*, London and New York 1980.) Also G.Chantraine, 'J.Clichtove: témoin théologique de l'humanisme parisien. Scolastique et célibat au XVIᵉ siècle', *RHE* 66, 1971, 507-28.

88.*Non est autem essentialiter annexum debitum continentiae ordini sacro, sed ex statuto Ecclesiae; unde videtur quod per Ecclesiam potest dispensari in voto continentiae solemnizato per susceptionem sacri ordinis* (*Summa Theologiae* II-II, 2.66, a.11).

89. For the Tridentine doctrine of the ministry, see *inter alia*: E.Boularand, 'Le sacerdoce de la loi nouvelle d'après le decret du Concile de Trente sur le sacrement de l'ordre', *BLKE* 56, 1955, 193-228; K.Becker, *Der priesterliche Dienst*, Vol.2, *Wesen und Vollmachten des Priestertums nach dem Lehramt*, QD 47, Freiburg 1970; A.Duval, 'Les données dogmatiques du Concile de Trente sur le sacerdoce', *Bulletin du Comité des Études* 38-39, vols.3-4, Paris 1962, 448-72; G.Fahrnberger, *Bischofsamt und Priestertum in den Diskussionen des Konzils von Trient. Eine Rechtstheologische Untersuchung*, Wiener Beiträge zur Theologie 30, Vienna 1970; A.Ganoczy, ' "Splendours and Miseries" of the Tridentine Doctrine of Ministries', *Concilium* 8, 1972, no.10, 75-86; H.Jedin, *Geschichte des Konzils von Trient*, four vols, Freiburg 1949-75; 'Das Leitbild des Priesters nach dem Tridentinum und dem Vaticanum II', *TuG* 60, 1970, 102-24, and *Vaticanum II und Tridentinum. Tradition und Fortschritt in der Kirchengeschichte*, Cologne-Opladen 1963; P.Fransen, 'Le Concile de Trente et le sacerdoce', in *Le Prêtre, Foi et Contestation*, Gembloux-Paris 1969; L.Lescrauwaet, 'Trente et Vaticanum II over het dienstpriesterschap', *Ons Geestelijk Leven* 47, 1970, 194-205; J.Pegon, 'Episcopat et hiérarchie au Concile de Trente', *NRT* 82, 1960, 580-8; H.Reumkens, *Priesterschap en presbyteraat volgens het concilie van Trente* (doctoral dissertation), Tilburg 1974; E.Schillebeeckx, *The Eucharist*, London 1968; *Handbuch der Dogmengeschichte*, Freiburg 1969, Vol.VI-5.

90. See A.Duval, 'L'Ordre au concile de Trente', in *Le Prêtre, Foi et Contestation*, 277ff.

91. The bishop of Avignon, see *Concilium Tridentinum* (ed. Societas Goerresiana), Freiburg 1901-61, Vol.9, 83.

92. See Denzinger-Schönmetzer, 1771-8: *de capita*: 1763-70. Above all:

Hoc autem (sacramentum ordinis) ab eodem Domino Salvatore nostro institutum esse, atque apostolis eorumque successoribus in sacerdotio potestatem traditam consecrandi; offerendi et ministrandi corpus et sanguinem eius, necnon et peccata dimittendi...' (Denzinger-Schönmetzer 1764). And: *'Si quis dixerit, in Ecclesia non esse hierarchiam, divina ordinatione institutam quae constat ex episcopis, presbyteris et ministris, a.s.'* (Denzinger-Schönmetzer 1776; to be compared with Vatican II, *Lumen Gentium*, no.28).

93. Speeches by the bishops of Modena and Ugento, *Conc. Trident.* 9.81 and 30.

94. See e.g. P.Fransen, 'L'autorité des conciles', in *Problèmes de l'autorité*, Paris 1962, 59-100, and 'Le concile de Trente' (see n.89 above).

95. See A.Rohrbasser (ed.), *Sacerdotis imago. Päpstliche Dokumente über das Priestertum von Pius X bis Johannes XXIII*, Fribourg 1962.

96. See H.Brémond, *Histoire littéraire du sentiment religieux* 3, *L'école française*, Paris 1921; L.Cognet, *La spiritualité française au XVIIe siècle*, Paris 1949; id., 'De la dévotion moderne à la spiritualité française', Paris 1958.

97. For Cyril, PG 76, 1398, Christ is priest on the basis of his manhood. Elsewhere it is the opposite, PG 68, 625. See Clement of Alexandria, *Protrepticus* XII, 120,2 (GCS, *Clement of Alexandria* I, 84); and earlier Eusebius, *De incarnatione* IX, 9.1-6. However, P.Galtier has shown that this new Alexandrian view radically went against the whole of the previous tradition: 'La religion du Fils', *RevAscMyst* 19, 1938, 335-75, esp. 352.

98. Augustine, *Litt.* 3.8, CSEL 34, 655.

99. Quoted by P.Pourrat, *Le sacerdoce: Doctrine de l'Ecole Française*, Paris 1943, 44ff.

100. J.H.Newman, *Select Treatises of St Athanasius*, 2, Oxford [2]1888, 245f.; see H.E.Manning, *The Eternal Priesthood*, London [20]1931.

101. See J.Crehan, 'The Dialektos of Origen and John 20.17', *TheolStud* 11, 1950, 368-73.

102. *Lumen Gentium*, 31 and 36; see also 23,25,28.

103. Thomas still rightly called the baptism of the Spirit the *radix* of the whole of the Christian life (*in Sent.* d.22, 1.2,a.2, sol.1).

104. 'Through the *ordo* the priests are consecrated to God in a new way' (*Presbyterorum ordinis*, no.12). See P.J.Cordes, *Sendung zum Dienst: Exegetisch-historiche und systematische Studien zum Konzilsdebat 'Vom Dienst und Leben der Priester'*, Frankfurt 1972, 202. From the abundance of post-Vatican literature on the question see above all A.Acerbi, *Due ecclesiologie: Ecclesiologia giuridica ed ecclesiologia di communione nella 'Lumen Gentium'*, Bologna 1975; H.L.Legrand, 'Nature de l'Eglise particulière et rôle de l'évêque dans l'Église', in *La charge pastorale des évêques*, Unam Sanctam 74, Paris 1969, 115ff.; P.Krämer, *Dienst und Vollmacht in der Kirche*, Trier 1973; K.J.Becker, *Wesen und Vollmachten des priestertums*, QD 47, Freiburg 1970; Y.Congar, Preface to B.D.Marliangeas, *Clés pour une théologie du ministère: In persona Christi, In persona Ecclesiae*, Paris 1978, 5-14. Even the insertion of the concept of *communio hierarchica* (*Lumen Gentium*, nos.21 and 22 and above all *Nota praevia*) alongside the concept of the church as *communio* cannot bring any real harmony between *sacramentum* and *ius*;

see a precise study of this lame concept in Cordes, *Sendung zum Dienst*, 291-301. The reasons for these unevennesses become clear from the *Expensio modorum* in the decree *Presbyterorum Ordinis*!

105. Jerome, *Dialogus contra Luciferianos* 21, PL 23, 175.

Part Four

1. *Lumen Gentium*, no.28.

2. This synod (1972) is the third synod since Vatican II. Officially it is called the 'second synod', because the previous one was an 'extraordinary synod'.

3. *Le ministère sacerdotal* (Rapport de la Commission Internationale de Théologie), Paris 1972. The six points are to be found there on pp.125f.

4. *'Itinera fidelitatis sunt semper et necessario itinera creativitatis... Duae theologiae de proposita quaestione nobis offerentur: una quae initium sumit a conceptu sacerdotii, altera vero a conceptu ministerio sacerdotali...Bene prae oculis habeamus praesentem crisim sacerdotii solvi non posse ex theologia ex qua ex parte crisis orta est'* (speech at the synod).

5. Patriarch Maximus V.Hakim, successor to Maximus IV who was at the Second Vatican Council, clearly said in a speech at the synod: 'Pour nous, que nous le voulions ou non, de par l'extension géographique de la chrétienté, de par la fin de l'ère coloniale et le réveil des nationalismes légitimes, l'ère d'une Eglise identique et nivelée est définitivement passée. Nous sommes entrés dans l'ère des Eglises locales, dont la variété fait beauté et dont l'unité autour du Successeur de Pierre, n'est pas et ne peut plus être uniformité.'

6. *'Conamen facere ut systema quoddam intra aliud systema majus reformandi, sine mutatione systematis majoris, est utopicus'* (speech at the synod).

7. *'Tempus est ut dimittamus curam, nos ad mundum adaptandi – id quod termino vernaculo* aggiornamento *expressum est. Nunc est tempus ut, Christum sequentes, aliis duces simus'* (speech at the synod).

8. The final text has an insertion aimed at giving this aspect its full value: 'to the degree that this earthly process contributes to a better ordering of society' (see *Expensio modorum, Gaudium et Spes*, ch.3, Part I, p.236). The final text now runs: 'But the expectation of a new earth must not weaken the concern to develop this earth; rather, it must strengthen it. For it is here that there grows the body of the new family of mankind which is already to some degree in process of giving a foreshadowing of the final kingdom. Thus although development on earth must be carefully distinguished from the kingdom of Christ, they are most profoundly involved in the kingdom of God in so far as they can contribute to a better ordering of human society' (*Gaudium et Spes*, no.39). Half an hour's *lectio divina* in the documents of Vatican II would have been most appropriate for the synod agenda.

9. Mgr A.Tortolo (Argentina): *'Unus Pater, invocata collegialitate, petivit ne clauderetur ianua. In nomine istius collegialitatis, liceat petere ne ianuam aperiatur.'*

10. *'Expedit quod caelibatus libera optione assumetur, habita ratione speci-*

atim dignitatis personae humanae, "numquam enim homines tam acutum ut hodie sensum libertatis habuerunt"' (*Gaudium et Spes*, no.4). '*Hic est etiam consensus maioris partis cleri nostri, prout in investigationibus* (encuestas) *patet'* (Mgr Felipe Santiago Benitez, Paraguay).

11. There is no explicit mention of a 'principle of selection' but the speeches clearly come very near to that. It is formulated most clearly by Mgr P.J.Schmitt (Metz), speaking in the name of the synod of French bishops: 'En raison de l'union personnelle du prêtre à Jésus-Christ et de sa consécration à la mission, *nous appellerons* au sacerdoce presbytéral *ceux qui*, par la grâce de Dieu, sont disposés a ce don total que constitue le célibat consacré dans "l'ésprit évangélique". En retour, nous nous sentions nous-mêmes engagés, avec tout le Peuple de Dieu, à leur offrir les conditions humaines, spirituelles et apostoliques d'une ministère qui corresponde au don de toute leur vie.' This is clearly an abandonment of the obligation that anyone who wants to become a priest should be celibate, but on the other hand the charisma of celibacy, already present and freely accepted, is regarded as a principle of selection for the choice of priests by the hierarchy. This spirit, then, at least makes a difference.

12. '*Moti sumus potius praesertim ex hac consideratione: ut (caelibatus) retineat maximum valorem signi quem habet, opportet... etiam ut in omnium communi aestimatione videatur esse talis, ablata omni obscuritate vel dubio... Propter hanc rationem, membra Conferentiae Antiliarum sentiunt ordinationem aliquorum hominum qui iam matrimonio sunt iuncti medium esse nostris diebus hos facere animo verre libero et generoso, a nemine coacto*' (speech by Mgr S.Carter).

13. 'Ainsi que l'on s'abandonne pas au gré de chacun le charisme du célibat. Il courait de trop grands risques' (Mgr B.Oguki-Atakpah, from Togo). One of his arguments was: 'En tout cas, on ne m'a encore montré ici à Rome la tombe de la femme de Pierre ou de Paul'; for him this was a providential sign for the celibacy of the priesthood. I am aware of the 'humorous' value of such 'arguments', but this nevertheless reveals their 'ideology'.

14. '*Ego certe non sum ex iis qui aliquo modo poetico vel nimis optimistico consideret statum de facto quoad caelibatum sacerdotalem... Sed idem valet etiam pro statu matrimoniali...*' (speech).

15. 'On a l'impression que tout tourne autour de la sexualité, sous prétexte que le mariage est un grand sacrément' (Mgr B.Oguki-Atakpah).

16. Mgr J.Gran, living amongst married Lutheran pastors, gave this evidence: 'In Scandinavia, where nearly everybody is Lutheran, the clergy are normally married men. Divorce, desertion and the like rarely occur. Most of the pastors appear to be truly spiritual persons, not inferior to our Catholic priests. Moreover, they often possess a maturity which must stem from their family responsibility. Their wives are very much part of their vocation...' Although the bishop said this in a speech in connection with the practical section, after him some bishops nevertheless painted the following picture of the disasters which would occur if married men were to be ordained: divorce, birth control, abortion,

polygamy, priests' children who might behave badly or even become hippies, nepotism, and so on.

17. Himself convinced that the celibacy of the priesthood should be strictly maintained, Mgr J. Diraviam, Archbishop of Madhurai (India), nevertheless made the following remark, which is worth considering: 'The decision of the Synod will not be acceptable for lack of credibility of the Synod, if the question has not been examined freely and without prejudice as though the decision was already settled beforehand.'

18. With reference to the Pope's letter of 1 February 1970 to Cardinal Villot, Cardinal Samore said: *'Haec Summi Pontificis verba manifeste eius voluntatem patefaciunt, quae disceptationem circa caelibatum sic dictum optionalem omnino excludit... Quapropter nec admittitur disceptatio qualiscumque in hac Synodo de readmissione ad ministerium sacerdotale illlorum qui ad statum laicalem reducti fuerint et matrimonium inierint.'*

19. *'Mihi, aperte dicam, pressio quae semper vehementior fit ab una parte sacerdotum minime videtur signum temporis per quod Deus loquitur Ecclesiae'* (speech).

20. This prayer was written by Ann H.Heidkamp; unfortunately I no longer have a reference to the original.

21. E.Schüssler Fiorenza, 'For Women in Men's Worlds: A Critical Feminist Theology of Liberation', *Concilium* 171, 1984, 32; see also her great work, *In Memory of Her*, New York and London 1983.

22. E.Schüssler Fiorenza, 'For Women in Men's Worlds', 32.

23. See Mary Dwyer, *New Woman, New Church, New Priestly Ministry*, Rochester 1980; D.Gottemoeller–R.Hofbauer (eds.), *Women and Ministry*, Washington 1981; Monica Furlong (ed.), *Feminine in the Church*, London 1984.

24. See my *Het ambtcelibaat in de branding*, Bildhoven 1965; G.Denzler, *Das Papsttum und der Amtszölibat*, two vols., Stuttgart 1973, 1976; H.-J.Vogels, *Pflicht-zölibat. Eine kritische Untersuchung*, Munich 1978; R.Gryson, *Les origines du célibat ecclésiatique du premier au septième siècle*, Gembloux 1970, and 'Dix ans de recherches sur les origines du célibat ecclésiastique', *RTL* 11, 1980, 157-85; N.Grévy-Pons, *Célibat et nature. Une controverse médiévale*, Paris 1975. See also the early study by R.Bultot, *La doctrine du mépris du monde*, Louvain -Paris 1963ff.

25. See e.g. PL 54, 1204.

26. See R.Kottje, 'Das Aufkommen der täglicher Eucharistiefeier in der Westkirche und die Zölibatsforderung', *ZKG* 81, 1971, 218-88; L.Hödl, 'Die *lex continentiae'*, *ZKT* 83, 1961, 326-54.

27. Civil: *Codex Theodosii* XVI 2,44; canonical: *Canones Apostolorum* 5.

28. *Acta Apostolicae Sedis* 66, 1954, 169f.

29. E.Fehrle, *Die Kultische Keuschheit im Altertum*, Religionsgeschichtliche Versuche und Vorarbeiten 6, Giessen 1910. Of course this author neglects Eastern influence on this Hellenism: see H.Jeanmaire, 'Sexualité et mysticisme dans les anciennes sociétés helléniques', in *Mystique et continence*, Études Carmélitaines, Paris-Bruges 1952, 51-60.

30. *Inter alia* (in addition to the standard literature on the Stoa and Neo-

Platonism), see a good short summary by G.Delling, s.v. 'Geschlechtsver-kehr', *RAC* 10, 1977, 812-29.

31. See A.Vööbus, *Celibacy. A Requirement for Admission to Baptism in the Syriac Church*, Stockholm 1951; K.Müller, *Die Forderung der Ehelosigkeit für alle Getauften in der alten Kirche*, Tübingen 1927; E.Schillebeeckx, *Het Huwelijk. Aarde werkelijkheid en heilsmysterie*, Vol.1, Bilthoven 1963, 171.

32. Jerome, *Ad Jovinianum* I, 20: PL 23,238; see also I, 34, PL 23, 256-8. See the same reasoning throughout the patristic literature, *inter alia* II Clement 14.3-5; 12.2,5, above all the book by the Pythagorean Sextus, which was a favourite among Christians (Origen, *Contra Celsum* 8,30), in which it is said that praying and sexual intercourse cannot go together and are by nature contradictory, so that castration is commended as the only way. This left a great impression on many Christians of the time. Origen himself adopted this means literally. See also in the same spirit Ambrose, *De officiis ministrorum* I, 50: PL 16,98; Innocent I, *Epistula ad Victricium*, ch.10, ch.20: PL 56, 523; *Epistulas ad Exsuperium* c.1, PL 56, 501; Pope Siricius, *Epist. ad Episcopos Africae*, PL 56, 728; Augustine, *De conjugiis adulterinis* II, 21: PL 486. Furthermore, in patristic literature we find the universal human complaints about married life in a frivolous sense, *inter alia* Ambrose, *De Virginibus* I, n.6, 25f.: PL 165, 195f.; Basil, *Epist*. II, 2: PG 32,224f.; Jerome, *Adversus Helvidium* 22: PL 23,206; Ambrose, *De viduis*, ch.13, n.81: PL 16.259; I,5: PL 1, 1282f. We also find this satyrical type of literature about marriage in the pagan writings of the time; see P. de Labriole, *Les satires de Juvénal. Étude et analyse*, Paris nd, 192-7. However, these universal human satires on married life, to be taken with a pinch of salt, served in patristic literature as the 'excessive motivation' for Christian abstinence, which at this time was clearly influenced by Hellenistic encratism or hostility to all sexuality.

33. Denzinger did not take this canon, which had such far-reaching influence on the Latin church, into his collection of 'important' church documents. See COD (ed. G.Alberigo *et al.*), Freiburg 1962, 174f. Furthermore, in its canon 7 this Council compels priests who are already legitimately married to send away their wives. This is completely incomprehensible in terms of the canon law of the church and in the light of the Bible. There is no thought as to the fate of the wife.

34. A precise study of this history can be found in M.Dortel-Claudot, 'Le prêtre et le mariage: évolution de la législation canonique des origines au XIIe siècle', in *L'Année Canonique* 17, 1973, 319-44; also E.J.Jonkers, 'De strijd om het celibaat van geestlijken van de vierde tot de tiente eeuw in het Westen volgens de Concilies', *Nederlands Archief voor Kerkgeschiedenis* 57, 1976-77, 129-44.

35. See the careful study, already cited in a previous chapter, by P.H.Lafontaine, *Les conditions positives de l'accession aux ordres dans la première législation ecclésiastique (300-492)*, Ottawa 1963, above all 71ff.

36. For the confiscation of goods in this connection see, *inter alia*, Synod of Pavia (beginning of the eleventh century), canon 3; Mansi, *Conc* 19, 353; Synod of Rome (1059): Mansi *Conc* 18, 897f.; Synod of Rome (1074):

Mansi, *Conc*20, 424; Synod of Amalfi (1089): Mansi, *Conc* 20, 624; the Second Lateran Council: Mansi, *Conc* 21, 526ff.

37. *Concilium Tridentinum* (Societas Goerresiana), Vol.9, 640, 660-9.

38.'Law of celibacy' is not my terminology but that of the official church documents, see *inter alia* the *Motu proprio* of Paul VI, *Sacrum diaconatus Ordinem* of 18 June 1967, where there is clear mention of *Lex caelibatus*, in *AAS* 69, 1967, 699, although as far as I remember this term is not to be found in the encyclical *Sacerdotalis Caelibatus*, itself dating from the same year; see *AAS* 69, 1967, 657-97.

39. J.Pohier, *Au nom du Père*, Paris 1972, 171-223.

40. See E.G.Blanco, *The Rule of the Spanish Military Order of Saint James, 1170-1493*, Medieval Iberian Insulas. Text and Stud.4, Leiden 1971.

41. See op.cit., above all 5,54f., 59, 83f., and the whole rule of the Order, pp.77-163.

42. See also J.Kerkhofs, 'Religeuzen, waarheen?', in *Kultuurleven* 51, 1984, no.3, 254-61; also *Pro Mundi Vita*, Bulletin 92, Brussels 1983, no.1.

Part Five

1. *Baptism, Eucharist and Ministry*, Faith and Order Paper 111 (Lima, Peru, January 1982), Geneva 1982.

2. *Sacerdotium Ministeriale*, in *Acta Apostolicae Sedis* 75, 1983.

Bibliography

(for details see Notes)

Part One, especially 2

J.Ash, 'The Decline of Ecstatic Prophecy in the Early Church', *TheolStud* 37, 1976, 227-52

M.E.Boring, *Sayings of the Risen Jesus. Christian Prophecy in the Synoptic Tradition*, Cambridge 1982

Y.Congar, 'Pneumatologie ou "Christomonisme" dans la tradition latine?', in *Ecclesia a Spiritu Sancto edocta*, Mélanges Théologiques G.Philips, Gembloux 1970, 41-63.

G.Dautzenberg, *Urchristliche Prophetie. Ihre Erforschung, ihre Voraussetzungen im Judentum und ihre Struktur im ersten Korintherbrief*, BWANT 104, Stuttgart 1975

J.Hermann, *Kurios und Pneuma. Studien zur Theologie der paulinischen Hauptbriefen*, Munich 1961

H.Kraft, *Die Entstehung des Christentums*, Darmstadt 1981

E.Schüssler Fiorenza, *In Memory of Her*, New York and London 1983

D.S.Wallace-Hadrill, *Christian Antioch. A Study of Early Christian Thought in the East*, Cambridge 1982

—, *Die Frau im Urchristentum*, QD 95, Freiburg 1983

—, *Leven uit de Geest*, Theologische peilingen, aangeboden aan E.Schillebeeckx, Hilversum 1974

Part Two, Section 1

K.Baus, 'Die Anfänge (zur frühchristliche Grosskirche)', in *Handbuch der Kirchengeschichte*, ed. H.Jedin, 1, Freiburg ³1965, 71-248

K.Berger, 'Volksversammlung und Gemeinde Gottes: Zu den Anfängen der christlichen Verwendung von "Ekklesia"', ZTK 73, 1976, 167-207

R.Brown, 'New Testament Background for the Concept of Local Church', *Proceedings of the CTSA* 36, 1981, 1-14

W.G.Doty, *Letters in Primitive Christianity*, Philadelphia 1973

P.Holmberg, *Paul and Power. The Structure of Authority in the Primitive Church as Reflected in the Pauline Epistles*, Coniectanea Biblica 11, Lund-Philadelphia 1980

E.A.Judge, *The Social Pattern of Christian Groups in the First Century*, London 1960

H.J.Klauck, 'Die Hausgemeinde als Lebensform im Urchristentum', MTZ 32, 1981, 1-15

D.Lührmann, 'Neutestamentliche Haustafeln und antike Oekonomie', NTS 27, 1981, 83-97

A.J.Malherbe, *Social Aspects of Early Christianity*, London 1977

W.A.Meeks, *The First Urban Christianities. The Social World of the Apostle Paul*, New Haven and London 1983

J.Neusner (ed.), *Religion in Antiquity*, Numen Suppl.14, Leiden 1970

W.H.Ollrog, *Paulus und seine Mitarbeiter. Untersuchungen zu Theorie und Praxis der paulinischen Mission*, Neukirchen 1979

J.Peterson, 'House Churches in Rome', VC 23, 1969, 264-72

S.Safrai and M.Stern (eds.), *The Jewish People in the First Century*, Philadelphia 1974

R.Scroggs, 'The Social Interpretation of the New Testament: The Present State of Research', NTS 26, 1980, 164-79

A.Schreiber, *Die Gemeinde in Korinth: Versuch einer gruppendynamischen Betrachtung der Entwicklung der Gemeinde von Korinth auf der Basis des ersten Korintherbriefes*, NTAbh 12, Münster 1977

E.Schüssler Fiorenza, *In Memory of Her*, London and New York 1983

J.H.Schütz, *Paul and the Anatomy of Apostolic Authority*, Cambridge 1975

Gerd Theissen, *Studien zur Soziologie des Urchristentums*, WUNT 19, Tübingen 1979

W.Wiefel, 'Die jüdische Gemeinschaft im Antiken Rom und die Anfänge des römischen Christentums', *Judaica* 26, 1970, 65-88

Part Two, Section 2

K.J.Becker, *Wesen und Vollmachten des Priestertums nach dem Lehramt*, QD 47, Freiburg 1970

U.Brockhaus, *Charisma und Amt*, Wuppertal 1972

R.Brown, *Priest and Bishop*, New York 1970/ London 1971

P.J.Cordes, *Sendung zum Dienst. Exegetisch-historische und systematische Studien zum Konzilsdekret 'Vom Dienst und Leben der Priester'*, Frankfurt 1972

J.Delorme (ed.), *Le ministère et les ministères selon le Nouveau Testament*, Paris 1974

J.Dupont, 'Les ministères de l'Eglise Naissante d'après les Actes des Apôtres', *Studia Anselmiana* 61, 1973, 94-148

J.H.Elliott, 'Ministry and Church Order in the New Testament', *CBQ* 32, 1970, 367-91

H.Frankemölle, 'Amtskritik im Matthäusevangelium?', *Biblica* 54, 1973, 247-62

J.Gnilka, 'Geistliches Amt und Gemeinde nach Paulus', *Kairos* 11, 1969, 95-104

P.Grelot, *Eglise et ministères. Pour un dialogue critique avec E.Schillebeeckx*, Paris 1983

F.Hahn, 'Neutestamentliche Grundlagen für eine Lehre von kirchlichen Amt', *Dienst und Amt*, Regensburg 1973, 7-40; id., *Der urchristliche Gottesdienst*, Stuttgart 1971

J.Hainz (ed.), *Ekklesia. Strukturen paulinischer Gemeinden. Theologie und Gemeindeordnung*, Regensburg 1972; id., *Kirche im Werden. Studien zum Thema Amt und Gemeinde im Neuen Testament*, Paderborn 1976

K.Kertelge, *Gemeinde und Amt im Neuen Testament*, Munich 1972

K.Kertelge (ed.), *Das kirchliche Amt im Neuen Testament*, Darmstadt 1977

H.J.Klauck, 'Das Amt in der Kirche nach Eph.4.1-16', *WuW* 36, 1973, 81-110

A.Lemaire, *Le ministères aux origines de l'Eglise. Naissance de la triple hiérarchie: évêques, presbytres, diacres*, Lectio Divina 68, Paris 1971

G.Lohfink, 'Die Normativität der Amtsvorstellungen in den Pastoralbriefen', *TQ* 157, 1977, 93-106

Gerd Lüdemann, *Paulus der Heidenapostel*, 2. *Antipaulinismus im frühen Christentum*, Göttingen 1983

J.Martin, *Die Genese des Amtspriestertums in der frühen Kirche*, QD 48, Freiburg 1972

J.Meier, 'Presbyteros in the Pastoral Epistles', *CBQ* 35, 1973 ,323-45

H.Merklein, *Das kirchliche Amt nach dem Epheserbrief*, Munich 1973

H.J.Michel, *Die Abschiedsrede des Paulus an die Kirche Apg.20,17-38*, Munich 1973

Petrus und Papst, ed. A.Brandenburg and H.J.Urban, Münster 1977

J.Rohde, *Urchristliche und frühkatholische Ämter*, Berlin 1976

R.Schnackenburg, *Der Brief an die Epheser*, Zurich-Cologne 1982

H.Schürmann, *Ursprung und Gestalt*, Düsseldorf 1970, 236-67

P.Stuhlmacher, 'Evangelium – Apostolat – Gemeinde', *KuD* 17, 1971, 28-45

A.Vögtle, 'Exegetische Reflexionen zur Apostolat des Amtes und zur Amtssukzession', in *Die Kirche des Anfangs*, Festschrift H.Schürmann, Freiburg 1978, 529-82

K.Walf, 'Das jüdische Schaliach-Institut. Rechtsinstitut und Ursprung des Apostelamtes?', in *Cristianesimo nelle Storia*, I-2, 391-9

R.Zolltitsch, *Amt und Funktion der Priester*, Freiburg 1974

And some collections:
Etudes sur le sacrement de l'Ordre, Lex Orandi 22, Paris 1957
Le ministère de la nouvelle alliance, Collection Foi Vivante 37, Paris 1967
Le prêtre: foi et contestation, Gembloux-Paris 1969

Part 3
From the Early Church to the Middle Ages

A.Adam, 'Bischof', *RGG* I, 1301ff.

O.Barlea, *Die Weihe der Bischöfe und Diakone in vornicänischen Zeit*, Munich 1969

K.Baus, 'Von der Urgemeinde zur frühchristlichen Grosskirche', in *Handbuch der Kirchengeschichte* (ed.H.Jedin), I, Freiburg 1962.

A.Beck, *Römisches Recht bei Tertullian und Cyprian*, Aalen 1967 = Halle 1930

J.Bleicken, *Lex publica. Gesetze und Recht in der Römischen Republik*, Berlin 1975

H.F.von Campenhausen, *Kirchliches Amt und geistliche Vollmacht in den ersten drei Jahrhunderten*, Tübingen 1953

E.Caspar, *Geschichte des Papsttums: von den Anfängen bis zur Höhe der Weltherrschaft*, 2, Tübingen 1933

C.Cochini, *Origines apostoliques du célibat sacerdotal*, Paris 1981

J.Colin, *Les villes libres de l'orient gréco-romain et l'envoie au supplice par acclamations populaires*, Brussels 1965

Y.Congar, 'Sur la trilogie Prophète-Roi-Prêtre', *RSPT* 67, 1983, 97-116

E.Dassmann, 'Zur Entstehung des Monepiskopats', *JAC* 17, 1974, 74-90;

—, *Sündenvergebung durch Taufe, Busse und Martyrerfürbitte in den Zeugnissen frühchristlicher Frömmigkeit und Kunst*, Münster 1973

—, *Charakter Indelebilis*, Cologne 1973

G.Deusen, 'Weisen der Bischofswahl in I.Clemensbrief und in der Didachè', *TuG* 62, 1972, 125-35

J.Fellermayr, *Tradition und Sukzession im Lichte des römisch-antike Erbdenkens. Untersuchungen in den Lateinischen Vätern bis zu Leo dem Grossen*, Munich 1979

R.Frei-Stolba, *Untersuchungen zu den Wahlen in der römischen Kaiserzeit*, Zurich 1967

J.Gascou, *La politique municipale de l'Empire Romain en Afrique proconsulaire de Trajan à Septime Sévère*, Rome 1972

O.Heggelbacher, *Vom Römischen zum Christlichen Recht. Juristische Elemente in den Schriften sgn. Ambrosiaster*, Freiburg 1959.

Elisabeth Herrmann, *Ecclesia in Re Publica*, Frankfurt-Bern 1980

S.Hirschfeld, *Die kaiserlichen Verwaltungsbeamten vom Augustinus bis Diokletian*, Berlin 1905

G.Krüger, *Die Rechtsstellung der vorkonstantinischen Kirchen*, Stuttgart 1935

K.Lübeck, *Reichseinteilung und kirchliche Hierarchie*, Münster 1901

K.Lütcke, *'Auctoritas' bei Augustin*, Stuttgart 1968

D.Magie, *Roman Rule in Asia Minor to the End of the Third Century after Christ*, two vols., Princeton 1950

A.Monahan, *Royal and Papal Power*, New York 1974

O.Perler, 'Der Bischof als Vertreter Christi nach den Dokumenten der ersten Jahrhunderte', in *Das Bischofsamt in der Weltkirche*; Stuttgart 1964

R.Reynolds, *The Ordinals of Christ from their Origins to the Twelfth Century*, Berlin – New York 1978

T.Ring, *Auctoritas bei Tertullian, Cyprian und Ambrosius*, Würzburg 1975

L.Schick, *Das dreifache Amt Christi und die Kirche. Zur Entstehung und Entwicklung der Trilogien*, Frankfurt 1982

J.Straub, 'Zur Ordination von Bischöfen und Beamten in der christlichen Spätantike', *JAC Ergänzungsband I*, 1964, 336-45

J.Vogt, *Das Kirchenverständnis des Origenes*, Cologne 1974

—, *Constantin der Grosse und sein Jahrhundert*, Munich [2]1960

Middle Ages

General

M.Bloch, *La société médiévale*, two vols, Paris [2]1949

L.Génicot, *La spiritualité médiévale*, Paris 1971

—, *Les lignes de faîte du Moyen-Age*, Doornik [3]1961

J.Leclerq, *Aux sources de la spiritualité occidentale*, Paris 1964

J.Le Goff, *La civilisation de l'Occident médiévale*, Paris 1964

R.W.Southern, *Western Society and the Church in the Middle Ages*, Harmondsworth 1979

—, *The Making of the Middle Ages*, London 1953

A.Vauchez, *La spiritualité du moyen âge*, Paris 1975

See generally *The Cambridge Mediaeval History*, eight vols., Cambridge 1911-63

Carolingian and Ottonian period

L.Halphen, *Charlemagne et l'empire carolingien*, Paris 1947

C.Heitz, *Recherches sur les rapports entre architecture et liturgie à l'époque carolingienne*, Paris 1963

J.A.Jungmann, *Missarum Solemnia*, two vols, Vienna [5]1962

P.Riché, *Les invasions barbares*, Paris 1953

—, *La vie quotidienne dans l'empire carolingien*, Paris 1973

C.Vogel, *Le pécheur et la pénitence au Moyen Age*, Paris 1969

—, *La discipline pénitentielle en Gaulle, des origines à la fin du VIIe siècle*, Paris 1952

Tenth and eleventh centuries

R.Bultot, *Christianisme et valeurs humaines. La doctrine du mépris du monde en Occident, de saint Ambroise à Innocent III*, two vols, Paris 1963-64

G.Duby, *Adolescence de la chrétienté, Paris 1967*

—, *L'an mil*, Paris 1967

A.Fliche, *La réforme grégorienne*, three vols., Louvain 1924-37

Fliche-Martin, *Histoire générale de l'Eglise*, 8. *Réforme grégorienne et la reconquête chrétienne (1057-1123)*, Paris 1940

Twelfth century

M.D.Chenu, *La théologie au XIIe siècle*, Paris 1957

G.Dumoutet, *Corpus Domini. Aux sources de la piété eucharistique médiévale*, Paris 1942

H.Grundmann, *Religiöse Bewegungen im Mittelalter*, Hildesheim ²1961

G.H.Haskins, *The Renaissance of the XIIth Century*, Cambridge 1928

J.Le Goff, *Hérésies et sociétés dans l'Europe préindustrielle, XI-XVIIIe siècle*, Paris 1968

T.Manteufel, *Naissance d'une hérésie: Les adeptes de la pauvreté volontaire au moyen âge*, Paris 1970

L.Mumford, *Technics and Civilization*, London 1934

G.Paré, A.Brunet and P.Tremblay, *La renaissance au XIIe siècle*, Paris – Ottawa 1933

H.M.Vicaire, *L'imitation des apôtres: moines, chanoines et mendiants (IV-XIIIe siècle)*, Paris 1963

Modern times

H.Bremond, *Histoire littéraire du sentiment religieux*, 3. *L'Ecole Française*, Paris 1921

I.Cognet, *La spiritualité française au XVII³ siècle*, Paris 1949

—, *De la dévotion moderne à la spiritualité française*, Paris 1958

P.J.Cordes, *Sendung zum Dienst* (see above, Part Two, Section 2)

A.Rohrbasser (ed.), *Sacerdotis imago. Päpstliche Dokumente über das Priestertum von Pius X bis Johannes XXIII*, Freiburg 1962

Index of Biblical References

Index of Names

Abbon of Fleury, 286
Acerbi, A., 290
Acqua, A.dell', 216
Adam, A., 277
Aigrain, R., 271
Albertus Magnus, 190
Alfrink, Cardinal, 216, 222, 223
Amalarius of Metz, 161
Ambrose, 134, 147, 294
Ambrosiaster, 73, 153, 272, 284
Anselm, 173
Aphraates, 282
Arius, 129
Arnold of Brescia, 72
Ascarza, Santos, 231
Ash, J., 272
Asten, P. T. van, 217, 225, 226
Athanasius, 129, 147, 277
Audet, J. P., 272, 276, 289
Augustine, 132, 134, 142, 144, 147,
   148, 170, 202, 282, 283, 290, 294

Barlea, O., 278
Baroni, A., 216
Bartoletti, E., 212
Basil, 147, 283
Baumeister, T., 284
Beauvais, Vincent de, 192
Beck, A., 278
Becker, K. J., 146, 288, 289, 190
Benitez, F. S., 292
Berger, R., 146, 283
Bérulle, P. de, 3, 4, 193, 202
Bévénot, M., 282
Beyschlag, K., 272
Bieler, I., 285
Blanco, E. G., 295
Blank, J., 275
Bläser, P., 279
Bonaventure, 179, 190, 274
Boring, M. E., 272
Bornkamm, G., 276
Botte, B., 278, 280, 282, 283, 284
Boularand, E., 289

Brandis, L., 276
Brandon, S. G. F., 18, 270
Brémond, H., 290
Brockhaus, U., 27
Brown, R., 273, 274
Brox, N., 273
Bultot, R., 293
Burchard of Worms, 285

Calvin, J., 199
Campenhausen, H. F. von, 284
Carmichael, J., 18, 270
Carter, S., 223, 226, 292
Chantraine, G., 289
Charlesworth, M., 275
Clement of Rome, 61, 69, 70, 125,
   126, 128, 204, 271, 276, 290
Clichtove, Josse, 190, 195, 196, 197
Colin, J., 283
Cognet, L., 290
Congar, Y., 146, 156, 279, 283, 285,
   288, 290
Connolly, R., 284
Conway, Cardinal, 225
Cox, R. J., 287
Crehan, J. H., 285, 286, 290
Crouch, J. E., 271
Cullmann, O., 18, 270
Culpeper, R. A., 274
Cyprian, 130, 131, 144, 145, 151,
   152, 153, 278, 282, 284
Cyril of Alexandria, 202, 290

Damme, D. van, 274, 280
Dassmann, E., 272, 276, 284
Dautzenberg, G., 271
Davids, A., 275
Dekkers, E., 283
Delorme, J., 284
Denzler, G., 293
Deusen, G., 272
Dionysius, Ps.-, 121, 158, 185, 279
Diravian, J., 293
Dominic, 181, 182, 183, 184